# WHO'S GOING TO READ THIS ANYWAY

?

# WHO'S GOING TO READ THIS ANYWAY?

KERRIGAN • MATTHEWS • WEBB

**4**TH
EDITION

Holt, Rinehart and Winston of Canada, Limited

Toronto

**Canadian Cataloguing in Publication Data**
Kerrigan, Donna, 1952–
Who's going to read this anyway?

4th ed.
Previous eds. by Ray Matthews and Gary Webb.
ISBN 0-03-922670-0

1. English language - Rhetoric. I. Webb, Gary.
II. Matthews, Ray. Who's going to read this
anyway? III. Title.

PE1408.K47 1991          808'.0427          C90–093032–2

Holt, Rinehart and Winston of Canada, Limited is grateful for the evaluations provided by the following educators.

Tom Decker
*North York Board of Education*

Marion Dennis
*Durham Board of Education*

Wendy Fish-Dunphy
*Lanark County Board of Education*

Rick Hallam
*North York Board of Education*

Bonita Kersey
*Centennial College*

Peter Miller
*Seneca College*

Colin Morris
*Mohawk College*

Senior Acquisitions Editor: Heather McWhinney
Developmental Editor: Iris Coupe
Publishing Services Manager: Karen Eakin
Managing Editor: Liz Radojkovic
Editorial Co-ordinator: Marcel Chiera
Copy Editor: Brenda Missen
Cover and Interior Design: Cundari Group Ltd.
Typesetting and Assembly: True to Type Inc.
Printing and Binding: Webcom Ltd.

Printed in Canada

    2   3   4   5        95   94   93   92

# Preface

For some strange reason, people in school (instructors and students alike) often forget that the real purpose of writing is *to communicate a message to someone*. Whenever this purpose is forgotten, the "in-class composition" becomes nothing more than an exercise in creating "in-class compositions": students view writing as the search for or repetition of a magic formula for an impersonal grading machine that is searching only for "grammatical correctness," not for what is really being communicated. Instructors, on the other hand, tend to look only for the students' ability to use the language "correctly" within the very narrow limits of the classroom setting. They return the paper with so few reactions about the message that was actually being conveyed to a real reader that the whole process reinforces the students' assumption that writing is an exercise whose consequences go no further than filling a blank page with words. In the long run, students come to view courses in writing as obstacles to be overcome rather than aids to career development.

Yet writing that is done anywhere other than in school always has a real reader and a real purpose that are quite clear and important to the writer. An accountant may be motivated to write in order to convince an employer that some change should be made in the operation of a business; a salesperson may want to explain a certain action to someone who is going to be judging the value of that action; or a technologist may want to explain how to operate a machine in such a way as to avoid confusion, frustration, and perhaps physical injury. In short, in the world outside of the school, the reader suddenly emerges as a "real" person.

Interesting things begin to happen to people's written communications as soon as they become aware of the reader. The writer thinks no longer in terms of grammatical errors, but in terms of the message that is really being communicated to the reader: Has a task been explained clearly enough to be understood by a stranger who has never done this task before? Have any terms been used that might be clear to the writer, but vague to someone else? Is the time sequence clear to the reader? Has the background to the problem at hand been presented clearly enough for the reader to grasp the significance of the recommendations of the report? The questions that the writer begins to ask in these situations go on and on, but they always come back to one central focus: how well will the reader understand what I really mean to say?

Moreover, as the writer struggles to clarify the ideas for the reader, something that at first may be quite surprising begins to happen: the old problems of "grammar" begin to disappear. Mistakes in grammar, it is soon realized, result chiefly from the writer's failure to take into consideration either the knowledge that the reader possesses about the topic being written about or the way in which the writer views that topic. For example, "pronoun reference" errors such as "They do not like me at the college" result from the writers' failure to remember that although they know who "they" are, the readers may not. When writers really become concerned about the message they are communicating, their choice of words and the order in which they appear, sentence structure and its impact, and all of the other elements that go into good writing suddenly become very important.

Frequently, college and high-school students are not fully aware of the importance of good writing in their future careers. The greatest barrier to students' professional advancement most frequently stems not from an inability to handle the work in their chosen profession, but from an inability to handle the written language that is called for by the job. Reports, memoranda, business correspondence, and the many other forms of written communication are vital to success in all professions. Recently, we encountered a case in which a college student was refused a job in construction work because his inability to spell correctly would stand in the way of his advancement to a higher position within the company at a later date. Even situations that call for conveying oral instructions or explanations require many of the same skills of audience analysis, organization, and word selection that are so important in writing.

On the other hand, many instructors seem to believe that good writing skills can be acquired through the boring process of memorizing "rules of grammar" and doing grammar exercises. Yet all that anyone except an expert learns from doing grammar exercises is how to do grammar exercises. How many times does it happen that students register near-perfect scores on grammar tests and then proceed to write an essay that proves to be virtually incomprehensible to anyone?

In this book, we approach the development of writing skills from the point of view of writing as an act of communication. From this point of view, the key to successful writing lies in fulfilling two prerequisites that are frequently forgotten: (i) you must identify clearly for yourself exactly what it is that you want to communicate and (ii) you must identify clearly to whom you wish to say it. Only when you have established these guidelines can you approach your topic in such a way as to achieve effective communication. In the process of clarifying and elaborating your ideas for your reader, you will almost always "correct" your own grammar because *all* that the various rules of grammar do is to provide generally applicable guidelines to the clear, logical presentation of ideas to a reader. If at any time you are in doubt about whether a construction actually conveys the message that you want it to, check it in the grammar section at the back of this book.

The articles that appear in this book have been selected from a wide range of contemporary newspapers and magazines. Not only do they deal with topics that we hope will interest students and stimulate further writing, but each reflects a unique approach to the problem of presenting information and opinions to readers who have different levels of background knowledge about the topic. In other words, each of the authors deals with exactly the same kinds of problems that you are going to be facing whenever you write. The Style and Structure questions that accompany each article are designed to help you see how that particular author has tried to deal with the material in such a way as to communicate the message to the reader effectively. The Thinking and Writing sections are designed to give *you* an opportunity to do the same things with your ideas on the topic. The Warm-up exercises that accompany each article will help you prepare your ideas and sharpen your language skills.

Any words in the Style and Structure and/or Thinking and Writing sections that appear in boldface (e.g., **thesis**) are defined in the last sections of the text. Consult the index for the exact page numbers.

## Publisher's Note to Instructors and Students

This textbook is a key component of your course. If you are the instructor of this course, you undoubtedly considered a number of texts carefully before choosing this as the one that will work best for your students and you. The authors and publishers of this book spent considerable time and money to ensure its high quality, and we appreciate your recognition of this effort and accomplishment.

If you are a student, we are confident that this text will help you to meet the objectives of your course. You will also find it helpful after the course is finished, as a valuable addition to your personal library. So hold on to it.

As well, please don't forget that photocopying copyright work means the authors lose royalties that are rightfully theirs. This loss will discourage them from writing another edition of this text or other books, because doing so will simply not be worth their time and effort. If this happens, we all lose — students, instructors, authors, and publishers.

And since we want to hear what you think about this book, please be sure to send us the stamped reply card at the end of the text. This will help us to continue publishing high-quality books for your courses.

# Acknowledgements

For kind permission to reprint copyright material, acknowledgement is hereby made to the following:

David Suzuki, author of "Monster Threatening Earth Is Us";
Neil Sandell, author of "Roller Coaster Heaven";
*Maclean's* for "Confronting Pornography" by Mary Janigan;
*The Globe and Mail*, Toronto, for "Baby, It's Yours" by Jennifer Hunter;
*Psychology Today* for "From Quill to Computer" by Robert Sekuler, copyright © 1985 (P.T. Partners, L.P.);
Brenda Rabkin, author of "Repeat Performances," reprinted from *Homemaker's Magazine*, May/June 1988;
*Discover* for "The Making of a Wasteland" by Mayo Mohs, © Discover Publications;
*Alberta Report* for "An Alternative to Incarceration" by Greg Heaton, Lori Cohen, and Patrick McManus;
Judith Haines, author of "Still Scared of the Dentist?" reprinted from *Canadian Living*, November 26, 1988;
Sidney Katz, author of "The 'Science' of Astrology is All Wet";
Rona Maynard, author of "Why Men Are Mad As Hell," reprinted from *Chatelaine*, December 1988;
*Humanist in Canada* for "Power and Control: Why Men Dominate Women" by Rick Goodwin;
*The Futurist* for "The Coming of an Information Society" by Edward Cornish, published by the World Future Society, 4916 Saint Elmo Avenue, Bethesda, Maryland 20814, USA;
Clarence Reynolds and *Discover* for "Muscling In on Madness," © 1988 Discover Publications;
Andrew C. Revkin and *Discover* for "A Car with a Mind of Its Own," © 1988 Discover Publications;
*American Banker* for "Living and Dying with AIDS: A Banker's Story" by Hank E. Koehn;
Judith Finlayson, author of "Math's Multiple Choices," reprinted from *Homemaker's Magazine*, January/February 1988;
*Psychology Today* for "Let the Punishment Fit the Crime" by Philip Brickman, copyright © 1977 (PT Partners, L.P.);
*Humanist in Canada* for "Judy" by Esther Kershman Muhlstock;
*Compass: A Jesuit Journal*, 10 St Mary Street, Suite 300, Toronto, Ont. M4Y 1P0, for "Deliberate Strangers" by Charlie Angus and "Education for One World" by Jack Costello;
*Discover* for "The Nuclear-Winter Threat" by Tom Levenson, © Discover Publications;
*The Globe and Mail*, Toronto, for "Is Plea-Bargaining So Bad?" by Leo Adler, a criminal-defence lawyer in Toronto;
Emil Sher, author of "Words That Wound";
*The Niagara Falls Review* for "I'm Making It!" by Shawn Dalgleish;
*Technology Review* for "The Low-Skill Future of High Tech" by Henry Levin and Russell Rumberger, copyright 1983;
Bruce Headlam, author of "Stop the Music," which originally appeared in *Saturday Night*;
Angela Heinrich, author of "Some Still State Flatly the Earth's Not Round";
Brian Weagant, author of "Teen Runaways: Should We Force Them Home?" reprinted from *Chatelaine*, September 1988;
*The Globe and Mail*, Toronto, for "Turning Down the Danger" by Ellen Roseman;
*Western Report* for "Peace at Any Price on Vancouver's Georgia Viaduct" by Ted Byfield;
Velvet Shelvock, author of "Lighting Up and Looking Cool;"
*Time* for "In the Beginning: God and Science" by Lance Morrow, © 1979 Time, Inc.;
Barry Estabrook, author of "Fashionable Ideas," reprinted from *Equinox*, November/December 1988;
Susan Hirshorn, Montreal-based journalist specializing in consumer affairs, author of "Where's the Bargain?";
*The Saturday Evening Post* and *Reader's Digest* for "Policewomen on Patrol" by Cynthia Brouse, adapted from "Policewomen on Patrol," *The Saturday Evening Post*, © 1975, The Curtis Publishing Co., and reprinted from the August 1988 issue of *Reader's Digest*;
*The Globe and Mail*, Toronto, for "If You Toss In a Dollar He'll Do Tricks";
*Alberta Report* for "The Kiddie-Vote Campaign" by Stephen Lequire and Mathew Ingram;
the *New York Times* for "Earth's Biggest Blast" by Walter Sullivan, © 1979 New York Times;
Mrs A.M. Paton and *Reader's Digest* for "A Cry for the Beloved Country" by Alan Paton, reprinted from the August 1988 issue of *Reader's Digest*;
*Newsweek* for "What TV Does to Kids," © 1977 Newsweek Inc. reprinted from the February 1977 issue;
*McCall's Magazine* for "Respect: At the Heart of Successful Marriage" by Annie Gottlieb, copyright © 1986 WWT Partnership;
Ivor Shapiro, author of "Second Opinion," which originally appeared in *Saturday Night*;
Sue Calhoun, author of "When P.E.I. joins the Mainland";
*Reader's Digest* for "Acid Rain: Scourge from the Skies" by Robert Collins, © 1980 by The Reader's Digest Association (Canada) Ltd., reprinted from the June 1980 issue of *Reader's Digest*;
Fran Rider, author of "Integrated Sports: A Question of Fair Play," reprinted from *Chatelaine*, February 1988;
John Colapinto, author of "Crowd Control," which originally appeared in *Saturday Night*;
W.P. Kinsella, author of "How to Write Fiction," which first appeared in *The Globe and Mail*.

# Contents

Thematic Table of Contents      xi

Monster Threatening Earth Is Us   *David Suzuki*      1

Roller Coaster Heaven   *Neil Sandell*      5

Confronting Pornography   *Mary Janigan*      9

Baby, It's Yours   *Jennifer Hunter*      19

From Quill to Computer   *Robert Sekuler*      26

Repeat Performances   *Brenda Rabkin*      33

The Making of a Wasteland   *Mayo Mohs*      41

An Alternative to Incarceration   *Greg Heaton, Lori Cohen, and Patrick McManus*      45

Still Scared of the Dentist?   *Judith Haines*      50

The "Science" of Astrology Is All Wet   *Sidney Katz*      57

Why Men Are Mad as Hell   *Rona Maynard*      61

Power and Control: Why Men Dominate Women   *Rick Goodwin*      71

The Coming of an Information Society   *Edward Cornish*      79

Muscling In on Madness   *Clarence Reynolds*      88

A Car with a Mind of Its Own   *Andrew C. Revkin*      92

Living and Dying with AIDS: A Banker's Story   *Hank E. Koehn*      97

Math's Multiple Choices   *Judith Finlayson*      106

Let the Punishment Fit the Crime   *Philip Brickman*      115

Judy   *Esther Kershman Muhlstock*      119

Deliberate Strangers   *Charlie Angus*      124

Education for One World   *Jack Costello*      131

The Nuclear-Winter Threat   *Tom Levenson*      139

Is Plea-Bargaining So Bad?   *Leo Adler*      143

Words That Wound   *Emil Sher*      148

I'm Making It!   *Shawn Dalgleish*      152

The Low-Skill Future of High Tech   *Henry Levin and Russell Rumberger*      157

Stop the Music   *Bruce Headlam*      165

Some Still State Flatly the Earth's Not Round   *Angela Heinrich*      172

Teen Runaways: Should We Force Them Home?   *Brian Weagant*      177

Turning Down the Danger   *Ellen Roseman*      182

Peace at Any Price on Vancouver's Georgia Viaduct   *Ted Byfield*      186

Lighting Up and Looking Cool  *Velvet Shelvock*    191
In the Beginning: God and Science  *Lance Morrow*    195
Fashionable Ideas  *Barry Estabrook*    202
Where's the Bargain?  *Susan Hirshorn*    209
Policewomen on Patrol  *Cynthia Brouse*    216
If You Toss In a Dollar, He'll Do Tricks  *The Globe and Mail*    221
The Kiddie-Vote Campaign  *Stephen Lequire and Mathew Ingram*    224
Earth's Biggest Blast  *Walter Sullivan*    230
A Cry for the Beloved Country  *Alan Paton*    234
What TV Does to Kids  *Newsweek*    241
Respect: At the Heart of Successful Marriage  *Annie Gottlieb*    247
Second Opinion  *Ivor Shapiro*    251
When P.E.I. Joins the Mainland  *Sue Calhoun*    259
Acid Rain: Scourge from the Skies  *Robert Collins*    270
Integrated Sports: A Question of Fair Play  *Fran Rider*    278
Crowd Control  *John Colapinto*    283
How to Write Fiction  *W.P. Kinsella*    291
**Who's Going to Read This Anyway?**    296
**Planning Your Written Communication**    297
**The Writing Stage**    303
**Proofreading Your Composition**    310
**A Short Guide to Punctuation**    330
**Commonly Confused Words**    344
**Spelling**    356
**Index**    365

# Thematic Table of Contents

**BETWEEN GENDERS**
Repeat Performances     33
Why Men Are Mad as Hell      61
Power and Control: Why Men Dominate Women      71
Math's Multiple Choices      106
Policewomen on Patrol      216
Respect: At the Heart of Successful Marriage      247
Integrated Sports: A Question of Fair Play      278


**GROWING PAINS**
Baby, It's Yours      19
Repeat Performances      33
Still Scared of the Dentist?      50
Judy      119
Education for One World      131
I'm Making It!      152
Teen Runaways: Should We Force Them Home?      177
Lighting Up and Looking Cool      191
The Kiddie-Vote Campaign      224
What TV Does to Kids      241
How to Write Fiction      291


**ETHICS, MORALITY, AND THE LAW**
Confronting Pornography      9
An Alternative to Incarceration      45
Living and Dying with AIDS: A Banker's Story      97
Let the Punishment Fit the Crime      115
Deliberate Strangers      124
Education for One World      131
Is Plea-Bargaining So Bad?      143

I'm Making It!    152
Stop the Music    165
Teen Runaways: Should We Force Them Home?    177
Peace at Any Price on Vancouver's Georgia Viaduct    186
Fashionable Ideas    202
Where's the Bargain?    209
A Cry for the Beloved Country    234
What TV Does to Kids    241
Second Opinion    251

## OTHER PEOPLE/OTHER VIEWS

An Alternative to Incarceration    45
The "Science" of Astrology Is All Wet    57
Living and Dying with AIDS: A Banker's Story    97
Judy    119
Words That Wound    148
I'm Making It!    152
Some Still State Flatly the Earth's Not Round    172
Fashionable Ideas    202
A Cry for the Beloved Country    234

## OUR PASTIMES

Roller Coaster Heaven    5
Baby, It's Yours    19
From Quill to Computer    26
The "Science" of Astrology Is All Wet    57
Muscling In on Madness    88
Stop the Music    165
Turning Down the Danger    182
Lighting Up and Looking Cool    191
If You Toss In a Dollar, He'll Do Tricks    221
What TV Does to Kids    241
Crowd Control    283
How to Write Fiction    291

## OUR FUTURE

Monster Threatening Earth Is Us       1
From Quill to Computer       26
The Making of a Wasteland       41
The Coming of an Information Society       79
A Car with a Mind of Its Own       92
Education for One World       131
The Nuclear-Winter Threat       139
The Low-Skill Future of High Tech       157
When P.E.I. Joins the Mainland       259


## THE WORLD AROUND US

Monster Threatening Earth Is Us       1
The Making of a Wasteland       41
The "Science" of Astrology Is All Wet       57
Education for One World       131
The Nuclear-Winter Threat       139
In the Beginning: God and Science       195
Earth's Biggest Blast       230
When P.E.I. Joins the Mainland       259
Acid Rain: Scourge from the Skies       270

# Monster Threatening Earth Is Us

**by David Suzuki**

Science-fiction writers have long recognized that an invader from outer space 1
could unite all earthlings in a battle against a common enemy.

Imagine that as that alien runs across the planet, it crushes an acre of 2
forest with each step, scrapes a wide swath of topsoil, blows noxious carbon
compounds into the upper atmosphere, and sprays toxic chemicals into the
air, water, and land. We would instantly declare a global crisis endangering
all life on Earth and marshal all of our forces to do battle with the threat.
Today, we are facing precisely those dangers, yet we are doing little to counter
them.

That's because the monster is us. Consider the straight facts, the ones about 3
which there is no controversy.

We are overrunning the planet like an out-of-control malignancy. There 4
are far more of us than any other large mammal on the planet, and we
keep adding to our numbers by 90 million every year.

We are destroying our soils. Twenty-five billion tons of agricultural topsoil 5
are swept away annually. That's seven percent of the globe's good growing
land every decade. As well, vast areas are being degraded by poor land use.
A report by Senator Herbert Sparrow in June 1984 concluded that Canadian
farms are mining our soil, degrading it by failing to replace the organic content
of farmland. Consequently, since 1984, global food production has declined
each year. And this is precisely at the time that human population is exploding.

The devastation is unrelenting. Every five minutes around the clock, 365 6
days a year, a major shipment of chemicals crosses an international border
to be disposed of somewhere, somehow; no place on this planet is free of
the toxic debris of technology. Every minute, 50 to 100 acres of tropical
forests are destroyed, and the rate of destruction is accelerating. Every year,
at least 20 000 species disappear forever, and the rate of extinction is speeding
up. Every year, in spite of two decades of research and contention, acid rain
sterilizes thousands of lakes and kills whole forests.

In addition, greenhouse heating of the planet is being caused by human 7
beings through our use of fossil fuels (which release carbon dioxide), our
farming of cattle (which produce methane), and our production of chemicals
(such as CFCs). Warming is already under way, and the agricultural and eco-

logical consequences over the next decades will be totally unprecedented and unpredictable. Even after CFCs are completely eliminated, ozone thinning will continue for years as CFCs already in use escape into the air.

8      The 1978 UN-sponsored Brundtland Commission on world environment and development documented the obscene disparity between the industrialized nations and the Third World. Making up only twenty percent of the world's population, industrialized countries consume 80 percent of the planet's resources and generate most of its industrial toxins and wastes. Any attempt by the Third World to achieve a level of affluence comparable to ours will be suicidal.

9      The challenge, then, is clear. We in the industrialized world must abandon immediately the notion that we must have continued growth, greater consumption, and more material goods. We are already using an immoral amount and we, not the Third World, are the major cause of the current environmental crises.

10     At the same time, we have to help the developing countries raise their standard of education and living in order to reduce their birth rate and avoid exploiting environmentally destructive technologies such as dams, coal burning, CFC refrigerators, etc. Out of pure self-interest, we have to pay to ensure a higher standard of living and more efficient and ecologically benign development in developing countries. We share this finite world with all other people and can no longer treat the disadvantaged of the earth as recklessly as we have in the past.

11     Stanford University's Paul Ehrlich points out that people can make major changes swiftly. After Pearl Harbor, we sacrificed, we cut back, we changed our lifestyle, and we fought for survival. Today, "we face a million ecological Pearl Harbors at once," Ehrlich says, "and that's the scale of public response that's needed now."

12     We are now in a war to save this planet. Small groups all over the country are drawing their own battle lines, but federal muscle is essential. There is money and personnel — military defence should be redirected to environmental defence while our soldiers can fight oil spills and PCB fires or help to reforest and rehabilitate damaged ecosystems. The war metaphor is appropriate — we are battling to keep the planet livable for our children.

13     In the science-fiction stories, human ingenuity and courage usually win out over the aliens from outer space, but this isn't make-believe — it's real and the monster is here.

# Style and Structure

1.   Write a one-paragraph description of this essay's intended reader. Support your conclusions with specific references to the text.

2.   (a) Write a short summary of Dr. Suzuki's **thesis**.

(b) Identify the sentence in the introduction that presents this **thesis** to the reader.

3.   (a) Explain three advantages Dr. Suzuki gains by using the science fiction analogy in his introduction.

(b) Why would Dr. Suzuki not reveal the identity of the alien invader until the third paragraph?

(c) Given the intended reader, why is his use of this science fiction analogy appropriate? For what kinds of readers do you think this analogy might be less effective? Why?

4.   (a) Write a point-form summary of the topic dealt with in each paragraph in the body of the essay (paragraphs 4 to 12).

(b) Does each of these topics relate to the **thesis** announced in the introduction? Does the essay have unity?

(c) These topics are grouped together into two sections, each of which presents one aspect of the **thesis**. What aspect is dealt with in each section? Why might Dr. Suzuki have chosen to present these sections in the order that he has?

5.   In what ways does paragraph 13 act as an effective **conclusion** for this essay?

6.   Dr. Suzuki uses a number of techniques to gain the reader's acceptance of his ideas.

(a) Identify two examples of Dr. Suzuki's use of the following types of supporting arguments:

(i)  citing an authority;

(ii) statistics.

For each, explain the reasons for its effectiveness in convincing the reader.

(b) Choose any paragraph in the first section of the body. How many facts does Dr. Suzuki provide concerning the topic dealt with in that paragraph? What is the effect of providing so many specific details in each paragraph? How does this quantity of detail affect the reader's acceptance of the suggestions in the second half of the essay? Why?

(c) Identify four examples of the subtle use of emotionally charged words (e.g., "malignancy") to develop the reader's almost unconscious agreement with the essay's ideas. Explain the effect achieved by each.

(d) What special technique does Dr. Suzuki use in paragraph 6 to drive home the urgency of the situation? How well does it work? Why?

(e) What is the effect of his using the first person plural ("we," "our," and "ours") throughout the essay?

(f) How do his references to Pearl Harbor in paragraph 11 affect the reader?

# Warm-up

Together with three or four others from your class, use the library to research measures that are being taken (or could be taken) to overcome one of the ecological problems mentioned by Dr. Suzuki.

Working on your own, write a short report of your findings. Then, with the others in your group, use your reports as the basis for a five to ten minute group presentation to the class.

# Thinking and Writing

a.    Sometimes when we read essays like this one we feel helpless in the face of such global problems. Yet, as Dr. Suzuki points out, if we are going to avoid ecological disaster, each and every one of us is going to have to make changes in our way of life.

Write an essay that suggests one action that everyone in your community could practise to help in this war. Try to convince your reader to implement your idea.

**Audience:** the average person living in your community.

When you have completed your final draft, share it with several others in the class; see how many of their suggestions you can adopt into the way you live.

b.    Write an essay outlining a program that could be implemented by the municipal, provincial, or federal government to fight one of the environmental problems described by Dr. Suzuki.

**Audience:** a politician in a position to influence government policy.

Send a copy of the final draft to your local representative at the appropriate level of government and ask for comments on your suggestions.

# Roller Coaster Heaven

## by Neil Sandell

It lasts 114 seconds. A white-knuckle, heart-in-your-mouth, dizzying, tizzying, scream-at-the-top-of-your-lungs 114 seconds. By Terror Standard Time, it's an eternity. I stagger off hoping the bloom will return to my ashen cheeks, perhaps by next month. My guide, Tim Sykes, doesn't budge from his seat. Grinning from ear to ear, he waits for one more ride. At least one more. 1

Tim is a roller coaster aficionado. The objects of his affection are the coasters at Crystal Beach Park in Ontario's Niagara peninsula. With the Giant, the second-oldest roller coaster in North America, and the Comet, a middle-aged but feisty 42-year-old, Crystal Beach comes as close to roller coaster heaven as you can get. 2

Heaven, and the pursuit thereof, was the whole idea at Crystal Beach from the beginning. One hundred years ago, the site attracted revival camp meetings. Over the then-sparkling waters of Lake Erie, the faithful travelled by excursion steamship from nearby Buffalo, New York, for a day of religion and recreation. This early version of R&R soon gave way to worship of an earthier variety. By the 1890s, Crystal Beach had turned into a full-fledged amusement park complete with sideshows. A ferris wheel was built, along with a scenic railway, and finally, in 1916, the wooden-trestled Giant roller coaster. 3

Today, the Giant is venerated by coaster buffs from around the world. A plaque from American coaster enthusiasts commemorates its seventieth birth-day. But the Giant almost didn't make it that far. In 1982, Crystal Beach Park was caught in the interest rate squeeze and fell into receivership. Devotees despaired. They flocked to Crystal Beach for one last ride on their cherished coasters. They filmed the Giant and the Comet for posterity. 4

Then, a trio of businessmen plucked Crystal Beach from the brink. The coasters were saved. Now, if anything, they're more secure. In 1986, attend-ance at the park soared by 54 percent, and in 1987 by another 28 percent. By the end of summer 1988, between 325 thousand and 350 thousand people had visited Crystal Beach. 5

The Giant is like an old friend to Tim Sykes. He figures he has ridden it at least 100 times. It's what is called a side friction coaster. Coaster con-noisseurs care about such things. Simply put, the trains aren't bolted to the rails. The sheer weight of the cars keeps the coaster on track. Unlike the 6 banked curves of a modern coaster, the corners are flat. Sykes says the Giant is like a big comfy sofa. It's slow and smooth, and its charm is nostalgic.

7    But the Comet is Sykes' first love. Sykes got hooked on roller coasters nine years ago. He had read about the Crystal Beach Comet in a *Weekend Magazine* article listing "100 Best Things About Canada." One thrilling ride, and he was smitten.

8    Since then, the 31-year-old dental technician from Cambridge, Ontario, has travelled to Nashville, San Diego, Coney Island, and Myrtle Beach, South Carolina, in pursuit of his hobby. The Crystal Beach coasters stand up to the best. The Comet is "fast from start to finish. They run it flat out, and that is one of the joys."

9    The Comet is routinely rated among the top ten coasters in the world. At 35 metres, its highest arch affords a spectacular, if brief, *reconnoitre* of the countryside. Its first big drop plunges the equivalent of ten storeys. The coaster reaches a heart-stopping 100 kilometres per hour. You feel as though you're plummeting into Lake Erie. If you have your eyes open.

10    Sykes says there's a technique to riding a coaster like the Comet. "You have to ride with the ride. If you fight it, hold your head down, or close your eyes, you'll end up getting bumped pretty good. What you have to do is look for the hills. If they're going down, you just kind of float."

11    Float indeed.

12    It's hard to imagine, but the Comet was built to replace a more terrifying coaster, the legendary Cyclone. It was dismantled after only twenty years. According to folklore, the Cyclone was so frightening that the park employed a nurse to attend to woozy passengers.

13    Tim Sykes says he relishes the legend surrounding the ghost coaster. It lives in his imagination, kindled by memories passed on by his father. In his collection of coaster memorabilia, Sykes prizes the ageing postcards of the Cyclone. As Sykes waits patiently for another spin on the Cyclone's "tame" successor, he laments the fact that he was born too late to ride the original as his father did.

14    It's a pity, I agree. Chances are, Tim Sykes wouldn't have needed the nurse.

## Style and Structure

1. (a) Sandell begins his essay with the words "It lasts 114 seconds." What is "It"? Where do you discover this information?

(b) What is your immediate reaction to the first paragraph? Is the writer successful in grabbing your interest? If so, how has he managed it?

2.    What is the role of paragraphs 2 through 5? How different would the tone of the essay have been if the writer had begun with paragraph 2, instead of with the introduction he devised?

3. (a) Write out paragraph 6, sentence by sentence. What is the unifying factor that holds these sentences together?

   (b) Can you suggest ways in which the unity of the paragraph might be improved? Rewrite the paragraph, illustrating your suggestions.

4. (a) Throughout the essay, the writer gives a fair amount of technical information about the functioning of roller coasters, particularly the Comet. Do you think readers interested in roller coasters want this sort of information? Explain your opinion.

   (b) How successful do you think the writer has been in presenting this technical information in a readable fashion? Why?

5.    Very likely, Sandell could have written his essay without employing the figure of Tim Sykes at all. Yet Tim plays an important role. In one well-developed paragraph, examine the role of Tim Sykes, using specific references to the essay.

6. (a) Examine the **topic sentence** of each paragraph as a means of determining what that paragraph is about. Then, devise an outline of the essay, one such as Sandell might have used if he had been working from an outline. Into how many sections do you find the essay divided?

   (b) Make a list of the **transitional devices** Sandell uses throughout his essay. Comment on the effectiveness of these devices in helping the reader to follow the thread of meaning from section to section.

# Warm-up

Discover some of the techniques that good writers use to convey heightened emotions to their readers. Find a sample of writing that contains very emotional passages and answer the following questions about it.

(i)   What emotion does the passage attempt to evoke?

(ii)  How many strong action verbs can you identify in the passage? (Write a list.)

(iii) How many colourful adjectives? (Write a list.)

(iv)  How are sentences structured to suit the action?

(v)   How are paragraphs structured to suit the action?

(vi) Roughly, on a scale of one to ten, with ten being "most successful," how would you rate the writer's success in conveying the emotion in (i) to the reader?

Read aloud to the class the passage you have chosen. Then, after all passages are read, hold a class discussion, focussing on comparing your answers to questions (i) through (vi) above.

# Thinking and Writing

a.    Even very good writers acknowledge the challenge of describing an emotion-filled experience in such a way that the reader is not put off — either by the personal nature of the experience or by the lavishness of the language used to describe it. The trick is to write so that the readers share the experience, even if they have never had the opportunity themselves.

List some "white-knuckle" experiences you have had and choose one. In a small group, relate the experience aloud so that your listeners get some insight into the emotions the experience stimulated for you. You may wish to jot down a few notes beforehand, concentrating on how you can introduce the subject so that your listeners are brought into the experience itself.

Write your descriptive essay, following Sandell's example of providing some nonemotional information about the subject as well. Be sure that your reader is informed, not just emotionally affected, by your writing. **Audience:** people who may not have had the experience themselves.

b.    In his essay, Sandell mentions an article that appeared in *Weekend Magazine*, entitled "100 Best Things About Canada." Draw up your own list of five "best things" — specific attractions either in Canada or in your immediate area. Using your list as the basis for an outline, write an essay developing each of the five examples.

Throughout the essay, keep in mind the value of drawing the reader into the experience of the attractions. Be careful to provide an appropriate introduction, so that your readers know what unifying principle ties the examples together. You might consider developing your essay as a list, numbering each example. **Audience:** someone who is not familiar with these attractions.

Send your final essay to a local tourism board.

# Confronting Pornography

## by Mary Janigan

Thirty-odd years ago, when the Supreme Court of Canada declared that D.H. Lawrence's novel *Lady Chatterley's Lover* was "not obscene," it dropped the legal shackles that had previously censored a tender, erotic love affair. *Lady Chatterley*, now a classic, seems almost virginal by today's permissive standards. Now, private acts — and private parts — are publicly available across Canada in books, films, videotapes, and magazines. *Hustler*, for one, features graphic pictorials of a lesbian encounter and of an aroused heterosexual couple who are engaged in explicit foreplay. Even those represent only mainstream, soft-core samples from the $50-billion North American porn industry, which spews out an estimated 540 different magazines and thousands of videos across the country every month. From Halifax to Vancouver, that societal shift is provoking an intense debate over censorship — and the limits of freedom of expression.  1

The battle is breaking out everywhere. It encompasses politicians, feminists, academics — indeed, most Canadians. In British Columbia, feminist social activists such as Jancis Andrews are bombarding the provincial attorney general's department with the names of tapes depicting rape, torture, and incest, available at the Red Hot Video chain, in an attempt to bring its products under the control of the B.C. Classification Board. In Manitoba, concerned parents forced the provincial education department to withdraw a planned sex education course because it did not present notions of "right" and "wrong" in sexual behaviour. In Newfoundland, the influx of sex videos has prompted the St. John's police to lay more than 50 charges against several video distributors over a period of two years, with 56 other charges pending. And in Toronto, the 1984 Festival of Forbidden Films opened with 100 banned films from 25 nations, only to find that some of them had also been banned by Ontario's censor board.  2

The issues raised by those and other related events are polarizing key groups in almost all segments of Canadian society. Feminists such as Maude Barlow, a former federal Liberal government adviser on women's issues, contend that the deluge of pornography debases women and threatens their safety. Other feminists, including author June Callwood, argue that it is dangerous to give governments more power to control the media. The arts community is also  3 divided. In 1984, 1115 furious members of the Alliance of Canadian Cinema, Television and Radio Artists (ACTRA) cancelled a recent decision by their union executive that could have discouraged union members from participating in productions involving excessive violence and abusive sexual behaviour.

4      There is no consensus on what to do about controlling pornography, least of all among academics. Some of them flatly declare that violence in the media generates violence in the real world. Others deny the existence of any causal link. Politicians, too, are buffeted by the confusing messages they receive. The Gallup organization has reported that two-thirds of Canadians say that television violence may adversely affect youngsters. And in February 1983, 58 percent of Canadians supported censorship of television programs, especially pornographic and violent shows. Said Eastern Passage, Nova Scotia, fisherman Stanley Purdy: "TV is terrible. It should be censored more thoroughly, especially the obscene parts." But politicians also note the contradictory evidence of the marketplace. Between 1965 and 1980, the sales of pornographic magazines in Canada skyrocketed by 327 percent, to $15.4 million from $3.6 million. In the United States, box office receipts of violent horror and science-fiction movies shot up by 600 percent from 1970 to 1984, according to the Washington-based National Coalition on Television Violence.

5      One of the most vociferous pressure groups clamouring for political change is the police. They claim that media violence is partially to blame for the deaths of six on-duty policemen, all occurring during a two-month period in 1984. They cite the case of Metro Toronto Const. David Dunmore, who was shot and killed by eighteen-year-old Gary White. Friends said that the killer was fascinated by the violent movie *First Blood*, in which star Sylvester Stallone, an army veteran, engages in hand-to-hand combat with the police force of a remote U.S. town. When White shot Dunmore, he was wearing army fatigues, as Stallone does in the film.

6      Societies have been censoring perceived threats to state stability or public morality ever since the power of the written and visual message began to be understood. In the fourth century B.C., the Greek philosopher Plato argued for the banishment of all poets because he claimed they lied about gods, heroes, and men — and hindered the development of virtue in individuals and justice in the state.

7      The Alberta education department has scrapped certain textbooks as teaching materials after an audit found sexist or racist biases in French and Ukrainian readers already in use. That decision highlights probably the largest single reason that the debate over censorship is sharper and more rancorous than ever: more diverse interest groups are detecting more types of threats

to their values. Ethnic and religious groups are challenging the way they are portrayed in everything from Shakespeare's *Merchant of Venice*, which offends some Jews, to snack food commercials that depicted Mexicans as lazy. Meanwhile, conservative lobbies continue to object to explicit material because they perceive it as a threat to a family-oriented society. But the most powerful pressure comes from women, who have emerged as a strong political interest group at a time when mass-market pornography has become more violent and more degrading. Many women contend that other types of sexually explicit material, both printed and on film, are a threat to their rising status and dignity.

The feminist proponents of censorship have redefined the traditionalists' definition of obscenity. They do not object to erotica — portrayals of sex between affectionate men and women — but they do oppose material that degrades or violates women, especially if it includes sexual violence. Declared Eileen Hendry, the former acting president of the Canadian Advisory Council on the Status of Women: "I have no trouble with censorship when I know that the results of this type of pornography are damaging and tragic." 8

Indeed, feminists are among the most divided groups on the issue. Callwood, for one, argues that rather than fighting degrading porn, women should concentrate on acquiring even more economic power. "People do not beat up equals but inferiors," says the best-selling author and civil libertarian. "Men do not push around women who make as much money as they do." Still, because of her anticensorship stance, Callwood claims that she has been ostracized by many feminists and has resigned from two national women's organizations. 9

Politicians, conscious of the changing definitions of obscenity and of the new distinctions that the public is drawing between erotica and violent porn, are now attempting to change the laws on the subject. They have three main federal tools at their disposal: the Customs Tariff, which prohibits the import of books or visual material of an "immoral or indecent character"; the Canada Post Corporation Act, which limits prohibited material from coming into Canada; and the Criminal Code, Section 159, which makes it an offence to sell or distribute obscene material. Many critics argue that the code is inadequate because its definition of obscenity is too narrow: it says that obscenity exists only when there is "undue exploitation" of sex or sex coupled with crime, horror, cruelty, or violence. 10

But censorship in Canada falls under both federal and provincial jurisdictions. The provinces can empower municipalities to enact bylaws regulating the display of pornographic materials. Recently, municipal politicians in Dorval, Que- 11 bec, persuaded local retailers to keep porn magazines five feet above floor level and block everything but the magazine title with a barrier. That move convinced Quebec politicians to empower other municipalities to enact similar legislation. More significant are the powers of the censor boards in the eight provinces that have them: they range from Manitoba's liberal classification system, which merely warns viewers of the type of content, to Ontario's strict censorship board, which cuts and bans without a trial. The Ontario board's actions are the most controversial and far-reaching, because most films enter Canada through that province, and other provincial boards usually maintain Ontario's cuts.

12    Because of those powers, Ontario inevitably finds itself facing the hardest-fought battles over film cuts. Now the opponents of censorship are challenging the legality of Ontario's censoring process with a powerful new weapon: the Charter of Rights and Freedoms. In 1982, the Ontario Censor Board banned public screenings of several films, including Michael Snow's *Rameau's Nephew*, an experimental work on perceptions that included a brief scene of penetration, and *Not a Love Story*, a National Film Board documentary on pornography. Soon after that, the Ontario Film and Video Appreciation Society, a group of arts organization administrators, filmmakers, and civil libertarians, sprang into existence. The film society promptly challenged the board's fundamental right to cut and ban films. In divisional court in 1983 and in the Ontario Court of Appeal the following year, the society's lawyers argued that the constitutional "freedom of expression" was being curtailed by a board that used only vague, subjective "community standards." They said that that was not a reasonable limit to a sacred right. Both courts backed the society's position.

13    Four months after the February 1984 decision, the censor board unexpectedly intervened in a new area. On May 31, Ontario censors seized two British videotapes from the avant-garde Toronto art gallery A Space, arguing that the board has authority over public showings of videos and that the gallery should have submitted the tapes for prior approval before showing them. The gallery protested vigorously. Ontario County Court judge Douglas Bernstein added strength to the anticensorship forces when he ordered that the tapes be returned because the censors did not have a warrant. Bernstein ruled that the Charter guarantees freedom from such unreasonable search and seizure. But the judge did not have to touch the sensitive issue of the censor board's authority over art galleries. A Space co-ordinator Douglas Sigurdson continues to maintain that the province does not have the right to censor art before it is shown.

14    The censors also have to deal with the shifting and confusing nature of

community standards. The country's censor boards tried to adapt to community standards the notorious film *Caligula*. The variety of rulings that resulted was staggering. British Columbia and Quebec allowed the U.S. edition, which featured twenty more minutes of violence and explicit sex than a British version. Five other provinces approved the British version, but in one — Alberta — police subsequently charged distributors with obscenity under the Criminal Code. Nova Scotia banned the film altogether.

The *Caligula* example reflects the ambiguity that haunts the issue of censorship. Community standards differ widely. And the question of what is "undue" exploitation of sex is still largely a subjective judgment. Former Ontario censor Michele White says, "Some men who find lesbian sex between *Playboy* bunny types just fine are appalled by male homosexual sex acts." 15

Meanwhile, the flood of sadistic, graphic material continues to grow. As a result, the police are demanding better weapons and tougher penalties to wage war on porn. And they are seeking a more forceful message from the public. As Insp. John Lucy of the Vancouver police department told *Maclean's*, "The police are paying more and more attention to the issue, but I think that clear public opinion is sorely lacking." 16

In the forefront of the pressure for tougher laws is Ontario's groundbreaking Project P. Formed in 1975, the four-member group of two Ontario Provincial Police officers and two Metro Toronto police officers is the country's first antiporn squad, offering courses to police and other law officers on how to recognize and charge obscenity. The officers of Project P have become active proponents of the need for an expanded definition for obscenity that includes violence and degradation. Project P's Cpl. Ronald Kirkpatrick says that most provinces now draw a legal line between simulated sex acts and such acts coupled with violence. As a result, sex with violence, hard-core sex, bestiality, and pornography involving children can be considered obscene. The courts have confirmed Project P's judgment on the issue: since 1975, the squad has lost only four out of 450 cases. Kirkpatrick said that Quebec and British Columbia are more tolerant: provincial police mainly restrict obscenity charges to kiddie porn, bestiality, and violent sex and coercion. But violence without sex remains largely free from censorship. "You could have a three-hour documentary about disembowelling babies," says Kirkpatrick with visible disgust, and police officers would not be able to stop its distribution. The officer added that most pornography users become "desensitized" and begin to crave more explicit and violent material. "The public at large is unaware how far things have gone," he declared. "Our tolerance changes because stuff sneaks up on us. Every month [the distributors] push the law and we try to push back." 17

18      Central to the concern of police and other procensorship forces is their belief that porn affects behaviour. Whether or not they are right is a question that has driven a nation-wide wedge into the academic community. At the heart of the controversy are a series of dramatic studies by leading North American academics whose results are both fascinating and disturbing. In 1981, two University of Manitoba researchers, Neil Malamuth and James Check, showed two sexually violent films, with rape scenes, to half of a group of 115 students and two nonviolent films to half of another 115 students. Subsequent questionnaires indicated that males who saw the sexually violent films revealed increased acceptance of violence against women. (The changes in female attitudes were insignificant.) Then, a 1982 study by Americans Dolf Zillmann and Jennings Bryant that exposed 160 male and female subjects over a six-week period to degrading but nonviolent pornography concluded that all members of the group became less supportive of women's liberation, more inclined to give lighter sentences to convicted rapists, and more distrustful of their partners in extended relationships. One of the most respected professors in the field, Ed Donnerstein of the University of Wisconsin, says that there has been sufficient serious research to justify the conclusion that pornography influences behaviour.

19      But the debate is not closed. York University sociologist and feminist Thelma McCormack, for one, is vehemently opposed to increased censorship — and she insists that the recent studies do *not* show any direct link between sex offences and pornography. McCormack argues that because men become desensitized, "It does not mean that they are *doing* anything." As well, she contends that there is no conclusive proof that the media can change attitudes, and that the media rarely change behaviour. "Researchers are now saying that porn does not cause aggression but it reinforces attitudes that condone aggression," she added. "Well, there is a big step between attitudes and behaviour." Criminologist Cyril Greenland of the University of Toronto, an expert in sex offenders, is even more blunt. "To the best of my knowledge, there is no causal relationship," he says. "Life is much more complicated than that. They [sex offenders] may be turned on by porn but the existence of porn does not compel them to act."

20      While the question remains unresolved, the belief that films and books affect behaviour still lies behind the call for more censorship — and indeed the basic justification for all censorship. Ontario censor Mary Brown contends that pornography is changing the face of Canadian society. She says that the incidence of violent sex films has more than doubled in the past year. The Ontario Censor board's monthly list of requested cuts contains almost as many

violent scenes ("eliminate two poles through man's eyes — graphic") as sexual scenes. Brown says that the current controversy over censorship is obscuring the real problem — the nature, not the control, of the product. "Porn is being force-fed into our culture," she says.

But Callwood said that the urge to censor is simply the urge to avaoid   **21** the unsettling, the unpleasant, and the disturbing. People reach for censorship as a "big white bottle of pills" to cure society's ills, said Callwood, but it is really a "big white ball of cotton that will cover our eyes from the realities of the world." Indeed, the desire to suppress what is perceived to be a threat has caused governments all over the world to censor various kinds of expression. According to PEN, the international writers' organization, at least 500 writers are currently imprisoned in countries from the Eastern Bloc to the Third World for their controversial works.

The results of government censorship are on view at the Festival of Forbidden   **22** Films. Each film shown either has been banned in its home country for political, religious, or moral reasons, or else government forces have hindered the filmmaker in his or her work. The festival's selection has included the 1976 Israeli film *The Black Banana* — director Benjamin Hayeem's satire of religious practices that the Israeli government suppressed because it offended that country's politically powerful religious groups. The festival also tried to run *In the Realm of the Senses*, a 1976 Japanese film that is both sexually explicit and violent — as well as being a powerful critique of the decadent elements in Japanese society. The Ontario Censor Board banned the film because of its explicit sex. "The amazing thing is how many times great film artists have been censored," said festival chairman Marc Glassman. Added Wayne Clarkson, director of Toronto's internationally acclaimed Festival of Festivals — which has had its films banned with numbing regularity ever since it began in 1976: "The price that we pay for censorship is a far greater price than those films inflict."

Increasingly, critics are concerned that those with the power to censor are   **23** banning films for political as well as social reasons. For instance, the Ontario Censor Board restricted showings of the British rock video *Two Tribes* by the group Frankie Goes to Hollywood to those over eighteen. The board claimed that the tape was too violent, but many observers countered that its content was clearly satiric: *Two Tribes* showed U.S. President Ronald Reagan and former Soviet leader Konstantin Chernenko in a vicious, groin-grabbing catfight. In the United States, the trend to political censorship appears even more clear cut. During the Reagan administration, government officials ordered National Film Board films on acid rain and nuclear war to be labelled as "government propaganda" and moved to curb the freedom of expression of its federal employees. The *New York Times* revealed that more than 120 000 federal workers had signed agreements to submit for censorship any speech, article, or book that they produce on U.S. intelligence gathering.

24        Both the advocates and the foes of censorship base their cases on a judgment of what causes society the most harm. Many Canadians, angered by sadistic and vulgar pornography, argue that a government must be able to protect the dignity and interests of its citizens. Others, alarmed by the prospect of surrendering more freedom to governments, contend that banning books and films will not make society safer or solve the real problems of its weaker members. It is a philosophical struggle that began before the first Chinese emperor held his book bonfire in 213 B.C. — and burned the humanist writings of the great sage Confucius. And it will continue as long as governments attempt to decide what freedoms and rights must be curbed for the greater good of society. The choice is one that no responsible legislator makes easily — and history is littered with ample evidence of their mistakes.

## Style and Structure

1. (a) Identify the sentence in paragraph 1 that best captures the **thesis** of the essay as a whole.
   (b) What contrast is stressed in paragraph 1? How is this "grabber" appropriate to the theme you have identified?
2. (a) How does Janigan emphasize the scope of the censorship debate in paragraphs 2 and 3?
   (b) Based on the information contained in paragraphs 1, 2, and 3, what assumptions does the writer make about the intended reader's previous knowledge about the censorship debate?
   (c) Why is it a good strategy to place the information contained in paragraphs 2 and 3 at this point in the article?
3. (a) What three types of offensive material does Janigan classify in paragraphs 4 to 9?
   (b) Given her assumptions about the intended reader's previous knowledge, why does the author feel it necessary to identify these three classes of offensive materials?
4. (a) In paragraphs 10 to 15, what levels of government does Janigan identify as having the power to censor?
   (b) What "censoring" tools does she identify as being available to each level of government?

(c) Why does she deal with the provincial level (censor boards) last?

(d) Given the topic announced in paragraph 1, why does Janigan spend so much time on the censor boards?

5. (a) How does the type of information presented in paragraph 18 affect the reader's attitude toward "the conclusion that pornography influences behaviour"?

(b) How does the type of information presented in paragraph 19 affect the reader's attitude toward the conclusion that pornography does *not* influence behaviour?

6. (a) What defence of censorship does Mary Brown offer in paragraph 20?

(b) What danger of censorship does June Callwood stress in paragraph 21?

(c) How do paragraphs 22 and 23 illustrate Callwood's argument in paragraph 21?

(d) What effect does the order of presentation of the information contained in paragraphs 20 to 23 have on the reader?

7.  Why does paragraph 24 make an excellent **conclusion** for the article?

# Warm-up

1.  Examine the movie listings in one of the large-circulation daily newspapers available in your community. Draw conclusions about the standards (e.g., language, violence, sexual content) used to classify or restrict movies for certain audiences. Write a one-paragraph report of your findings.

    **Audience:** someone who has not thought much about the ways movies are classified.

    Compare your paragraph to those written by two or three of your classmates. How do their conclusions compare to yours? Suggest to them any additions or clarifications that might help them convey their ideas more effectively to readers. Revise your own paragraph, taking into consideration the suggestions made by your classmates.

2.  Working with the rest of the class, prepare a formal debate on the following resolution:

    > Violence, of any kind, should be censored in movies and television.

    Half the class should write single paragraphs, each presenting *one* argument that supports the resolution; the other half should write single paragraphs, each presenting *one* argument that opposes it. Based on these paragraphs, each group will develop the arguments to be presented by three debaters for each side. Each debater should have enough material for a two- to three-minute presentation.

After the debate, revise your paragraph so that it takes into account any objections you have heard raised against it.

# Thinking and Writing

a.   Janigan quotes Inspector John Lucy of the Vancouver police department as saying, "The police are paying more and more attention to the issue [of the censorship of pornography], but I think that clear public opinion is sorely lacking."

Survey at least ten people to find out whether or not they support censorship. If they support censorship, ask them to define what types of materials they would like to see censored (e.g., scenes depicting explicit sex, scenes depicting sex and violence combined, scenes depicting violence without sex, scenes depicting homosexual activities). If they do not support censorship, ask them to define how such materials as those listed above should be dealt with.

Make certain that the types of people you survey are diverse enough to be representative of members of your community (i.e., that they represent different age levels, types of employment, sexes).

Write an essay in which you explain your findings.

**Audience:** someone who is involved with trying to enforce censorship in your community and would be interested in knowing more about "community standards" in your area.

Send a copy of your essay to the public relations department of the local police force.

b.   Write an essay in which you explain your opinions on the role that should be played by a provincial censorship board in determining which movies should be shown in theatres, which videotapes should be rented or sold, and which magazines and books should be sold in your community.

**Audience:** someone who is familiar enough with the subject and holds a view so opposed to yours that you will have to offer concrete evidence and well-reasoned arguments to support your view.

# Baby, It's Yours

## by Jennifer Hunter

Simone Robin Hunter Cruickshank is a very privileged little girl. A West Coast baby, she has acquired a taste for smoked salmon and salmon caviar sushi. Her cupboard and drawers are stuffed with adorable clothes that carry trendy labels such as Bravo, Esprit, Roots, and Beaver Canoe. Many were bestowed by wealthy great-aunts too young to be grandmothers. For Simone's third birthday last June, her mother (me) and father bought her a $25 green dinosaur cake and a Fisher-Price kitchen for $100. The thirteen pint-sized party guests left with $4 loot bags and appetites sated by Häagen-Dazs ice cream. By the time my husband and I realized what had happened we'd blown at least $200 on the birthday bash. Okay, so I felt several twinges of guilt when I looked at the bills. But since I have the income, I told myself, why not give my only child the best? Besides, my mania for buying her things isn't unique. 1

Thousands of other working women and men, affluent children of the prosperous 1950s and 1960s, are lavishing extraordinary amounts on their offspring. Says one mother, whose basement is filled with Little Tikes toys: "You get the same kind of jollies buying luxuries for your child as you do for yourself." Indeed, retailers have stocked their shelves with so many entrancing items for youngsters that parents almost feel guilty not buying. One father sighs: "It's tough to go out for a walk and avoid the stores." 2

Businesses catering to the under-twelve group are burgeoning; designer clothing boutiques, bookstores, video outlets, and toy shops have sprung up to serve this strategic consumer segment. Retail marketing expert Len Kubas estimates the children's market has grown to a $3.5-billion-a-year phenomenon in Canada. 3

Split families are one reason why we are buying so much for our kids. A third of Canadian marriages end in divorce, and dual households for kids demand dual toy boxes. In families where Mom and Dad remain a unit, it's Mom who does most of the buying, and guilt is often a motive. Three out of five women who have preschool children are in the work force and feel torn between double duties as mothers and career women. They shop to relieve the stress of their inner conflict. "Last week I spent $30 on a train for James," says Alison Pickard, 30. "He wasn't feeling well and I sent him to school. I felt guilty." Sandra Ross-Dixon, 40-year-old mother of two, says: "I try to make up for not being there. So I'll buy things like Speak & Spell 4 or other educational toys so they'll have something stimulating to do when I'm not at home."

5    Many first-time moms are older, often in their 30s, before their children are born, which means that they are discovering the bliss of motherhood after having established their careers. Not only do they have a lot of disposable income by then, they also have fewer children than their parents did — an average of 1.7 per family. The children become that much more precious. Take the example of Tory Dickinson, a charming, sunny two-year-old. The treasured first-born of working parents, she spends her days in OshKosh overalls and Weebok sneakers. One of her favourite toys is a plastic child-sized shopping cart. "You work hard and you convince yourself the only reason you're working so hard is for the money, so you can spend it on your child," says her mother, securities lawyer Sheila Murray, 32. "When I was growing up you'd go out shopping once or twice a year. You'd get one pair of shoes and one pair of jeans. You'd get gifts on your birthday and at Christmas. With Tory, Dave and I very often go out on the weekend and get her shoes or clothes. She is more indulged."

6    Another mother, a university professor, confesses that when she goes out shopping for her eight-year-old and three-and-a-half-year-old she can easily spend up to $200. "I have a bag in my cupboard with four unopened toys and six new books. It's like I have this garrison mentality. My mother-in-law has a house full of food, just in case. I have a house full of toys, just in case." Her own mother has splurged on the children, too, buying an elephant slide and chipping in for a $240 Little Tikes playhouse.

7    Grandparents have become a big factor in boosting retail spending on the under-twelve set. Canadians over the age of 45 are the most prosperous group in the country, with money to burn. They have fewer grandchildren to indulge than their parents did and have had to wait longer for them. Simone's maternal grandmother was 57 when her first grandchild arrived. Mine was just 48 when I arrived on the scene. Grandparents hanker after the opportunity to bestow upon these long-awaited grandchildren the material benefits they could never afford to give their own kids. Ede Ross, 70, has eleven grandchildren, all under the age of ten. She recalls that when her four children were young, they had three sets of clothing. "One on, one in the laundry, and one that was clean." Now her grandchildren are outfitted in designer clothes, many of which were bought by Mrs. Ross herself. "I don't need to buy a lot of things for myself. And I love to see my grandchildren nicely dressed."

8    Practically every weekday, the enormous shopping mall in the Toronto suburb of Mississauga, Square One, is filled with jeans-clad mothers pushing

strollers, and relaxed-looking grandparents browsing through the stores. One area of the mall, Kid's Place, is devoted strictly to children. It has twelve shops selling toys, shoes, clothing, and baby furniture. In the window of a store called Mom & Me is a corduroy jump suit (size two) with a Pierre Cardin label. It's $73. "When parents need something unique for their children they don't mind spending the money," says Sophie Dawod, the store manager. Naturally, the spending boom has been like manna from heaven for retailers and manufacturers. Even though there were fewer kids between the ages of five and twelve in 1986 than in 1980, retail spending on those kids steadily increased by twelve percent a year, says Glenn Asano of Micromedia Ltd. His company has recently completed a study aimed at companies who want to capture a greater chunk of the children's market. "Children are big business today," the study notes. "The 1980s mini-boom created a huge new demand for trendy, expensive baby and children's clothes, accessories and toys that didn't exist in the 1970s."

What's more, kids are demanding, picky, and ruthlessly status-conscious. The study goes on to say: "Children aged nine to twelve have a high level of awareness of the status associated with brands and brand names. This is largely attributable to the pressure they feel from their peers to wear fashionable clothing. When children are actually buying, or are influencing the purchase, they are more likely to choose a quality, brand-name product. Hence, it is important for marketers to plant the first seeds of brand loyalty at an early age." The advice would seem insidious if it were not based on the plain truth. Marlee Ross-Bakker, a Vancouver mother, comments, "I have a niece who is thirteen who will only wear Esprit and Benetton. You don't want to be the only mother who is not letting her kids wear that." 9

Kids, of course, start picking up brand and status consciousness in the cradle, from their parents. There are, for instance, right baby strollers and wrong baby strollers, and the right ones cost $350. Perego stroller salesman Doug Ineson says he is no longer selling utilitarian pushcarts for babies; he is "selling fashion." 10

Parents have extended their generosity to hairdos, books, records, birthday parties, and other forms of entertainment. Derek London, a Vancouver hair-salon owner, opened a children's salon called Headz at the back of a trendy children's boutique two years ago. Boys and girls can watch Pee Wee Herman on video while they get their hair cut by London's stylists. Some little girls even get perms. "It's the only business I've ever opened that's paid for itself in a year," he says. He charges between $15 and $25 for a cut and shampoo and his 600 clients allow him to bring in roughly $5000 a month. Some 11 of the more style-conscious moms are allowing their public-schoolers to get their hair streaked. London says, "If mother is blonder than daughter, she wants her child to look more like her." One Toronto mother says her husband was aghast to learn that she planned to spend $25 on her three-and-a-half-year-old daughter's haircut. "But I know if you have a horrible haircut you look horrible," the mother says. "I want my daughter to look wonderful."

12    Kids' show biz has become a big item, too, and singers such as Raffi and Sharon, Lois, and Bram are hounded like rock stars for autographs and a pat on the head. The Vancouver Children's Festival, a week-long feast of songs and fun, has been mimicked by fifteen other such festivals in North America. Sales of children's cassette tapes have become so lucrative that the Children's Book Store in Toronto will soon open a second store specializing in cassettes and videos. Raffi's latest album has even been released on CD. Meanwhile, the store sells $2 million worth of kids' books a year. Fourteen years ago it was the only store of its kind in Canada. Now there are 55 others, and Coles Book Stores Ltd. is opening a chain just for children called Active Minds. There are no Canadian statistics on children's book sales, but in the United States, sales grew 160 percent from 1982 to 1987. The boom, say the book-sellers, started only about five years ago.

13    A huge demand has developed for clowns and musicians at birthday parties ($75 to $90 a party), for parent–tot gym classes, which teach parents how to play with their kids ($80 for ten sessions), and for educational toys. Creative Kids, which sells toys à la Tupperware in mothers' homes, is projecting sales of $4.5 million this year. Last year, sales were $2.5 million. "Our best party was $2500 in one evening," says Ivana Kuttas, the company's public relations manager. "I do know consultants who said they were surprised at some of the people who spent money. But I guess when it comes to your children, you're not as rational as you are in other areas of your life."

14    What is this spending spree doing to our kids? Plenty, say children's experts Lynne Williams, Henry Berman, and Louisa Rose. In their book *The Too Precious Child*, they see overspending as a symptom of something more. Having waited longer than previous generations to have children, many couples throw themselves into parenthood with heightened expectations. They hold an ideal of parenthood that resembles Glinda the Good Witch in *The Wizard of Oz*, who grants a child's every wish with a wave of her wand. But in return for giving their children so much, they expect perfect children. This places a burden on the child that may be intolerable for some. "Excess produces excess," the trio writes. "Excessive involvement may lead to a surplus of guilt; excessive adoration may result in the extreme self-absorption of narcissism.

And this thesis is borne out empirically every day in psychiatrists' offices around the country, where victims of too-intense parenting attempt to examine their insatiable need for achievement, their unreasoning feelings of failure, or their difficulties in sustaining relationships."

Are we creating a generation of overindulged juvenile basket cases? When I watch Simone heedlessly splashing paint on her Roots sweat pants, I don't really see a *too* precious child. Most of the time — usually when she gets a good nap — she is a co-operative three-and-a-half-year-old, loving, sensitive, and self-assured. Maybe the child experts have a point. But maybe, if we can instill our children with a sense of balance, a social conscience, and respect for others, all our spending may not do them too much harm. In any case, steering clear of the stores may prove far too difficult for a generation of baby boomers born to shop.

15

## Style and Structure

1. (a) How would you describe the opening strategy Hunter uses in her essay?
    (b) What is your immediate reaction to "Simone Robin Hunter Cruickshank"? How do you think the writer intends you to feel? How might you have felt if the child had been introduced simply as "Simone"?
    (c) Judging by your own reactions, to what sort of readership do you suppose the writer means to appeal?
    (d) In using her own case as a starting point, Hunter sets up certain expectations in the reader. Discuss the effectiveness of this technique under the following criteria:
       (i) credibility;
       (ii) objectivity;
       (iii) stimulation of interest.
2.    Throughout the essay, the writer refers to a number of resources, quoting frequently from both named and unnamed sources. Count the number of sources that she cites. What effect do you believe this technique has on the reader?
3. (a) Hunter gives several reasons why the children's market has grown so rapidly in Canada in recent years. Identify what these reasons are and in what paragraphs they are found.
    (b) How do the **topic sentences** of these paragraphs help you to identify the information in (a)? Comment on the usefulness of each.

4. (a) This essay takes a cause-and-effect approach to the subject of parents' spending on their offspring. Determine which parts of the essay are devoted to the investigation of causes and which to effects.

   (b) Would you say that the development is consistent?

   (c) Discuss what improvements, if any, you would like to see in the development of causes or of effects.

5.    Throughout the essay, the writer provides a great many figures to indicate costs, ages, numbers of clients, and so on. What is the overall effect of these figures? What is your personal reaction to the numbers cited?

6. (a) Examine the last paragraph of the essay. Jot down in your notebook a list of the issues covered, sentence by sentence. What is your opinion of the **unity** and **coherence** of this paragraph? (See pp. 301 and 302).

   (b) Rewrite the body of the paragraph, using three of four sentences while retaining the original **topic** and **concluding sentences**. Compare your paragraph with the one in the essay and discuss which you prefer and why.

# Warm-up

Preliminary research can help a writer to confirm personal suspicions and get "a fix" on what is actually happening in the world. One method of preliminary research involves checking newspapers and advertisements. In preparation for the following essay, check to see what is selling, and at what prices, in children's clothing and services.

Imagine a typical middle-class child of a certain age. Make a list of the new clothes, toys, furnishings, and/or services that this child might require during a month. Next, consult advertisements, newspaper articles, and consumer reports to list what products will best satisfy those hypothetical needs. If possible, indicate the range of prices; for instance, haircuts for children may be advertised at $5 to $25. From your lists, write a paragraph summary indicating trends in kid-consumerism.

# Thinking and Writing

a.    The writer asks us a leading question: "Since I have the income, why not give my only child the best?" The best, in this case, was a $200 birthday party for a three-year-old.

Many people, including experts, feel that overindulging children, regardless of family income, is a bad idea. The writer suggests a few of the undesirable results throughout her essay. Review the points that she makes and compose a list of four reasons why you believe that extreme generosity to one's children may be a mistake.

With your list as a guide, develop an outline for an essay in which you argue that giving the best is not always the wisest choice. Use four paragraphs for the body of your essay, one for each of the reasons on your list. Try to provide as many real-life examples as possible to illustrate your ideas.

**Audience:** affluent parents who are unaware of the possible results of their spending habits.

Send a copy of your final draft to an instructor of family life studies or sociology for in-class discussion.

b.  Every generation seems to feel that its youngest members are the worst examples humanity has ever seen. To some people, the suggestion that kids today are "demanding, picky, and ruthlessly status-conscious" has a certain ring of validity. Others are quick to point out that all children, whatever age they are born into, are self-centred and out merely to please themselves — that this is what childhood is all about. Are children of the 1990s any more demanding than children of any other age?

To answer this question, visit a shopping mall and speak to several store managers about children's fashions and accessories. Find out about trends and prices, and the influence children have in their parents' purchasing decisions. Ask if the managers have found appreciable differences in buying behaviour for children in the last five years. Also, be careful to note the behaviour of shoppers as a clue to the answers you are seeking.

With the results of your investigation, develop a descriptive essay to answer the question of whether or not children are now more demanding.

Variation: Write a compare/contrast essay, in which you use examples of your own and your friends' spending habits when you were pre-teenagers, showing how these habits were different from or similar to those you see in pre-teens today. Be as objective as possible, giving plenty of examples to demonstrate your ideas and showing the opinion of your parents as well.

**Audience:** people in your own age group who are wondering about the future of today's children.

# From Quill to Computer

## by Robert Sekuler

1  Every advance in technology manages somehow to transform the creative process. Improved fabrication of steel forms stimulated a new vision of architecture's possibilities. Developments in electronics gave musicians unimagined creative freedom and artistic control. Now, a relatively new technology, word processing, may be transforming the art of writing. It is too early to predict all the ways in which writing will change, but we can get some clues by looking at research in cognitive psychology and by studying the experiences of people who use word processors.

2  The range of available word processors is large. They vary in size from one small box weighing less than four pounds to a deskload of heavy equipment; their costs are similarly variable — from about $1000 up to $20 000. But, basically, they are all the same: electronic devices that allow you to type, store, modify, and print text.

3  The differences between writing longhand, typing, and word processing are readily apparent even to the most reluctant first-time user of a word-processor. Writing with paper and pencil is slow, laborious, and downright painful in time. Composing on a typewriter helps with speed and physical comfort, but correcting a typo, inserting a new sentence, or repositioning a paragraph requires messy erasure, fumbling with correction fluid, or "cutting and pasting" — physically relocating a misplaced paragraph with scissors and tape.

4  The word processor accomplishes these and several other tasks electronically, and consequently can transform writing in three distinct ways: it can ease the mechanical drudgery of writing; it can enhance our motivation and willingness to spend time writing; and it can produce qualitative changes in the way we go about writing.

5  Nearly all how-to books on writing stress the importance of revision, typically advising "revise, revise, and then revise some more." Many writers treasure the tools of revision — erasers, scissors, tape, correction fluid, and wastebasket — almost as much as they value the implements of production — pencils, pens, and typewriters. But, while teaching freshman composition a few years ago, I rediscovered what teachers of English have long known: most people have a strong aversion to revision. Teachers may deplore this reluctance to revise, but it is easily understood. Ordinarily, revision is both difficult and tedious.

A word processor certainly can make cleaning up typos, misspellings, and   6
punctuation errors easy to do. But good prose, of course, is not just a collection
of neatly displayed and properly constructed sentences; to lead the reader
from one idea to the next, naturally and without hesitation, the writer must
provide appropriate road signs — clear transitions and connections between
sentences, paragraphs, and larger sections.

Though these transitions are often as hard to produce as the elements them-   7
selves, research has shown that readers (and writers) pay a price when writing
does not flow smoothly. Marcel Just and Patricia Carpenter, cognitive psychologists at Carnegie-Mellon University, presented readers with two sentences
— either adequately or inadequately linked — as in the following pairs.
1. (a) It was dark and stormy the night the millionaire died.
   (b) The killer left no clues for the police to trace.
2. (a) It was dark and stormy the night the millionaire was murdered.
   (b) The killer left no clues for the police to trace.

As the participants read, Just and Carpenter tracked their eye movements   8
and found that, on average, readers spent half a second less on the second
pair of sentences than on the first pair. Why? In the second pair, the transition
is clear: the writer uses the phrase "was murdered" in the first sentence
to set the reader up for "the killer" in the second sentence. When transitions
are missing, you must stop and mentally create them yourself — a distracting
and time-consuming task. If you can imagine reading an entire article with
sloppy connections not only between sentences but between paragraphs and
collections of paragraphs, you can see why good transitions are so important.

How would a word processor help? As Peter Wason, a psychologist at Uni-   9
versity College, London, observes, "Writing is difficult for some people because
they try to do two incompatible things at the same time: say something,
and say it in the most acceptable way." In *Writing with a Word Processor*,
William Zinsser suggests that you forget links and transitions initially. Concentrate instead on "letting your creative motor run the full course at full
speed; repairs can always be made later." Following Zinsser's advice, you can
mark each place where a transition might be needed (say, with an "XXX").
Later, you can instruct the word processor to locate each "XXX" and display
the surrounding text, and then you can develop and insert the needed transitions. Many people, in fact, do the same thing when composing with pen,
pencil, or typewriter, but the whole process is less convenient than it is with
a word processor and therefore less likely to get done.

Word processors are also helpful because they make it easy to get a clean   10
printed copy of your latest revision. Andrew Fluegelman and Jeremy Hewes,

authors of *Writing in the Computer Age,* argue that getting clean copies on demand offers positive psychological benefits. The copy's attractive, professional appearance provides reinforcement: when you have been really struggling with the text, the clean copy holds out a promise of better times ahead. Also, the clean copy makes it easier for you to review the material as any other reader would, without interruptions from complex marginal notes and messy insertions and deletions.

11    Word processors make an important contribution, improving motivation not only during revision but also during the entire writing process. Once beginners overcome their fear and awe of word processors, they realize that these imposing gadgets can make writing more bearable for several reasons. For one, word processors eliminate one of the more perplexing obstacles for many writers — the blank sheet of paper that seems to stare back reprovingly. Some people claim that a blank word-processor screen actually evokes less terror than does a blank piece of paper. Since few word-processor screens display the equivalent of an entire 8½-by-11-inch page, Fluegelman and Hewes say you can fill a screen faster than you can a sheet of paper, in effect dividing the chore into smaller, more manageable subtasks.

12    One friend of mine, however, is bothered less by a blank page or screen than by another common problem — writer's block. When he's stuck on one part of an article he must write, he quickly detours to another part that will be easier to complete. Not only does the detour give his writer's block sufficient time to work itself out, but when he's finally got all the parts completed and in place, the word processor can remove all telltale marks of the chaos from which his article emerged. Many people take similar detours when writing longhand or on a typewriter, but both methods tend to promote thinking in one direction — from a document's beginning to a document's end. Inserting material into something you've already written is possible but, again, not convenient.

13    Though the mechanical and motivational effects of the word processor are powerful in their own right, they may prove minor compared to one potential effect of this new technology: changing the way we think about the writing process itself. To appreciate this fully, we'll have to consider what creative writing is.

14    Many textbooks and teachers describe creative writing as a series of clearly defined steps. According to this view, you pick a manageable topic, do the required research, compose an outline, flesh out that outline, and, finally, polish what you have written. Though this view encourages the idea that writing can be taught and learned in simple and convenient chunks, many

cognitive psychologists — and many successful writers — have a different understanding of the writing process.

The novelist E.M. Forster put it well, asking: "How do I know what I think until I see what I say?" Kurt Vonnegut makes the same point when he observes that when writing, he feels like someone who is "watching a teletype machine in a newspaper office to see what comes out." Fine, for the creative genius, you might say, but what about the average person?    15

Psychologists Linda Flower and John Hayes of Carnegie-Mellon University asked college students to write essays on women's rights or abortion and, at the same time, to describe aloud what they were doing. Their research suggests that good writers do not do as much detailed mental planning as we might think. In fact, Flower and Hayes found that writers often did not know precisely what they would write until they had written it.    16

Though these findings are somewhat discomforting, suppose that they are true. What are the implications for writing on a word processor? Because it makes it easier both to produce and to modify our writing, a word processor may also make it easier to find out what we think.    17

One way to understand this is to consider what Susan Horton, a professor of English at the University of Massachusetts, calls reformulation. In *Thinking Through Writing*, Horton likens revision to tinkering and reserves the term "reformulation" for significant changes in organization, structure, and clarity. Reformulation, then, is a form of creative play, requiring intuition and experimentation. Reviewing the text, you may feel that a change is needed at a particular place without knowing precisely what that change should be.    18

One way of resolving this dilemma is to ask a series of "what if" questions. This type of question has been popularized by computer programs, such as VisiCalc, used for financial planning. In such programs, the user enters all the relevant data and assumptions — for example, interest rates. The program then projects an outcome based on those data and assumptions. You can then ask a "what if" question by telling the computer to recalculate its projections based on some changed assumption: what if interest rates rise, for example.    19

These programs encourage the same kind of playful, creative experimentation that an experienced word-processor user comes to depend on. You simply examine what you have already written and then try various "what ifs" — "What if I invert this sentence . . . move this paragraph . . . delete this phrase?" and so on. If you've made an improvement, it can be retained; if not, you can try again. By making alternative reorganizations more accessible, a word processor encourages you to experiment where you probably would not bother on a page of typed manuscript.    20

21    A word processor can certainly help an individual to write, but often writing involves collaboration with others. Though there haven't been any formal studies, in my experience a word processor can prove equally helpful when collaborating with another author.

22    When Randy Blake, a colleague at Northwestern, and I collaborated on a textbook, we divided the chapters between us and worked separately to prepare very rough first drafts. When a rough draft was ready, we sat down together at one word processor, using one keyboard but two display screens so that each of us had an unimpeded view of the action. Then we took turns reading aloud, revising and reorganizing the text in tandem. The idea was to encourage joint work before the text had become too polished and therefore resistant to change. Working together in this way, we generated far more "what if" questions than we would have singly. The result is a text that not only reads well (we're told) but appears to be seamless; reviewers say they can't tell who wrote what.

23    There's little doubt that, when used properly, a word processor can be a valuable tool for writing. But like all stories, this one has another side that should not be ignored. Some writers become so entranced by these devices that the new-found power to revise turns into an obsession. When that happens, the word processor tends to resemble its counterpart in the kitchen — the food processor. Perhaps you know, as I do, cooks who can't resist using their marvellous toy, so that everything they create is sure to be very well sliced, diced, or pureed.

24    There's a lesson here, not just for cooks and writers, but for all of us. No matter how powerful the technology we may have to help us, we still need good judgment and self-control.

## Style and Structure

1. (a) Identify the paragraphs that form the introduction to the essay, and underline the sentence or sentences that best state the **thesis** of the essay.
   (b) What does the inclusion of paragraphs 2 and 3 tell you about the writer's assumptions concerning his intended reader?
   (c) Why would the author include the information contained in paragraph 4 at this point in the essay?
2. (a) List the three types of revisions identified by the writer in paragraphs 5 to 10. How many paragraphs does he devote to the discussion of each type of revision? What does the more developed discussion of one type of revision tell you about the writer's assumptions concerning his reader?

(b) What aspect of the topic does Sekuler deal with in paragraphs 7 and 8? Given the intended reader, why would the author choose to employ the studies he does? (This essay originally appeared in a magazine directed at people interested in psychology.)
3. (a) What advantage of the word processor does Sekuler develop in paragraphs 11 and 12?
   (b) How does the author effect a smooth **transition** from the previous topic to this one?
4. (a) What advantage of the word processor does the author develop in paragraphs 13 to 22?
   (b) Why would the author choose to deal with this particular advantage as the final one in the body of the essay?
   (c) How do the sentences in paragraph 13 assist the reader to understand the essay? Identify any other sentences in paragraphs 14 to 22 that serve the same purpose.
   (d) What information does Sekuler present in paragraphs 14 to 16? What information does he present in paragraphs 17 to 20? Why would the author present the information in this order?
   (e) What is the relationship between the information contained in paragraph 22 and that contained in paragraph 21? What purpose does the inclusion of paragraph 22 achieve?
5. Often a **conclusion** is simply a summary of the main points made in the body. What alternative approach to a **conclusion** has Sekuler used in paragraphs 23 and 24?

# Warm-up

1. One problem with learning how to word process is the shortage of computers in schools. Write a one-paragraph summary of the state of computer availability in your school and its ability to allow every student to learn word processing.
   **Audience:** a school administrator.
   Send copies of the paragraphs created by the entire class to the administrator in your school who is responsible for computer access. Invite the person to your next class to discuss the situation. (You may want to revise your paragraph and resubmit it after the discussion.)
2. Working in groups of seven or eight, survey one another to see how many of you actually do revise your work (as Sekuler advises in paragraphs 18 to 20). If you do, discuss how thorough the revision is

(e.g., do you revise only for spelling and then simply recopy the paper?). If you do not revise, explore your reasons for not doing so. Write a report on your findings.

**Audience:** the rest of the class.

When you have finished, work with the others in your group to create a short oral presentation on your group's findings. Be prepared to lead a short discussion following the presentation. (Afterwards, you may want to revise your report before handing it in to your instructor.)

When all the groups have finished their presentations, have a general discussion about the problems and, more importantly, the benefits of doing revisions.


# Thinking and Writing

a.   Write an essay in which you explain, based on your own experience or that of people you know, whether or not the use of word processors improves the quality of written communication. Outline specific cases in which improvements have or have not occurred. If you do not use a word processor yourself, interview one or two users about the changes that processors have brought to their writing.

**Audience:** people who know little about word processors but would like to know whether they will improve their writing skills.

b.   Marian Kester wrote the following in an essay entitled "The Awful Price of the Computer Age":

> Apart from offices, a boom in word processor sales has been occurring amongst writers. Some say they couldn't function without their Apple II. The belief seems to be that the machine, if it will not actually write the material, is at least conducive to writing. That's like saying a crutch is conducive to walking.

Write an essay in which you support or attack Kester's comment.

**Audience:** someone who is in charge of designing the writing courses at your school and has been considering the purchase of word processors for student use.

Send a copy of your final draft to the person in charge of the English curriculum at your school.

# Repeat Performances

## by Brenda Rabkin

For many of us, getting married is the ultimate sign that we have attained independence from our families. We are now free to make choices and take on responsibilities based on our own wishes. Yet the pattern of our marital relationships will likely bear a strong resemblance to the one we observed between our parents, even when we consciously wish to change it. Why should this be so? 1

There are two major familial influences that will have shaped us by the time we declare ourselves ready to marry: the relationship between our parents, and the way we came to view ourselves as a result of having grown up in a particular family. "How we see ourselves gets translated into what we want, expect, and demand of our partners," says Francine Klagsbrun, author of *Married People: Staying Together in the Age of Divorce* (Bantam, 1985). Were we constantly criticized and put down, leading us to believe that we were unworthy of being loved? Or were we so indulged and overprotected that we could not possibly see ourselves as strong and independent? How did we work out a way to win approval for ourselves? 2

By providing the opportunity for intense closeness, marriage often simulates and reawakens the relationship we had with our parents. In many ways, it is as though we have never left home. So much of what has gone into making us who we are is buried under the thick overlay of family heritage that we are often unaware of these formative components and how they have affected us. The ghosts of our family's past will not only determine our choice of partners, but will also play a significant role in influencing the dynamics of the relationship. In other words, marriage is a perfect stage on which the ghosts can emerge and dance. 3

In *Intimate Partners* (Random House, 1987), a book about how love relationships are formed and how they change during marriage, author Maggie Scarf notes that a couple will often conspire — albeit unconsciously — to restage some version of a family drama that has special meaning for each of them. "It's as if family dilemmas that had never found their satisfactory resolutions needed to be resurrected in the real world, so that different individuals could work on those problems once again." 4

What Scarf found so astonishing is that these resurrected dramas emerge with a decided inevitability, even when the couple makes a deliberate choice not to repeat them. She cites the example of a woman whose father was 5 never able to find secure employment. Her mother had to work hard as a secretary to support the family, and the daughter vowed to do better for herself. She married a professional who was committed to climbing the corporate ladder. But in mid-life, her husband became disenchanted and opted for the challenge of running his own business. The venture was a failure, and the woman was forced to accept a low-paying job in order to make ends meet.

6    The strong connection between generations is nowhere seen as clearly as in the choices we make in intimate partners and how we behave in relation to those partners. We are all familiar with the expressions "He married his mother" and "She married her father." Although there may be some folk wisdom here, we seldom marry duplicates of the opposite-sex parent. What is perhaps more accurate, according to Robin Norwood, author of *Women Who Love Too Much* (Pocket Books, 1985), is that through our choice of partner, "we are able to replicate the atmosphere of childhood already so well known to us, and use the same manoeuvres in which we are already so practised. This is what for most of us constitutes love." As adults we involve ourselves in relationships where we can re-create the challenges we faced as children, this time in an attempt to master them.

7    Norwood believes that until we realize what we are doing and work on changing ourselves, the struggle to re-create and triumph over painful family experiences is one we are doomed to lose and repeat. It also explains why so many people seem to develop a pattern of entering unhealthy relationships with unloving partners. This is especially obvious in the case of women who grew up with an alcoholic parent. Feeling unloved and unworthy because they didn't get the nurturing they needed, these women often choose emotionally remote men upon whom they can lavish unlimited attention and resources in the hope that they will be appreciated and loved.

8    Norwood based her findings on counselling work she did with women who came from dysfunctional homes. A "dysfunctional" home, by her definition, is host to one or more of the following: drug or alcohol addiction, physical or emotional abuse, and seemingly benign behaviour including compulsive eating or cleaning. Other homes that qualify as dysfunctional are ones in which the parents are competitive with each other or with their children, or there is one parent who cannot relate to others in the family. Extreme rigidity about money, religion, or use of time, and minimal displays of affection are other symptoms. The environments in these homes don't promote the expression of honest feelings and intimacy. Consequently, children from such homes "are to some extent damaged in their ability to feel and relate."

But who among us is not? To one degree or another, we all bear the
scars of imperfect parenting, of hurts and disappointments never assuaged,
never healed. We may succeed in covering them up through our attempts
at denial or control, but in situations where we feel vulnerable or defenceless,
they will surely be exposed. A case study will help to illustrate the problem.

9

Catherine grew up in a family that was dominated by her mother, a strong,
intelligent, capable but highly critical woman who cowed her family into sub-
mission through excessive displays of emotion, especially anger. Her father
was a kindly man, gentle and soft-spoken, who appeared to adore his wife,
but who hardly related to his daughter at all. He always seemed to be away
at work.

10

From her mother, Catherine learned what it meant to be a woman, and
she modelled herself after her. A gifted child, she distinguished herself in
school and earned praise for her accomplishments. She became strong, out-
going, ambitious, and independent. When she was 24 she met Hugh, who
at 26 was in the process of carving out a brilliant career as a lawyer. Though
emotionally withdrawn and quiet (qualities that reminded Catherine of her
father and so made her feel safe because she was choosing what was familiar),
he adored Catherine for her intelligence and energy. Hugh's mother was somewhat shrewish and his father was easygoing. He and Catherine had so much
in common. They fell madly in love and were married a year later.

11

Catherine had no difficulty in assuming the major responsibility for the
efficient running of their household, while at the same time excelling in her
demanding job as a teacher. When two children came along and added to
the load, she simply pedalled harder.

12

But Catherine seethed with resentment and expressed it with the only
emotion she knew well — anger — at everyone and everything. She came
to believe that there was something fundamentally wrong with her. Why,
in such enviable circumstances, could she not feel happy? If she could just
accept things without complaint, then maybe her situation would improve.
Nevertheless, no matter how much she accomplished or how hard she worked,
her anger would not disappear. Hugh became quieter and more withdrawn,
which served only to fuel her rage. Finally one day Catherine asked him
for a divorce.

13

How could a union that began with so much hope and love end in such
pain and bitterness? Sadly, what happened to Catherine and Hugh is very
common among couples in conflict. "It is a fact of marital reality, well known
to experts in the field, that those qualities cited by intimate partners as having

14

first attracted them to each other are usually *the same ones that are identified as sources of conflict later on in the relationship*," says Maggie Scarf.

15    Perhaps because of the anger that Hugh saw his mother unleash toward his father, who shrank in its wake, he was determined to detach himself from Catherine's anger, so that he would not be victimized by it. It was easy for him to be gentle and quiet, because he never saw himself as angry — just like his father, who was the only role model he had of how a husband should act with an emotionally overbearing wife, which was now his view of Catherine.

16    For her part, Catherine could never see herself as soft and kindly, because she would then be vulnerable to her mother's wrath. Her mother in turn was behaving the only way she knew in the presence of an emotionally absent husband, which was now what Catherine perceived Hugh to be. They had both unwittingly re-created the most negative aspects of their parents' marriages.

17    To save their marriage from the painful deadlock of feelings they had created by means of these trade-offs, both Hugh and Catherine would have to realize that they'd done this — no easy task, admittedly. They then would have to take responsibility for the particular behaviours they had renounced and given over to the other for expression. They would have to learn to recognize the good and the bad in each other, and in themselves, rather than the either/ or situation regarding anger and control that they had devised.

18    "When it becomes possible for partners to take on the unfinished work of childhood and to re-own parts of the self that once had to be disavowed and discarded," says Scarf, "then marriage becomes a therapeutic relationship in the best, most gratifying sense of that word. It becomes a place in which old wounds can be healed."

19    While it is true that we are shaped by our family histories, we are not doomed to repeat them. If we are comfortable with them and function well and happily, then we have no reason to change them. But if the ghosts of our past diminish our lives, then that pain can and should serve as the signal for change. And change is frightening, because it involves departing from what is familiar, even if familiarity means hell. Nor are there any guarantees that change will necessarily create an improvement. But if the pain is great enough, to change or not to change is no longer the issue. Survival is.

20    How do people depart from their hurtful family histories? "They stop fooling themselves by denying that they have problems," says Francine Klagsbrun. "Then they look for the sources of their pain. . . . Although for some people expert treatment is necessary, I believe people can look at themselves and

say, 'Hey, what's happening? Why am I doing this?' I believe people can recognize, if they want to, the ways in which they repeat early family behaviours."

One way of recognizing these behaviours is simply to be on the lookout    21
for them. What counterproductive family patterns are we emulating? For example, whenever Sarah got into an argument with her husband she would
withdraw, wounded and sulking, and wait for him to make the overtures
of reconciliation, which he inevitably did. In the early years of their marriage,
it gave her a small sense of triumph and reassurance when he approached
her, but after ten years of marriage she began to feel frustrated and victimized,
and found herself looking for subversive ways to express her power. Overspending on their joint charge accounts became her favourite method.

"One day it just hit me," says Sarah. "I was behaving exactly like my mother,    22
who was a very passive and manipulative woman. My father indulged her
and treated her like a child. I swore I'd never be like her, and here I was,
my mother all over again. I knew that if I wanted power and respect in
my marriage, I was going to have to act like an adult. I started to stand
up to John when we had disagreements and to say what I really wanted,
or what I was feeling. And boy did he listen! It's made things a lot easier
for him too."

People can also change the perceptions they have of their family histories    23
by acknowledging their more positive aspects. For example, in her marriage
to Hugh, Catherine re-enacted her mother's unbridled anger and her own
fear of expressing gentler emotions. But what she ignored was her mother's
ability to be compassionate, loving, and supportive of her father, and her
skill at being expressive and feminine with him. He was unfailingly understanding of her and respectful toward her. To her own surprise, Catherine
saw that her parents actually had a successful marriage, one she did want
to emulate.

Today Hugh and Catherine are struggling to revise the destructive, polarized    24
patterns they established early on in their marriage. "If not for therapy, we
wouldn't be here today," says Catherine. "We had hit rock bottom in our
marriage. We were both so immobilized by pain that all we could do was
blame each other." Therapy helped them identify the issues that needed work,
and to understand how they had originated. The rest was up to them. "I
believe that therapy can only take you so far," explains Catherine. "There
comes a point where you have to translate what you've learned into action.
It was a big step for me to say to Hugh, 'I'm frightened and I need your
help.' And for him to say to me, 'I get really mad when you get bossy,
but I don't know how to deal with it.' But it's a relief to both of us to

know that we can express those feelings."

25    It can be very reassuring to know that there are positive features in one's family background to choose from as an alternative to replaying old, hurtful scripts. But what if they're not there, no matter how hard one tries to find them, because the negatives are so overwhelming?

26    "In a situation like that at least we can learn that we know what we *don't* want to be," says Marcia Jacobs, who practises psychotherapy in Vancouver. "And that requires risk because then we are stepping out into the void, into the unknown. But it's only when we're there that we can allow space for positive changes to take place. That is what creating our own lives is all about. People can learn to play roles other than the ones they were raised with. And once they do and find greater satisfaction, they also come to see that they don't have to be victimized by old family scripts. They can write their own."

27    A large part of coming to terms with family ghosts is understanding that they may never completely disappear. They will always be lurking in the wings, waiting for that angry word, that cold glance, that helpless expression, to make their reappearance. But we can choose not to give them centre stage by recognizing that within each of us are strengths and weaknesses for which we alone are ultimately responsible.

# Style and Structure

1.    Rabkin's essay deals with relationships between men and women. Primarily for whom do you feel the essay was written? Give at least three reasons for your answer.

2.    Identify the **thesis statement** in this essay. Where does it occur? How helpful do you think its placement is for the reader?

3. (a) Make note of the number of questions Rabkin uses throughout her essay. Where do they occur?

   (b) Consider the value of a question by suggesting why the writer might have chosen to use this technique.

   (c) Occasionally, instructors of writing will insist, "Don't ask me; *tell* me." In other words, do not use questions unless you are quoting a research source. To what extent would you agree with this advice?

4. (a) The essay includes a number of case studies as examples. Discuss the

effectiveness of this technique in terms of the following:

  (i) credibility;

  (ii) reader interest;

  (iii) clarity;

  (iv) general appeal.

(b) Count the instances where Rabkin shows research regarding marriage problems. How many individual sources does she cite? How often does she refer to each? Using the same four considerations as above, discuss the effect of using multiple sources of supporting research.

5. (a) Discuss what a **concluding sentence** should do for a paragraph. Point out which of the **concluding sentences** in this essay are particularly effective, referring to them by paragraph number, and outline reasons for your choices.

  (b) An old philosophy of paragraph writing (which can also apply to essay writing) is that first you tell your readers what you will tell them, then you tell them, then you tell them what you told them. Comment on the effectiveness of this model.

6.   In paragraph 3, Rabkin introduces a "ghost" metaphor, which she repeats in paragraph 19 and then again in the **conclusion** of the essay, paragraph 27.

  (a) How does the "ghost" metaphor help the reader to understand the text? Besides helping the reader to understand, what other effect might the use of this metaphor have?

  (b) How does the use of this metaphor in the **concluding paragraph** affect the reader?

# Warm-up

Do you make an effort to use concluding sentences in your own writing, or do you generally rely on the material presented in the paragraph to carry its own meaning? Reading over a recent essay, count up the number of paragraphs in which you used concluding sentences. Devise conclusions for those paragraphs that you believe could be improved in this way. When you are finished, give both your first and your revised copy to a classmate and ask for comments on the effectiveness of your improvements.

# Thinking and Writing

a.  For many of us, getting married is the ultimate sign that we have attained independence from our families. (paragraph 1)

"Ultimate," however, does not mean "only." Usually, we see the process of declaring independence from one's family as having several stages and as being achieved (if ever) only over a number of years.

Draw up a list of milestones — those occasions that you see as important in the process of becoming independent. Consider those events that you believe are more or less common throughout your social circle. Using an outline drawn from your list, write a process-analysis essay in which you demonstrate that "leaving home" is a slow process. (You may wish to make this a personal essay, using your own experiences as examples, but be sure to show the process as being one largely familiar to most within your social circle.)

**Audience:** members of a junior high-school health or family life class.

b.  Many of us have had the opportunity to see marriages within a family, marriages in which the partners act in patterns that seem to be almost pre-determined. As this essay points out, familiar marital dramas may "emerge with a decided inevitability, even when the couple makes a deliberate choice not to repeat them." (See paragraph 5.)

If you have seen a case of "repeat performance," write a compare/contrast essay in which you outline the major similarities, as well as differences, between the marriages. For this essay, do some research on the phenomenon of repeated marital behaviours, perhaps using the sources mentioned in this essay (if they are available to you), as well as this essay itself. Use at least three quotations, properly documented, in which you show how research predicts your observations.

**Audience:** those wanting to marry in the near future. Note, however, that these may be the people most difficult to convince, usually because they tend to have plans and expectations that may not be entirely realistic.

# The Making of a Wasteland

## by Mayo Mohs

The fires are elaborate undertakings, choreographed destruction. A virgin trop- 1
ical rain forest is too wet under its canopy simply to put to the torch. Men
with axes and chain saws must first fell many of the trees, let them dry
in the sun, and only then set fires that clear thousands of acres at a time.
Afterward, if they are farmers, they plant their crops in the ashes, rich with
the fertilizing chemicals released from the burnt logs. If they are cattlemen,
they may sow a crop of hardy Australian grass to turn it into grazing land.

Yet this wholesale razing of the forest produces only short-lived profits. 2
The ash disappears quickly. Denuded of its protective canopy and deprived
of its fertile carpet of decaying plant life, the thin topsoil typical of much
of the Amazon basin is soon washed away or leached out by tropical down-
pours. Within a few years it can support neither man nor beast. The farmer
and the rancher must cut still deeper into the forest, leaving behind only
desolate scrub land, or even near-desert.

The Amazon basin is immense. The great river, second only to the Nile 3
in length, rises in the Peruvian Andes and meanders 6500 kilometres to the
sea, draining some 7 million square kilometres of land through its vast web
of tributaries. About 324 million hectares, 46 percent of the basin, is rain
forest — a third of all that remains in the world. Just since the Second World
War, almost half of the rain forest in the tropical belt girdling the earth has
disappeared, lost to logging, farming, ranching, mining, and road building.

Estimates of exactly how much rain forest is being lost or irretrievably 4
changed range from 8 million to 20 million hectares each year — between
one and two percent of what is left. In the Caribbean, where Columbus first
wrote in awe about the rain forests of Hispaniola, they are all but gone.
They are dwindling fast in West Africa, Southeast Asia, and Central America.
Only in Zaïre and the Amazon is there a chance to save large, unspoiled
tracts.

What is lost is literally irreplaceable. Notwithstanding the cliché, the jungle 5
does not reclaim its own. Even where healthy second growth arises, the species
it breeds are not the same. A primal tropical rain forest reaches back through
epochs of evolution. Its flora and fauna reflect the drift of continents and
the ebb and flow of ice ages. The sheer abundance of plant and animal species
in any rain forest is staggering. In the 1970s, Ghillean Prance, a tropical botanist

at the New York Botanical Garden, counted 235 species of trees in a one-hectare patch of rain forest in the Amazon; a comparable parcel of New England woodland might yield ten. Scientists fear that as the forest disappears, a million species could become extinct by the year 2000 — many of them before they are even found and named, let alone studied seriously. Potential foods, medicines, and valuable products for agriculture and industry may be lost without them, along with a lode of unique genetic material that researchers are just beginning to mine.

6    In the Amazon, one singular species is succumbing to disease and dispossession. The Indians, the aboriginal human inhabitants of the rain forest, numbered as many as nine million in the basin in 1500. By 1900, only one million were left, and now there are only 200 000. More than one hundred tribes have become extinct in this century; others are certain to follow.

7    Because the Amazon rain forest is so vast, its loss would pose other dangers. Scientists estimate that the respiration processes of forest trees and plants return at least half of the rainfall that drops on it to the air, to fall again and again within the same region. As the forest shrinks, the Amazon basin could dry out irreversibly, grow warmer, and shift weather patterns in the United States and Canada, pushing the grain belt northward. The widespread burning of rain forest could also compound the buildup of carbon dioxide in the atmosphere, intensifying the threat of a greenhouse effect that could warm the global climate, melting polar ice caps and raising sea levels dramatically.

8    The Brazilian government is finally beginning to worry about the rain forest's future. Brazilian scientists of the National Institute for Amazonian Studies have joined Americans of the World Wildlife Fund in a twenty-year effort to determine how much rain forest must remain intact in a single piece if its thriving life is to survive. Meanwhile, development continues. A far-flung network of huge hydro-electric projects, together with mammoth new mines, may carve up the forest even more quickly than did earlier schemes.

## Style and Structure

1. (a) After reading the essay, write a one-sentence summary of its main **thesis**.
   (b) Identify in paragraph 2 the sentence that best captures the theme you have identified.
   (c) What is the relationship of the rest of paragraph 2 to this sentence?
2. Since the author states his theme in paragraph 2, why does he preface it with the information contained in paragraph 1?

3. (a) Why does the author choose to include the information contained in paragraphs 3 and 4 at this point in the essay?
   (b) What does the inclusion of the information contained in paragraphs 3 and 4 tell us about the intended reader of this essay?
4. (a) What three consequences of the "wholesale razing of the forest" does the author deal with in paragraphs 5, 6, and 7?
   (b) Why does the author choose to present these consequences in this order?
   (c) What further conclusions about the intended reader of this essay can be made from the information in these paragraphs? How does the author stress the relevance of the destruction of the tropical rain forest to this reader?
   (d) Why in paragraph 5 does the author refer to "a comparable parcel of New England woodland"?
5. Identify a number of words and phrases employed by the author that reveal his attitude to the subject.
6. (a) What two approaches to the management of the Brazilian rain forest are contrasted in the concluding paragraph?
   (b) These two approaches could have been presented in a different way. For example, read the last two sentences of paragraph 8, and then read the first two sentences of the paragraph. How does this changed order affect the "message" of the paragraph?

   Given the main **thesis** of the essay, the writer's attitude toward it, and the reaction the author wants to create in the intended reader, which order of presentation makes for the more effective conclusion?

# Warm-up

1. The people involved in projects such as those described by Mohs are not inhuman monsters out to destroy the world. Write a one-paragraph character sketch of your idea of a typical Brazilian farmer or rancher who clears these huge tracts of land.
   **Audience:** a conservationist trying to understand the thinking of Brazilian farmers in order to find ways of persuading them to change.
2. In paragraph 5, Mohs uses a comparison between the rain forest and something with which his intended reader is probably more familiar to help drive home his point. Write a one-paragraph comparison that will help the same reader grasp the significance of the statistics on the natives contained in paragraph 6.

Test the efficiency of your paragraph by having two or three people from outside the class read it. Try to judge from their reactions the extent to which your efforts have been successful. Try another version of the paragraph on one or two more people and compare the results.

Finally, exchange paragraphs with two or three classmates and compare the effects you have achieved.

# Thinking and Writing

a.   Identify a local project that is now having or will soon have a negative impact upon the environment (e.g., deforestation, conversion of farm land to other uses, the dumping of untreated sewage and/or wastes, or the use of chemical sprays). Write an essay that explains the project and its impact.
**Audience:** someone who knows little, if anything, about the project.

b.   Write an essay in which you explain the probable motives and attitudes of people who promote, or participate in, projects that have a negative impact upon the environment. Go on to suggest realistic measures that could be taken to convince such people to abandon or modify such projects.
**Audience:** someone who may not have thought about the long-term effects of such projects.

Send a copy of the final draft of your essay to a minister in the provincial or federal government whose department deals with these types of projects.

# An Alternative to Incarceration

## by Greg Heaton, Lori Cohen, and Patrick McManus

Indians comprise 10 percent of the 12 500 inmates in Canada's penitentiaries 1
but only 2 percent of the country's population. On the Prairies, Indians make
up about 5 percent of the population but 32 percent of inmates. According
to one study, a Saskatchewan treaty Indian boy turning sixteen in 1976 had
a 70 percent chance of at least one trip to prison by the age of 25. The
startling disproportions are blamed on alcoholism, poverty, welfare, and the
failure of North American Indians to assimilate into white European society.
The problems are obvious. The solutions, unfortunately, are not.

In August 1988, however, a nine-member committee of the Canadian Bar 2
Association released a study that proposes an extraordinary solution. The gist
of the report, written by University of British Columbia law professor Michael
Jackson, is that traditional western notions of crime, justice, and punishment
are incompatible with aboriginal culture and values, and must be replaced
by a parallel justice system largely controlled by Indians.

Professor Jackson argues that Indians are the victims of three centuries 3
of social, economic, and political dispossession and deprivation. The European
colonization of North America not only usurped native ownership of the land,
he suggests, but also undermined their culture and imposed a foreign criminal
justice system. Poverty, alcoholism, and crime are not the only results. Infant
mortality rates are 60 percent higher than the national average. Violent death
rates are three times the national average. The suicide rate among natives
is six times the national rate. Professor Jackson concludes that native self-
government is vital to native survival, and that a justice system run by natives
can be accommodated as part of the process of self-determination.

The system proposed by Professor Jackson would borrow from Indian tra- 4
ditions where practical and would be implemented by natives as much as
possible. He concedes that serious offences — murder, for instance — and
cases involving non-native victims must remain within the purview of main-
stream courts. But many crimes that take place on reserves could be handled
by the community. The mechanisms should reflect the diversity of tribal tra-
ditions. In some cases, native justices of the peace, in concert with band elders,
could arbitrate disputes, dispense justice, and mete out punishment. In the
Dene and Inuit cultures, where egalitarian social values reject awarding
decision-making authority to individuals, community consensus would serve
as judge.

5      Punishment would also reflect native values. Jail, says Professor Jackson, does not have the same stigma for natives as it does for whites. So "creative solutions" such as banishment or community service are necessary. For those natives who do end up in jail, the report recommends separate native-run correctional facilities.

6      Winona Stevenson, associate professor of native studies at the University of Saskatchewan, explains the principles of conciliatory justice as practised by the Plains Cree before the arrival of white settlers. In the case of a murder, for example, the killer and the victim's family would meet with a communally chosen moderator. In the village's Great Lodge — a giant structure that served as a kind of community centre, church, and court — the parties would pray, negotiate, and smoke the revered tribal pipe. "In the presence of such a sacred object," says Professor Stevenson, "anger had to be dropped." Retribution for a murdered son was usually two or three horses.

7      Professor Jackson's report is welcomed by Henry Quinney, an elder at the Saddle Lake Reserve, 80 miles northeast of Edmonton, who has been trying to establish an on-reserve, traditional disputes-settlement system. The 2500-member band, two-thirds of whom are under 25, is plagued with alcohol-related crime. "When our people go to court," says Mr. Quinney, "there's always a reason behind it. But with the adversarial system you have to have a lawyer and you can't really talk for yourself." He thinks native offenders should be judged by tribal elders. They would insist on alcohol counselling, if necessary, and seek reconciliation between the offender and his victim. Punishment, if any, would likely include some form of community work, often in the service of the injured party.

8      In a number of recent trials involving natives, courts have been asked to consider traditional, community-based justice systems in rendering judgments. In 1986, in the Northwest Territories community of Arctic Bay, a 21-year-old Inuit man was found guilty of raping his fourteen-year-old cousin. At sentencing, territorial court judge Bourassa heard that the "inumarit," or council of elders, could "rehabilitate the offender and reconcile the offender, the victim, and the community." Thus, he imposed a minimal sentence. But Judge Bourassa's decision was later overturned by the Alberta Court of Appeal, and the man was sentenced to eighteen months' imprisonment. A majority of the Appeal Court found that Arctic Bay is in most respects a modern community profoundly influenced by modern technology and culture. Thus, the inumarit is not "a remnant of ancient culture," capable of enforcing "traditional ultimate sanction on the offender. . . . [The inumarit's] counselling service [cannot]

replace the sentence of imprisonment which is required in virtually all cases of major sexual assault."

While the Appeal Court questioned the legitimacy of traditional native justice systems, other observers worry that self-government and an independent native justice system are socially divisive — tantamount to the creation of a nation within a nation. Others argue that special judicial treatment for Indians will invite other ethnic minorities, for instance, communal sects such as Hutterites and Doukhobors, to seek similar consideration. 9

Nonetheless, Professor Jackson remains optimistic that a parallel justice system can and will work, in concert with the development of Indian self-government. "Colonialism has run its course," he says. "The mindset of this country has been toward assimilation as a historical process, not only inevitable but desirable. This has to change. Eventually, Indians will not be a disadvantaged group, but they will always be a distinct society." 10

# Style and Structure

1.  All of the other "Style and Structure" sections in this book present questions we developed. For this essay, *you* will develop the questions.
2.  Divide into three or four groups of approximately the same size. Each group will develop a series of ten questions. These questions should guide others through
    (a) the essay's organization (the introduction, the sections of the body, the conclusion, and paragraph structure), stressing any unique or striking things the authors have done,
    (b) specific strategies used to give impact to the ideas (statistics, citing authorities, examples, etc.), and
    (c) specific writing techniques used to communicate the ideas effectively (transitions, variations in sentence length, word choice, etc.).
3.  Use the following questions as a guideline as you decide which features of the essay to highlight: What strategies employed in this essay would our readers find beneficial in their own writing? How can we word our question to help them appreciate the strategies we have selected? (You might also find it helpful to review some of the questions we used in the "Style and Structure" sections for other essays.)
4.  Working together as a group, examine the questions developed by each

of the other groups. Evaluate each according to the following marking scheme:

|  | Weak | Good | Very Good |
|---|---|---|---|
| Examination of Overall Structure | 1 | 2 | 3 |
| Examination of Paragraphing | 1 | 2 | 3 |
| Examination of Style, Word Choice, and Special Features | 1 | 2 | 3 |
| Examination of Adaptation to Reader | 1 | 2 | 3 |
| Usefulness of Features Highlighted | 1 | 2 | 3 |

Final Grade   __/15

Submit the list of questions your group has produced to your instructor.

# Warm-up

1.  In groups of three, act out a conciliatory meeting such as that described in paragraph 6. One person will be the victim (or victim's parent), the second will be the criminal, and the third will be the moderator. Assume that the criminal has either stolen (and spent) the victim's life savings or murdered a child. Try to negotiate a mutually satisfactory solution.

2.  Write a paragraph in which you describe the advantages or disadvantages of this type of conciliatory justice.
    **Audience:** someone who has never heard of this approach to justice.

    Let the others in your role-playing group read your first draft before you revise it. Ask them for specific comments on strong and weak areas they find in your presentation of the ideas. (Do not be satisfied with "It's okay, I guess." Ask for specific comments.)

# Thinking and Writing

a.   Professor Jackson argues that Indians are the victims of three centuries of social, economic, and political dispossession and deprivation. The European colonization of North America not only usurped native ownership of the land, he suggests, but also undermined their culture and imposed a foreign criminal justice system. (paragraph 3)

Most Canadians, however, have been taught to think of the settling of Canada in terms of European immigrants coming to an empty land. We seldom hear of the highly developed societies that existed all across the country thousands of years before the arrival of Cartier and Cabot.

Write an essay that explains the impact of European settlement from the point of view of the native people. Do not worry about including specific historical events. Concentrate, instead, on the general impact of *one* of the following: possession of land; religious and cultural beliefs; education of children in ways their parents desire; or the self-image that comes from being part of an independent culture.

**Audience**: an average non-native Canadian who thinks of the history of Canada as beginning with the arrival of Cartier or Cabot.

b.   In the last paragraph of the essay, Professor Jackson is quoted as saying, "The mindset of this country has been toward assimilation [i.e., incorporating the native people into white society] as a historical process, not only inevitable but desirable. This has to change. Eventually, Indians will not be a disadvantaged group, but they will always be a distinct society." A separate justice system run by native people is part of this change.

Write an essay that answers the question, "Can a separate system of justice for native people, run by native people, be achieved in Canada?"

**Audience**: someone who is not aware of the problems faced by the native people.

Send a copy of your final draft to the public relations office of the Department of Indian Affairs in Ottawa or to the public relations officer at your local Indian Friendship Centre.

# Still Scared of the Dentist?

## by Judith Haines

1     "I can remember going to the dentist as a child. It was a little wee back door in a dark stairway in a dark, scruffy-looking office, and there seemed no end of excruciating pain involved. It took a lot for me to go up those stairs. I was ab-so-lute-ly terrified." These visits to the dentist happened over 35 years ago but they're still a vivid memory for Brian Gordon. Until recently this 45-year-old Ottawa police officer avoided dentists like the plague and would tremble when just walking by a dentist's door. When he did occasionally drag himself to a dentist, it was only to have a decayed tooth pulled — a lesser evil, it seemed, than the wrenching pain of a toothache.

2     As many as 40 percent of us avoid the dentist because we're afraid, according to the Canadian Dental Association. Avoidance can mean staying away entirely or visiting only when we absolutely have to. And even those among us who see our dentists regularly often express fear or dislike of these health practitioners and their treatments. Why *is* this?

3     Aside from the obvious reasons of discomfort and occasional pain, we may fear dentists because we regard our mouth as one of our most personal body parts, and we don't want it invaded. From the moment we're born, our mouth is special, indeed vital, to us. We use it to receive nourishment, to tell our mom and dad when we're happy, wet, or unwell, and to explore the fascinating tastes and textures of our world. As we grow, the mouth becomes one of our main vehicles for communicating with others. It can win friends and influence people, soothe hurt feelings, and, yes, get us into trouble. Our mouth is an integral part of our personality.

4     It is also very sensitive. Consider that a hair stuck inside a sock can go undetected by our foot, but let it enter our mouth and it is noticed immediately. It's that kind of sensitivity that gets our knees knocking at the thought of going to the dentist. A hair is one thing, but a drill, a pick, or a needle? Forget it. "People tend to have an oral fixation," says Dr. David Donaldson, head of oral, medical, and surgical sciences and director of dental clinics at the University of British Columbia's school of dentistry. "They don't mind you working on their ears, the backs of their necks, their hands, or their toes, but for some reason they have this fear of someone working in their mouths."

Working in your mouth. The words conjure up an image of being tipped 5 back, your open mouth filled with probing hands and instruments. You're unable to speak. What if you feel a sneeze coming on? What if you want to ask a question? You can if you've worked out a signal with your dentist beforehand: "If I want you to stop, I'll raise my left hand," you might say. But if you haven't worked out signals, then what? "Can I move my arm?" you wonder. "What if I hit his arm and he jabs some instrument into me? Oh, no, maybe I should just keep quiet."

But there's a cost to keeping quiet: vulnerability. And when we feel vul- 6 nerable, or not in control, we feel frightened. "There's a sense of helplessness in the dentist's chair," says Vancouver clinical psychologist Dr. Lee Pulos. "Anytime you feel helpless, any kind of probing or intrusion is going to create discomfort." The answer, he says, is self-confidence. "In the old days, people were conditioned to give their power away to those in authority. But I think patients are now realizing that the more sense of mastery they bring into any kind of situation with a professional and the more in charge they are, the more they're going to accelerate the healing and get-well response." He defines the get-well response as the ability to manage pain, overcome the gagging reflex, and relax.

But no matter how assertive we are, we're still suckers for horror stories 7 about dentists. And whether it make sense or not, we often let such anecdotes affect our attitudes. "My dentist!" a friend will say, "He just loves inflicting pain." And why are we so ready to laugh at the disturbing message in cartoons like *Herman*, where the dentist causes his patient no end of suffering and won't hesitate to stick his arm down a throat to retrieve a dropped instrument? "Dentistry seems funny because we fear it," says Donaldson.

There's a big difference, though, between the jocular anxiety many of us 8 express when we talk of the dentist and the immobilizing fear experienced by people like Brian Gordon. For them, reality has been terribly skewed by a traumatizing experience, often in childhood, of pain or humiliation, poor dentistry, or a negative dentist–patient relationship. And after a time, it's not just the memory that prevents these people from going to the dentist, but the guilt that they've let themselves go and are the worst case of neglect a dentist will ever see. "Everyone," says Donaldson, "thinks he or she is the worst."

But no matter how painful the memory or frightening the expectation, shun- 9 ning the dentist can only make matters worse, for the health costs are considerable. Tooth decay, the number one cause of tooth loss in children, and gum disease, the number one cause of tooth loss in adults, can affect our ability to chew and speak, and detract from our appearance and overall health. Yet, all this is preventable.

10    One year ago, Brian Gordon finally contained his fear long enough to book an appointment with his sister's dentist. He was fed up with his teeth and his appearance. A number of his teeth were either decayed or broken, and while he was eating one day, his gums started to bleed — a sign, he recognized, of gum disease. Nervously arriving for his appointment last November, he expected to find a dozen people in a cramped waiting area and the dentist hurrying from room to room. Instead, he entered a cosy, uncrowded reception area with an array of children's books on the floor and a welcoming pot of coffee brewing. He was greeted by friendly, unhurried staff and addressed by his first name. During his first dental appointment in years, he was not expected to undergo any dental procedures. He simply sat and talked with Ottawa dentist Dr. Arthur Conn and his staff. He spoke of his dental health and fears, his work, and his interests. For him it was like emerging from a long, dark tunnel. And to his considerable surprise, he felt himself relaxing.

11    For anyone fearful of dentists and dental care, making and keeping that first appointment is a tough step. Once they get themselves to an empathetic dentist and get to know the staff, though, frightened patients are often amazed that they were so nervous about going in the first place. Winnipeg dentist Dr. Dee Marvin feels there are two reasons for this: "One, dentistry has changed quite a bit; and two, in your imagination anything you worry about over time gets worse and worse and worse — kind of like a boogeyman."

12    Bernadette O'Driscoll of Niagara-on-the-Lake, Ontario, is 26 years old and hasn't been to a dentist for seven years. The boogeyman that keeps her away is the memory of a dentist in another city and his painful extraction of one of her wisdom teeth. "When he put the needle in to freeze me, I passed out," she says, "and he had to give me oxygen to bring me around. When he started working on the tooth, it wasn't frozen and I could feel everything. He was so rough. He just didn't care. At least, that's how I saw him." For a moment, she's back there. Then she adds, almost wistfully, "I have a good dental plan, and if I wasn't afraid, I'd go to the dentist. I always think that when I get old I'm going to have to have false teeth. I mean, I would never want to lose my teeth, but. . . . "

13    While a poor relationship with our dentist can keep us from seeking dental care, a good relationship is at the core of successful fear management. When we feel comfortable with our dentist, we communicate better. On the other hand, if we feel that the person we're dealing with doesn't understand what

we're saying and how we feel, our fear will likely persist. It pays to put a lot of energy into finding a professional who will take the time to work with you. Ask friends, co-workers, and those who work in dental offices whom they recommend. Most dentists and patients agree that word-of-mouth is best.

Seasoned Vancouver dental hygienist Gail Thorp-Moa says that the fearful patient's first visit to a new dentist should be strictly social. "Come in and meet the people," she says. Be sure to explain to the staff that you have fears. It's particularly helpful if you can be specific about the kind of incident that sparked your anxiety. Marvin also suggests writing down your fears at home so that you can more clearly articulate them at your appointment. For instance, saying you're scared of needles is helpful, but it's more helpful still to say: "I'm afraid of needles because they hurt me" or "I'm afraid of needles because I stay numb for so long and I dribble and I feel embarrassed." Most people are afraid of needles, drills, and pain. But a significant group of people are afraid of other things, such as having their teeth cleaned. Unfortunately, many dentists consider cleaning a relaxing, anxiety-free procedure and schedule it for the patient's first or second appointment. 14

Offering individualized treatment to the fearful patient is the dentist's responsibility; making choices that feel right for you is yours. Depending on the dentist, you may have many or a few treatment options to choose from. Strategies dentists employ in their offices generally reflect their personal styles and skills. More doesn't necessarily mean better, nor will the same technique be appropriate for every fearful patient who walks through the door. But whatever strategies are used, the goal is to make the patient feel comfortable in the dentist's chair. 15

Helping fearful patients feel at ease is the focus of the pain and anxiety control program at the University of British Columbia's school of dentistry. There, says David Donaldson, students learn how patients acquire fears, as well as the different methods of anxiety control. Donaldson underlines that if you decrease anxiety, pain is also decreased. "It's been shown that people who are very anxious feel pain more than people who are relaxed," he says. "So the idea is to get your patient to relax before you start having to use local anesthetics or anything else." 16

The program teaches, and employs through its dental clinics, two approaches to managing patients: psychological and pharmacological. Psychological strategies include modelling, in which phobic patients watch nonfearful patients receive dental treatment; densensitization, in which patients are gradually exposed to more involved dental procedures; and quick induction hypnosis. Pharmacological approaches include administration of drugs orally (a patient might 17 take a drug such as Valium the night before, then again an hour before a dental procedure), intravenously (sedative medication is injected into a vein), and by inhalation (the patient relaxes after breathing nitrous oxide).

18    Where in this battery of drugs do the patient's coping skills come in? you might ask. Donaldson says the drugs are not a substitute for coping. Intravenous medication, for instance, is not given routinely to a patient. But it *can* be used to break the fear cycle. Given in low concentrations it simply relaxes the nervous patient. Once patients have had one successful dental experience, he says, most won't require the medication at their next visit.

19    As for using intravenous medication as general anesthesia, Donaldson says it should only be used for patients who cannot be treated otherwise. And because it has risks, it is normally done in a hospital setting, where appropriate monitoring is available. "But even more to the point," he stresses, "people don't get over their fear of dentistry if they're put to sleep. It's not a learning process."

20    Fear of dentistry is hardly new. But programs like Donaldson's are helping more fearful patients get the attention they need. "What's happening now is that we're reaching people we couldn't reach before," he says. And having a university-based treatment program benefits more than the patients; it also exposes dental students to the fearful population. Quick to recognize this, the school of dentistry at Dalhousie University in Halifax is looking at the development of a special needs centre for people such as those afraid of dental procedures. "Ideally the centre would have a three-pronged approach — teaching, treatment, and research," says Dr. Christopher Hawkins, a periodontist and assistant professor in the department of restorative dentistry. Still at the proposal stage, the idea for the centre emerged during the school's curriculum review, which is still under way.

21    People like Brian Gordon, who had the strength to finally seek help for his paralysing fear, would find such a centre a blessing. Having experienced the slow deterioration of his teeth along with a good chunk of his self-esteem, he admits that the will to change is only the first step on the road back to dental health; the next is finding empathetic and knowledgeable professionals.

22    After considerable restorative work that included five root canals ("They didn't hurt a bit!"), Gordon is feeling pretty good about himself these days. His friends tell him he's smiling more, but he's surprised: "I've always smiled," he insists. Then he adds, "Well . . . I *may* be opening my mouth more now."

# Style and Structure

1. (a) This essay begins with the narrative of a 45-year-old police officer who had a terror of dentists. Rewrite the introduction, giving, instead, a history of dentistry or a definition of fear. Which introduction is more effective? Why?

    (b) Why might the writer have chosen a mature police officer as an example, rather than, say, a teenager or a senior citizen? What readership might this writer be trying to reach in using the introduction she has?

2. The writer points out, "As many as 40 percent of us avoid the dentist because we're afraid, according to the Canadian Dental Association." What effect does such a statement have on the intended reader?

3. (a) At the end of paragraph 4, the writer reports one resource as saying " . . . for some reason they have this fear of someone working in their mouths." Paragraph 5 begins "Working in your mouth." Why does the writer use a **sentence fragment** here? Do you believe that the use of a fragment is unacceptable bad grammar in this case?

    (b) Discuss the purpose served in shifting the pronoun from "they" (paragraph 4) to "you" (paragraph 5).

4. (a) The writer begins paragraphs 6, 7, and 9 with "But." Discuss the effectiveness of this strategy.

    (b) For variety, suggest different opening strategies for each of the paragraphs mentioned.

5. The writer begins and ends this essay with the story of Brian Gordon, the fearful police officer. In contrast, in paragraph 12 she introduces another case, that of Bernadette O'Driscoll. The writer does not follow through on this second case, but leaves it hanging with a quotation from the subject herself: "I mean, I would never want to lose my teeth, but. . . . " Discuss what purpose the writer might have in mind in leaving this case without a conclusion. Do you believe the strategy is successful?

# Warm-up

A writer's powers of observation are probably the most valuable assets to the trade. Request a tour of a local dentist's office and pay careful attention to the environment that has been structured there. Make notes to describe the waiting room and the treatment rooms, taking care to observe all the details. After the tour, use your notes to write a descriptive paragraph in which you show your reader what the dental office is like and what impressions it is likely to give patients.

Exchange paragraphs with fellow students and discuss the different impressions that each writer drew from the same environment. What do these differences tell you about the writers' attitudes as they approached the dental office?

## Thinking and Writing

a.  Reread Judith Haines' essay, making a list in your notebook of the reasons she gives for patients' fear of dentists.

In paragraph 15, Haines advises that "offering individualized treatment to the fearful patient is the dentist's responsibility." As a concerned consumer of dental health services, write an essay discussing ways dental staff can help patients to overcome fear and receive treatment. You may want to consider such factors as

(i) environment;

(ii) behaviour of the staff;

(iii) treatment procedures.

**Audience:** members of the dental profession.

Send a copy of your essay to your dentist or to the dental sciences faculty of your school, and ask for comments.

Variation: Humour is often seen as one of the more common defences against fear. (See also paragraph 7.) Try writing your essay from a humorous point of view.

b.  One of the supporting resources quoted in this essay suggests that people "who are very anxious feel pain more than people who are relaxed." It follows that the more comfortable you as a patient can make yourself, the less traumatic a visit to the dentist will be.

Write a "how-to" essay in which you outline a step-by-step method of reducing anxiety, both before you enter the dentist's office and once you get there. As you think about the steps to take, consider the points Judith Haines makes throughout the essay about why patients are fearful. Try to anticipate your reader's difficulties and provide reassurance that those fears are both common and avoidable.

**Audience:** any adult who is fearful of dentistry.

# The "Science" of Astrology Is All Wet

by Sidney Katz

Indian astrologers have exultantly claimed that they foretold the assassination of prime minister Indira Gandhi on October 31, 1984. Two pieces of evidence are offered as proof. The first is the prediction published in an astrology magazine that "an elderly person who is holding a very important position, or has in the past, could be afflicted and even pass away." The second is a horoscope of Mrs. Gandhi cast in 1980 by a prominent Indian astrologer, Pandit Parsal, who predicted that her immediate future was bright but that beyond September 1984 the outlook was more gloomy.    1

Both these "proofs" are a far cry from specifying that the Indian prime minister would meet a sudden, violent death. Nonetheless, millions of people in Canada and elsewhere will probably be impressed by this triumph of prognostication, because the belief in astrology is profound and widespread. Astrological books sell by the zodiac-load.    2

Because the demand for astrological services has so expanded, many astrologers have become specialists. Some devote their time to personal horoscopes, others to predicting the future of corporations. There are astrology specialists in Canada who claim special skills in advising you who to hire and who to fire, in advising you which friend is a suitable candidate for a relationship, in telling you which are the best and worst days for your pet, in advising you on selecting a perfume that reflects the *real* you.    3

Several times in the past I have conducted a retrospective check on the performance of various prominent astrologers and arrived at a firm conclusion: as prognosticators, astrologers are dismal flops.    4

I once reviewed a list of seventeen predictions made about the future of well-known public figures by Jeane Dixon, a syndicated columnist who appears in the *Globe and Mail* and a number of other newspapers. The following are some of Ms. Dixon's forecasts: assassination attempts would be made against Richard Nixon; Senator Henry (Scoop) Jackson would win immortal fame (Henry who?); Jane Fonda would face tragedy; following the death of John F. Kennedy, his widow Jacqueline would never marry again.    5

This last forecast was also made by another popular astrologer, Zoltan Mason, in these words: "Jacqueline will go to her grave as a widow because this    6 is what the stars destined for her at the time of her birth." When Jackie married Aristotle Onassis a few weeks later, Mr. Mason angrily defended his prediction. "I was right! I was right! Do you call her marriage to Onassis a real union? A young woman married to an old man?"

7    For years, Carroll Righter was touted for his special aptitude in foretelling the fortunes of prominent personalities. He gave a sterling demonstration of this gift on April 11, 1971, when he published the horoscope of J. Edgar Hoover, then director of the Federal Bureau of Investigation. He noted that "Hoover will face a very satisfactory 1972, in terms of health, effectiveness, and all-out happiness." On May 2, 1972, Hoover died, presumably in perfect health and a state of all-out happiness.

8    The best way to assess the validity of astrology as a science is to gather up 100 articles and books on the subject and read them carefully. You will soon be impressed by the extent to which the various writers contradict each other. For example, the "authoritative" Encyclopedia of Occult Sciences assures us that Librans (born between September 24 and October 23) are aesthetic souls, adoring flowers, jewels, music, and ornate clothes. Oscar Wilde was a Libran, but how do we explain the disposition of another Libran, Mahatma Gandhi? We're also told by the encyclopedia that people born under the sign of Leo (July 24 to August 23) are ambitious and heavy-handed and that their fortunes rise and fall suddenly. This seems like a pretty good claim when you consider that Caesar and Napoleon were Leos. However, so was Mae West. And how is it that Adolf Hitler and Julie Andrews share the same astrological sign?

9    One *might* think that such discrepancies would try the faith of the credophile.

## Style and Structure

1.    What is the effect on the reader of the writer's use of quotation marks around the word "proofs" in the first sentence of paragraph 2? How does the rest of the sentence drive home his specific objections to the astrological predictions in paragraph 1?

2.    In paragraph 2, Katz makes the point that, in Canada, "belief in astrology is profound and widespread." Why does he follow this statement with the information contained in paragraph 3?

3.    What is the relationship of paragraph 4 to the main theme of the essay?

How does paragraph 4 prepare the reader for the information contained in the remainder of the essay?

4.  What type of evidence does Katz present in paragraphs 5 to 7 to disprove the validity of astrology as a reliable prognosticator? Is there enough evidence presented to convince an objective reader to accept Katz' argument? Give reasons to justify your answer.

5.  The writer's choice of words in paragraphs 5 to 7 particularly reveals his attitude toward astrology. In one sentence, summarize Katz' opinion of astrology. Quote examples of words and phrases to justify your answer.

6.  What type of evidence does Katz present in paragraph 8 to disprove the validity of astrology as a reliable prognosticator? Is there enough evidence presented to convince an objective reader to accept Katz' argument? Give reasons to justify your response.

7.  Considering the content of the essay and the writer's attitude toward it, does paragraph 9 act as an adequate **conclusion**? Justify your answer.

# Warm-up

1.  Work with a group of four or five classmates to create a questionnaire that will reveal how widespread the belief in astrology really is. Be sure to build in checks to see if people say one thing but practise another (e.g., some people may tell you that they do not believe in astrology but read their horoscopes in the newspaper every day).

    Have eight to ten people answer your questionnaire. Get a good cross section of your community.

    Compile the survey results obtained by your group. Working on your own, write a report to the rest of the class on your group's findings.

    From the reports written by the people in your group, select the one that is most complete and most easily understood. Make overhead projections of it to use as the basis for a brief oral presentation of your findings to the rest of the class. After the presentation, revise your own report into a final draft.

2.  Write a paragraph that uses an example to argue for or against the reliability of astrology.
    **Audience:** your classmates.

    Get together with two or three others in the class and compare paragraphs. Are the examples well used?

# Thinking and Writing

a.    Using newspapers in the library, make a record of the past week's horoscope predictions under your astrological sign. Write an essay in which
you compare these predictions to the events that actually occurred on
these days, and draw conclusions about the accuracy of astrology used
in this way.
**Audience:** the person who made the predictions.

Send a copy of the final draft to the writer of the horoscope in care
of the newspaper or magazine in which it was predicted.

b.    In his article, Katz argues against astrology by using examples. Write
an essay that uses other ways of arguing either for or against the validity
of astrology. (For example, you might explain the scientific basis of astrology; the state of knowledge about stars and planets when astrology
first began as compared to what is known about them today; or the
ignorance of ancient peoples concerning heredity and/or psychology.)
**Audience:** someone who would disagree with your stand.

# Why Men Are Mad as Hell

## by Rona Maynard

The Toronto aircraft technician was feeling burned. His Canadian Auto Workers' local was sponsoring a course in Wen-Do, a self-defence technique designed for women. His dues had helped to fund the event, which would be held at his union hall. But men would not be welcome.

When the women gathered for the course on September 12, 1987, the aircraft technician asked to join them and was turned away by the female instructor. He asked to observe the class and again was refused. But he was ready for a long battle. He had In Search of Justice (ISOJ), a militant men's-rights organization, in his corner, and the group has taken his cause to the Ontario Human Rights Commission. The complaint: sex discrimination against men.

Nonsense, retorts Marilyn Walsh, a director of Wen-Do Women's Self-Defence. She points out that both the Canadian Human Rights Act and the Charter of Rights and Freedoms permit special programs for disadvantaged groups — and that women ought to qualify when it comes to street-fighting skills. "Most rapes happen to women," says Walsh. "Most spousal abuse happens to women. Yet, women in general don't participate in contact sports, don't learn to defend themselves." She adds that men can choose from literally dozens of other martial-arts courses.

So what? demands Ross Virgin, founder and president of ISOJ. He compares Wen-Do to an employer who refuses to hire blacks or Jews on the grounds that thousands of others would be glad to do so. If ISOJ wins its case against Wen-Do, its next target will be the luxurious all-female McGill Club, where Toronto's elite businesswomen meet for saunas and white-wine spritzers.

Only yesterday, gender bias was a women's issue. But after nearly two decades of government-funded efforts to advance women's status, an outspoken new breed of male activist claims that women now get all the breaks. Men are calling themselves the oppressed group. And they charge that women's drive for equality has become a selfish vendetta against men. "It's okay for women to force their way into men's clubs," says Virgin. "It's okay for women to join men's teams. But God help you if you reverse the genders."

Across North America, hundreds of groups campaign for men's rights. Most pursue a single goal: a better deal for divorcing fathers who want a chance to raise their kids and a break from alimony payments. Such men account for roughly 80 percent of ISOJ's 2100 recruits nation-wide. But Virgin, a 42-year-old health-care worker who has never been married, expects them to fight a mightier foe than any ex-wife — the National Action Committee on the Status of Women (NAC).

7    He plans the crusade from a spartan command post in a suburban Toronto industrial mall. The decor consists of men's-rights slogans ("Alimony should not be a lifetime sentence") and a colour blowup of a man permanently scarred when his wife threw a pot of boiling water at him. Unlike NAC, which this year boasts $611 211 from the federal purse, ISOJ has made do with donations from members ever since its inaugural meeting back in 1972. But tough odds don't daunt Virgin, who is betting that most of the four million people NAC claims to represent have little use for its official pronouncements.

8    He could be right, to judge from the response to his own agenda. Twenty percent of ISOJ's incoming phone calls are from supportive women — the mothers and partners of put-upon men. Meanwhile, legislators, politicians, and talk-show hosts pay increasing attention to his attacks on every plank of the feminist platform.

9    •**Rape**    Feminists insist that a victim's sexual history has no place in the courtroom. Men counter that it may be essential to a fair trial for the accused. At trials for any other crime, defence lawyers routinely grill witnesses about past experiences that might cast doubt on their testimony. According to Virgin, a history of one-night stands suggests that a woman who says she has been raped has in fact "enticed" the defendant.

10    •**Sexual abuse**    Conventional wisdom holds that kids never lie about abuse. Virgin claims that they often do, destroying the reputations of innocent people — most of whom are male. His group will help prepare a defence for any man accused of molesting a child, no questions asked. And his ideas are clearly spreading. Last summer, the 22 000-member Ontario Public School Teachers' Federation announced that it would take legal action on an accused teacher's behalf, once he is cleared in court.

11    •**Sexual harassment**    Men's rightists say that they are sexually victimized at work. As they tell it, most sexual harassment complaints come from office temptresses who told co-workers "no" while signalling "yes." ISOJ argues that a woman's written "no," delivered to the alleged harasser, should be a condition for a human-rights investigation. The proposal appals feminists, who say that women going public with complaints need protection from retaliation by their harassers.

12    •**Wife assault**    One million Canadian men beat their wives, says a study pub-

lished last year by the Canadian Advisory Council on the Status of Women. Virgin, who accuses anti-male researchers of jumping to conclusions, guesses that the actual number is about 2000. He wants more attention paid to the battered husbands whose stories are dismissed by incredulous police officers, and he is currently helping three ISOJ members to lay charges against violent wives.

•**Alimony**   Now that more than half of Canadian women hold jobs, few divorced women have the right to financial support from their ex — or so the men's movement contends. Dismissing feminist concerns about unskilled homemakers catapulted into the job market, its leaders say that alimony discourages women from working and shortchanges second wives. And judges are listening. Increasingly, they limit spousal support to three years, even for longtime homemakers.

13

•**Pay equity**   If women want equality at work, say men's rightists, they should accept the same deal that men do. That means no affirmative action, no paid maternity leave, and, above all, no government programs to fatten women's paycheques. Fumes Virgin: "Any pay based on your genital organs is sex pay, the same as prostitution."

14

Whenever activists like Virgin condemn the women's movement, one issue is bound to surface — male-bashing. Feminists, they say, portray all men either as violent, lecherous exploiters of helpless women or as cold, selfish lovers. U.S. author Shere Hite, whose latest 922-page study consisted mainly of women's gripes about their partners, has men's tempers boiling over. "Feminists are realizing that cranking the male-as-monster myth pays terrific dividends," says Brian Demaine, a Montreal teacher and prominent men's activist. "Male hate explains why women aren't equally represented in the better-paying professions, in politics, in the arts, in sports — you name it. Male hate is the answer to every perceived failure."

15

Men are not alone in charging that feminism has gone too far. After all, Hite's critics include female scholars who accuse her of biassed research techniques. Paid maternity leave, which Canadian feminists would like to see lengthened, strikes many female lawyers in the United States as discriminatory — and ultimately dangerous to women because it may discourage employers from hiring them.

16

Meanwhile, an emerging female elite is negating the feminist image of oppressed womanhood. If a woman has the right degrees and the drive to make them work, she has options undreamed of by men. Like it or not, many employers expect less commitment from a woman than they do from a man

17

— especially when she becomes a mother. The female lawyer who reduces her hours to nurture a baby must give up her hopes for partnership but not for society's approval. A male colleague who takes the same step will be viewed as a wimp. Amid growing evidence that neither sex truly has it all, some mothers are deciding, as one female MBA sums up, that they "wouldn't be a man for anything."

18    Does the men's movement have a legitimate case? Are feminists demanding more than just equality? It might seem so at first. But whatever men's rightists may say, equality is not their goal. Their arguments are based not on reason or fairness, but on corrosive anger at women.

19    Pat Marshall is not easily shaken. As head of Toronto's Metro Action Committee on Public Violence Against Women and Children, she knows how to keep cool under fire. But she admits to being frightened in May 1988, when she spoke at a public forum on sexual assault. ISOJ sent a delegation of about twenty men, one of whom shouted "Bull!" throughout a rape victim's account of her ordeal. The same man interrupted Marshall's own remarks with screams of "Nazi! Nazi! You're Gestapo!"; it took five men to restrain him. The mood turned so ugly that the organizers nearly cancelled the forum, and the women in the audience did not dare walk to the washroom alone. "It was an assaultive experience for all the women taking part," recalls Marshall.

20    That night, Virgin took the microphone to cite two of his favourite statistics: 60 percent of sexual-assault charges result in acquittals, compared to sixteen percent of other criminal charges. Virgin uses these figures, which he says he was given by the U.S. Federal Bureau of Investigation (FBI), as proof that lying women drag hundreds of innocent men into court. But the FBI denies any knowledge of the figures, and no comparable Canadian data are available. While most feminists admit that sexual-assault cases have an unusually high acquittal rate, they offer another explanation: the courts' reluctance to believe the victims.

21    Stacy Michener, a counsellor at the Toronto Rape Crisis Centre, points out that the courts expect more supporting evidence in a sexual-assault case than they do for almost any other crime. "But there's seldom any corroborating evidence, because men pick and choose places where there are no witnesses. So it's his word against hers. The courts look at the way she dresses and her lifestyle, and decide she's not the kind of woman they should put him away for."

22    Rightly so, if you ask Virgin. He took heart from the dismaying news, reported last spring by Rhode Island researchers, that 50 percent of junior

high-school students believe that a woman who walks alone at night in "seductive" clothing is asking to be raped. "Thank God for the wisdom of young children," writes Virgin in an unpublished manuscript entitled *Rape: Fact or Fiction?* He overlooks the fact that men ought to be able to control their libidos. But that's hardly surprising given his belief that unsatisfied male lust constitutes a "medical problem" warranting free government-run prostitution.

When men's rightists do have a point, they swathe it in distortion. For instance, ISOJ's complaint against Wen-Do cites a 1985 U.S. survey showing that women are as likely as men to use violence against their partners. The study purportedly proves that abused women have no need for all-female courses in martial arts. **23**

Tell that to Jan Stets, a sociologist at Washington State University and an expert on violent relationships. She and fellow sociologist Murray Straus, a co-author of the very survey quoted by ISOJ, have recently found that marital and cohabitational violence seems to have a greater impact on women than on men. Women spend more time in bed and report more stress and depression. "Research [on violent women] is being used to cut off funds for women's shelters, ignoring the fact that women are being battered," worries Stets, who adds that existing studies raise more questions than they answer. Are women at last rejecting the taboo against female aggression? Are they only defending themselves against men who strike the first blow? Are abused men downplaying their pain in an effort to appear manly? So far, researchers have proved just one point: abused men need attention and support. **24**

The irrational rage of men's rightists is nowhere more evident than in their own publications. *Equality*, a now-defunct Montreal newsletter, once parodied the 23rd Psalm as a divorced woman's hymn of praise to her alimony cheques: "My Cadillac tank runneth over." But divorced women splurging on Cadillacs are the exception. More than half of divorced and separated mothers raise their kids in poverty. **25**

What does the men's movement really want? A return to the 1950s, suggests an essay in *Equilibrium*, another defunct Montreal newsletter. It blames employed mothers for most of society's ills: drug abuse, divorce, youth suicide, teen runaways, and street crime. The problem, it says, is that women have forsaken their rightful job: "making life worth living." **26**

If women don't work, they will be hard pressed to support themselves in the event of a divorce. But consistency is not the movement's strong point. Virgin, who thinks that day care hurts children, nevertheless considers it the perfect career for displaced homemakers. "If there's so much demand for day **27** care, these women can open up centres in their homes and set their own price." What this approach to child care would mean to kids and women does not trouble him. "Icicles hang from each chamber of my heart," he smiles.

28    It is tempting to dismiss men's rightists as a sick joke. But what they reveal about relations between men and women is no longer a laughing matter. Only a few years ago, when "androgyny" and "commitment" became media buzzwords, men and women seemed close to a truce in the sexual battles that followed feminism's rise the 1960s. Now, hostility runs higher than ever. Until men and women understand the feelings that divide them, "equality" will remain a rhetorical device for extremists of both sexes.

29    At most, ten percent of men give women's quest for independence their whole-hearted support, concludes U.S. journalist Anthony Astrachan in his 1986 book *How Men Feel*. When Astrachan factored in all the men backing the feminist dream for pragmatic reasons, he still came up with a modest total of about 35 percent. What holds men back is fear: of exposing their own weakness, of losing other men's support, and of humiliation by women.

30    Feminists have long chastised men for refusing to share power. But while men still dominate political parties and corporate boards by a huge margin, the average guy has no power to share. He needs to view women as his inferiors, and the more heated their demands for a shot at the top, the more painful his awareness of his status on the bottom. The result, says Astrachan, is rage, denial, and "compulsive fantasies of power" that may erupt in wife beating at home or in sexual harassment on the shop floor. A male metalworker admitted to Astrachan, after a few beers, that he liked to harass women at work — and that sexual attraction had nothing to do with his advances. "Especially if she's the kind who works extra hard and talks like she wants extra credit for it, I don't mind showing her who's really stronger."

31    Women's assault on male job bastions threatens men on two fronts. History has shown that any job loses status when large numbers of women move in (time was when the public looked up to clerks). And men feel constrained by women's presence, especially blue-collar workers. They may not be less enlightened about women than managers and professionals, but they have traditionally been less inhibited about expressing sexual attitudes through off-colour jokes and crotch shots on walls. Man after man lamented to Astrachan: "With a woman on the job, I can't talk the way I want to."

32    The macho bond derives its force from men's shared distrust of women, which is based on biology and entrenched by cultural patterns. Ever since primitive people made female idols with swollen bellies, women's power to

bear children has filled men with awe. And women's time-honoured responsibility for rearing children has pitted the sexes against each other.

U.S. psychologists Dorothy Dinnerstein and Nancy Chodorow unravelled     **33**
the process during the late 1970s. Simply put, mother is the first source of
comfort and of prohibition for sons and daughters alike. She inspires passionate
devotion and searing resentment in children of both sexes. But sons, unlike
daughters, must forsake her for a more appropriate role model — the father.

A boy's rebellion against his mother, whom he loves and fears more than       **34**
anything or anyone else, unleashes a maelstrom of loss and betrayal. Alarmed
by his own emotions, he shuts them away. But in his adult relationships
with women, he unconsciously re-enacts his childhood tragedy again and again.
He may demand too much from his partner, or withdraw from an argument
into angry silence.

This is the behaviour that Hite's latest book describes in some 900 pages.     **35**
And even if she exaggerates its extent, what it means is clear enough. Women
and men will not be loving equals until children have two active nurturers.

Almost a decade has passed since Betty Friedan, in *The Second Stage*, urged     **36**
feminists to stop measuring their progress in terms of equality with men.
She pointed to a more urgent challenge — the restructuring of social institutions — and she predicted that men would be essential to the task. So
far, neither sex has answered the call. The women's movement, perhaps under-
standably, has focussed less on shared parenting than on expanded day-care
services to promote women's participation in the workplace. The men's movement, sadly, has encouraged men to seek custody after divorce, but not to
be active fathers during marriage.

Surely women and men can fare better as a team. Here's to the day when     **37**
none of us need worry about defending ourselves from the opposite sex.

# Style and Structure

1. (a) Write down the number of the paragraph that contains the **thesis state-
     ment** of this essay.
   (b) What effects do the paragraphs preceding the **thesis statement** have on
     the reader? What reasons might the writer have for placing them ahead
     of her **thesis statement**? What does her choice of this order of presentation
     tell you about the attitudes she believes her readers will bring to her
     **thesis**? Is this strategy an effective way of dealing with the intended
     reader? Give reasons for your answer.

(c) List the kinds of writing and the kinds of intended readers for which this type of introduction would be *appropriate*.

(d) List the kinds of writing and the kinds of intended readers for which this type of introduction might be *inappropriate*.

2.    In paragraphs 1 to 17, identify three ways Maynard presents her information to show objectivity toward male activists. Give one example from the essay for each. How does this objectivity affect the reader? How does it affect the impact of the attack contained in the second half of the essay?

3.    Paragraph 18 acts as a **transition**.

(a) What change in approach to the subject takes place in this paragraph?

(b) What reasons might Maynard have for starting the paragraph with two questions?

(c) How does the wording of the third sentence prepare for the coming change?

(d) How does the development of the ideas in this paragraph reflect the development of the ideas in the essay as a whole?

4.    Identify three techniques that Maynard uses in paragraphs 19 and following to convince her reader that "their arguments are based not on reason or fairness, but on corrosive anger at women" (paragraph 18). Give one example from the essay for each.

5.    Identify ten words or phrases that Maynard uses in paragraphs 19 and following to influence her reader against the arguments of male activists (e.g., "dismaying news" in paragraph 22). How effective is this subtle use of diction? Why?

6.    Maynard's **conclusion** is not a simple summary of the essay or restatement of her **thesis**. What does she do in her **conclusion**? Is it an appropriate way to conclude this essay? Is it effective in conveying her overall message to the reader? Give reasons for your answers.

7.    Nowhere in the essay does Maynard use the word "I." Yet her opinion of the male activists' movement is obvious.

(a) What effect does keeping her arguments in the third person ("he," "she," and "they") have upon the reader? Would her arguments have been more effective or less effective if she had written them in terms such as "I think . . . ," "I believe . . . ," or "I know of men who . . . "? Why?

(b) Under what circumstances would it be better to use the subjective "I" approach in your own writing? When would the objective approach be more effective?

# Warm-up

1.   This essay ends with the statement, "Surely women and men can fare
     better as a team." Working with the entire class, make a list of specific
     ways and specific situations in which women and men could fare better
     if they improved their teamwork. Select one item from the list and write
     a paragraph that explains how the teamwork could be improved.
     **Audience:** your classmates.

     Give a copy of your paragraph to a group of five or six people in
     your class. Lead them in a five- to ten-minute discussion of your
     suggestions.

     Make any revisions to your paragraph that might be necessary to clarify
     your suggestions. Distribute copies of the final draft to the group members
     so they can create small booklets that will be circulated through the
     class.

2.   In groups of five or six people, create a short questionnaire that will
     allow you to judge the attitudes of men and women in your community
     toward Virgin's ideas. Have eight or nine people answer the questionnaire;
     try to get a cross section of different people. When you have finished,
     compile the survey results gathered by everyone in your group.

     Write a short report of your findings aimed at the other people in
     your class.

     Make overhead projections of the report that best summarizes the
     results of your group's survey. Use these overheads as the basis for a
     short oral presentation to the class. (Make notes on the presentations
     made by the other groups so you can use the results in the "Thinking
     and Writing" section. Ask questions about any points that may not be
     clear to you.)

# Thinking and Writing

a.   One of Maynard's sources, Anthony Astrachan, estimates that 35 percent
     of men, at most, support women's quest for independence. Even some
     women would seem not to support it, since 20 percent of the calls
     Ross Virgin receives are from women.

     Based on your own experiences with the people you know, write
     an essay in which you examine the support given by men and women
     to the search for women's equality and independence. Take into con-

sideration factors that might affect people's support, such as education and age.

**Audience:** someone involved with the women's movement.

b.   Maynard suggests that "what holds men back is fear: of exposing their own weakness, of losing other men's support, and of humiliation by women."

Write an essay in which you explain the role these factors and any others you can identify play in keeping men from supporting the search for women's equality and independence.

**Audience:** someone involved directly on one side or the other of this debate.

Send a copy of your final draft to someone in your school or community who is involved with the ISOJ or the National Action Committee on the Status of Women. Ask for a response.

# Power and Control: Why Men Dominate Women

## by Rick Goodwin

As a counsellor in a re-education program for abusive men, I recently worked with a man who was convicted of assault causing bodily harm. The charges stemmed from an incident where he beat his wife severely on Christmas Day with their children present. Asked to explain his actions, he told the court he was upset that morning because his wife allowed the children to open their presents before he got out of bed. 1

Before we pass judgment on this man and look for the psychological rationale for his behaviour, let us examine the greater social context in which this man and his family live. Their world is one in which women are half the population, perform two-thirds of the work, receive one-tenth of the world's income, and own only one-hundredth of the world's property. This assault was not the only injustice this woman has ever faced — simply because she was a woman. 2

The unjust treatment of women should not be news, nor the fact that this man's abuse and the relative privileges bestowed on men in society are intertwined. If we search for reasons why this disparity exists between the sexes in the first place, we must understand why men maintain their position of power over women. 3

At least ten percent of all women are victims of physical assault inflicted by their husbands or common-law partners. In Canada, this translates to close to a million women. In response to the unmet need for intervention with the batterers, I co-founded New Directions, a counselling service for abusive men. In addition to working directly with the abusers, we conduct many workshops on the issue of men's violence. The question I am most frequently asked by social workers, community groups, and even abused women themselves, is, simply, "Why do the men do it?" 4

It is not an easy question to answer because we still do not fully understand all the causes of wife battering. In our work with close to 300 abusive men, however, one factor has emerged as one root cause of men's violence against women. For men who batter, their purpose is simple: to gain power and control. 5

Every month, my colleague and I offer an information session for prospective clients. One of the things we do in this two-and-a-half hour workshop is 6 to ask the men outright what causes their violence. They are usually quick to respond: "She provoked me," "I was drunk at the time," "I lost control," "My psychiatrist told me I was insecure," "I was abused as a kid," "She was making a fool out of me." But when we ask them what they gain from their abusive behaviour, the group is usually silent, or may insist they don't get anything from it. This begs our response: "If you don't get anything from it, why do you do it?" Silence.

7    After attending the information session and an individual interview, the men may begin a 24-week program of group counselling based on a preset curriculum. In these sessions, we present various psycho-educational exercises designed to examine the components of both physical and emotional abuse. Throughout the program, we must always steer the group back to the heart of the issue — that men don't need to be abusive, that they *choose* to be because violence as a means of control works. We let them know that accepting this fundamental truth and abandoning their excuses is the first essential for them to stop their violence.

8    This isn't easy. While batterers may experience some negative and painful consequences of their actions, they have much to gain. For example, the men benefit from the forced acquiescence and subservience of their mates. The abuse affirms their own sense of superiority. The acts of violence can also protect men from dealing directly with their insecurities about themselves and their relationships. Abusive behaviour, of any type, is often used by men to reinforce their "male privilege" in the relationship. The attitude that a man is "king of the castle" is still very much with us.

9    This work has made me grapple with some disturbing truths. Abusive men are not much different from most men. Contrary to popular belief, they are not sick, pathological, or psychotic. They have been socialized in the same male-dominated society as the rest of us. While men who batter certainly differ as to the extent and expression of their need for power in relationships, it would be folly to think that the rest of us are immune to this need. Just as we all need to critically examine issues of discrimination because we live in a racist society, all men need to come to terms with issues of power as they relate to the women in their lives.

10   Some may find this surprising. Yet, much of our culture is characterized by relationships of domination and subordination, not only of men over women, but of industrialized countries over Third World nations, of lighter skins over dark, of rich over poor. In the age of Rambo, we implicitly believe we can obtain what we want by supremacy and force. As part of this process, we spend a lot of energy classifying individual perpetrators of injustice as

"deviants" or "criminals." Their behaviour, however, is simply a concrete manifestation of the destructive and darker aspects of the human psyche.

This theme of domination is endemic to our society, particularly in the area of male–female relationships. The imperialism over women engulfs both marital relationships and gender politics. Much like the issue of wife battering, the analysis of this power differential has emerged from the feminist movement. As a result, we now know that masculinity and femininity are socially constructed entities, and that tendencies toward domination are an integral component of the male "social" identity. Before we can diagnose the origins of male dominance, however, it is imperative that we examine the psychology of men. **11**

Noted feminist writer Susan Griffin employs the term "chauvinist thinking" to describe men's perception of women. Men all too often regard their own masculine attributes as superior when compared to traditional feminine qualities. This allows men to oppress and exploit women as beings who are inherently "inferior." Griffin refers to this cognitive polarity as a "delusion" that men desperately need to hold on to. The blinders of this ideology distort the perception not only of women's lives, but of men's lives as well. By denigrating "feminine" qualities and projecting them exclusively onto women, men reject important aspects of their own psyches, since expressions of "female" emotions and qualities do not conform with notions of traditional hypermasculinity. We see this clearly in the way boys insult each other. They use put-downs like "sissy," "girl," "wimp," and "fag" to call one another's masculinity into question. The ultimate insult for a male is to suggest that he is not a male! **12**

Patriarchal culture dictates that men must live with this strict and confining definition of heterosexual masculinity. Any substantial variance will not be tolerated. The feminine "other" symbolizes the inadequacies, fears, and aversions of this macho ideal. For men to hold true to traditional masculinity they must not only reject this "dark side" of themselves, but condemn it as well. Only by purging any "female" qualities can the purity of masculine identity be upheld and unquestioned. Women are not the only ones maligned by this process. Gay men and "effeminate" men also fall victim to this masculine imperialism. . **13**

For oppression to work, the "other" must be objectified and discounted. In South Africa, the Afrikaners have to perceive blacks as less intelligent, less civil, and less governable to substantiate apartheid. Likewise, an abusive man will no doubt refer to his partner as "the wife," "my old lady," or simply "her." In this process, he denies her true identity by making her some sort **14** of appendage or possession. Similarly, pornography is employed as a kind of propaganda of misogynist ideology. As Andrea Dworkin states, "Male power is the raison d'être of pornography: the degradation of the female is the means of achieving this power."

15    Not surprisingly, male power has its roots in the socialization of boys in our culture. For males to develop their gender identity, they must undergo a radical transformation from total vulnerability and dependence as infants to an adult display of complete mastery over both themselves and their environment. Like girls, boys must dissociate themselves from their mothers, who represent the entire world from which they came. This is essential for children to create their own sense of self. Yet boys must also separate themselves from this primary bond as they become aware of their maleness. Subsequently, boys learn to bury their "feminine" qualities as characteristics that are associated with mother. What boy hasn't been told not to show his pain because "only girls cry"?

16    As boys remove themselves from their mothers, they begin to identify with the more distant male figures in their lives. Fathers, brothers, or the male roles portrayed in society give boys a clear role model of masculinity. Their emotionality must be renounced, as well as any interest they may have in "girls' stuff." Boys are discouraged from any traditional feminine roles of nurturing as they enter the competitive and aggressive world of men. The modern-day archetypes of He-Man, G.I. Joe, and Captain Power permeate a boy's perception of the impenetrable world of men.

17    From an early age, boys learn that aggression is a legitimate means of resolving conflict. Be it in sports, the schoolyard, policing, or war — or, as Andrea Dworkin states, "[in] the mythology of heroism" — violence is acceptable. What boy doesn't want a toy gun or soldier? Now we have water pistols that look like Uzis. The toy industry markets war toys exclusively for boys. As a child playing road hockey, I vividly recall my friends and me throwing down our sticks and staging fights because this is what we saw on television. Similarly, the schoolyard bully may be emulating his abusive parents, and the batterer may be repeating his father's behaviour toward his mother.

18    This continuum of dominance, aggression, and violence isn't just a replay of witnessed events or a resolution of conflict. It also gets results. The potential of this power transforms the individual man from a position of relative powerlessness to one of complete control. Nobody messes with John Wayne or the Equalizer.

19    Male domination allows men economic advantage, as women make only $0.64 for every dollar men earn, and can give them sexual liberties as

expressed by sexual harassment and assault. Historically, men's physical and emotional needs have been met by women — mothers, girlfriends, housewives, maids. Men control women not only in monopolizing discussions but in politics and business as well. Perhaps the question should not be "Why do men batter?" but "Why do they feel they need to?"

When men batter, they discount their partner's selfhood on a daily basis.   20
Society can be accused of the same crime, in that it has historically failed to respond to, much less identify, the victims of this male terrorism. Yet, things are changing for the better, now that we are no longer silently ignoring the needs of abused women. As a result, batterers are slowly being confronted. If we demand that abusers be held accountable for their behaviour, we must also demand the same from the police, the courts, and other powers-that-be. It becomes painfully apparent that to change abusive men we must change our abusive society.

Part of this process of change must involve redefining power as an either-   21
or concept. It is not a choice for men to consider that the only other alternative to having power over women is to be powerless. One of the greatest fears for abusers is that they will be "walked all over" by their partner if they give up their control. This false choice permeates our culture. We must strive instead for a society that honours a position of "power-from-within," a situation of mutuality and egalitarianism that honours all involved. By reclaiming the original definition of power as "to be able," we can evoke a sense of empowerment in both men and women. Since abuse cannot occur between equals, we must first restructure both interpersonal and gender equity.

We've got a lot of work to do before we can herald a major change. We   22
are on the right track in addressing male violence by establishing programs for batterers; however, male abuse of power is an issue for *all* men to consider, not only those involved in violence programs. All too often, even those who receive counselling only modify their use of controlling behaviours. Much fanfare can be made over men's reduction of physical violence while they are in treatment. Unfortunately, many of the men only develop more subtle and sophisticated forms of verbal and psychological abuse to maintain their control. Feminists and social workers alike need to give more thought to what the mandate for these groups should be, in addition to what constitutes success.

Men's programs will not stop patriarchy. At best, they can provide a blueprint   23
for change, if men *choose* to change. Batterers' groups deliver a strong message to society that men are responsible for their violence, and that their behaviour is unacceptable. We must not, however, be seduced into believing that therapy can be the vanguard of an egalitarian society. Male dominance must be rec-

ognized and rooted out wherever it is found in society. As men, we must start challenging each other in our sexism, as well as providing ourselves with support in our struggle to break free from it.

24    If we want to achieve equality between the sexes, then we will have to give up our power and control over women. It's only fair. Men are now beginning to question the psychological costs they pay to maintain their male dominance. Perhaps this is a start. What we do know is that, as men, we must begin the difficult process of relinquishing our masculine prerogatives. If not, whether we batter or not, our collusion with male violence will continue.

# Style and Structure

1.  (a) In his title, Goodwin suggests he is writing about the relationship between men battering women and power and control. Where in the essay does he actually make a direct statement about this relationship?

    (b) What purpose is served in delaying this **thesis statement**?

    (c) Do you feel that his strategy of repeating the title in the **thesis statement** is an effective one? Would you alter either the **thesis statement** or the title?

2.  (a) The opening sentence of this essay contains a personal statement: "I recently worked with a man who was convicted of assault causing bodily harm." What purpose do you think the writer has in mind when he makes such a statement?

    (b) Students are sometimes advised to avoid making "I"-statements. Explain whether you think this is a general rule, or whether it applies only to certain situations.

    (c) Can you suggest situations where an "I"-statement is especially effective?

3.  (a) Goodwin makes good use of **topic sentences** throughout the essay. Identify which ones are particularly effective in focussing the reader's attention. Explain the reasons for your choices.

4.  (a) Writers in several fields, sociology among them, have occasionally been criticized for using too much jargon in their communications. With the help of a dictionary, explain what jargon is. Do you find evidence of this habit in Goodwin's writing?

    (b) Identify those words you believe to be jargon. Do you think their use could have been avoided? Use a dictionary or thesaurus to suggest alternatives.

(c) Examine the effect of jargon. Survey classmates about how they felt when reading the passage(s) you have identified and together make a list of reactions. What advice might nonexperts give to professionals who write?

5. (a) From paragraph 12 on, the writer makes frequent use of quotation marks: "female" emotions, "dark side," "effeminate" men, "female" qualities, and so on. Discuss Goodwin's probable intention in using these quotation marks.

   (b) Do you find that the quotation marks help or simply get in the way? Give reasons for your decision.

6. (a) Examine paragraph 19: "Male domination allows men economic advantage, as women make only $0.64 for every dollar men earn. . . . " Would you judge this paragraph to have strong **unity**? **Coherence**? (See pp. 301 and 302.)

   (b) Rewrite the paragraph, starting with the **concluding sentence**, adding appropriate **transitional words**, and devising a new **concluding sentence**. Compare your reworked paragraph with the original and decide which is better, and why.

# Warm-up

Many writers begin the essay-writing process by telling a story or recalling a vivid scene from the past. Take a few moments to remember a scene of children acting with violence, which you have either seen in real life or read about in literature. Tell (don't read) the story to the class, taking time to represent the scene as vividly as possible. As you are telling your story, try to note its effect on your listeners. Often, when a story strikes a respondent chord, listeners will nod or otherwise indicate agreement.

After all the stories are told, examine, as a class, which ones are especially effective and why. Discuss how you might use the storytelling technique as preparation for your next essay.

# Thinking and Writing

a.  Goodwin points out that he remembers playing road hockey, when the players threw down their sticks and staged fights because they had seen such behaviour on television. He suggests, "From an early age, boys learn that aggression is a legitimate means of resolving conflict" (paragraph 17).

Make a list of three occasions when, as a child, you might have acted out aggression as you had seen others do, or perhaps occasions when you saw others behaving aggressively in imitation of a parent or other role model. For each occasion, jot down as many of the details of the scene and the behaviour as you can remember. Now, taking Goodwin's statement (above) as your **thesis**, and your examples as evidence, develop an essay in which you argue that children pattern their behaviour after a given model.

**Audience:** someone who would question the validity of this thesis.

b.    Although most of us would think of abusive people as sick or abnormal, Goodwin makes the point that abusive men are not much different from others: they are not "sick, pathological, or psychotic" (paragraph 9). Perhaps what we need, then, is a better profile of an abuser.

Write an essay in which you describe a hypothetical abuser, using information from Goodwin's essay and giving examples to illustrate your case. Suggest what sort of man he is, what his background might be, and how he views himself and the world. You may want to consult some standard sources, such as journals of psychology and/or sociology, to get other expert opinions to validate your case.

**Audience:** young women who believe spouse abusers are easily recognized.

# The Coming of an Information Society

## by Edward Cornish

Many new technological systems will flood into our lives during the 1990s, but those in communications and computers may have the most revolutionary consequences. These new systems promise transformation in the ways we work, learn, play, shop, and manage our everyday lives.

No new technological breakthroughs are required for this transformation: the devices are already available and have begun to move into homes, offices, and factories. As this happens, the communications revolution long anticipated by scientists and engineers will actually occur.

To understand the information revolution, it is useful to look back at a few of the great historical landmarks in the collecting, synthesizing, and transmitting of information. If the computer is defined as any device for storing and processing information, it has an ancient history. Nature developed protoplasmic computers — brains — hundreds of millions of years ago. Animal brains evolved steadily through the eons, though far more slowly than have electronic brains. The human brain, which appeared approximately two million years ago, represented a major advance over earlier models and gave enormous power to the species possessing it. This remarkable "wet computer" was almost certainly accompanied by a major breakthrough in communications — human languages. Thanks to these powerful computing and communicating abilities, man became the dominant animal on earth.

The next great breakthrough in information technology did not occur until about 10 000 years ago with the invention of writing, which made it possible to encapsulate information and transmit it through time and space. With writing, information could be stored outside the brain and accessed years later for processing in another brain. The information could also be transported thousands of kilometres in its exact form — without being distorted by repeated passage through different human brains. To be sure, the method of transmitting the message was slow: a messenger proceeding on foot, horseback, or boat. Still, the communication system — primitive as it seems by modern standards — enabled the Roman emperors to govern territories ranging from Britain to Egypt.

Down through the ages, stupendous efforts were exerted to speed up communications. In the 1400s, the Incas had a system of messengers, each of whom ran about one-and-a-half kilometres at top speed to the next messenger; this relay system enabled a message to travel at the rate of about 240 kilometres per day across the Inca kingdom. No significant improvement on the Inca system occurred until the nineteenth century, but pre-electronic communications systems enjoyed one last moment of glory — the Pony Express. Started by the U.S. government in 1860 to carry the mail from St. Joseph, Missouri, to the Pacific coast, the Pony Express lasted only sixteen months but made a lasting impression on American consciousness. The "ponies" were actually horses, stationed sixteen to 24 kilometres apart. Each rider rode three animals successively, covering at least 53 kilometres before passing the mail pouch to the next rider. The fastest trip ever made took seven days and seventeen hours, but the regular schedule was ten days — hardly better than the Incas' system.

6    The telegraph, developed commercially in the 1840s, made communications virtually instantaneous over hundreds, even thousands, of kilometres. But the telegraph stopped at the water's edge. Though the news of Abraham Lincoln's assassination could be transmitted by telegraph instantaneously to California 4800 kilometres away, it could not cross the Atlantic. As a result, news of Lincoln's assassination took twelve days to reach London.

7    By the early twentieth century, the telephone had largely replaced the telegraph, and cables linked Europe to America. Marconi patented his radio in England in 1896, but it was not until the 1920s that radio became a major medium of mass communications. Franklin D. Roosevelt, with his "fireside chats," turned radio into a major medium of politics in the 1930s. Motion pictures, which had evolved from the nickelodeon into the great silent pictures of the 1920s, began to talk in the early 1930s and had blossomed into colour by the end of the decade. Television, demonstrated experimentally as early as 1927, began to enter U.S. homes after the Second World War. During the 1950s, television swept into homes at a stupendous rate: in 1950, less than ten percent of homes had television; by 1960, more than 90 percent of homes had succumbed to the one-eyed monster.

8    While radio and television were expanding furiously, developments were occurring elsewhere that seemed initially to have little bearing on mass communications. Large businesses and governments had vast amounts of information that needed to be handled economically and swiftly. One approach to information-handling was to use punched cards that could be manipulated mechanically, thereby making it possible to retrieve needed information more quickly. Rapid data-handling became particularly important to the U.S. military, which was trying to figure out ways to aim and launch missiles over very

great distances. Human mathematicians operating with paper and pencil were simply too slow to perform the necessary calculations quickly enough. Nor could clerks get information from file drawers as fast as was required. So the military began putting funds into the development of electronic calculators — devices that later became known as "electronic computers" and then simply "computers." The experimental computers of the late 1940s and early 1950s were very large, often occupying a good-sized room, and were monstrously expensive. Furthermore, they were extremely stupid by today's standards. But during the 1950s, 1960s, and 1970s, the capabilities of the computers to manipulate data increased dramatically; equally dramatic was the decrease in their cost.

At first it seemed that only large government agencies like the U.S. Census 9 Bureau could use computers, and that computers could be used for only a few purposes, such as solving certain types of mathematical equations. But as people gained more and more experience with computers, the electronic "brains" began to perform more and more tasks. And a funny thing began to happen: the computers began to "talk" to each other and to human beings by means of telephone lines, and telephone companies began to use computers to keep track of long-distance communications. So the barriers that once separated communications and computers into two fields began to break down. By early 1980, U.S. officials were in a serious quandary because the Communications Act of 1934 authorized the Federal Communications Commission to regulate electronic communications, but the Commission found it virtually impossible to find a legal formula that clearly distinguished between communications and data processing. In effect, technology had made obsolete the laws that were designed to regulate it!

The convergence of communications and computers is natural since both 10 deal with information. Computers store and manipulate information; communications systems transmit the information from one point to another.

The importance of information is hard to overstate because we use infor- 11 mation as the basis for all action. Without good information, we may blunder disastrously, but with it, we can reach our goals quickly and easily. Thus, better communications and information systems hold a tantalizing promise: they may be able to help us solve many of the problems besetting the modern world.

The speed of progress in computers has astounded almost everyone. Musing 12 on microcomputers, Stanford University economist Edward Steinmuller has been quoted as saying, "If the airlines had progressed as rapidly as this technology, the Concorde would be carrying half a million passengers at 32 million kilometres an hour for less than a penny apiece!"

13   A writer for the *Washington Star* went even further:

> Had the automobile developed at a pace equivalent to that of the com-
> puter during the past twenty years, today a Rolls Royce would cost
> less than $3, get one million kilometres to the litre, deliver enough
> power to drive the Queen Elizabeth II, and six of them would fit
> on the head of a pin!

14   Such statements may seem to be mere hyperboles, but the microcomputer
revolution has awed even its proponents. One expert, Adam Osborne, wrote
a book called *Running Wild*, since that is what he said the microcomputers
were doing. Osborne said neither government nor big business (nor anybody
else) could halt the breathtaking advance of the silicon chip.

15   The rapid increase in the ability of computers to store and manipulate vast
amounts of information led to speculation as early as the 1950s that computers
might someday challenge the traditional paper-based information systems. Why
couldn't the information in our daily newspapers be put into a computer and
sent electronically into people's homes without the present cumbersome system, which involves the cutting down of vast forests for paper, the use of
gas-guzzling fleets of trucks, and battalions of vendors and carriers? Why
couldn't the contents of libraries be stored in computers so that the information
could be accessed by users almost anywhere?

16   During the 1960s, studies were made by the Library of Congress and numerous other institutions to determine what role computers might play in
sorting and disseminating information. Many of the studies could be sum-
marized as follows: yes, computers were technically capable of doing many
of the things suggested by their enthusiasts, but the technology was insuf-
ficiently advanced to make most such projects economically desirable. Still,
there were exceptions to that rule. For example, the Library of Congress
decided it would be desirable to computerize its card catalogues, and, during
the 1970s, libraries in the United States and elsewhere adopted computers
for many of their book-handling procedures. In effect, the libraries computerized "information about information" — titles and authors of books, reference numbers so books could be located, and so on — while leaving the
bulk of the information in the form of books and other materials on paper.

17   Newspapers also began to adopt computers, and, by 1980, major newspapers
all over the United States were thoroughly computerized. Instead of using
a typewriter, a reporter types his or her article on a computer console, and
the information is stored in the computer while various editors work on it.

Instead of using pencils to edit copy typed on paper, the editors edit copy on a video display screen, a device looking much like a television screen but showing text instead of pictures. The system allows an editor to carry out all normal editorial tasks: words can be deleted, inserted, shifted about, and so on. Once an article is ready to print, the computer generates the electronic signals needed to control the typesetting operation. But, in its final form, a modern newspaper is still a collection of large paper sheets on which articles and advertisements have been printed in ink.

The truly electronic newspaper — a contradiction in terms since it is    **18** *paperless* — appeared in Britain in the late 1970s. As happens so often in technological innovation, the breakthroughs did not come from the traditional provider of the service. Instead of British newspapers pioneering the electronic newspaper, the British post office and the British Broadcasting Corporation (BBC) established information services that could be described as electronic newspapers: news can be called up on a video screen and read whenever one wishes. For instance, a subscriber may select "headlines" and then press the appropriate buttons on the mechanism (which is about the size of a pocket calculator). The headlines then appear on the screen. After reading them, the viewer can call up other subjects such as "foreign news," "consumer news," "people," "weather," and so on. An electronic "newspaper" may have hundreds of pages of information in its memory.

The broadcast versions of the electronic newspaper, such as the BBC's,    **19** allow the viewer to call up a wide variety of information that is being broadcast simultaneously. The viewer has the feeling of being able to interact with the system, but the interaction is really limited to the electronic equivalent of looking at different pages in a printed newspaper. By contrast, the electronic newspaper provided by the British post office has the technical feasibility of allowing the reader to contact the editors of the newspaper. The reason is that the post office's electronic newspaper is transmitted by telephone lines; being two-way, the system allows a viewer to ask for any information in the post-office memory bank. Many thousands of pages of information can be made available, since the system is not limited by the constraints of the airwaves. The post-office system, because of its enormous information capacity, provides a bridge from the electronic newspaper to the electronic library. The contents of hundreds of thousands of books can now be put onto computer tape, and people can have the material displayed on their home viewing screens.

The terminology of the new electronic information systems is unsettled,    **20** but the word "teletext" is often used to suggest a system employing a television signal for transmission, while "viewdata" (or "videotext") is often used in cases where the information is transmitted by cable or telephone lines. However, these terms are still used rather interchangeably.

21    No one knows how rapidly the new electronic information systems will catch on. So far, the British systems have not proved outstandingly popular, in part because of the substantial costs involved. But as more people acquire home computing equipment (for whatever reason), the way will be open for the electronic information systems to move in more strongly.

22    Conceding probable defeat, newspapers are now actively trying to get into the electronic act themselves. Eleven major newspapers, including the *New York Times*, *Los Angeles Times*, and *Washington Post*, have been selected to join a national computer data network and will supply their entire editorial material every evening to a service based in Columbus, Ohio. The service, CompuServe Information Service, is available to anyone with a home or office computer at a time-sharing fee.

23    The electronic newspaper system began when the *Columbus Dispatch* joined the program. Subscribers can call up any of the articles in the newspapers, and the newspapers will receive twenty percent of the time-sharing charge levied on the subscriber. Initially, only editorial copy will be supplied, but the newspapers are expected to sell national ads on the computer media soon.

24    Another experiment is under way in Coral Gables, Florida, where Knight-Ridder Newspapers is supplying news, advertising, and other consumer services via 200 personal computers installed at no cost in selected homes. If viewers want to order goods they see advertised, they can type messages in their terminals to say where they want the goods delivered, along with the necessary credit-card information.

25    The growing use of computer terminals may greatly speed up the arrival of the electronic newspaper. The Source Telecomputing Corporation of America, based in McLean, Virginia, allows its subscribers to access all kinds of information, including the United Press International dispatches from around the world and the *New York Times* Information Bank. In addition, Source subscribers can post messages on an electronic bulletin board, send messages to each other, and play electronic games. The availability of these other services means that people have a variety of reasons for acquiring a computer terminal that, once acquired, can be used for accessing newspaper-type information.

26    The advent of electronic information systems means that people will be able to get more up-to-date information in their areas of interest than is possible with the present publishing methods. Already, book publishers are recognizing the challenge of electronic publishing and are moving into the field themselves. U.S. elementary and high schools spend a substantial amount on computer-

based equipment. Textbook publishers are putting material into computer form so that more people can get computerized instruction.

Meanwhile, in the scholarly world, computers and telecommunications are having a wide variety of impacts. For instance, two authors thousands of miles apart may use a computer as a communications link while they are collaborating on a "paper." Each author suggests ideas, paragraphs, clarifications, and so forth, and watches for misspellings by the other. Eventually the "paper" is completed, and the question then becomes what to do with it. One approach would be to put it into a traditional journal printed on paper. Another approach, however, would be to keep the article in the computer and let other scholars access it by means of their computer terminals. In this way, the paper would go only to those really interested in it, and a large amount of paper and mailing costs would be saved.

The concept of networking has emerged as one of the most exciting ideas in the information area. In a sense, the concept is so natural that one might wonder what the excitement is all about. Networking really implies little more than a shift in the way we view the storage of information. Information can be stored in a large central location, such as a huge computer. However, the same information might be stored in smaller computers at a wide variety of locations. The arrival of microcomputers, which can be bought by ordinary people, has meant that it is possible for a person working in a basement to develop a computer program and/or data base that many other people can use. When a system is connected into a network linking up other people's systems at other locations, the individual computer user suddenly has access to enormous resources and also becomes a resource for other people on the network. An individual in the network can be both a user and a supplier of information transmitted by the network.

Hundreds of computer networks are now springing up all over the United States. In some instances, these networks may consist of nothing more than a few individuals who share an interest in something. In other cases, the networks have thousands of individual and organizational members and have easy access to vast stores of information. The networks make it possible for ordinary people to access huge data banks, such as the Index Medicus (medical index), maintained by the National Library of Medicine in Bethesda, Maryland. As these networks grow, each individual will have increasingly easy access to more and more information. To an increasing degree, we will all be able to find out almost everything we want to know about anything whenever we want it.

The impacts of the communications revolution will continue to be pervasive, unsettling, subtle, and mysterious. On the one hand, the new technologies in communications and computers — sometimes abbreviated to "compunications" — will help us to save energy, prevent crime, drive more safely, do more of our work at home, and remove much of the agony of such chores as preparing our income-tax returns. On the other hand, the compunications revolution may be expected to destroy many people's jobs and provide new opportunities for crime.

31    The information revolution may also change our views of ourselves. Down through the centuries, human beings have taken pride in their knowledge, even giving themselves the name *Homo sapiens* or "knowing man." But, already, some computers are smarter than human beings — at least in some respects. In 1980, human and computer chess players squared off at the National Conference on Artificial Intelligence, held at Stanford University in Palo Alto, California. Paul Benjamin, an expert-ranked human from New York City, won one game from a computer but lost a second. An exhausted Benjamin congratulated his opponent for its "brilliant tactical" play. "I was definitely inferior," he admitted ruefully.

# Style and Structure

1.    A good introduction contains a **thesis statement** and an indication of the approach to be taken in the body of the essay. Underline the **thesis** of this essay.
2.    In paragraph 2, the writer hints at his approach to the topic when he says, "The devices [1] are already available and [2] have begun to move into homes, offices, and factories." Does Cornish maintain this approach consistently in the following sections?
   (a) British systems: paragraphs 18 to 21
   (b) American systems: paragraphs 22 to 29
      (i)  Does the author describe the systems?
      (ii) Does he show how they are moving into homes, offices, and factories?
3.  (a) What aspect of the subject does Cornish develop in paragraphs 3 to 14?
   (b) In paragraphs 12 and 13, what do the quoted comparisons accomplish?
   (c) From your answers to 3(a) and 3(b), draw up a profile of the intended reader.
4.    Paragraphs 30 and 31 form the **conclusion** of the essay.
   (a) What function does each of these paragraphs serve?
   (b) Are both of these functions legitimate for a **conclusion**? Why?

# Warm-up

1. List three or four ways in which *Homo sapiens* is *superior* to any computer, no matter how powerful it may be. Then write a paragraph that explains *Homo sapiens'* superiority.
   **Audience:** your classmates.

   Join with a group of four or five others in the class. Look at all of the paragraphs produced by the group and select two for presentation to the rest of the class: (1) the one that is the most creative and (2) the one that is the most impressive. Put them onto overheads and make your presentation.

2. Keep a journal that records every instance that your life is touched by a computer in any way in a 24-hour period. Watch out for hidden contacts such as bank transactions, television effects, and supermarket scanners.

   Write a paragraph that explains how far computers have flooded into your life.
   **Audience:** someone who has read Cornish's article.

   Compare your paragraph to two or three written by classmates. Have they found computers in places you did not suspect? Are their conclusions similar to yours? Make suggestions to one another for improvements in the way you convey your messages, then revise your paragraph into its final form using these comments as a guide.

# Thinking and Writing

a. The article presents a variety of uses of "compunications." Choose the one most attractive to you, and write an essay explaining its advantages in such a way that your readers will want to have a terminal in their home.
   **Audience:** someone who knows nothing of the new compunications systems.

b. Cornish says, "These new systems promise transformation in the ways we work . . . " (paragraph 1). Write an essay on the positive and negative effects such systems may have on the profession for which you are preparing.
   **Audience:** someone presently working in the profession you have chosen.

   Send a copy of your essay to the person in charge of training you for this profession.

# Muscling In on Madness

## by Clarence Reynolds

1   It's no secret that for many bodybuilders and athletes, popping steroids goes hand in hand with pumping iron. Anabolic steroids — synthetic versions of the male hormone testosterone — allow users to develop more impressive pecs and delts than they could by weight training alone. But the quest for brawn may play havoc with the brain. Psychiatrists Harrison Pope Jr., at McLean Hospital in Belmont, Massachusetts, and David Katz of Harvard Medical School report that steroid use can lead to major psychiatric disturbances.

2   In the past, attention has focussed on the physical toll exacted by steroids. In men, steroids can cause breast development, shrinking of the testes, and decreased sperm production; in women, they can lead to deepening of the voice, growth of facial and body hair, clitoral enlargement, and menstrual irregularity. Long-term risks in both sexes include liver damage, hypertension, and atherosclerosis.

3   Much less attention has been given to the mental effects of steroids. Anecdotal evidence, however, suggests that the drugs can lead to unusually aggressive and irritable behaviour. When two patients turned up at McLean Hospital with steroid-induced psychosis, Pope and Katz decided to investigate.

4   The psychiatrists interviewed 41 bodybuilders and football players who admitted having used the drugs. (Although steroids can't be legally obtained without a prescription, they are there for the asking on a thriving black market.) Thirteen of the athletes reported that they had experienced manic or near-manic behaviour during steroid use. The most common symptoms were hyperactivity and inflated self-esteem, which increased their drive to train harder and intensify their workouts. They also described episodes of grandiose and reckless behaviour. One 23-year-old man bought a $17 000 sports car while taking the oral steroid methandrostenolone. When he stopped the drug, he realized he could not afford the payments and sold the car. A year later, during another steroid cycle, he impulsively bought a $20 000 sports car. Another respondent, convinced of his own immortality, deliberately drove a car into a tree at 65 kilometres per hour while a friend videotaped him.

5   Five subjects also experienced severe psychotic episodes. One person had auditory hallucinations that lasted for five weeks; another became extremely paranoid and thought his friends were stealing from him; yet another developed

the grandiose delusion that he could lift his car and tip it over. These episodes ceased when they stopped taking the drugs. "We're not exactly sure what causes the mood changes," says Katz, "but we do believe that somehow these drugs disrupt the normal functioning of neurotransmitters in the central nervous system."

Although steroids are sometimes prescribed for medical purposes (to treat        6
men with low testosterone levels, for example), the doses are generally lower than those used by athletes, and Pope and Katz think that psychiatric manifestations are much less likely to occur. Athletes often "stack" steroids, taking up to five or six different kinds, including oral and injectable drugs and even veterinary preparations.

Since many athletes are wary of discussing their steroid use, says Katz,        7
it's difficult to assess how common such psychiatric disturbances are. "But we're convinced that there's a huge subculture out there using the drugs. We've only touched the tip of the iceberg."

# Style and Structure

1. (a) Judging from the vocabulary used throughout this essay, who would you think is included in the intended audience?
   (b) Make a list of any words you do not immediately recognize and guess at the definitions from context by reading the passages in which they occur. Check a dictionary to see how accurate your guesses are.
   (c) Reviewing your list in (b), do you think the writer does a good job of showing the meaning of the words chosen through the context in which they occur?
   (d) Do you believe the use of these unusual words is necessary for the overall effectiveness of the essay? Put a check mark beside each of the words in your list that you believe is essential to the essay.
2. In this short essay, how many different **organizational approaches** have been used? What would you say is the overall **organizational approach**? (See pp. 301–302)
3. In the **concluding paragraph**, the researchers state that it is difficult to assess the psychiatric side effects of steroids because athletes are wary of discussing their use. Has the writer managed to show that there is not a large body of evidence to back up the essay? How?

# Warm-up

Many writers begin their essay-writing process by highlighting questions that people have about a certain issue. Draw up a list of at least five questions that people have concerning the use of steroids. Be sure that your list covers the entire breadth of the issue, not just a single interesting aspect.

When you have completed your list, discuss what is achieved by writing down the questions. How might the reader of an essay on the topic benefit if the writer brought out these questions? Discuss with classmates.

# Thinking and Writing

a.    It has been suggested that we live in a society that believes there is a chemical cure for every problem. You're feeling down? — Have a drink! Feel a cold coming on? — Take a megadose of Vitamin C! We pour chemicals into our bodies, onto our foods — even onto our lawns to keep them problem-free. To the outsider, it would seem that we have enormous faith in chemicals.

Write an essay, developed by example, in which you inventory the ways a typical family responds to its problems with chemical solutions. You do not need to have all the answers or to be fully aware of all the implications of the family's use of chemicals. Do try, however, to raise thought-provoking questions for your readers about lifestyles and chemical dependencies of all sorts.

**Audience:** the average Canadian who is unaware of the extent to which we use chemicals.

b.    The essay outlines a number of unpleasant side effects that steroids produce, and yet we hear almost daily about athletes using these banned substances to increase their stamina and ability. We must assume that, although these athletes are aware of the dangers, their desire to win is greater than their fear of the drugs' side effects.

What is this drive to win all about? Is it always the admirable impulse to overcome obstacles and achieve excellence in whatever field? Or is it something less healthy, something that a great number of us don't have and are just as glad?

Write an extended-definition essay, in which you examine the competitive drive. Develop your essay with numerous examples, but be sure to use appropriate transitions and to state your thesis clearly.

**Audience:** aggressive young people who have not considered all the implications of competitiveness.

# A Car with a Mind of Its Own

## by Andrew C. Revkin

1   Automobiles in 2001 "are not going to be fat or flat," says Chuck Gordon, vice president in charge of GM's design staff. "They'll be lean and graceful and smooth and round — but not *fat* round."

2   But sleekness aside, 2001 model cars from GM and other manufacturers will not look all that different. They'll still have four wheels, four rubber tires, piston engines, and a chassis that's predominantly steel.

3   The biggest change in the car of 2001 will be under the hood, in the electronics. Most cars will have a powerful integrated electronic nervous system and central brain that will do everything from monitoring the slightest engine hiccup to preventing tires from spinning out on ice or skidding in a panic stop. Most mechanical systems in the car will be aided by, if not replaced by, electronics. Today about ten percent of a vehicle's value is represented by electronics. By 2001 that figure may jump to 25 percent — even more in luxury and high-performance models.

4   Unlike the flashy all-digital displays of the early 1980s, the electronics of tomorrow will be less for show and more for function. That's not to say that the automobile of 2001 will lack sophisticated electronic conveniences. Chris Magee, chief engineer for advanced vehicle technology at Ford, envisions a luxury-car owner walking out to the garage carrying a personalized, programmed card that automatically unlocks the door, starts the car, and adjusts the radio, seat, and steering wheel to preprogrammed preferences. And the car, armed with the knowledge of when the driver leaves for work, may even turn itself on when it's chilly, to warm up ahead of time.

5   Electronics will be the basis for new safety features. Sensors will scan blind spots in order to warn the driver of anything from a passing car to a child crouching behind the rear bumper. GM and other companies are developing systems for enhancing vision at night and in fog. One proposal is a dashboard screen that displays an infrared picture of the road ahead, like the image on a military night-vision scope. Cruise-control systems will probably be augmented with station-keeping technology: the distance between a car and the car ahead will be measured, and if the gap gets dangerously narrow, the brakes will automatically go on.

6   Of all the changes that advanced electronics will make possible, perhaps none is more fundamental to driving than total traction control. The antilock

brakes that have already appeared in luxury cars will probably be standard by 2001, says Robert Eaton, president of GM Europe. These computer-controlled devices monitor the speed of each wheel. If a wheel starts to lock, the brakes instantaneously ease up, then clamp down again just as fast when the wheel starts to move. The other half of traction control is antislip acceleration, which is something like antilock braking in reverse. The computer monitors wheel speed as the car accelerates, and the moment a wheel starts to spin out on a patch of ice or sand, power to that wheel is reduced briefly until traction is regained.

The four-stroke internal-combustion engine, patented in 1862, will still be the dominant power plant by the turn of the century, though its inventor would hardly recognize it. The hottest engine parts will be made of ceramics or novel metal alloys. The carburetor, which blends air and vaporized gasoline before they enter the engine cylinders, will be all but extinct; in its place will be the computer-orchestrated fuel-injection system already available in many cars.   7

The engine itself will be wired up with sensors that track everything from the amount of oxygen in the exhaust (to ensure efficient combustion) to vibrations in each cylinder (to sense engine knock and adjust the fuel–air mixture or ignition timing). Nissan has already developed the latter device: etched on a microchip are ten strips, each of which resonates with vibrations of a certain frequency, as a tuning fork does; it sends a signal into the circuit if any abnormal vibrations are picked up.   8

By 2001 manual transmissions will be all but extinct. Engineers have long dreamed of a continuously variable transmission, in which the abrupt transition from one gear to the next is eliminated. A continuous transmission may be developed by the turn of the century, but it will probably not be able to power full-size cars; the technology will be limited to very light, low-power vehicles.   9

Even the most basic of automotive systems, the suspension, will be overhauled with new technology. By 2001, many off-road vehicles and a growing number of conventional cars will offer active suspension, in which a computer responds instantly to potholes or cobblestones, moving each wheel up or down to compensate for irregularities in the road. One GM prototype of an off-road vehicle can move its wheels as much as ten inches; it can "step" over a fallen log. According to an engineer who recently drove a Ford sedan equipped with active suspension on a rough, cobbled test track, "you can race at 80 kilometres per hour with very little disturbance to the driver. Try that in a regular car and you'll have trouble holding on to the wheel."   10

11    One innovation that may have to wait is "drive by wire," a system like the one now used in jet fighters and innovative commercial aircraft. Instead of a physical connection between, say, the gas pedal and the engine, the link would be electronic, via fibre-optic cables or wires. Stepping on the gas pedal would no longer pull a cable attached to a throttle; it would send a digital instruction to the throttle via computer. But some engineers argue that this type of system would be not only too costly but also too risky. It may be annoying when a loose wire or faulty microchip means your radio doesn't work, but if you can't accelerate at a crucial moment, you're in real trouble.

12    Engineers agree that any advance in technology is only as good as it is reliable. "If you're first with something that works *most* of the time, that's as good as being last," says Magee. Although it may seem that the auto industry constantly recalls cars to fix one problem or another, the experts say cars have steadily become more reliable. "There have been some glitches," says Eaton, "but the trend is very clear. Look at tires. There was a time when you didn't take a vacation without more than one spare in the trunk. By 2001, the reliability of tires may be such that you won't carry a spare at all. We're already selling a significant number of Royal Seals with sealant compound inside that automatically fixes most punctures." If the spare tire survives at all, it may be there just to make consumers feel a bit safer.

13    Yet even in newfangled designs, there's at least one feature that will likely remain unchanged well into the next millennium. It's a feature that works so well in modern autos and other forms of transportation that it has defied all attempts to improve it. "I was at the airport yesterday," says Jordan, "and here comes this big sophisticated jet, full of advanced electronics — with two ordinary windshield wipers flopping back and forth."

## Style and Structure

1.   Based on evidence drawn from Revkin's approach to his topic, list three or four characteristics of this essay's intended reader.

2. (a) Identify the essay's **thesis statement**. What aspect of 2001 model cars does Revkin announce he will discuss?

   (b) Given the intended reader you have identified, what is the purpose of the paragraphs that precede the **thesis statement**?

   (c) Which paragraphs in the body of the essay make no mention of the topic Revkin announced in the **thesis statement**? What techniques does he use to hide this lack of **unity** from his reader? Is he successful?

2.   How does the order in which Revkin presents his paragraphs reflect his general appeal to or concern for his reader's interests?

3. (a) Choose any four paragraphs in the body of the essay. Identify the **topic sentence** in each. Explain in one or two sentences how the ideas in the rest of the paragraph relate to the **topic sentence**. How does this relationship affect the reader's understanding of the ideas in the paragraph?

   (b) Identify the **concluding sentence** in each paragraph you choose. If any do not have **concluding sentences**, write ones that would be appropriate. How do these sentences help the reader?

4.   Revkin faces a problem common to anyone writing about a highly technical subject. He has to translate specialized ideas and vocabulary into terms the nonspecialist can understand. Identify three places in the essay Revkin has accomplished this objective. For each, explain what technique he used and why he was successful.

5.   In his **conclusion**, Revkin takes a different approach to the standard one of summarizing or commenting on the points made in the body. What does he do? How successful is this approach in helping the reader come to grips with the essay's central topic?

# Warm-up

1.   Part of the problem in writing about familiar things — whether they are highly technical or not — is that we unconsciously assume others know what we are writing about and forget to include information they need to understand our point.

   Select a device with which you are very familiar. It may be something highly technical, like the zoom lens on a camera, or something much more common, like a retractable ballpoint pen. Write a one-paragraph description of how the device works.

   Give someone the paragraph to read, together with the actual device whose operation you have described, in order to review your success. Ask your reader to examine the device and determine how it works based only on your written description.

   Make notes about places in the paragraph that give your reader trouble. If the person simply cannot follow your description, provide more details or describe the process in other words. When your reader understands the process completely, revise your paragraph into a final draft.

2.    Write the text for a large newspaper advertisement in the year 2001 selling a car such as the ones described by Revkin in his essay. Try the ad out on some of your classmates to see if it would attract them to a dealer's showroom.

# Thinking and Writing

a.    Take a careful look at the cars in your school's parking lot. Based on what you see, write an essay that explains what people are looking for in the cars they buy (e.g., simple transportation, image, durability). Illustrate your points with specific examples drawn from three or four cars that seem to be typical.
**Audience:** the same intended reader as addressed by Revkin in his essay.

b.    Revkin's projections make an interesting contrast to suggestions made by Ivan Illich, a critic of the car industry. Illich calls for cars of the future to be built for endurance and durability, and to have "no frills" rust-proof bodies designed for safety and ease of maintenance, limited upper speeds and simple engines with low gas consumption, and modular components that owners can repair by plugging in new units; in short, he calls for cars to become simple tools for work and transportation.

Based on what you know about the reasons people have for buying cars, write an essay explaining the types of cars that will be popular in the year 2001. Will they be like the ones Revkin describes, like Illich's suggested workhorse, or something completely different?
**Audience:** the average Canadian car buyer.

# Living and Dying with AIDS: A Banker's Story

## by Hank E. Koehn

*Hank E. Koehn died of AIDS on September 29, 1987.*

At approximately 2 p.m. on Friday, February 20, 1987, my world came to an end in the San Jose, California, air terminal. 1

I had been in the San Jose area on a two-day business trip. Like most of my out-of-town visits, it consisted of two speaking engagements. 2

A week earlier, my doctor had convinced me I should have a test for the human immune deficiency virus that causes AIDS. He felt the results would allow him to treat me with greater knowledge. I had rejected the test. I suppose, like many other men, I was avoiding the information that I already suspected. 3

On Friday the 20th, I was scheduled to call my doctor for test results. I made the call while waiting for my flight to Los Angeles. The doctor informed me the test was positive. 4

I had AIDS. 5

With almost clinical detachment, we made an appointment for early the following week. According to the doctor, I "would have to be watched." 6

At the end of that visit, I, almost casually, mentioned that I was having difficulty using my left hand. For several weeks I had assumed this was due to some muscle I had pulled in my shoulder. 7

At my mention of this problem, my doctor sat up and took notice. After several questions, he said that this could indicate a serious problem linked with AIDS. The difficulty with the hand might be due to brain damage as a result of the now-active AIDS virus. 8

An appointment was made for me to have a magnetic resonance scan of my brain the following afternoon. That test required placing my head and shoulders inside a tubelike device that seemed to belong on a *Star Trek* movie set. 9

Within a day, the scan would indicate that there was a lesion on the right side of my brain. It could be the result of a tumour, or, more probably, the AIDS virus attacking my brain directly. 10

11    The doctor explained this in a cool, efficient manner. But, at the same time, he unwittingly transmitted the subconscious emotional message that I had a terminal condition — my future consisted of certain death.

12    It was arranged for me to go to the hospital for a complete diagnosis as soon as possible. Much to my doctor's displeasure, I delayed while I turned over my client commitments to an associate and visited my attorney to arrange matters — should I not leave the hospital alive.

13    On the day I left home to go to the hospital, I took a final look at my liquidambar tree; it was budding and I thought it was highly probable that I would never see the tree with all of its leaves.

14    The hospital stay was not unpleasant. However, the multitude of tests did little to change my outlook for a limited future. They indicated the brain lesion was due to toxoplasmosis infection.

15    This protozoan is usually present in all of us, but our immune systems keep it in check. In my case, the infection in my brain was slowly taking away my ability to use my left hand and arm. Dressing and daily living became a one-handed exercise.

16    On the day I was to leave the hospital, I had my first seizure. My arm and hand jumped around for about fifteen seconds as a result of "short circuit" signals from the infected area of the brain. Utterly terrified, I was then told that this could become a common event — which it did — and I received my first capsule of Dilantin.

17    I left hospital convinced my days among the living were indeed numbered. The doctors were surprised at my acceptance of my limited prospects. I said I had led a full, happy, productive, and successful life. I did not feel cheated and could therefore face my impending demise calmly.

18    I had prepared myself for death and resolved to get on with it. I decided two things: I would most likely not live beyond the end of the year; and, when I thought it was time to die, I would merely get into bed and stay there. These feelings and an all-encompassing resignation remained with me for several weeks. My calmness was the result of an accepted certainty.

19    During this same period, I decided that I would no longer work. I couldn't bear the thought of having a seizure in the middle of a lecture. Also, I felt I would be rejected when the word got out that I had AIDS. I was sure that most of my clients would be appalled at accidentally learning about my choice of lifestyle.

20    I then decided to be comfortable in my remaining days. This decision led to two discoveries. First, I had lost my sense of self-worth, which I had not

considered linked to my career. Indeed, I found I had little personal identity outside my work life.

Second, without my work, I had lost interest in the outside world. As    21
a futurist and a social observer, I had previously spent most of my time watching and reading about change.

With no work to do, I was no longer reading and watching video. Instead,    22
my days became empty. To fill the time, I began to sleep all day, as well as all night. Weeks before, while in the hospital, I had found that I could stare at "nothing" on the ceiling for many hours.

In retrospect, the frightening fact was that I was very content doing nothing.    23
Everything, including reading, became too much of an effort. Nothing seemed worthwhile, since I had only a limited number of days. Because of my relatively strong personality, there was almost no one to challenge my approach to my remaining time among the living.

I was well cared for in a comfortable home. I still felt deep inside that    24
resignation seemed the civilized approach to my remaining life.

Then one day, while talking with a friend, I asked again if he didn't think    25
I had become oo resigned, too easily. As we explored this thought, I became convinced ' had given up too quickly — even if giving up was the obvious course of action. From that point on I began to explore the alternatives. I had already been receiving some counselling to stabilize my emotional state — which I felt was stable without help.

To my surprise I found that, upon reflection, my inner needs were spiritual    26
or metaphysical. When I mentioned this thought to more friends during the next few days, I found that during illness they had reached the same conclusions in their own lives. It was suggested that I read several books, including one written by Louise L. Hay.

Ms. Hay, a metaphysical healer, had been working successfully with both    27
cancer and AIDS patients. Her Wednesday-night meetings held in Plummer Park had become legends in the gay community. I acquired several of her tapes and began to play them several times a day.

Slowly I began to understand that my future was in my own hands —    28
perhaps mind is actually a better word. This is strange considering that, as a futurist, I had told my clients, "If you can dream it, you can do it." Louise Hay reminded me that each of us has the capacity to invest tomorrow with the thoughts we have today.

After a period of time spent listening to the meditation tapes, my attitude    29
began to shift from resignation to a belief that I could play a major role in

healing myself.

30    About this time, I developed an overwhelming urge to visit the ocean. I wasn't sure why I needed to see the ocean, but the need was very real.

31    We stayed in a Laguna Beach hotel that directly overlooks the surf. When I sat in a lounge chair, looking down at the waves, I realized why I had wanted to come to the sea. The pattern of the waves began placing me in a relaxed state.

32    My mind began to float and I recalled a long-forgotten feeling from early life, when I was an only child without parents. I had felt abandoned, and this feeling would be repeated both in my teen years and in two adult relationships.

33    My overpowering fear, now as a grown man with AIDS, was that I would once again be abandoned. This sudden, ocean-induced awareness shocked me. I had not realized I feared abandonment, at least not consciously. I realized how productive my visit to the ocean had been, and I returned home resolved to learn more about myself and healing myself.

34    The attempt to reach my inner mind and understand its abilities and effects on my life became a challenge, the biggest I had ever encountered.

35    I began to reach out to others who had attempted mentally to influence their health and well-being. To my amazement, many of my friends had accepted this line of thinking. They suggested several books that discussed the self-healing process.

36    There were many moments when I felt that I was succeeding as I reached deep inside myself for understanding and direction. There were many more moments of failure, but I continued on by reminding myself that I had shaped my career through personal determination for many decades — and had been successful.

37    I resolved that, at some time, I would place myself on a religious retreat in my own home as I began my spiritual search for a meaningful identity. It became clear that, whoever I became at the end of my odyssey, I would be far different from the person I was when I was diagnosed with AIDS. Obviously, it was time for me to make a transition in my life. I felt that having AIDS could be turned into a positive experience.

38    During the months since I had been diagnosed, I found that for the first time in my life I cried easily. I had never cried before — it isn't considered appropriate for a man to do so in our society.

39    My crying was not the result of fear as much as an emotional expression or outlet for pent-up anger and frustration. When my friends were very kind

to me, I would cry then also. I had never thought that so many people would come forward openly expressing love for me. This saddened me because I had never understood how they felt about me.

I was frequently overpowered by a feeling of being all alone in a strange, dark place. Along with the crying and the loneliness, I developed an almost desperate need to be hugged and held closely — almost as if I were a small child.  40

I was being transformed from an independent person into someone who could no longer walk alone, who needed help to shower and to get to bed at night. My feelings and attitudes became so different that they seemed to belong to someone I didn't know.  41

The massive change in so short a time left me confused and surprised. I was not prepared either to understand or to control this new individual. For this reason alone the future would be very different, with a new set of values and objectives.  42

Even the closet full of executive suits now seemed to belong to someone else. Frequently I would wake up still believing I could hop out of bed and jump into the shower. Obviously, I had not adjusted to my new body and wondered how long it would take for the present reality to dissolve the memories and actions of over 50 years.  43

The last few months have brought the steady loss of my ability to use my left hand, arm, and leg. Over a period of 120 days I watched my disability grow until I could no longer move freely under normal circumstances. I progressively became more crippled and more useless.  44

Standing up became a high risk, as I fell into objects around my home. Once I lost the use of the arm and leg on the same side of my body, canes were useless, and the manipulation of a wheelchair became a one-armed event.  45

AIDS is perceived to alter the life of one person, the patient. This is not true, since the patient slowly becomes dependent upon someone else — finally needing help all day, all week.  46

Thus the disease destroys the quality of life for two people, because the care giver of the AIDS victim is also relentlessly held hostage by the disease, trapped in a round of simple but indispensable tasks.  47

If there is anything worse than having AIDS, it is caring for the person who has AIDS. The "significant other" can do little but wonder, "How long will this go on?"  48

The patient watches while the care giver's life and freedom become more restricted, in the name of love; the relationship becomes one of self-imposed  49 duty. It is difficult to say who is the victim and who hurts the most. Joy slowly seems to vanish in the eyes of both the patient and the care giver. The disease dominates every discussion and action.

50   Over five months, I have learned how to help myself and take responsibility for my healing. Conversations with others have provided information concerning possible therapies and drugs to fight the disease. How others cope with the challenge of AIDS gives clues and direction to my own efforts to maintain a civilized quality of life. The overriding challenge is, "How can I be less of a burden on my care giver?"

51   Accepting care and understanding limitations are skills one must learn. Expectations must be adjusted to a new reality.

52   It was a great challenge for me to learn to reach out to others and to accept their concern and love.

53   Fortunately my many friends, including business associates and clients, have come forward to express their love and willingness to help. Indeed, I have been surprised by their deep concern for my present and future well-being. I have received dozens of calls conveying love, hope, and encouragement. To date, no one has been appalled by the knowledge of my preferred lifestyle during the past twenty years. I have deeply felt the love of others who I never thought would call and say "We love you."

54   My preferred life of 54 years is gone. Even if I were to go into remission or be given a cure, that life is over. My concern with my spiritual needs and metaphysical well-being is now central to my existence.

55   I can now empathize with terminally ill cancer victims and the helpless feelings of the elderly as they are forced to depend on others for their daily existence. I'm not sure what I'll be like when I complete this passage, except that I will be very different, able to accept my needs and the love of others.

# Style and Structure

1. (a) Write a one-paragraph profile of the intended reader of this essay. Use evidence from the essay to support your conclusions.
   (b) Write a one-sentence summary of the essay's central topic.
   (c) How do the first five paragraphs of the essay relate to the central topic you have identified?
   (d) Would a single-sentence **thesis statement** such as your summary be a more effective way of introducing the topic to Koehn's intended reader? Justify your answer.

(e) Which strategy would have been more appropriate if the essay had been written for an academic journal? Why?

2. Many magazines and newspapers, like the one in which "Living and Dying with Aids" first appeared, use techniques to make their contents look easy to read. One is to break paragraphs into one- or two-sentence blocks. These blocks are then printed as if they were separate paragraphs.

   Examine paragraphs 46 to 48 in this essay, for example. They could be combined to form a single unified and coherent paragraph. All the elements are there: a **topic sentence** (in paragraph 46), relevant details in the body, and a **concluding sentence** (in paragraph 48).

   Identify two other passages in the essay where the same technique has been used. For each, identify the **topic** and **concluding sentences**. Then explain briefly how joining the shorter blocks together would create a unified and coherent paragraph.

3. This essay uses the process-analysis format; i.e., it analyzes and explains the process of change that Koehn went through after his diagnosis. (See p. 302 for a further explanation of the process-analysis format.)

   The most difficult tasks in writing a process analysis are (1) identifying the unique stages in the process and (2) creating appropriate paragraphs for them. Even when the paragraphs present natural stages, some writers forget to use **topic** and **concluding sentences** to guide the reader through them.

   (a) Examine the body of Koehn's essay for any paragraphs that do not fit into the natural order of the process he went through. If you find any, suggest ways in which they could be changed to make them fit better (e.g., placing them elsewhere in the essay, adding a sentence, or providing a **transition**).

   (b) Choose any two **topic sentences** from paragraphs in the body of the essay. Explain how each helps the reader understand that paragraph's stage in the process.

   (c) Choose any two **concluding sentences** from paragraphs in the body. Explain how each helps the reader understand that paragraph's stage in the process.

4. Koehn faces a problem in dealing with some readers who might not be sympathetic to the gay lifestyle. Why could this problem be particularly acute in paragraphs 46 to 50? What techniques does he use in these paragraphs to avoid alienating these readers?

5. (a) How effectively do the last two paragraphs of the essay act as a **conclusion**? Justify your answer.

(b) What is the relationship between the statement made in the last sentence of the **concluding paragraph** and that made in the opening sentence of the essay? Is this an effective technique to use in a conclusion? Why?

# Warm-up

Working with a group of four or five others, choose one of the following topics and, if necessary, do some background research on it in the library:
(i) the way AIDS develops in victims after they have contracted the virus;
(ii) the people who are in "high-risk groups" for contracting AIDS;
(iii) a history of the spread of AIDS;
(iv) the risk for the average Canadian of contracting AIDS.

On your own, write a one-paragraph explanation of the topic that can serve as a handout for all of your classmates. Then, as a group again, select the paragraph that best explains the topic and distribute copies of it to everyone else in the class.

# Thinking and Writing

a.  Write a process-analysis essay in which you explain the changes a person undergoes during one of life's major transitions (e.g., going from childhood to adolescence, moving away from home for the first time, or moving to a new town or a new school). Be sure to use specific details at each stage in the process.
    **Audience:** someone who has never gone through the experience and who may not be sympathetic to the problems encountered.

b.  Koehn writes, "[Early in my illness] I was sure that most of my clients would be appalled at accidentally learning about my choice of lifestyle" (paragraph 19). Later, however, he is able to write, "Fortunately my many friends, including business associates and clients, have come forward to express their love and willingness to help. . . . To date, no one has been appalled by the knowledge of my preferred lifestyle . . . " (paragraph 53).
    Write an essay in which you explain whether or not most people in our society would have this type of sympathetic reaction if they dis-

covered that a friend or business associate had AIDS. Give reasons for the reactions you identify.

**Audience:** someone who deals with AIDS patients and is sympathetic to their problems.

Send a copy of your final draft to a group that provides support for AIDS victims in your community.

# Math's Multiple Choices

## by Judith Finlayson

1    The world has been transformed in the past twenty years. Geared to microchips, floppy disks, and video display terminals, today's society demands a higher degree of mathematical skill than ever before. But, sadly and even dangerously misinformed about the realities of the working world, many teenaged girls across the country are repeating their mothers' mistake, a mistake that has propelled the majority of Canadian working women into low-paying, dead-end jobs. In high school, they are dropping out of science and math.

2    Today, a background in math is required for most high-paying technical jobs in fields such as computer technology and microelectronics, as well as for many apparently unrelated professions such as law, interior design, and urban planning. Some companies require Grade 12 math for all entry-level positions, even for caretaking jobs.

3    The need for mathematical competence has been heightened not only by the extraordinary technological change of the past two decades, but by social change as well. Women have entered the work force in unprecedented numbers. They can also expect to stay there — from 25 to 45 years, even if they choose to marry and have children as well as a job outside the home. And they should anticipate changing careers at least twice during that time.

4    As Donna Stewart, educational co-ordinator for WomenSkills, a Vancouver organization devoted to education and research on women's work, warns: "Whole fields of work are shrinking or disappearing entirely. We export enormous amounts of work to countries where labour is cheap, or we give it to machines. One result is that greater levels of competence are required, even for low-level jobs."

5    It's not surprising that a research report published in 1987 by the Economic Council of Canada stressed the value of flexibility in today's workplace. Not only are better-educated and highly skilled women more likely to benefit from technical change, but the report also concluded that their adjustment may be dependent upon how successfully they enter nontraditional occupations. It is important to note, however, that both higher education and nontraditional work are increasingly linked with competence in math.

6    Consider, for instance, that a minimum of high-school math is often required for entrance to university courses such as nursing, teaching, and law. It is

also mandatory for many social-science courses such as psychology and sociology, as well as for admission to a substantial number of community college courses. The problem is, female students tend to drop math and sciences as they progress through high school. This fact has led educators to conclude that math is an "invisible filter" denying females entry into the growth-related industries of the future.

Math and science avoidance in females is generally acknowledged as a serious issue, but unfortunately there are no national statistics that document the full extent of the problem. Research by the Toronto Board of Education, however, shows that even at the introductory level, the ratio of students in computer science courses is two-thirds male to one-third female. By Grade 13, approximately two-thirds of girls in Toronto schools have dropped out of maths and sciences. 7

"I'm still seeing the Cinderella myth at work," says Arlene Day, a resource teacher for equality in education with the Manitoba Teacher's Society. "Even though they see their mothers working outside the home because the family needs the money, girls are refusing to believe that the same thing will happen to them. They're still aiming for clerical jobs. Most are not even acquiring the computer skills that are necessary to be successful at office work." And her view is echoed in *What Will Tomorrow Bring?*, a 1985 Canadian Advisory Council on the Status of Women report that concluded, "adolescent girls still see their lives in very traditional and romanticized terms." 8

Statistics confirm that the majority of women (almost 60 percent) hold clerical and service-sector jobs, which are generally low paid, offer little potential for advancement, and may be in danger of becoming obsolete. Although women have made serious inroads into some male-dominated professions, such as business, medicine, and law, they are still segregated outside the more scientific fields, such as engineering and computer science. According to Statistics Canada, at the university level, the majority of women remain concentrated in the traditional fields of study, such as education, nursing, and the humanities. The pattern also holds true for community colleges, where most women continue to study secretarial science, community and social services, nursing, education, and the arts. 9

"To some extent, women have succumbed to the myths about women's work," comments Donna Stewart. "They want to be helpers and to work with people. They may be avoiding nontraditional jobs and careers that require a sound basis in math because they haven't seen the human context to these jobs. Social service agencies need to balance their books. And no one builds bridges alone. You're part of a team." 10

11    Women who avoid math may be ignoring more than the human context of working with numbers. Mathematical training has been linked with high-salaries and job security in fields that have been targeted for future growth. Engineering technology, a profession that is 92 percent male, is one example of this trend. Two years after graduating from community college, an engineering student can expect to earn $20 000 a year. Perhaps more importantly, engineering technologists who reach the senior level will likely make more than $30 000 and, if they rise in management, they can earn up to $50 000 annually.

12    Compare these salaries to those in a female-dominated field. Ninety-nine percent of secretaries are female. Not only is their average salary just $14 100 two years after graduation from community college, but according to a 1983 Labour Canada report, even those who reach senior levels earn on average under $20 000.

13    This kind of wage discrepancy alarms educators who see girls avoiding math. "Nowadays, a math and science background is necessary for most of the higher-paying jobs," says Linda McClelland, a science teacher at Crescent Heights High School in Calgary. "And girls are losing out on these credentials at the same time that more and more women are entering the work force. In addition, there is a rising number of women supporting families on their own who really need to earn a decent wage."

14    Tasoula Berggren, an instructor of calculus and linear algebra at Simon Fraser University in Burnaby, British Columbia, points to at least 82 careers for which math education is a prerequisite. Last November, she organized what she hopes will become an annual conference, Women Do Math, for girls in Grades 9 and 10 and their parents. Four students from each of 85 Vancouver schools were invited. "I thought we would get 100 people," Berggren recalls, "and 300 registered, with many more schools asking to bring more students."

15    Berggren designed the conference not only to introduce girls to women professionals but to provide an introduction to basic mathematical concepts. "Once they see the application of calculus — how a formula can give them the volume of a lake — they find it exciting. They say, 'This is great, I'm enjoying math!'"

16    She stresses the necessity of constant parental encouragement, something that Myra Novogrodsky, co-ordinator of women's labour studies at the Toronto Board of Education, observes does not come naturally. She is conducting a new program designed to make parents of Grade 7 and 8 girls aware of the importance of math and science education to their daughters' futures.

17    "I usually begin the workshops with a true-or-false quiz designed to test

awareness," she says. "I've discovered that a lot of people haven't thought much about the implications of social change. They still think that most girls will live in a nuclear family and be secondary wage earners, if they work outside the home at all."

One result of this misconception is that many parents have lower career    **18**
expectations for their daughters than for their sons. Their attitude is reinforced by negative role modelling, which can include apparently innocuous statements such as "Women don't have a head for figures" or "Her mother can't balance a chequebook." These stereotypes can seriously undermine the confidence of girls who may have an interest in technical subjects or nontraditional work.

"By Grade 10, I knew I was mechanically oriented, but people said that    **19**
physics was too hard for me and I believed them," recalls Heather Bears, who is currently studying electronics technology at Red River Community College in Winnipeg. As a result, after graduating from high school, she spent two unsatisfactory years in the work force doing odd clerical or child-care jobs. Career counselling finally revealed her scientific aptitude and motivated her to return to high school as an adult student. Not only did she make up her physics courses, but she earned straight A's.

Today, as a second-year electronics student, she still feels the negative effects    **20**
of gender roles. "When I entered the course there were only two other girls and approximately 100 guys. There was a real sense that we were bucking the system and it was scary. At its most basic, I'm only five-foot-two and most of the male students are in the six-foot range."

Although Bears admits that it is difficult being a pioneer — "some teachers    **21**
pick on us and others favour us" — the satisfaction of doing what she finds fulfilling is worth the price. "If I had one piece of advice for girls in high school, it would be, 'Don't be afraid to enter a man's world.' I believed people who said I couldn't do it because I was a girl, and that's what held me back."

MaryElizabeth Morris, a math teacher at Castle Frank High School in To-    **22**
ronto, believes that the "my mother/my self syndrome" can also influence a girl's career expectations. "A woman who does low-level work could undermine her daughter's success because she might not convey the sense that work can be a rewarding experience," she says. "If her mother is a poor role model in terms of job satisfaction, a girl may cling to the Cinderella myth because she doesn't see work outside the home as desirable."

Studies such as *What Will Tomorrow Bring?* show that professional mothers    **23**
tend to be positive role models for their daughters. But mothers who don't work outside the home can also encourage their daughters to develop an interest in traditionally male domains by organizing scientifically oriented ex-

cursions, such as a visit to a science museum, or by doing traditionally masculine tasks.

24     "We live on a farm, so my mother is a real handyman," says Robin Chant, a Grade 12 student at MacGregor Collegiate Institute in MacGregor, Manitoba, who excels at maths and sciences. "I think one of the reasons I do well in math is because, like her, I enjoy figuring things out."

25     Chant was the only girl in her physics class last year and there is only one other girl in this year's math class, compared to nine boys. "Most of my girlfriends have dropped math because they think it's too hard," she says. "They all want traditional jobs as secretaries and day-care workers. They plan to get married and have kids. I'm different because I really want to have a career."

26     Myra Novogrodsky believes that if mothers are to help their daughters overcome their negative outlook toward math, they must become aware of and overcome their own negative feelings. If parents "suffered" through math class themselves, they may convey their anxiety and inadvertently undermine their children's performance. Equally important are the role models that girls receive outside the home.

27     "It's hard for girls to accept the message that they can have high career aspirations and study maths and sciences if they don't see any other women doing it," says Linda McClelland. "We need more female math and science teachers as role models, as well as more women in nontraditional careers."

28     All the women math and science teachers interviewed for this article strongly agreed. Moreover, those who kept statistics on the ratio of males to females in their classes reported that the fact that a woman was teaching the subjects had a positive effect on girls.

29     "In the past there was usually only one female student in senior-level physics," recalls Shelagh Pryke, who teaches all the physics classes at Kwalikum Secondary School in Qualicum Beach, B.C. "Now as many as 42 percent of my students are girls, and I know the fact that I'm a woman who is married with a family has played a role in this change. The girls see that it's socially acceptable to be a woman who is interested in science."

30     Lydia Picucha, a math and science teacher at Mount Elizabeth Junior and Senior Secondary School in Kitimat, B.C., shares this point of view. "I've been teaching here for seven years and I know my female students relate to the idea of a woman who enjoys her work and takes her career seriously. As a result, most of my female students — about 70 percent — have continued with science into Grade 11, when girls normally start dropping out."

31     The lack of female teachers as role models is complicated by the way maths

and sciences are taught in schools. Mathematics, for example, may alienate girls because it is typically taught in a masculine style. John Clark, co-ordinator of mathematics at the Toronto Board of Education, says, "Math is usually presented as a search for the right answer rather than as a process of enquiry. Some sociologists believe that females have a more collaborative style. They want to work by consensus and talk with other people."

Whether or not there is any inherent difference between the male and     **32**
female aptitude for mathematics remains a hotly debated issue. However, there is no doubt that the way girls are socialized undermines whatever natural ability they might have. For example, the kinds of throwing, jumping, and mechanically oriented play that boys engage in actually prepares them for an understanding of maths and sciences.

Consider the game of baseball. Most boys catch balls better than most girls     **33**
simply because by constantly playing ball sports they have learned how to estimate where the ball will land and, therefore, how to position their hands. What is less obvious is that this skill requires an understanding of the relationship between distance, force, and velocity that serves them well once they begin to study physics.

At the Institute of Child Study, a school that operates in conjunction with     **34**
the University of Toronto's Faculty of Education, teacher Robin Ethier confirms that there is a division of play along gender lines by the time the children arrive at kindergarten. "The boys choose blocks and sand to build large spaces, whereas the girls prefer small paper projects," she says. "The few girls who prefer large motor-skill projects really stand out. They are identified as tomboys."

Even so, Anne Cassidy, the Grade 5 teacher at the school, says she is     **35**
not aware of a gender difference in her students' approach to maths and sciences. To some extent, she believes the school's emphasis on intuitive and personalized learning has helped minimize the difference. Classes are small and teachers strongly encourage children to learn through their own activities. For example, to teach the law of averages, she might ask her class to count up the pennies all seven grades collected for UNICEF over Hallowe'en. When she asks her students to work out approximately how much each grade collected, they soon realize that to get an average they must divide the total number of pennies by the number of classes. In the end, they discover the mathematical formula all on their own.

This kind of hands-on learning validates the children's own observations     **36**
about the world. It also reinforces their sense of themselves as autonomous problem solvers, a skill linked with success in math. Parents can play an im-

portant role in helping their children develop this problem-solving ability by transforming daily activities into informal lessons in maths and sciences. Children should be encouraged to play mathematically oriented games such as backgammon and chess. Cooking is an excellent activity for teaching fractions as well as the principles of chemistry. Similarly, carpentry teaches measurement and spatial concepts, and comparing sizes and prices at the supermarket can turn even shopping into a learning experience.

37     "People make the mistake of trying to introduce new math concepts with paper and pencil," according to Dr. Ada Schermann, principal of the Institute of Child Study. "Start with a game or a fun activity such as cooking, gardening, or playing a mathematically based card game like 21. Then children don't think they're being taught, and the learning comes naturally."

38     Girls' poor problem-solving abilities have been linked to the fact that they are not usually encouraged to assert themselves as individuals. So perhaps it's not surprising that they begin to retreat from maths and sciences during their teenage years. During this period their willingness to consider a non-traditional career also wanes.

39     It must be the responsibility of parents and teachers to erase the myth that an interest in math makes a girl "different" or "unfeminine." From preschool to high school, maths and sciences should be as natural and nonthreatening subjects of study as English or history. Without a solid grounding in these subjects, the doors of opportunity will slam shut for yet another generation of young women — and, unfortunately, unemployment figures are the numbers *everyone* understands.

# Style and Structure

1. (a) What is the overall **organizational approach** of this essay: narrative, descriptive, cause and effect, or compare/contrast? (See pp. 301–302.)
   (b) Having established the overall approach, identify other approaches Finlayson employs to support her opinions.
2. (a) In making her point, the writer cites a number of sources throughout the essay. Identify each of these sources and classify them as
     (i) professionals;
     (ii) institutions;
     (iii) nonprofessionals.
   (b) In a fully developed paragraph, explain how well you believe these sources serve the writer's purpose. Examine the appropriateness of the sources,

the number of citations given, and the effect upon the reader.

3. (a) In paragraphs 11 and 12, the writer presents two career paths, one dominated by men and the other dominated by women. What do you believe the writer is hoping to accomplish?

(b) Where has the writer obtained her statistics about salaries? How might these statistics affect the reader?

(c) One of the primary rules about comparisons is that the writer must compare like things — not apples and oranges, as the old saying goes. Is the writer comparing apples and oranges in this case? (Suggestion: how might the comparison have changed if the writer had chosen nursing as a career dominated by women?)

4. Finlayson often employs a technique of making a statement and following it with examples to illustrate. Identify three instances of this technique. In each case, how does it aid the reader?

5. (a) What is the main point of this essay?

(b) Does the writer manage to give both a positive and a negative picture of the situation? How?

(c) Do you believe it is important to give the reader encouragement by pointing out the possibilities for success, even when dealing with what seems to be a very significant and widespread problem? Why?

# Warm-up

Giving and following instructions are essentials in game playing, as well as in many of life's more important functions. Choose a board or card game, preferably one that would help teach mathematical concepts. Divide into small groups and teach the game using clear and concise instructions. Members of the group must listen closely to the instructions.

Test your success by playing the game. Count the number of times instructions have to be repeated to gauge how clearly you explained the rules and how well the participants listened. Compare with other groups and discuss.

# Thinking and Writing

a. In her essay, Finlayson points to the advice of Dr. Ada Schermann: "People make the mistake of trying to introduce new math concepts with paper and pencil. Start with a game or a fun activity such as cooking, gardening, or playing a mathematically based card game like 21" (paragraph 37).

Choose a mathematical concept that a primary school child would need to learn and devise a game that would allow the child to learn that concept. For instance, you might select working with volumes, and then work out a game in which the child would want to know how to halve a cookie recipe.

Write an essay in which you explain the workings of the game you propose and the concept you wish to illustrate. Be as creative as possible, remembering that kids are severe judges of what is fun.

**Audience:** Children and parents who are anxious to make mathematics an integral part of their family life.

b.     In paragraph 18, Finlayson speaks of stereotypes that reinforce the myth that women cannot do math, or that they are not interested in the subject. Make a collection of cartoons, jokes, or household sayings that seem to substantiate the writer's opinion that these stereotypes are damaging to girls' confidence in handling mathematics.

Outline and write an essay in which you argue that stereotypes are having a negative effect, using your collection as examples. Be sure to write a clearly defined thesis statement and, if possible, suggest how girls can overcome the image portrayed in these stereotypes.

Here is an example to get you started on your collection!

## For Better or For Worse by Lynn Johnson

For Better or For Worse. Copyright 1982. Universal Press Syndicate. Reprinted with Permission. All Rights Reserved.

**Audience:** Grade 9 or 10 girls who are thinking of dropping out of maths and sciences.

Send a copy of your final draft to a high school guidance department for comment.

# Let the Punishment Fit the Crime

## by Philip Brickman

When a thief in Chicago stole a motorcycle, the press reported, the victim, 1
who knew the thief, was not particularly interested in seeing the thief punished,
just in getting his motorcycle back. By the time the police caught the thief,
he had sold the motorcycle. He received a suspended sentence. The victim
was told he would have to sue the thief if he wanted his money back.

What is wrong with this story? It does not satisfy our sense of justice because 2
justice means that everyone gets what he or she deserves. Justice should mean
helping victims as well as punishing offenders. This story and our criminal
justice system ignore the problem of restoring fairness for victims as a principle
of justice.

We set two primary goals for our criminal penalties. We want them to 3
deter crime and we want them to rehabilitate criminals. In theory, these two
goals should go together, since they amount to saying that we want to keep
crime from happening in the first place, through deterrence, and to keep crime
from happening again, through rehabilitation.

In practice, these two goals seem incompatible, since the harsh penalties 4
that might work as deterrents offer little hope for rehabilitation, while the
supportive treatments that might work as rehabilitation seem inadequate as
deterrents.

Curiously, however, neither deterring crime nor rehabilitating offenders is 5
a principle of justice. Our sense of justice requires that penalties be propor-
tionate to their crimes.

Suppose we took restoring fairness as the first principle of our criminal 6
justice system, instead of either deterrence or rehabilitation. What would such
a system look like?

Simply put, offenders would be given sentences whose purpose, in the end, 7
was to restore both the loss that the victims had suffered and the loss that
society suffered through its investment in preventing, detecting, and punishing
crimes. Where possible, this could involve labour directly related to recovering
property, repairing damage, or making streets safer. More generally, it might
involve contributing earnings from specified tasks to a general fund whose
purpose was to compensate victims.

In informal systems, where victims and offenders are known to one another, 8
restoring fairness is the common penalty that satisfies all concerned and pre-

serves the social bond. It is typical of penalties that are meted out in healthy families.

9        Restitution as a principle of justice appeals to both liberals and conservatives. Liberals like the idea that the penalty involves something more meaningful than just going to prison. Conservatives like the idea that the penalty involves holding offenders responsible for their actions and making them pay for their crimes. It appeals to people on moral and emotional grounds. It appeals to people on practical grounds, in that it offers some hope of helping both the victims and the offenders, as well as society.

10      Restitution can work in the service of both deterrence and rehabilitation. The cost of making restitution should substantially outweigh the potential gain of the crime, since both the victim's pain and suffering and society's costs of enforcement may be included. At the same time, the act of making restitution should serve to restore not only the offender's sense of himself or herself as a worthwhile member of society, but, even more crucial, society's sense of the offender as well, in a way that punishment alone could never do. The penalty can and should involve real cost for the offender, but the novel and critical feature is that it should also involve creating something of value in both society's eyes and the offender's own eyes.

11      The idea of compensating victims can be distinguished from the idea of restitution by offenders. There are many crimes with victims needing help where offenders are unknown. Even if an offender is caught and convicted, restitution at best takes time, while the victim's needs are immediate. The solution is to use state funds to compensate victims, while offenders either replenish these funds or provide other services.

12      To be successful, the principle of restitution must be implemented in a way that is not seen as exploitation of offenders in the service of existing class interests. Most offenders are poor, and many victims are rich. It is doubtful that making restitution to a corporation such as an insurance company will have much meaning for people who do not see the corporation as a victim in the first place. It is certain that chain gangs and corrective labour camps do not supply work from which either victims or offenders derive any sense of meaningful restitution. They are merely punishment and should be plainly so named. Restitution that is psychologically valuable will have visible and tangible effects that can be seen by victims, offenders, and society.

13      Although not widely known, laws for victim compensation have been enacted in a number of countries (including England and New Zealand) and a growing number of states (including New York and California), while experimental programs for offender restitution are under way in Georgia, Iowa,

and Minnesota. Preliminary results are encouraging, but they represent only a beginning. Much remains to be learned about tailoring sentences to both society's needs and offenders' capacities, and we have yet to work out how to allow prisoners to work without threatening jobs for anyone outside prison. These are reasonable tasks for social science and social policy. It is unreasonable to leave the field of criminal justice to the bankrupt debate between deterrence and rehabilitation.

# Style and Structure

1.  For what reasons does Brickman open his essay with the particular illustration that he chooses?
2.  Underline the **thesis statement** and draft a plan of the essay's organization.
3.  Trace the development of the writer's argument in paragraphs 3 to 6. Show how this development is logical.
4.  What is the relationship of paragraph 7 to paragraph 6? How do paragraphs 8, 9, and 10 relate to paragraph 7? How do paragraphs 11 and 12 relate to paragraph 7?
5.  In what ways does paragraph 12 function as a good **conclusion** for the essay as a whole? How does the author by his choice of words in the last two sentences attempt to win the reader over to his point of view?

# Warm-up

1.  Select a crime that is reported on tonight's newscast or in today's newspaper. Write a short essay that applies to this crime the principles of justice outlined by Brickman in paragraph 7.
    **Audience:** officers of the local police department.

    In a workshop setting with a group of three or four others, review the essay that each has written. Help the writer prepare for final revisions by identifying points at which the intended reader may have trouble understanding the ideas. In addition, look for improvements to the wording that will help overcome any preconceived ideas an intended reader might have about the content.

    Revise your essay and send a copy of the final draft to the public relations department of your local police force. Ask for comments.

2. Use the library to research the effectiveness of jail sentences in dealing with the type of crime you have identified in exercise 1. Write a paragraph reporting on your findings.

   **Audience**: officers of the local police department.

   Review this paragraph in a workshop setting as you did your earlier essay, revise it, and send a copy of the final draft, along with your essay from exercise 1, to the police department's public relations officer.

# Thinking and Writing

a. The benefits that Brickman outlines for the victim, the criminal, and society are needed nowhere more than in dealing with the crimes of murder and rape. However, no crimes offer greater difficulties to the judge who has to determine the sentence for a particular offence and to convince the general public that his or her sentence is "just" to all those concerned.

   Write an essay in which you assume the role of a judge who is sentencing a person for one of the following crimes; outline the sentence that you would give in accordance with Brickman's "restitution" and justify this sentence to the general public who may, at present, prefer punishment or revenge:

   (i) a woman with three children who has killed her husband in a fit of rage during a domestic quarrel;

   (ii) a man who has no previous convictions and has before this offence been considered to be an ideal "family man," who has been convicted of raping a woman whom he had never met before.

   **Audience**: the "average" newspaper reader.

b. Write an essay in which you outline and present evidence to substantiate your personal point of view on the value and effectiveness of basing our system of criminal justice upon a theory of restitution such as Brickman proposes. Use concrete examples and logically developed arguments to support your thesis.

   **Audience**: someone who works in a field related to criminal justice (e.g., lawyer, judge, police officer, or social worker).

   Send a copy of your essay to a person employed in one of the positions listed under "audience," or to your MP or MPP.

# Judy

## by Esther Kershman Muhlstock

I knew a culture shock awaited us when we moved with our three little  1
children from a walk-up four-room apartment to a four-fireplace, huge dream
house. Spacious, on a quiet and charming street, with a Superior Court judge
living beside us on one hand and a senator on the other, in a completely
French Canadian neighbourhood with lovely green lawns and a beautiful park
a few doors away.

I had perfect confidence in our Judy, age seven, already in the second-  2
year program of the Jewish People's School and staunchly Jewish. I was sure
she would skilfully handle this multi-language and multi-religion situation. So
would Naomi, our four-year-old, who had declared to me, "Mother, you know
that everybody in the world is Jewish, but some people talk French."

Judy had been playing with the judge's daughter. She confided in me, "I  3
have been teaching Marie Hebrew. She's fine when she says 'David,' but she
has a terrible time pronouncing 'Chaya.' Their family must be immigrants."

I had to laugh. Marie's great, great grandparents had come to Canada in  4
the 1700s. In Marie's family's eyes, we were the invaders, the immigrants.

One morning, shortly after we had settled in, the doorbell rang furiously.  5
There were about fifteen children in our doorway, with Judy in front. She
was holding an old shoe box in her little hands. In the box, lined with grass,
lay a tiny bird, moaning. It had fallen out of a tree and was hurt.

"Help it, Mummy," Judy implored. The children began to clamour.  6

With all those eyes focussed on me, what else could I do? I got an eye  7
dropper, forced the baby bird's mouth open, and forced a few drops of milk
into it.

"C'est tous ce que je peux faire, mes chéries," I told them. Marie took  8
possession of the bird and they all left.

Shortly after, Judy came running in, tears streaming down her face. "What  9
does 'noyer' mean? Does it mean 'to drown'? Marie's father said it would
be kinder to drown the bird. He says the bird is crying for its mother. Please
don't let them drown the bird, Mother, please!" she pleaded.

"Ask the children to come back and I'll talk to them," I suggested.  10

The news had spread, and a much larger group came to the garage door.  11
"C'est contre la religion de le noyer. Il faut l'aider à vivre," I told them.

Dramatizing the situation, I fed the little bird some of my children's vitamin drops, assuring them at the same time that I would get some bird seed at the pet shop for the little bird.

12    On returning from some errands later in the afternoon, as I approached the house, the crowd came fairly flying at me. "Est mort, le pauvre petit," they shouted in chorus.

13    "That's too bad," I replied. "Let's scatter this bird seed I have brought," I suggested.

14    The children then pondered the question of interment. "Not in our garden, Judy," I said. "Why not the empty lot down the street?" That suggestion seemed satisfactory and the gang proceeded there.

15    At bath time that evening, I was informed of the progress of the grave-digging. "We all dug the grave and it's lovely. Someone plucked a flower from someone's garden and we put the flower on it."

16    In the morning, out sped Judy, and returned immediately. "All the kids are there, Mother, and now there are thirty-five flowers all over the grave," she shouted.

17    That evening, Judy appeared for her bath, nervous and irritated. "Do you know what THEY did? They gathered up all the flowers and formed them into a large cross on the grave. But when the kids all went home for their supper, Naomi and I went to the grave and arranged the flowers into a Jewish star," she whispered, secretly.

18    "Was that necessary?" I asked Judy.

19    "Yes," she replied. "It was also my bird."

20    The next day was Sunday. What with the *New York Times* with comics and a "round" visit with Daddy to the hospital, it was late morning before the children finally visited the grave site of the bird. They were back within five minutes.

21    "Mother," Judy exploded, "what do you think? They changed it into a cross again."

22    It was time for some talk. "Judy, is the air Catholic? Is the water French? Is the flower Jewish? God didn't make crosses or stars. God made people and birds and flowers. Only man made the other. Why not have a cross *and* a star? Then the bird would be everybody's."

23    She agreed a little reluctantly. "Come with me," she urged. We proceeded to the grave, the other children following. Judith carefully arranged the cross at the head of the grave and a Magen David, as best as she could, at the foot. There seemed to be general approval and I sauntered back home, a little disturbed.

At noon, the children came in beaming. "Mother," both children's words 24 tumbled forth. "We took off the cross and the star, and over the bird we made a big heart. Now, it is really everybody's bird."

The little bird has made us friends. 25

# Style and Structure

1. (a) A quick glance at this essay tells the reader that the paragraphs are very short. Give at least two reasons why, in your opinion, the writer has chosen to write this way.

   (b) How do you think the paragraphs in this essay compare with those of other essays in terms of effectiveness? Explain your reasons.

2. Is there a **thesis statement** evident in this essay? In a well-developed paragraph, explain the writer's strategy regarding **thesis** and the reasons why you believe this approach has been chosen. (The formal name for the approach is "implied thesis.")

3. (a) A great deal of the essay involves reported conversation of the characters involved. How useful is this technique in terms of reader interest? Why?

   (b) Much of the effect of reported conversation depends on how well the writer manages to portray a realistic sound. For example, most credibility is lost if small children are reported as speaking like learned scientists.

      How realistic is the conversation of the characters portrayed in this essay? Explain your answer by referring to specific portions of the text.

4. It is difficult to imagine a story in which nothing happens. In this story, what happens to the neighbourhood? to the family? In all, what progress is made? Why do you think so?

5. (a) There are three passages in the essay that are written in French. Why do you believe the writer has chosen to leave these lines untranslated?

   (b) If you do not understand French, what was your immediate reaction to the lines written in French? Assess the reactions of other classmates who do not understand the language. How are their feelings typical of people who encounter a language, culture, or religion they do not know? What bearing do their feelings have on the impact of the entire story?

6. (a) Volumes of philosophy and social science deal with theories about multicultural relationships. Why would this writer choose to write a short narrative about some small children from a mixed neighbourhood and their flower arrangements? In one paragraph, discuss the effectiveness of storytelling, comparing this narrative with non-narrative forms of expository prose.

# Warm-up

Perhaps no people on earth know better than Canadians the difficulties encountered when one is not entirely free to speak one's language of choice. Much has been written in the Canadian press about Anglophones not understanding Francophones, Francophones not understanding Anglophones, and governments restricting or promoting the free use of language, with or without agreement among voters.

Make a search of libraries and reading rooms for newspaper articles on language issues. Collect as many articles as possible, circulating them around the class to make sure you don't have duplicates.

Next, make a poster collage of headlines in order to give viewers a quick overview of the extent of the controversy and the range of emotions that are raised when language becomes a source of disagreement.

When you have completed your research, review the findings in a class discussion.

# Thinking and Writing

a. It has been suggested by a skilled storyteller that the only good reason for telling a story is to relate something that the author has felt deeply, whether it is joy, anger, wonder, or some other emotion. We might add that sometimes a good story is worth a thousand volumes of explanation.

Do you have a story about getting along in a bicultural or multicultural environment — a story perhaps about yourself, but especially one about which you feel deeply?

Write your story in essay form and try your hand at using direct quotes. Pay careful attention, especially in your final draft, to the correct punctuation of quotes. (Note: in this case, it is all right to keep an implied thesis, as long as the purpose of your essay is clear to the reader from the story itself.)

**Audience**: anyone concerned with keeping good relationships between different races and cultures.

Send your best stories to a local newspaper and ask if the editor would like to publish them.

b. As the story "Judy" illustrates, the cross, the star, and the heart are all powerful symbols, even to children. What exactly do these symbols mean? Why do they have the potential both to unite and to break apart? What is a symbol?

Taking this essay as an example, discuss the power of symbol in a well-developed cause-and-effect essay. Discuss why people adopt symbols and what effect their use has.

**Audience**: adults who recognize such symbols but do not think much about either their meaning or their power.

# Deliberate Strangers

## by Charlie Angus

1  It's Saturday night and the kids want a movie. At the local video store, row after row of neatly packaged carnage assails the eyes. *The Toolbox Murders*, *Sorority House Massacre*, and *Three on a Meathook* compete with such old-time classics as *Texas Chainsaw Massacre*. There are video covers featuring victims being hunted with knives, chainsaws, hooks, and drills.

2  As you search in vain for an old Disney classic, the kids are crying out to see Jason. Jason? Who is Jason? They hand you a video called *Halloween*, a film that has spawned four sequels and countless imitations. The basic story line is rarely changed, movie to movie: a psychopath named Jason dons a mask and mutilates local teenagers.

3  "He's sort of a cult hero," the guy behind the counter explains.

4  Okay, so vampires, werewolves, and things that go bump in the night have always been part of our folklore. People love a good ghost story and always have. Bram Stoker's Dracula, the most famous figure in horror history, has been frightening people for generations.

5  It can be said that horror provides a way of synthesizing unexplainable evil. Tales like *Dracula* provide a safe way of confronting the darker side of human relationships. The reader is able to step over the line of the great unknown, comforted by the fact that the beast is always defeated in the end. The reign of darkness is broken by dawn, and Nosferatu is foiled in his evil plans.

6  Hollywood accepted this basic premise of horror for years. The heroine was always rescued from the fate of the undead, and Bela Lugosi always died before the credits rolled. But then, in 1960, Alfred Hitchcock released the film *Psycho*, and nothing has been the same since. For the first time, the monster in a horror film was another human being — a psychopath. Hitchcock tapped a growing fear that strangers could be monsters. Howling at the full moon was replaced with the brutal depiction of Janet Leigh being slashed in the shower. A generation of filmgoers would never feel the same again about closing the shower curtain. In this one scene, Hitchcock changed forever the way viewers perceive fear.

7  A trip to the video store is enough to realize how far-reaching the effects of *Psycho* have been. Supernatural monsters have been replaced by Jason and the genre of psycho killers. The techniques of presenting horror have also

continued to change. In the 1970s, Brian DePalma released *Dressed to Kill*, which used the camera as if it were the eyes of the killer. The audience was allowed to share in the excitement of the hunt, the gore of the kill. Our focus has been shifted from the thrill of stopping the villain to the thrill of hunting down the victim. The modern horror movie has taught us to be wary of seemingly tranquil country roads. Who knows where someone might be waiting with a chainsaw or an axe?

Horror has made a clear shift from identifying with victims as subjects to    8
regarding them merely as objects. Is this shift a harmless flight into fantasy, or have the borders of our culture, the substance of our collective soul, been altered? Welcome to the age of Jason, an age when the serial killer has become a cultural hero.

Meet Ted Bundy, all-American boy. He was popular and good-looking, and    9
it was said that he had an almost Kennedy-like charisma. A former employer described Ted Bundy as a man who believed in the system. In particular, Ted believed in success. At one time he studied law. In 1972, he completed his degree in psychology and worked at a crisis clinic in Seattle.

Over the next four years, he raped and killed as many as 50 women.    10
When finally apprehended after murdering two women and assaulting a third in a Florida sorority house, Ted Bundy became an instant celebrity. His trial was a classic event of the 1980s. Two hundred and fifty reporters, representing readers on five continents, applied for press credentials to the first televised murder trial in history. ABC News set up a special satellite hookup to bring the trial to 40 million American living rooms — a television horror drama.

The man of the hour did not let his public down. Bundy presented a persona    11
that was charming and witty. When interest seemed to wane, he resorted to outrageous stunts for the cameras. The case moved further into the realm of absurdity when Bundy announced to the court that he had married a woman who fell in love with him during the trial. Those who missed such highlights the first time round could relive the experience when *The Deliberate Stranger*, a made-for-TV dramatization, was shown on prime time. Even radio claimed a piece of the pie with the songs *The Battle of Ted Bundy* and *Just Say It Ted*. Ted Bundy found the success he had craved.

The hype of the trial and Bundy's celebrity status served to underline Amer-    12
ica's fascination with serial killers. Bundy was a star in the quickly growing field of *lustmord*: killing for the thrill of it. Historically, there have been occasional instances of serial killers, but such cases were rare. According to Elliot Leyton in *Hunting Humans*, in the period between 1920 and 1950, the United States did not average more than two serial killers a decade. In

the 1960s, this number rose to five (for an average of one new serial killer every twenty months). In the 1970s, the number of known serial killers rose to seventeen (for an average of one every seven months). Between 1980 and 1984, the figure jumped to 25 known serial killers, signifying a new serial killer every 1.8 months.

13     The rise of serial killers is disproportionate to population growth and to the increase in the murder rate in general. Newspapers are full of information on the latest killers, their particular "styles," their kill ratios in relation to existing "records." The Son of Sam, the Hillside Stranglers, John Wayne Gacy, Henry Lee Lucas, Charles Ng, the Green River Killer, Clifford Olson — countless books, movies, and articles chronicle the exploits of these killers with a fascination that borders on adulation.

14     Ted Bundy became something of a spokesperson for this new breed of killer. He showed the world that psychopaths are not deranged. Most serial killers have passed previous psychological testing. They are well liked and never socially suspect. Psychopaths, however, relate to other human beings as objects. They lack the ability to empathize. Psychopathy is the extreme form of self-centredness.

15     The testimony at the trial underlined how easily such a disordered personality could fit in with social convention. At the time of Bundy's arrest, his friends were unable to reconcile the man they thought they knew with the brutal murderer described in the press. "He was one of us," one friend explained. Although it was overshadowed by the revelations of murder and mayhem, this detail is a key to unlocking the world of Ted Bundy. As a young Republican, as a yuppie, and as a brutal killer, he was one of us. His killings, like everything in his life, were a mirror image of the world around him.

16     After his conviction, Ted Bundy spent many hours being interviewed by his biographers, Hugh Aynsworth and Stephen Michaud. Calmly and dispassionately, he articulated the roots of his murderous inclinations: "If we took this individual from birth and raised him, say, in the Soviet Union or Afghanistan, or in eighteenth-century America, in all likelihood he would lead a normal life. We're talking about the peculiar circumstances of society and of the twentieth century in America." Ted Bundy knew he was a psychopath. Perhaps we all have some of the psychopath in us.

17     This is an age of impersonal violence. Television has brought saturation bombing in Vietnam, genocide in Cambodia, sniping in Beirut, and street wars in Los Angeles into our homes. Every night around suppertime, the living room is filled with footage of strangers killing strangers. Our response to

tragedy has become shallow. Horrified for a minute, interested for an hour, we soon turn our attention from the dead and dying on our screen. The victims have become merely objects eliciting prurient interest instead of subjects eliciting heartfelt empathy. We no longer relate to them as human beings. Neither did Ted Bundy. "What's one less person on the face of the earth anyway?" he asked his interrogators.

Ironically, while becoming numb in the face of death, we are still aroused    18
by violence. We have witnessed the deaths of thousands, both real and imag-
ined. We have been spectators in an endless parade of shootings, stabbings, bombings, burnings, and stranglings. In the realm of fiction, Jason is just the latest in a long line of cultural figures who testify to the power of violence in solving problems, settling scores, and putting zest into one's day. What makes fictionalized killing palatable is that the audience doesn't have to relate to those killed. Bad guys are dispatched with style and the audience is spared the messy details about grieving families and friends.

Ted Bundy did not kill to solve problems or expiate childhood trauma.    19
He killed to possess status goods. His victims were all socially desirable women. "What really fascinated him," Bundy said, "was the thrill of the hunt, the adventure of searching out his victims. And to a degree, possessing them as one would a potted plant, a painting, or a Porsche. Owning, as it were, this individual."

In his world view, sex and violence were simply two faces of the same    20
coin. "This condition," he told his interrogators, " . . . manifests itself in an interest concerning sexual behaviour, sexual images. . . . But this interest, for some unknown reason, becomes geared toward matters of a sexual nature that include violence." The stimulation we receive from media violence and sex rests on our ability to see others as objects. They become commodities to be consumed. "Once the individual had her [the victim]," Bundy explained, "where he had, you know, security over her, there would be a minimum of conversation . . . to avoid developing some kind of relationship."

This is indeed an era of peculiar circumstances. The days when one's neigh-    21
bours were like family are long gone. We do not know our neighbours; perhaps we are not even interested in knowing them. This rift has been the price paid in the pursuit of commodity culture. In advanced capitalist societies, every-thing has a price, and every obligation is judged by its ability to advance individual interests. The ties of community, family, and even marriage have been weighed in the balance and found wanting. The modern ethic chooses pleasure over obligation, career over community, the self over the other. We have become a culture of deliberate strangers.

22    Serial killers are nurtured in this breakdown of community. In the absence of strong social interrelationships, the alienated mind begins to perceive others as objects for personal gratification, whether financial, sexual, or violent. On a spiritual level, *lustmord* is the logical extreme of our cultural sickness. Murder has become the ultimate act of self-worship. Gone are the crimes of passion, the relationships gone wrong, the fated love affairs. The killings reflect a cold brutality, the sterile control of subject over object.

23    Ted Bundy went to his death on January 24, 1989. His execution served as a gruesome conduit of hate and media sorcery. Two hundred reporters, camped out near the grounds of the prison, detailed every aspect of Bundy's date with the electric chair as if it were a major sports event. Cheering crowds gathered outside the prison gates. Street vendors reported a brisk trade in "I like my Ted well-done" T-shirts.

24    In the eyes of the public, it was not a fellow human being who was dying, but an object, a thing fit for ridicule and murder. His public revelled in the gruesome details, spurred on by reports of his fear and remorse. In the end, it was as mechanical and empty as his own crimes, again the sterile control of subject over helpless object. Ted Bundy died reaffirming America's belief in murder. No wounds were healed, no victims' families made whole once again. The beast is not dead but remains lurking in the gulf between neighbours. The electric chair and the cheering crowds serve only as reminders that Ted Bundy was one of us.

25    Ted Bundy was not a monster. He was a human being, and his path toward the ultimate in evil is a path that is well trodden in our culture. He made the choices that commodity consciousness dictates: pleasure, self-worship, and alienation from true relationships. His obsessions with violence and death were extreme, but the path that led there is a path we have all walked in our viewing and in our minds. If Ted Bundy's life and death are to have any meaning, we have to realize that the pursuit of self-interest is not a harmless choice. It fundamentally affects the fabric of human relationships. It is time to repair the bonds of community and stop being deliberate strangers.

## Style and Structure

1. (a) In paragraphs 1 to 4, the writer establishes a chatty tone. Point to those words or expressions that seem to invite the reader into an informal discussion.

(b) Why do you think the writer has chosen this strategy for his introduction? Given the overall purpose of the essay, why might such an introduction be particularly fitting?

2. (a) A change occurs in the fifth paragraph, where the writer begins a different approach. Which one of the **organizational approaches** does he use here? Why? (For **organizational approaches**, see pp. 301–302.)

   (b) In paragraph 9, Angus again changes the tone and direction of his essay by focussing on Ted Bundy, an American serial killer. As a reader, do you find these changes to be disturbing from the point of view of **unity** and **coherence**? Explain your answer.

3. (a) List the films that Angus mentions or alludes to in his essay.

   (b) The impact of the examples the writer uses will diminish greatly if few readers recognize them. How well known are Angus's examples? Have you or your friends seen or heard of any of these movies? What can you say about the success of Angus's examples in terms of recognizability?

4. (a) In paragraphs 23 and 24, the writer compares Ted Bundy's death to the death of his victims, but also suggests that the crowds thirsting for details were much like Bundy himself as he committed his crimes. As a reader, how did you react to this **conclusion**? Did you feel shocked or insulted, or did you see the **conclusion** as reasonable given the argument that preceded it?

   (b) Examine the text of the essay one more time. How has the writer set the reader up for the conclusions he draws?

5. (a) Is there a **thesis statement** in this essay? If so, where did you find it?

   (b) What do you think is the writer's strategy in dealing with a **thesis**? Explain your answer with reference to the essay itself.

# Warm-up

Violence, like beauty and pornography, may be in the eye of the beholder. What seems violent to one person does not always seem violent to the next.

What is violence? Write a paragraph in which you define what violence is for people of your age category. Compare your definition with those of your classmates, and see if you can agree upon a single definition of violence.

# Thinking and Writing

a.  Angus has a theory that we have become a culture of deliberate strangers. He suggests that "the days when one's neighbours were like family are long gone. We do not know our neighbours; perhaps we are not even interested in knowing them" (paragraph 21).

Is this true? Do people not know their neighbours, except perhaps in the most superficial way? List the number of your neighbours you know at least well enough to speak to on the street. Look back over your list, and put a check mark beside the names of those you feel you know very well (that is, you know all the members of the family and have visited several times over a year). Next, compare your list with those of your classmates to discover if there is a trend away from close neighbourhood bonds. What can you conclude about Angus's theory?

Using the results of your investigation and discussion, write an essay in which you prove or disprove the following thesis: "We have become a culture of deliberate strangers."

**Audience:** the local police or members of Neighbourhood Watch or Block Parents (if there is such an organization in your area).

b.  When we discuss the most unattractive features of our society, our tendency to accuse television of playing a major role is almost automatic. Angus, for instance, points to television as being largely responsible for an age of impersonal violence.

Does television deserve the bad press it gets? Examine TV programming to determine whether there is a large proportion of violence offered to viewers. Write an essay showing which programs fit your definition of violence. Be sure to design your essay around a clear-cut thesis statement.

**Audience:** members of your peer group who may be unaware of the real level of violence in television viewing.

# Education for One World

## by Jack Costello

From Plato to John Dewey, philosophers of education have insisted that a system of education can be effective only if it takes account of social conditions. Young people, they all agreed, must be trained for the society in which they are to live. So most educators have conscientiously transmitted their cultural heritage while trying, with greater or lesser success, to relate it to their own times. 1

But something has happened on the way to the future that neither Plato nor Dewey nor anyone in the centuries between them could have foreseen. Two historical factors are distinctive about our situation: first, the massive acceleration of all forms of change, and second, what can be called a "loss of faith" in our civilization on the part of its own members. It has become increasingly difficult to educate for a changing world. 2

After Alvin Toffler's *Future Shock* detailed the speed of change in our high-tech society, many were relieved to see that their anxieties had some basis in fact. Change that used to take a century began happening in a generation by the eighteenth century and is now occurring at two or three times that speed. Take, for instance, our consciousness of AIDS and *glasnost*, neither of which was a major factor in our world a few years ago. 3

In 1949, when he was almost 60 years old, the Scottish philosopher John Macmurray gave a talk on education reflecting on the devastating impact the First World War had on European civilization's experience of itself as a stable and rational social order. He confessed to his audience, "I have been trying to catch up with a process of change that is too fast for me, and falling steadily behind — faint but pursuing. Ever since 1919, I have felt that I was educated for a world in which I have never lived; and have had to live in a world for which I was never educated." 4

Most of those who are middle-aged or older recognize themselves in this confession. They were given an education in cultural ideals, career goals, scientific theories, social values, even notions of the right order of the world that were meant to last a lifetime and beyond. But they now find themselves shaken by what has happened to these notions in "real life." The world that produced these ideas is no longer the world they live in. Along with Macmurray, they have had to scramble to re-educate themselves, feeling all the while that the world will always be moving faster than they can follow. 5

6    This leads quite naturally to the loss of faith that characterizes our society. By faith, I do not mean primarily belief in a set of doctrines, but the shared meanings and purposes that direct our choices as a society and give us the capacity to act according to them. At root it must be religious. This faith is gone. Its disappearance is due partly to the breakup of the stable, nineteenth-century world and its world view that Macmurray described, and partly to our failure in the twentieth century to find new terms for a faith that can direct us. Because of that vacuum in our collective soul, we feel fragmented, drifting, caught up by events and technology rather than being directed by any unified purpose that engages our whole heart and soul. We have lost a capacity to choose and to act together, because without faith there is no common principle of valuation, and therefore no unity of purpose. This makes us a fearful and a grasping people. We define our problems in economic terms, constantly serving the economy as if it were some cruel ancient god demanding sacrifice. The truth is that we will never resolve our economic troubles until we have solved the dilemma in our spiritual life that produces them. And the same can be said for our quandary about how to educate ourselves and our children at this time.

7    Thus, education today carries a special burden: we want to educate our children to live well while having little collective wisdom to share with them about what the good life is or how to achieve it. At the same time, we are trying to educate them for a society that will be culturally very different from our own. No wonder educators are confused.

8    I am convinced we will get a fix on sound educational objectives only if we can come both to some shared faith in what the "way to genuine life" is for our world at this time and to some capacity to live graciously and creatively with constant change.

9    The search for a new faith for society could also be expressed in this religious form: In what direction is the Spirit of God leading the world at this time? If we can discern this direction and ally ourselves with the Spirit to bring this about, then we will have a sure (though moving) relationship to our own centre into which much change can flow without destroying our personal unity or making us constantly feel nostalgic.

10   The basic issues facing education in our society are contained in these questions: What is the way to fuller life for our world at this point in history, and can we choose to co-operate in that direction? If this is a fair appraisal of our dilemma, then we must reject any view that suggests the basic purpose of education today can be expressed by focussing simply on learning the her-

itage of the past, meeting the needs of the individual, preparing for careers, or simply acquiring "tools" or "skills" for survival.

The very fact that the world one generation ahead is so hard to foresee reveals that we ourselves live and educate in a time of permanent cultural revolution. If this is so, and I believe it to be, then we have no choice but to consider education as cultural action. It must be education that shapes not only the way our children think about their own lives and goals but also the way they see the society they live in and the way they choose to judge it and act in it. And it must teach them not only to accommodate themselves to life as they find it but to be shapers of society itself, giving direction to its goals and structures that will lead to greater life. 11

Many people judge our era to be a time of revolution because the peoples of the world are in the process of becoming a "world society" beyond the framework of national sovereign states and their partial alliances that have held sway for so many years. For the past several decades, the nations of the world have moved into deep interdependence with one another in their economic affairs, in spite of their presumed independence. This economic interdependence is a fact of life that will not go away but can only increase. The reality of our world relationships calls desperately now for a corresponding political interdependence that will place all nations under some commonly accepted system of planetary law in relation to areas of shared concern. The time for such an international order is here — and overdue — if we are to avoid further wars and even greater destruction of our planet. Finally, our times call out for a celebration of our human interdependence as an end in itself. 12

Teaching our children and ourselves to articulate, own, and promote this human interdependence already beginning to shape our world should be, in my judgment, the most urgent educational objective in the dominant countries in the world today. Our times require nothing less than this: that the Western countries (the First World) and the Eastern Bloc (the Second World), along with Japan, learn to relinquish all claims to supremacy and begin to act in a genuinely co-operative and equal relationship with the rest of the world. 13

Our education systems must help us try to achieve this basic conversion. They must help us move from seeing ourselves simply as citizens of one country to embracing our participation in a world order in which membership is determined not by skin colour or a country's economic system but by our common humanity. 14

Implicit in this revolution in our self-image would be a commitment to 15 change the way we live and our educational goals and strategies from kindergarten to Ph.D. As John Macmurray observed, "We are committed not merely to seek for knowledge but to live by it; and not merely as individuals but as communities with the goal of becoming the single community of humankind."

16    When this basic objective for education is embraced, a new light falls on the more specific aspects of our educational efforts. First of all, it becomes clear that education must be a program for integration: a blending of learning and living. It becomes a challenge to apply our learning as a light for judging our way of living and as a help for finding ways of improving life. It fosters learning for cultural action that is at once critical and constructive.

17    This "critical" and "constructive" role of education can best be understood in relation to the current premises underlying our culture and our North American way of life. A conviction about the unitary nature of life on our planet and about the communal nature of human life leads to a belief in the unitary nature of all knowledge. We come to see that it's all meant to fit together and means something together. Once this belief takes hold, many questions and further convictions about our own society follow.

18    For example, it leads to a rejection of the opposition made in some religious — and business — circles between material and spiritual values, and works at showing the unity between them. It questions our liberal tradition in its separation of "private" and "public" morality and proposes the model of morality as a "seamless garment" in which the threads between individual and global issues are seen to be woven together. It challenges the split between thinking and feeling that leads to false categorizations of what is "objective" and what is "subjective" and wrongheaded views of what is masculine and what is feminine. It rejects the individual's — and the corporation's — separation of financial and career ambitions from concern for personal relations of intimacy and justice at home and in the larger community. It does all it can to formulate and propagate a genuine notion of the common good. Finally, even as it fosters a concern that each individual be free to hold and express his or her own views, it leads to the conviction that an educational process engaged in apart from belief and commitment is at best dangerous and at worst destructive.

19    If this conscious choice for world community is made in a school, then the administrators and teachers will constantly be educating their students not only toward an intellectual synthesis of all their studies but toward becoming an actual community in their life together. Utopian as it may sound, I believe that every school should aim at being a society of friends. After

some years teaching in secondary schools and university, I am convinced this is best achieved — and inevitably will be achieved — if and only if the members of the staff have such a relationship with one another. All good primary and secondary school teachers know that they are teaching people, not subjects, and that young people learn best by imitation and only secondarily by information. If staff members have a vision of community for the school as well as for the world, and celebrate it with one another in shared purpose and friendship, the students will pick that up by osmosis. The student becomes a junior member in a fellowship that already exists.

These are some of the standards of this new age that it is the task of  20
education to provide. There are, of course, vast limitations on our capacity to achieve them under the best of circumstances. First, this goal of educating for freedom in community is a value that has to be embodied in a new culture that still awaits creation. Second, it remains true that the major part of education is done, well or badly, in the home. If the home training is bad or if it is shirked, the school will be helpless. And this does not even address the issues of overcrowding, overworked teachers, and lack of money and resources.

I have merely hinted at the role of religion as an agent in shaping this  21
faith and as an element in education, but the transformation envisaged here is essentially a religious one. The desire to form one community is not a political desire but a deeply human one that goes beyond the political structures that need to be part of it. I have already noted that this human response can be related to nothing less than the impetus of God's Spirit in the world.

As for the teaching of religion, we should acknowledge that the concern  22
of educators today has to be not simply how to teach religion in the schools but how to teach religion in the schools of a civilization that has thrown religion over. This same civilization has simultaneously made choices that have resulted in the near-disappearance of the family. These losses are two sides of the same coin. If a society refuses to try collectively to heal this rupture in family life by reordering its values, it could be said that it is a society with its heart set against community. There is no room for religion in such a society — except as a rebellion and a refusal to accept that kind of life. This creative rebellion was already suggested in my earlier examples of how the critical spirit shaped by the desire for community might look on the operating "truths" of our society.

Finally, I return to John Macmurray to have the last word on how our  23
children might learn to live in a world of constant change. In the same talk mentioned earlier, Macmurray concluded, "If we are to provide an education

which will fit the children of today for the world they will have to live in, it must be one which embodies and expresses continuous transformation as the norm of life. It will not be enough to train them to adaptability so that they can make shift to live without stability while retaining the idea of stability as desirable. That is altogether too negative. What they need, in both the cultural and the technical field, is an education in which continuous transformation is both the law and the delight of life; a training which will make them happy and active agents in the transformation of their own society."

24    I believe that such an education is possible if we and our children can come to believe in the community we are being invited to build with our learning and our lives.

## Style and Structure

1. (a) In his introduction, Costello gives a historical overview of the philosophy of education. This, of course, is not the only way he might have chosen to begin. Referring to p. 303, write two alternative introductions for this essay. Choose which you prefer, and give your reasons.

   (b) Review one of your own recent essays and write an alternative introduction. Notice how the tone of the essay varies as the opening strategy changes. Comparing the two introductions you have now written for the essay, suggest what sort of readership might find each appealing.

2. (a) This essay is a challenging one, estimated at Grade 13 level on a standard index. How do you know that this is more difficult reading than you might have previously experienced in this text? Give at least four reasons for your answer.

   (b) For what sort of readership do you believe this essay was written? Why do you think so?

   (c) Do you believe that, given the readership you determined, the essay is written in a suitable style? Do you believe that the style and tone are suited to the nature of the subject matter?

3. (a) Paragraph 8 marks a change in the direction of the essay. What is the difference between the content of paragraphs 1 to 7 and that which follows?

   (b) Do you believe that this shift in direction is natural and necessary, or is this a flaw in the essay? Give reasons for your choice.

4. (a) In paragraph 18, the writer uses the word "it" repeatedly. Jot down in your notebook the number of times the word is used and the accompanying verb in each case.
   (b) What does "it" stand for? How do you know?
   (c) Do you find the use of the pronoun "it" in this instance helpful or misleading? If you are not happy with the effect, rewrite the paragraph to clear up the problem.
5. (a) The writer makes a significant effort to assist the reader by providing a number of **transitions** throughout. (See p. 308 for a definition of **transitions**.) Make a list of all the **transitions** you find in the essay.
   (b) Identify the **transitions** you believe are particularly effective and suggest why the writer found it necessary to include them.

# Warm-up

In his introduction, Costello outlines a part of the historical background of the philosophy of education, "from Plato to John Dewey." Practise this technique by writing a paragraph showing a brief historical view of one of the following:
  (i) the automobile;
  (ii) the postal service;
  (iii) tobacco;
  (iv) public libraries.

# Thinking and Writing

1. In paragraph 19, the writer lays out his vision of what a school should be. He suggests that young people learn best by imitation and that, "if staff members have a vision of community for the school as well as for the world, and celebrate it with one another in shared purpose and friendship, the students will pick that up by osmosis. The student becomes a junior member in a fellowship that already exists."

   Explore the idea of school as community. Looking at such aspects as relationships among faculty, administration, and students, list five characteristics such a "fellowship" might have. Using these five characteristics to form topics for the paragraphs in the body of your essay and adding an appropriate introduction and conclusion, write an essay in which you describe the sort of ideal school Costello has in mind.

**Audience:** a parent–teacher group or the Board of Governors of your school.

Send a copy of the final draft to the chairperson.

2.  The writer of this essay suggests, "Change that used to take a century began happening in a generation by the eighteenth century and is now occurring at two or three times that speed" (paragraph 3). Discuss with an older person the one most significant change that has affected his or her life. Investigate the process in which the change occurred and the effects it has had, keeping in mind that those effects may be positive, negative, or mixed.

Using the evidence of your conversation, write an essay in which you prove or disprove Costello's theory that the fast pace of change has led to the loss of faith that characterizes our society (paragraph 6).

**Audience:** a religious leader in your community.

Send a copy to this person and ask for comment on your ideas.

# The Nuclear-Winter Threat

## by Tom Levenson

Ever since Hiroshima and Nagasaki, most people have been grimly aware of the heat, blast, and radiation effects of nuclear weapons on human beings, structures, and the environment — and of the immensely greater holocaust that a full-scale nuclear war would bring. Now, studies suggest another catastrophic consequence of an all-out nuclear exchange, one that has been largely overlooked. At a meeting in Washington late in October 1985, scientists warned that soot, smoke, and dust from the explosions of less than half of the superpowers' nuclear arsenals could blanket the earth, block out the sun, and cause a prolonged, bitterly cold "nuclear winter." This climatic upheaval, the scientists warned, could threaten the survival of the human species.

Planetary scientist Carl Sagan reported that he and several colleagues had run mathematical simulations showing that the pall from burning cities, forests, and fuel stocks would create a dense cloud that could screen much of the Northern Hemisphere from more than 90 percent of the sun's light for as long as a month. Within two weeks of detonation, the surface of the earth could cool to $-25°C$ and remain that cold for several months. After several weeks, the cloud could reach the Southern Hemisphere as well. Full daylight and normal temperatures would not return for as long as a year.

Using the physicists' predictions, a team of biologists headed by Stanford's Paul Ehrlich gauged the ecological consequences of several levels of nuclear war. After a major conflict, involving more than three-quarters of the available strategic arsenal, the cold would devastate crops and other plant life, particularly if a war occurred during the spring or summer. Fresh water would freeze; hungry and thirsty animals would die. At the same time, the dark would limit photosynthesis, the process by which plants produce the chemical compounds necessary for life. In the oceans outside of arctic regions, the lack of sunlight would be felt immediately. There the food chain depends on microscopic plants that are extremely sensitive to changes in the amount of light they receive. On the land masses in the tropics, where most plants lack a reserve of stored energy, a substantial decrease in the amount of sunshine would quickly extinguish many species.

Says Ehrlich, "We doubt that these effects would kill off all humans immediately. But the survivors would face a radically different environment from that which they are used to." Over the decades that follow, he says, "we cannot exclude the possibility of the extinction of the human species."

5    These grim biological predictions depend on the accuracy of the mathematical techniques the physicists used to determine the climate changes, and some climate specialists have criticized Sagan's models for making too many assumptions about the behaviour of smoke and soot particles in the atmosphere. Says Joseph Smagorinsky, retired director of the geophysical fluid dynamics laboratory at Princeton, "The models aren't suited for this kind of calculation. Most models attempt to predict small departures from the present. I don't doubt that a nuclear war would have some serious effects on the climate, but I don't know what those would be."

6    Stephen Schneider, an atmospheric scientist with the National Center for Atmospheric Research in Boulder, Colorado, agrees with Smagorinsky in part. "The three great uncertainties are how much, how high, how wide a cloud you get. There are no real calculations for these." But, Schneider adds, "there is an enormous amount of soot available. The results Sagan and Ehrlich discuss are all well within the range of possible consequences."

# Style and Structure

1. (a) Identify the sentence(s) in paragraph 1 that best introduce(s) the main **thesis** of the essay.
   (b) If this essay deals with the nuclear-winter threat, why would the author choose to open it with a sentence on the heat, blast, and radiation effects of nuclear weapons?
2. How does the author arrange the information presented in paragraph 2 to dramatize the effects of the nuclear winter?
3. How, in paragraph 3, does the author stress for the average nontechnical reader the impact of a nuclear winter?
4. What is the effect of saving the information contained in paragraph 4 for this particular point in the essay?
5. (a) How in paragraph 5 does the author reveal his scientific objectivity?
   (b) How does the inclusion of paragraph 5 enhance the credibility of the essay?
6. Why do Stephen Schneider's comments in paragraph 6 form an effective **conclusion** for this essay?

# Warm-up

1. Place yourself in the position of someone living in your community in the midst of a nuclear winter. Choose one of the following topics:

    (i) the changes in the local environment;

    (ii) the changes in your way of life;

    (iii) the prospects for the community's survival.

    Discuss it with the others in the class who have chosen the same topic, and then write a short report.

    **Audience:** other members of the community affected by the nuclear winter.

    After you have written your report, join up once again with the others who worked on the same topic. Together, develop a short presentation that will drive home for the rest of the class the possible local impact of a nuclear winter.

2. Exercise 1 attempted to give personal treatment to a problem that we usually discuss in abstract terms. The drawback of abstract discussions is that they make the problems seem remote. Write a one-paragraph report on the benefits of personalizing such global problems as nuclear winter.

    **Audience:** someone trying to find ways to mobilize public opinion.

    Compare your paragraph with those written by others in the class.

# Thinking and Writing

a. One person who read this essay commented, "People have become so used to living with the threat of nuclear war that a new theory such as 'nuclear winter' won't even faze them. Instead of becoming indignant and demanding an end to the madness that threatens each and every one of them, they will try to ignore this new threat and mutter some nonsense about the individual's not being able to do anything to prevent it anyway."

    Write an essay in which you support or oppose this view of people's reaction to articles such as "The Nuclear-Winter Threat."

    **Audience:** someone who would oppose your stand.

b.  Write an essay in which you explain the role that Canada should play in the future of nuclear arms.

   **Audience:** someone who is involved in making policy decisions at the federal level.

   Send a copy of your final draft to your MP in Ottawa.

# Is Plea-Bargaining So Bad?

**by Leo Adler**

When the British Columbia Supreme Court ordered that the $100 000 trust    1
fund set up for the family of mass murderer Clifford Olson be declared null
and void, it threw a wrench into the whole legal system of plea-bargaining.
The fund had been set up by the Crown in return for Mr. Olson telling the
authorities where he had hidden the bodies of the children he murdered,
and for giving the Crown full details of these crimes to ensure his conviction.
This is not the first time that the Crown has made "deals." In Ontario, a
Mafia enforcer named Cecil Kirby has been granted full immunity, protection,
a new identity, a financial allowance, and other benefits for helping the Crown
prosecute the people who hired him to commit numerous crimes. Mr. Olson
and Mr. Kirby are simply the two most graphic illustrations of plea-bargaining
and the tactics used to gain convictions.

The courts have long recognized that if every accused pleads not guilty    2
and the Crown has to prove his guilt, our already overburdened courts would
cease to function beneath the sheer weight of trials. For this reason, discussions
are always being held among the Crown attorney, the police, the defence
counsel, and even the judges. Through the negotiations, trial lists and costs
are considerably reduced, issues clarified, and sentences are usually set within
acceptable legal principles.

For the most part, these discussions invoke the possibility of a plea to a    3
lesser offence, an agreed sentence range, or the withdrawal of other out-
standing charges. For the Crown and the police, a possible acquittal is averted
and an accused who is truly guilty is found guilty and made to pay the penalty.
The accused avoids the risk of a possible conviction for a more serious charge,
or is made aware of exactly what range of sentence he is facing. For the
witnesses, there is the benefit of not having to come to court and be subjected
to occasionally embarrassing cross-examination. It is true that the ultimate
decision is made by a judge — who can set aside, or ignore, a patently un-
conscionable plea or suggested sentence.

However, when that situation occurs (which is quite rare), the judge either    4
sends the case to another court, or gives his reasons for not complying with
the request, thereby allowing a higher court to decide whether he was wrong.
Significantly, in the Olson case, the trial judge was made aware of the "cash-

for-bodies deal," without which there could not have been a guilty plea or possibly even a conviction. The trial judge did not strike out the plea, thereby implying that he was prepared to abide by the arrangements.

5    Within the criminal justice system, the intricacies involved in plea-bargaining are founded on the reputations of the defence counsel, police officers, Crown attorneys, and often the judges. When an agreement is broken, it is more than simply bad form; it means a loss of reputation that forever marks the man who broke his word. He can never again negotiate or be trusted, and his usefulness to his clients is virtually at an end. The British Columbia Supreme Court, by overturning an agreement made in good faith, has thrown the entire system into a quandary. If agreements cannot be made and maintained, what is the point of making them?

6    The morality of plea-bargaining may be troublesome, but it is nothing compared to the immorality of not having a plea-bargaining system and of having to subject the parties, and the public, to proceedings they could otherwise be spared. We do not live in a perfect world where innocent people are never convicted, nor do we live in a perfect world where all criminals are caught and brought to justice. Our justice system may not be ideal for resolving disputes, but it is the best of all other options. What makes it the best is the continuing negotiation that usually leads to a correct resolution of a case.

7    With regard to Mr. Olson, the hard fact is that for $100 000 the parents finally know what happened to their children. Would the parents have preferred that the money not be paid, leaving them in the dark as to what happened? Without the $100 000, Mr. Olson might still be roaming the streets, murdering children. With the $100 000, society has assured itself that he will be behind bars for the rest of his life.

8    Is the moral and financial price really that high or that outrageous to ensure that this man never again sets foot outside jail? If the answer is no, then the deal was a good one and ought to have been upheld. If the answer is yes, then we must stop all plea-bargaining and admit that the Crown should have taken its chances without Mr. Olson's admissions, and that he may have been acquitted. This plea-bargain achieved its purpose. In that respect, it is no different from the hundreds of other plea-bargains made daily and that are not overturned by the courts.

9    There is nothing immoral or unethical about parties negotiating a resolution. It is called compromise and it happens in the real world as much as it happens within the criminal justice system. But it will not continue if individuals and

lawyers do not have confidence that their agreements will be upheld. And if this lack of confidence actually permeates the criminal justice system, it is justice that will suffer the most.

# Style and Structure

1. What is the relationship of the first sentence in paragraph 1 to the rest of the essay?
2. Why does the author follow the first sentence in paragraph 1 with the information contained in the rest of the paragraph? What does the inclusion of this information tell you about the intended reader of the essay?
3. Make a list of the three arguments presented by the writer to justify plea-bargaining in paragraphs 1, 2, and 3. Note beside each entry in your list whether the argument is based on practical or moral considerations.
4. What information is contained in the first sentence of paragraph 4? What information is contained in the second and third sentences of paragraph 4? By presenting the information contained in paragraph 4 in this order, what conclusion does the writer lead the reader to accept?
5. What information is contained in the first three sentences of paragraph 5? What information is contained in the last two sentences of paragraph 5? By presenting the information contained in paragraph 5 in this order, what conclusion does the writer lead the reader to accept?
6. Make a list of the three arguments presented by the writer in paragraphs 6, 7, and 8 to justify plea-bargaining in general and in the Olson case in particular. Note beside each entry in your list whether the argument is based on practical or moral considerations.
7. (a) In the first sentence in his **conclusion**, the writer claims, "There is nothing immoral or unethical about parties negotiating a resolution" (i.e., plea-bargaining). Review your lists of the arguments made in paragraphs 1 to 3 and 6 to 8. Do these arguments prove the claim made in the sentence quoted above?
   (b) Why do the last three sentences of paragraph 9 form a more appropriate **conclusion** for this essay? Why, then, does the writer choose to include the first sentence of the **conclusion**?

# Warm-up

1.  Working in groups of three or four, research one of the following topics
    in the reference section of the library. Two groups may end up doing
    the same topic, but be certain that each topic is covered.

    | | |
    |---|---|
    | Clifford Olson | Cecil Kirby |
    | Crown attorney | provincial supreme court |
    | Supreme Court of Canada | unconscionable plea |

    Working on your own, write a one-paragraph report on your topic
    for the rest of your class. Compare your report with those written by
    the others in your group and make any changes that might add to your
    readers' understanding of the topic. Then make enough copies of your
    report that, between those distributed by you and those distributed by
    the other members of your group, everyone in the class will have a
    report on your topic (but not one from each writer).

2.  Read paragraph 7 of the essay "Let the Punishment Fit the Crime" (p.
    115) and paragraph 6 of "An Alternative to Incarceration" (p. 45). Then
    write a short explanation of the possibility of applying the ideas contained
    in those essays to the Olson case.
    **Audience:** someone who knows of the Olson case but is not aware
    of the principles outlined in the other essays.

    Working with the class as a whole, create a list of arguments both
    for and against applying these principles. Revise your explanation so that
    it takes into account as many of the objections listed by the class as
    possible.

# Thinking and Writing

a.  Write an essay in which you explain whether or not the $100 000 trust
    fund achieved by plea-bargaining in the Olson case served the purposes
    of justice. In your argument, you might want to take into consideration
    the purpose of the police and the courts: is it to stop crime from recurring,
    to exact revenge, or to see that everyone affected by crime is treated
    justly and equally?
    **Audience:** someone who knows little if anything about the Olson case.

b.  Write an essay in which you argue that plea-bargaining either should or should not be used as a tool of the justice system. Whichever way you argue, consider the effectiveness of plea-bargaining for the justice system in dealing with crimes against property (e.g., theft, burglary, and fraud), crimes against society (e.g., smuggling, drug offences, and drunken driving), crimes causing bodily injury (e.g., assault and rape), and crimes causing death (e.g., murder and manslaughter).

**Audience:** someone who knows how plea-bargaining works but would argue against your position.

Send a copy of your final draft to the local Crown attorney's offices and ask for response.

# Words That Wound

## by Emil Sher

1     I lived in an African village for two years. As I search for words that are faithful to what I experienced, words that capture the poetry of rural Botswana, there's one that I won't use. On the printed page, it's an irritant to my eyes, a thorn that pricks at my skin. Spoken, it leaves a bitter taste in my mouth. The word is *primitive*.

2     Bobonong is a sprawling village nestled between the borders of Zimbabwe and South Africa. It's blessed with the most beautiful sunsets this side of heaven, and has all the characteristics many Canadians would call primitive. The Batswana build their traditional homes as they have for centuries, with round walls moulded from mud and thatch. With few exceptions there is no indoor plumbing or electricity. Villagers fetch water from communal taps. Women with perfect posture balance buckets on their heads in regal processions that wind through a maze of huts. Tired donkeys pull carts along unpaved roads as rough as the washboards used to scrub laundry. Meals are prepared over hot coals that flicker in the night like fireflies.

3     It could all look so "primitive." But I've learned that there are different ways of seeing. Life in industrialized countries comes with a risk: a severe case of myopia. We gaze at the Bobonongs scattered around the world through lenses framed in rigid assumptions. We see a way of life "less developed" than ours. We see people eating with their hands and smugly wave our forks. We see people walking comfortably in bare feet and tap our leather shoes.

4     As we look on in judgment of others, we lose sight of ourselves. I don't know how the Batswana would say "appalled," but I do know that's how many would feel if they saw how we treat the elderly amongst us. They don't ship the older ones in their communities to homes for the aged; there aren't any. In Botswana, the word "nuclear" had only one meaning for me: communal families of three generations, tightly bound by the spirit of collective care. Back home, where technology thrived, I knew that nuclear referred not only to families, but to weapons of destruction that could tear them apart. Mothers in Botswana would surely be puzzled and amused to learn that public breastfeeding is still taboo in Canada. They nurse their babies wherever they happen to be — on buses, in shops, in the comfort of a neighbour's yard. And no one bats an eye.

At the end of a long day, teenagers often gather in small groups. They 5
don't stand glued to new video games; they move to traditional dances. Some
keep the rhythm on a goatskin stretched over an oil can. Others wear rattles
around their ankles. A shoeless train of feet rumbles along tracks of dry soil,
and clouds of dust mingle with voices sweet and pure. Few of their younger
sisters or brothers have the electronic toys sold here in suburban malls. Re-
sourceful village children twist wire and empty beer cans into toy cars with
waist-high steering mechanisms that actually work.

The word *primitive* doesn't sit well with me anymore. I need to find one 6
that does justice to the way others live. For the pen *is* mightier than the
sword, and words have the power to wound.

# Style and Structure

1.  Write a one-paragraph description of the intended reader of this essay.
    Base your conclusions on specific evidence from the essay.
2.  (a) Write a one-sentence summary of this essay's central **thesis**.
    (b) How is this **thesis** introduced in the opening paragraph? What relationship
        does it have to the word *primitive*? What advantages does the author
        gain by using this approach? (The formal name for this approach is "implied
        thesis.")
    (c) Unless you are writing an essay specifically for publication in a popular
        magazine, you should never use an implied thesis. Why is a clear **thesis
        statement** preferable in more formal kinds of writing, such as business
        reports and academic essays?
    (d) How many words are there in each of the sentences of the opening
        paragraph? How does the variation in sentence length affect the reader?
3.  Identify four examples of words used in paragraph 2 that subtly convince
    the reader of the beauty and validity of Bobonong's way of life. In a
    sentence for each, explain how it adds to the reader's positive impression
    of the village.
4.  (a) Identify all of the references to sight in paragraph 3. How does this
        extended metaphor of sight help Sher drive home his point that there
        are different ways of seeing?
    (b) How does the sentence structure in the paragraph reinforce the impact
        of the extended metaphor?

(c) How does Sher try to convey to the reader that Bobonong is only an example that illustrates his **thesis**?

(d) What benefits does the author gain by using the pronoun "we," rather than "they"?

(e) Find three examples of words used in paragraph 3 that subtly convince the reader of the myopia (nearsightedness) that results from life in industrialized countries. In a sentence for each, explain how each achieves its effect.

5. (a) How does the first sentence in paragraph 4 gain its effectiveness as a **transition**?

(b) In paragraph 4, Sher uses a compare/contrast format but avoids a simple "we do this, they do that" approach. Instead, he sets up the contrast by having the reader examine North American life through the eyes of the Batswana. Identify one example of this approach in the paragraph and explain how it achieves its effect.

6. (a) What criticisms of North American society does Sher imply in paragraph 5? How is his use of extended description more effective than an explicit sermon would be?

(b) Why would the author choose to save the contents of this paragraph for last in the essay's body? What does this order tell you about his intended reader?

7. (a) In what ways does the final paragraph act as a **conclusion** for this essay?

(b) What is the effect on the reader of returning to the word *primitive*?

(c) How does the final sentence of the essay relate to the respect for people seen in Botswana and in industrialized countries? Why, then, might Sher have chosen to end his essay with that sentence?

8.    The standard advice to writers is not to use "I" in formal expository writing. What problems could arise in most writing situations if "I" is used? What enables Sher to avoid these problems?

# Warm-up

1.    Sher uses the definition of one word, *primitive*, as the focus of his essay. Choose a word that summarizes for you a particularly moving experience you have had. Make point-form notes on the ways this word summarizes the experience.

   Write a paragraph or very short essay that uses as its focus the word you have chosen.

**Audience:** someone who may not be sensitive to the possibilities of the word you have chosen.

Let two or three people in the class read your first draft. Try to judge from their reactions if there are any ways you could revise to improve its impact.

# Thinking and Writing

a.  Many words used in our society reflect the same kinds of prejudices as does "primitive." And we do not have to leave our own country to see this kind of prejudice at work. We hear words such as "on welfare," "deprived," and "underprivileged" applied to people almost every day.

Choose a group of people who you feel are affected by this kind of prejudice in our society. Write an essay that examines the positive aspects of their way of life (as Sher has presented those of the Batswana), pinpoint the reasons for the prejudice, and explain the problems caused by it.

**Audience:** a reader who is not aware that this kind of prejudice exists.

Send a copy of your final draft to an organization that represents the group you have identified or to a local newspaper (ask if the editor would be interested in publishing it).

b.  Sher's major criticism of industrialized societies centres on the breakdown of the family and the effect it has had on teenagers. Write an essay in which you either support or attack the validity of this criticism, at least in relation to Canada. Use specific evidence from your observations of family life and the behaviour of teenagers in your community to support your stand.

**Audience:** someone who does not realize that our society may have shortcomings in these areas.

# I'm Making It!

## by Shawn Dalgleish

*Shawn Dalgleish, a nineteen-year-old student at Niagara Falls Collegiate, spent four months completing an essay that chronicles the nineteen years he has lived with Cerebral Palsy. The essay won a province-wide competition and is reprinted here in its entirety.*

1   In March 1970, my older sister Linda ran home from school and raced upstairs to see her new baby brother. The crib was empty. The baby was still at the hospital in an incubator. He had tubes in his arms to feed him and tubes in his nose to help him breathe. The doctors said he was very weak and would probably die. Well, that was me — Shawn Dalgleish! I'm alive and making it!

2   Something had gone wrong inside my mother even before I was born. No one could have prevented it; it just happened. Somehow, the oxygen supply was cut off. When I was three months old, they took me to Toronto for assessment. I was diagnosed as having Atheroid Cerebral Palsy. This meant that I would have problems with muscle co-ordination, speech, and maybe even learning.

3   The doctors in Toronto told my mother that she could raise me until I was five or six years old, but then she would have to put me into an institution. I hate that word! My mother was angry and refused to believe the doctors. We have proved those doctors wrong. I have lived with my mother all my life and soon I will live on my own.

4   My independence means a lot to me. Much of my independence was learned at Lakewood Camp near Port Colborne, which is run by the Easter Seal Society. They have many workshops including archery, swimming, and canoeing. We stayed in cabins but often we slept in tents or under the stars. No matter what kind of problem you had, the counsellors always treated you like someone special.

5   Just this past summer, I spent three-and-a-half weeks in Toronto with a program calls TIPS, which stands for Teen Independence Program. There were kids with different kinds of handicaps. Some of us still write letters to each other. I made a very good friend there named Tiffany and we were together all the time except at night. At TIPS they taught us how to use a stove, a microwave, and a washing machine and dryer. Also, I learned how to get

around in a large city on my own. Cleaning my room, making my bed, and cooking for myself when no one is around are all things I don't enjoy doing, but they are a part of life. I'm just happy I can do these things on my own.

The biggest influence in my life has been my mother. She has made me   **6** what I am today. When I was little, she carried me everywhere and she taught me how to walk. When I started kindergarten at King George V, I took a taxi to school. My mom carried me out to the cab and the cab driver would carry me into school and set me on my no-speed tricycle. I still take a taxi to high school, but now my mother puts my computer outside on the driveway, goes back into the house, and shuts the door. I just give her a dirty look — especially on cold days. The driver carries my computer into school because I'm afraid I'll drop it.

I take four classes and my friends carry my computer to each class for   **7** me. If there is a fire drill, my friends pick me up and throw me over their shoulders. They've had to "rescue" me at least twice this year. I have a peer tutor who helps me with my school work. She does most of the typing for me because I only type about ten words per minute. She also corrects my spelling for me. Lisa treats me just like everyone else. She is more than a peer tutor — she is a friend. Two weeks ago, we went to a dance and the bouncer wasn't going to let me in because he thought I was drunk. Lisa told him to . . . !

It was in Grade 5 that I really realized that I couldn't do everything everyone   **8** else could do. My friends at school decided that they were going to sign up for ice hockey. That night I asked my dad if I could play hockey too. But my father told me that I wouldn't be able to skate like my friends, because my legs weren't strong enough to hold me up and I wouldn't have the balance to stay on my feet. This was the first time I realized I was different.

As I grew older I didn't have to worry about having CP until the day   **9** when I was thirteen and I went roller skating. I remember trying my hardest to be just like the other kids. I couldn't do it; I kept falling. I got so frustrated that I ran into the washroom and whipped my skates against the wall and started crying. It didn't seem fair.

One of the reasons why I had never worried about being different was   **10** that my sisters and mother and father treated me like a regular brother. We would bug each other and fight just like other brothers and sisters. And I knew that they loved me even when I was being a bratty little brother.

I'm now in Grade 12 and I can't wait to graduate next year. I've been   **11** working at the Minolta Tower for four years as a coin roller. When I graduate, I want to work for a year, save some money, and travel. Eventually, I would like to go to college and study music or horticulture. I like to have a good time with my friends. I like to joke around with them. But someday I want to be just like Terry Fox or Rick Hansen. I respect them because they both had a handicap but they did something with their lives.

12    I think that my CP has helped make me a better person. When people make fun of me, I just ignore them. I don't let them hurt me. I never feel sorry for myself, because I have so many friends, I don't need to worry about the people who don't understand.

13    In spite of my handicap, I've grown up with a full and exciting life. I've come to a major time and I have to choose the path I'm going to follow. I'm confident about the future because I have strengths in place of the ones I'm missing. I'm Shawn Dalgleish. I've made it and I'm still making it.

## Style and Structure

1.    This essay uses an interesting device by having what appears to be an introductory **thesis statement** ("I'm alive and making it") but maintaining an even more significant implied thesis.

     (a) Write a one-sentence summary of the implied thesis of this essay.

     (b) Why might an implied thesis be appropriate for an essay appearing in a newspaper or popular magazine?

     (c) Why would it be inappropriate for more formal writing situations such as business reports or academic essays?

2.    (a) Identify one or two passages in the opening paragraph that help establish the tone of the essay. How does this tone contribute to the reader's response to the **thesis**?

     (b) What effect does the introductory anecdote have upon the reader's reaction to the **thesis**?

3.    Given the probable reader of this essay, why is it a good strategy to include the contents of paragraphs 2 and 3 early on in the body?

4.    In writing his autobiography, Shawn could have used a chronological approach to organize it for his readers ("When I was born. . . . When I was two years old. . . . When I was thirteen. . . . "). Instead, he chose to organize it according to topics that relate to his **thesis.**

     (a) Identify the topics that form the major sections of the essay's structure.

     (b) How does each section relate to the writer's **thesis**? Are there any sections that distract the reader from the essay's central idea?

(c) How does the order in which the sections of the body are presented help the reader?

5. Shawn makes excellent use of **transitions** between paragraphs and sections. Identify two such **transitions**; explain the way each functions and briefly describe how it helps the reader to see the point being made.

6. How does Shawn incorporate humour in this essay? How important is it for the reader's understanding of the **thesis**?

7. This essay is one of the few exceptions in which the use of the first person ("I") is appropriate. Why?

# Warm-up

Shawn says, "When people make fun of me, I just ignore them" (paragraph 12). Write a one-paragraph explanation of why some people might behave in this insensitive way.

Exchange your paragraph with one or two other people in the class. How do your explanations differ? How valid are the different explanations? Are there any suggestions you can make that will help the others improve the presentation of their ideas?

# Thinking and Writing

a. Many people dislike the term "handicapped." For example, one person who read this essay commented that the only handicap this young man has is the reaction of some people he meets. Shawn seems to believe that what some would call a handicap may in fact be an asset: in paragraph 12, he writes, "I think that my CP has helped make me a better person."

Write an essay that explains how people's attitude to life is just as important as, if not more important than, their physical or intellectual capabilities.

**Audience:** one of those who has made fun of Shawn.

b. People with many different disabilities are being integrated into the school system and into society in general. The usual argument is that this integration will help *them*.

Write an essay that explains how the reverse may be true — how *those in contact with* people who have disabilities are the ones who will benefit most.

**Audience:** an average person in our society who has never had contact with people who have disabilities and may be apprehensive about doing so.

# The Low-Skill Future of High Tech

## by Henry Levin and Russell Rumberger

High technology has become the nation's latest white knight, heralded as a means of creating many new jobs at home and restoring our economic supremacy abroad. Politicians and editorial writers even look to high technology as a way of upgrading the skills of the American labour force and increasing worker satisfaction.

1

To fulfil this promise, policy makers have proposed vast changes in our educational system. The New England Board of Higher Education recently endorsed an ambitious proposal from three high-tech consultants that calls upon government and industry to raise $1 billion for high-technology education. The House of Representatives has already passed a bill that would provide $425 million to upgrade math and science education at the elementary, secondary, and college levels. Although most of the funds would be spent on improving the quality of teaching, $20 million is slated to recruit and train faculty in high-technology fields at junior and community colleges. The bill also provides at least $15 million to help develop programs in computer education. Other proposed federal legislation would provide tax credits to manufacturers who donate computers to schools; California already provides such credits on state taxes. Many states are also independently pursuing ways to increase the number of science, math, and computer courses required of all high-school graduates.

2

These proposed changes are based on two assumptions. First, future job growth in the United States will favour professional and technical jobs that require considerable education and training in computer-related areas. Second, high technology will require upgraded skills because workers will be using computers and other technical equipment.

3

Unfortunately, these assumptions are dead wrong. The expansion of the lowest-skilled jobs in the American economy will vastly outstrip the growth of high-technology jobs. And the proliferation of high-technology industries and their products is far more likely to reduce the skill requirements of jobs in the U.S. economy than to upgrade them. Therefore, America's policy makers should revise their educational priorities and place greater emphasis on a strong general education rather than a narrow specialized one.

4

The Department of Labor has projected a faster rate of growth for high-tech jobs than for jobs in other occupations in the 1980s. While total employment is expected to increase 22 percent in the next few years, employment

5

in data processing, machine maintenance, and computer programming are projected to grow between 70 and 148 percent.

6      But such percentage changes are misleading. The total number of new jobs generated in these and other high-technology occupations will be vastly outweighed by the number of jobs generated in other areas. For instance, the five occupations expected to produce the most new jobs are all in low-skilled areas: caretakers, nurses' aides, sales clerks, cashiers, and waiters and waitresses. No high-tech occupation even makes the "top twenty" in terms of total numbers of jobs added to the U.S. economy. While employment for engineers, computer specialists, and other high-technology professionals will grow almost three times as fast as employment overall, these occupations will generate only about seven percent of all new jobs during the rest of this decade.

7      Statistics on specific occupations reinforce this picture. Employment for computer-systems analysts will increase by over 100 percent, yet only 200 000 new jobs will actually be created. And while there will be 150 000 new jobs for computer programmers, some 1.3 million new jobs are projected for caretakers, nurses' aides, and orderlies. Indeed, in each of these categories alone, there will be nine unskilled jobs for every computer programmer.

8      As a whole, employment growth in the United States will favour the low- and middle-level occupations, according to the Labor Department. Jobs in all professional and managerial occupations will account for only 28 percent of all employment growth, less than in either of the previous two decades. In contrast, clerical and service occupations will account for 40 percent of total employment growth.

9      These estimates suggest that most job expansion will occur in areas that require little or no training beyond high school. Even if the number of high-tech jobs doubles or triples in the next decade, they will hardly make a ripple in the overall job market in America.

10     Job projections aside, there is no question that high technology will have a profound effect on many American jobs. Vast segments of the labour force are already finding their jobs altered by sophisticated computer technologies. Secretaries are trading in their typewriters for word-processing equipment, bookkeepers are using computerized financial spread sheets, purchase and inventory employees keep records on computerized systems, mechanics are using diagnostic systems employing microcomputers, and telephone operators now rely on computerized directories. But will the use of these new technologies require workers with more sophisticated skills?

Based on past experience, the answer seems to be no. Throughout the history of industrial production in this country, management has endeavoured to divide and subdivide work into repetitive, routine tasks for which unskilled and low-paid workers can be used. This approach was first advocated by Adam Smith in *The Wealth of Nations* and later refined by Charles Babbage, who argued that it was cheaper to hire many workers capable of performing dissociated tasks than to hire a single worker capable of doing them all.

11

Technology has generally been used to aid and abet this division of labour. More than twenty years ago, James Bright, a professor at the Harvard Business School, examined the effects of automation on job-skill requirements in industries such as metalworking, food, and chemicals. The general assumption then, as today, was that increasing levels of automation required increasing skills. However, Bright observed that the skill requirements of jobs first increased and then decreased sharply as the degree of mechanization grew. He found that in the long run, automated machinery tends to require less operator skill. Once operators master their particular machines, "Many so-called key skilled jobs, currently requiring long experience and training, will be reduced to easily learned, machine-tending jobs."

12

Our recent analysis of job-skill requirements in the United States supports Bright's conclusion. We compared Department of Labor data on job-skill training requirements for specific occupations in 1960 with more recent ones. We found that in spite of continuing advances in technology and the widespread shift toward automation, job-skill requirements have changed very little over the last two decades.

13

The impact of more recent technologies only reinforces this conclusion. Many of the jobs in the printing industry, for instance — typesetting, layout, and photo-engraving — have historically required highly complex craft skills. But over the last ten years, technological advances have enabled many of these operations to be performed by machines. The introduction of teletype-setting machines has eliminated many manual typesetting operations. Tasks that once required handling and proofing of metal plates and castings can now be done by computer. Many manual operations involved in reproducing photographs have been automated. Complete layouts can be duplicated and transmitted to distant presses with a high degree of precision. Taken together, these advances have sharply reduced the skill required of workers who remain in the composing room.

14

Computers, which are at the very heart of the high-technology revolution, provide another textbook example. Early computers were not only large and

15

expensive by today's standards; they required programmers and operators with fairly complex skills. But as computer languages become more "user-friendly," the level of skills needed to operate computers declines.

16     The new generation of office computers is specifically designed so that workers can use computers for a wide variety of tasks without any knowledge of computer languages. In the office, computers now perform many of the tasks formerly done by secretaries. Word processors can correct typing errors automatically by the use of electronic dictionaries, so letter-perfect typing and strong spelling skills are no longer required. In addition, each operator's performance can be monitored by the computer so that supervisors can instantaneously compare productivity among workers.

17     Ironically, high technology could be used to enhance the quality of working life and increase the level of worker skills. At General Motors, for instance, managers and workers meet regularly to discuss new assembly-line technology and analyze how it can be applied to give workers a greater sense of responsibility on the job. But whether these meetings will actually accomplish anything remains to be seen. Judging from the past, we have every reason to believe that future technologies will continue to simplify and routinize work tasks, making it more difficult for workers to express their individuality and judgment.

18     The danger signs are already evident in places such as Silicon Valley. Although some executives, programmers, and engineers are stimulated by their jobs, most workers in the valley are employed as office workers, assembly workers, and low-level technicians. Many are overeducated for their jobs and find little challenge from high tech. That may be why, according to a front-page story in the *San Jose Mercury*, one-third of all workers in the valley take drugs and drink on the job. According to local narcotics agents quoted in the article, drug users in these plants are believed to be largely responsible for thefts on the job as well as accidents.

19     Just as ominous is the possibility that high tech will eliminate more jobs than it creates. Researchers at the Robotics Institute at Carnegie-Mellon University estimate that in the next twenty years, robotics could replace up to three million manufacturing positions involving operating machinery, and potentially eliminate all eight million of these positions by the year 2025. The widespread use of computer-aided design may virtually eliminate the occupation of drafter in the not-too-distant future, a potential loss of 300 000 skilled positions. A study from the Upjohn Institute estimates that robots could eliminate three times as many jobs as they will create, and the director of advanced

products and manufacturing at General Motors predicts that the "factory of the future" will employ 30 percent fewer workers per car because of robotics. Even if laid-off production workers are retrained for high-tech positions, they may not be able to achieve a comparable income level. Placement counsellors in Michigan found that laid-off steel or iron workers retrained for high-tech positions and lucky enough to find jobs typically received wages at half their previous level.

Another danger from high tech is that it may facilitate the transfer of pro- **20** duction overseas, further reducing the number of jobs available in the United States. Much high-tech assembly requires no more than a primary education, and many countries in the world can provide workers with such qualifications at less than $1 per hour. Atari's announcement that it was shifting most of its manufacturing facilities to Taiwan and Hong Kong illustrates this danger. As a result of this move, some 1700 workers in Silicon Valley — middle managers as well as production workers — would be laid off.

Whereas past technical innovations primarily displaced physical labour, future **21** technologies, rooted in the microelectronics revolution, threaten to displace mental labour. Entire classes of skilled or semiskilled workers can be made obsolete by sophisticated software packages.

Obviously, high technology is not going to be a cure-all for our nation's **22** economic woes. And its potential impact on the workplace and society in general could be a lot more disturbing than we'd like to think. What, then, are its implications for education?

To begin with, an excessive emphasis on specialized schooling will not pre- **23** pare workers for the future. Although many workers will need to acquire new knowledge to adjust to technological change, they will probably have to learn different, rather than more demanding, skills. Most of these new skills can best be acquired on the job and through short training courses rather than through expanded science, math, and computer-programming studies.

In fact, in a survey of industrial employers in Los Angeles conducted for **24** the local chamber of commerce, Wellford Wilms, professor of education at UCLA, found that they prefer employees with a sound education and good work habits to those with narrow vocational skills. A similar survey of British companies seems to confirm employer preference for workers with a good attitude and a sound education.

In the future, technological advances will come at an increasingly fast pace. **25** Specialized job skills will be more rapidly rendered obsolete and the once-familiar work environment will change at a bewildering rate. We believe that the best possible preparation for adapting to this lifetime of change will be a strong general education. By that we mean a knowledge of different political, economic, social, and cultural tenets as well as the acquisition of strong analytical, communicative, and computational skills. These are essential for understanding the currents of change in society and for adapting to such change constructively.

26   This approach should also fulfil the need to provide a common educational background for all students that will best serve the democratic interests of our society. A democratic society requires that citizens be qualified to understand the major issues of the day, discuss them, and take appropriate action. Early specialization not only deprives students of the general knowledge and skills needed to adapt to a changing labour market; it also fails to provide the basis for democratic participation.

27   In a high-tech future, a solid basic education will become more, not less, important. The challenge of the schools will be to upgrade the overall quality of instruction by attracting the best talent society has to offer. This will require major curriculum improvements, competitive professional salaries, and a much greater commitment to educational quality on the part of teachers, parents, policy makers, and society in general.

# Style and Structure

1. (a) Upon what assumptions about the future job market in the United States is the American educational policy based? Give two reasons why the writers would choose to discuss these assumptions in the first three paragraphs of the essay.
   (b) What is the relationship between paragraph 4 and the preceding three paragraphs?
   (c) What is the relationship between paragraph 4 and the rest of the essay?
2. (a) In what paragraphs of the essay do the authors offer proof for the statement they make in the second sentence of paragraph 4: "The expansion of the lowest-skilled jobs in the American economy will vastly outstrip the growth of high-technology jobs"?
   (b) What type(s) of evidence do the authors use to prove the above statement?
   (c) The intended reader of this essay has probably been influenced by the "assumptions" about the job market presented by "politicians and editorial writers" as outlined in paragraphs 1 to 3. Why, then, is this type of evidence effective?

3.   What function does paragraph 9 serve in relation to the preceding four paragraphs?

4. (a) In what paragraphs of the essay do the authors offer proof for the statement they make in the third sentence of paragraph 4: " . . . the proliferation of high-technology industries and their products is far more likely to reduce the skill requirements of jobs in the U.S. economy than to upgrade them"?

   (b) What type of evidence do the authors use to prove the above statement?

   (c) Given the intended reader, why is this type of evidence effective?

5.   What function does paragraph 21 serve in relation to the preceding eleven paragraphs?

6.   In what paragraphs of the essay do the authors offer proof for the statement they make in the final sentence of paragraph 4: "Therefore, America's policy makers should revise their educational priorities and place greater emphasis on a strong general education rather than a narrow specialized one"?

7. (a) What reasons do the authors present for maintaining that "an excessive emphasis on specialized schooling will not prepare workers for the future" (paragraph 23)?

   (b) How do these reasons lead the reader to the conclusion that a strong general education is the best preparation for the future?

   (c) Why do the authors choose to define the term *general education*?

   (d) Given the society within which this essay was written, why do the authors switch from a discussion of the role of education in job training to the argument presented in paragraph 26?

8.   Does paragraph 27 form an adequate **conclusion** for this essay? How?

# Warm-up

1.   Working in a group with five or six classmates, select one of the topics listed below and research it in the library:

   (i) the number of "low-tech" jobs created each year in Canada for the most recent three years for which figures are available;

   (ii) the number of "high-tech" jobs created each year in Canada for the most recent three years for which figures are available;

   (iii) the skills that employers have reported they want most in job applicants;

(iv) the types of jobs that were most frequently advertised in the help-wanted ads in two newspapers over the past week.

Working individually, write a short report on your findings. Based on these individual essays, develop with your group a two- or three-minute presentation for the rest of the class. (You will use the information contained in these presentations in the next exercise. Make notes as you listen and ask any questions that will help you understand the points being made.)

After the presentation, revise your report into its final form.

2. Based on your report and on the notes you made during the presentations made in exercise 1, create a small booklet that could be given by a guidance counsellor to any student wanting guidance on what type of job training to pursue.

Send copies of your final draft to a guidance counsellor at your school or college and ask for comments on its usefulness.

# Thinking and Writing

a. Write an essay in which you explain how the future job-growth pattern outlined by Levin and Rumberger will affect the employment of people in the field for which you are training.

**Audience:** someone who is familiar with that field and who plays a role in deciding how many people will be trained for it.

Send a copy of your final draft to the instructor in charge of your educational program.

b. Write an essay in which you explain how the educational program in which you are enrolled should be changed if it is to incorporate the suggestions made by Levin and Rumberger in paragraphs 22 to 27.

**Audience:** someone who is in charge of designing your educational program.

Send a copy of your final draft to the chairperson, dean, or principal of your department or school.

# Stop the Music

## by Bruce Headlam

The people in Section 45 of Exhibition Stadium in Toronto were particularly courteous as they waited for the concert to begin. They applauded politely when the stadium lights dimmed. And they applauded when The Cure, a British quintet that had ridden the crest of the nihilistic punk movement ten years earlier, was chauffeured to the grandstand stage in two white extended Cadillacs. Near the front of Section 45, a punk couple in their late twenties took their seats, and their appearance — all dark make-up and razor-sharp Mohawk haircuts — was admired by a sea of less severe imitators. Even in Toronto, there is just not enough black clothing to go around. Behind the punks, two young men in baseball caps boasted that they had attended four concerts and the monster truck mania show, but they agreed that concerts were better because afterwards more girls went to McDonald's. Three girls in identical Cure T-shirts sat behind them, eating caramel corn and telling each other that so many kids at the concert were "like, so obnoxious."     1

Not all of The Cure's memories of their August 1 concert in Toronto will be agreeable. Three weeks earlier, the Hamilton City Council had passed a resolution recommending to Queen's Park that the group's song "Killing an Arab" be banned throughout Ontario. On July 13, Mayor Art Eggleton informed Toronto City Council that The Cure had agreed not to perform "Killing an Arab" at the CNE. The council then adopted Hamilton's resolution without dissent. A motion to circulate the resolution to every Ontario municipality with a population of 50 000 or more was also unanimously accepted. It took the council less than two minutes to support the suppression of the song. Even the girls in matching Cure T-shirts, when asked about the ban, agreed that it was, like, so unreal. But Eggleton was pungent in explaining his determination to ban "Killing an Arab": if the song were in printed form, he argued, it would be called hate literature.     2

"Killing an Arab" was written in 1976 by Robert Smith, The Cure's lead singer, under the inspiration of Albert Camus' existential classic, *L'Étranger* — a book that, like most books, appears in printed form, but has not yet been classified as hate literature. Smith read Camus in his "A"-level French literature course in an English secondary school. The song's lyrics describe the critical event of the novel: the senseless shooting of an Arab on an Algerian beach. In the song, the chorus, "I'm alive. I'm dead. / I am the stranger killing     3 an Arab," is repeated three times over a quirky bass line and Hollywood-style harem guitar solos. The novel is meant "to illustrate the utter futility of the central action of killing," Smith explains for the benefit of those of us without our "A" levels in French literature. Smith emphasizes that his intention, like Camus', was existentialist, not racist.

4    "Killing an Arab" attracted little attention when it was first released in 1977, but it happened to be re-released on a new collection of The Cure's singles after the American bombing of Libya in April 1986. When a student disc jockey at Princeton University broadcast the song with an anti-Arab crack, Arabs in the United States complained to Elektra Records, The Cure's recording label. In December 1986, Elektra and the American-Arab Anti-Discrimination Committee agreed that a sticker declaring that the song "has absolutely no racist overtones whatsoever" would be attached to the cover of all copies of the album. A week later, Smith — citing "brainless and irresponsible DJs" — requested that "Killing an Arab" be removed from all radio playlists.

5    In February 1987, The Cure's Canadian distributor, WEA Music of Canada, voluntarily started putting those same stickers on copies of the offending album sold in this country. In April, negotiations between WEA and Canadian Arab groups were undertaken under the auspices of the Race Relations Division of the Ontario Human Rights Commission. During those negotiations, WEA suspended distribution of the album. "WEA showed some sensitivity and positive corporate leadership," says Dennis Strong, then of the Human Rights Commission.

6    But the compromise reached in the United States came unstuck in Canada. The Canadian Arab groups were much less easily mollified than their American counterparts. Just a few months before, the Canadian Arab Federation had negotiated the removal of a boys' doll, "Nomad — enemy of Rambo," from Canadian and U.S. stores. They planned to be as tough with The Cure.

7    Rana Abdul Qadir, executive director of the Canadian Arab Federation, rejected the disclaiming sticker on the album cover: "The point is not [The Cure's] intention. The point is outcome. Ninety-five percent of people take this song in a negative way." Bernadette Twal of the Palestinian-Arab Association of Hamilton was even more adamant. "This song is a racist statement. . . . If the title were 'Killing a Jew' or 'Killing a Black,' it would not take so long to recognize this." Banning the song from further airing in Ontario would not be censorship, Twal claimed, because "it should not have been allowed in the first place."

8    As the group's Toronto concert neared, the Canadian Media Coalition, a lobby that claims to speak for minority ethnic communities, asked the Toronto

City Council to ban any further sales of the song and to forbid The Cure to play the song at Exhibition Stadium. George Imai, vice-president of the coalition, has no patience with freedom-of-speech protections for The Cure. "If the so-called guardians of freedom were in the place of a minority child, what would their attitude be? Would they allow racist statements to be hurled at them? If that is what democracy is all about, God help us. Under the guise of freedom of speech, art, and culture, people get away with this kind of crap."

Meanwhile, Twal was writing to Ontario's attorney general, Ian Scott, urging that "Killing an Arab" be charged as hate literature. Scott's reply conveyed the opinion of his office's Hate Literature Committee that no such charge was possible. "He adopted the same argument as The Cure," Twal angrily remembers. "The attorney general is a very dangerous man."     9

There is no law empowering mayors or city councils to dictate what can be sold or performed in their cities. But Mayor Eggleton unhesitatingly telephoned Bill Stockwell, chief general manager at the CNE, and asked him to stop the song. Stockwell asked The Cure's management to assure him that the song would not be played. The Cure's management said only that the song was not in The Cure's current repertoire, but Robert Smith told the *Toronto Star* that he had made no promises. "It is untrue we've agreed to anything of the sort. If we want to play it, we will play it."     10

Nevertheless, the song wasn't played.     11

What did the Hamilton and Toronto city councils think they were doing when, beyond their legal powers and in possible defiance of the Charter of Rights, they tried to ban a song? By the way, Canadian Arab groups offer only one specific example of a racist incident directly caused by the song: a girl at a private pool in Hamilton claims to have been taunted when the song was played over a loudspeaker. But Toronto Alderman Joe Pantalone believes that municipal governments have "a moral responsibility for advocating positions that affect citizens." Petitioning the Ontario government to ban The Cure's song, and attempting to enlist support from other municipalities, is exactly that sort of moral leadership, not — to Pantalone — unlike posting multilingual street signs, arranging cultural exchanges with foreign cities, and cancelling council meetings that fall on Jewish holidays.     12

When The Cure failed to play the song, an interesting thing did not happen: indignation. A few irritated rock'n'roll columnists let off steam, but otherwise "Killing an Arab" was censored without protest.     13

The Cure was the victim of two double standards. If "Killing an Arab" had been opera, theatre, or literature, it's hard to imagine any city council,     14 even Toronto's, attempting to ban it. The defenders of high art are so much more daunting than punkies.

15    And if anybody had suggested banning "Killing an Arab" because it was smutty, it's hard to believe The Cure would not have had some defenders. Censoring sex is at least controversial; but treading — or seeming to tread — upon the new taboos of race is uncontroversially forbidden.

16    And besides, the song was never very popular in Canada, where The Cure is better known for whiny odes to adolescent angst such as "Boys Don't Cry" and "In Between Days." The Cure have long abandoned their punk roots and now their unimpeachable coolness appeals to the junior-high, funny-haircut set, like the people in Section 45 who, after the band's third encore, were tired from dancing and eager to leave the stadium. The two guys in baseball caps left the concert early, no doubt to ensure themselves a good table at McDonald's. One of the girls in Cure T-shirts was sick, not from drinking but from all that caramel corn. Only the punk couple seemed disappointed that "Killing an Arab" was not performed. As they climbed the concrete stairs toward the exit, they sadly recalled braver days. "You know," said the man, "eight years ago, they would have played that song for sure."

# Style and Structure

Headlam's essay is very well written and extremely subtle in the way it communicates its real **thesis** to its readers. Nevertheless, some of the techniques he uses, such as the implied and delayed **thesis statement**, require sophisticated writing skills and are not appropriate to more formal writing situations.

1. (a) Examine the *last* three sentences in this essay. Why would the author want readers to leave the essay with these ideas foremost in their minds?

   (b) Reread the last paragraph's description of the crowd (immediately preceding the final three sentences of the essay). How do this description and the contrast it provides add to the significance of the ideas that conclude the essay?

   (c) Examine the description of The Cure with which Headlam begins the essay's last paragraph. How does this description affect the reader's insight into the ideas in the rest of the paragraph, particularly the one in the last sentence?

   (d) What is the main point the author is trying to convey to the reader of this essay: the fact that the song was banned? the history of the song? the change in The Cure? or something else? Write a short summary of his main point.

2. (a) List three things that we learn about each of the following in the first paragraph of the essay:
   (i) the people in Section 45;
   (ii) The Cure;
   (iii) the punk couple;
   (iv) the two young men;
   (v) the three girls.
   (b) What ideas is the author trying to drive home by including these descriptions in his opening paragraph? What additional insights into them does the essay's final paragraph give you?

3. (a) What function does paragraph 2 serve for the reader?
   (b) Of all the comments that would be available on the council's actions, what reasons might Headlam have for choosing to cite "the girls in matching Cure T-shirts"?
   (c) Headlam chooses his words very carefully in the last half of this paragraph to influence his readers in the subtlest of ways. Give the meaning of each of the following words:
   (i) suppression;
   (ii) even;
   (iii) pungent.
   Try replacing them with synonyms (such as "ban" for "suppression"). How does this rewording change the emotional impact of this section of the paragraph? What reaction is Headlam trying to elicit in his reader?

4. (a) What purposes are served by including paragraph 3's background information so early in the essay? Why, specifically, is it important that it come before the reader learns the history presented in paragraphs 4 to 11?
   (b) After examining each in its context, explain briefly why Headlam might include the following words and phrases in paragraph 3:
   (i) inspiration;
   (ii) existential classic;
   (iii) appears in printed form, but has not yet been classified as hate literature;
   (iv) senseless;
   (v) those of us without our "A" levels.

5. (a) Choose any four words or phrases in paragraphs 4 to 11 that influence

the reader's attitude toward the subject matter. Explain how each works. How effective is each in achieving its objective?

(b) Find three examples of words that Headlam uses to help the reader make **transitions** between the ideas in different paragraphs in this section of the essay. Explain how each does its job.

(c) Examine the quotations Headlam uses in paragraphs 4 to 11. Select one that *adds* validity to the speaker's stand. Select one that *undermines* the point the speaker is trying to make.

Explain how each achieves its effect. Would the same points have been made as effectively if Headlam had inserted some personal comment to guide the reader? Justify your answer.

(d) What effect does Headlam achieve by using a one-sentence paragraph (paragraph 11) contrary to the advice usually given to writers? In light of this effect, how would you advise budding writers about the use of one-sentence paragraphs?

6. (a) What purpose is served by beginning paragraph 12 with a question? Point out two ways in which the wording of the question attacks the council's stand.

(b) Writers will sometimes base an argument on a single example of a situation. How does Headlam point out the weakness of this strategy and use it to undercut his opponents? (What techniques might his opponents have used to prevent this attack?)

7. (a) In acting as a **conclusion** for this essay, paragraphs 13 to 16 function in several ways. What are they?

(b) Identify three techniques Headlam uses in paragraphs 13 to 15 to give added impact to his ideas. Explain the way each is used and the effect it has on the reader.

8. (a) How effective is Headlam's use of a delayed and implied **thesis statement** as a rhetorical device? Give reasons to justify your answer.

(b) What limitations does this device have? How would these limitations affect your own use of it?

# Warm-up

1.    Pay careful attention to the students entering your school tomorrow morning. Make notes on their appearance, behaviour, and general attitudes toward school. Write a one-paragraph description of the scene

(similar to the one with which Headlam begins his essay) that drives home a point about students and schools.

**Audience:** a general reader who has been out of school for some time.

Before you do your final revision, exchange paragraphs with several others in the class. How do their observations differ from yours? Do they have trouble understanding any parts of your paragraph?

2. Choose a song that you like. Write a one-paragraph description of the song that explains its significance and attractiveness to a reader who has never heard it. Headlam's approach in paragraph 3 may give you some ideas on how to describe your song.

Find one or two people who know the song and test your first draft on them. After you have revised it, try it on someone who does not know the song.

# Thinking and Writing

a. Headlam implies that young people have lost interest in fighting against rules imposed upon them, even when the rules are blatantly unjustified.

Identify a situation or incident in which young people have acted in a way that supports or contradicts this thesis. Write an essay in which you use this example to argue for or against Headlam's implication.

**Audience:** people in the age range of the audience described in the article.

b. Headlam's article seems to suggest that young people are kept from protesting by their interest in more material things such as Cure T-shirts or a good table at McDonald's.

Write an essay that explains *your* ideas on the reasons for young people's reactions to rules that are imposed upon them by various authorities.

**Audience:** someone in the same age group who is interested in activating student involvement with issues.

Send a copy of your final essay to the students' council in your school, your provincial students' organization, or the youth wing of one of the major political parties in your province.

# Some Still State Flatly the Earth's Not Round

## by Angela Heinrich

1  Long before Ferdinand Magellan first circumnavigated the globe in 1521, proving the earth was round, Babylonians believed the earth as they knew it was flat. Of the many ancient maps drawn on clay tablets, one unearthed in Iraq shows the earth as a disk surrounded by water with Babylon as its centre, dated 1000 B.C. Yet even after three great ages of scientific cosmology, consisting of the historical works of Aristotle, Copernicus, Newton, and Einstein, and the current space age, there are people who still believe the earth is flat.

2  The Flat Earth Research Society International has more than 3000 members worldwide, according to its 62-year-old president, Charles K. Johnson, who lives with his wife Marjory, the society's secretary, on a ranch in the Mojave Desert twenty miles from Edwards Air Force Base. Associated with the Covenant Peoples' Church, the society contends that Moses, Job, the prophets, and Jesus Christ all affirm the earth as flat, stationary, and the centre of the universe, not an orb revolving around the sun.

3  Descending from the Universal Zetetic Society of America and Great Britain, which was founded by Samuel Birley Rowbotham in 1832, the current society has an annual budget of less than $25 000. It conducts a research program, holds monthly meetings, and publishes a quarterly newsletter. Many may scoff at the absurdity of the flat-earth doctrine, but the Johnsons' spare bedroom, which serves as society headquarters, is piled high with correspondence from curiosity seekers and supporters alike.

4  It is a society for individuals whose outlook is "Zetetic," or characterized by the seeking of truth and the denial of "imaginary" theories. Members rely only on "provable" knowledge, and consequently believe that the "spinning ball" theory regarding the earth is absurd. They maintain that Australia is not under the world, Australians do not hang by their feet head down, nor do ships sail over the edge of the world to get there; they also assert that continental drift is really the result of the earth and water being "shaken asunder by God." Using the laying of the first Atlantic telegraph cable as an example, Mr. Johnson points out in one of his newsletters how the surveyor's plans and engineering reports show evidence that the Atlantic Ocean

has a level surface — not a curved one as astronomers have believed. The
society gathers information, disseminates its findings, and generally seeks to
"push forth the frontiers of knowledge in geophysical matters."

But what evidence is there to support such beliefs? From interpreting the 5
Bible literally, Mr. Johnson claims that the first flat-earth text was the Book
of Genesis. "In the beginning God created the world without form and void
(it had no shape, just water, no land, stretching forever). The land later created
is sitting in and on the water. The world is infinite, without an end or an
edge," he says.

In fact, "the four corners of the earth" is referred to several times in the 6
Bible, and it is with references like these that Mr. Johnson colours his news-
letter. He also believes Jesus was a flat-earther because he "ascended" to heaven.
If the earth were a spinning ball in space, there would be no up or down.

Of the people Johnson refers to as prophets and kindred souls, it is surprising 7
to note that he counts George Washington, Franklin D. Roosevelt, and Josef
Stalin among them. Washington, as a young land surveyor, may have used
procedures similar to those of earlier flat-earth experimenters; Roosevelt and
Stalin helped found the United Nations, whose emblem is taken from the
flat-earth map of the world.

Calling himself "the last iconoclast," Mr. Johnson aims to restore "sanity" 8
to the world by opposing "theoretical dogmatic assumptions." He considers
himself and his followers sane, free-thinkers who rely on observation and
common sense for their findings. The world, according to Mr. Johnson, is
"laid out in a circle, around the magnetic or north 'pole' with lands spread
out in a circle. Furthest anyone can go, comes to ice . . . any direction from
north is south . . . and you come to the ice . . . what is beyond is unknown."
He says that, 3000 miles overhead, the sun and moon, each 32 miles in
diameter, circle among the tiny planets. Another thousand miles up, Mr. Johnson's research indicates, is heaven.

While the society would welcome new members, Mr. Johnson suspects 9
that many prospective "followers" want to pay the ten-dollar membership fee
only as a joke, to be entertained rather than enlightened. In fact, the application
form stipulates that "we do not want members who are stupid, mindless,
brute beasts with two feet whose only aim is to scoff or in some way 'harm'
our work."

Even though the society is serious in its beliefs, it is open to ridicule. The 10
Flat Earth News is written in crude, sarcastic English and is in serious need
of editing. With its preachy, often religious tone adamantly condemning certain

scientific establishments and agencies, it has an explanation for every conceivable scientific theory or question. Mr. Johnson calls everything from the space program to the 1986 nonstop global flight of the Voyager a hoax. He accuses the National Aeronautics and Space Administration of brainwashing the public with fake photographs and "grade-Z movies" of simulated space flights — and of deceiving its own astronauts with "drugs that space you out." Even though Mr. Johnson states that the space shuttle is "a simple stupid old airplane carried piggyback and dropped over Lancaster," he does admit that the space program hasn't done the flat-earth movement any good.

11    He is often invited to speak at various Kiwanis and Rotary clubs, but, he says, "it's hard getting the locals to buy some of these theories." Nevertheless, Charles K. Johnson is determined to prove the world is flat. Like the unmoving earth and central figure of the universe, he is steadfast in his fight against conspiracies that say otherwise.

# Style and Structure

1.   Write a one-paragraph description of the intended reader of this essay. Base your conclusions on such evidence as the author's word choice, aspects of the topic covered, and general approach.

2. (a) Identify this essay's **thesis statement.**
   (b) What purposes do the other sentences in the introductory paragraph serve? How does their placement in relation to the **thesis statement** affect the reader?

3. (a) List four points presented in paragraphs 2 and 3 that might make the society appear more legitimate.
   (b) Given the reader's probable attitude to the society, why would Heinrich choose to begin the body of her essay with these points?

4.   Paragraph 4 opens with a definition of "zetetic." How does this opening affect the reader who may have prejudices against a society that believes the earth is flat? Why would the author want to achieve this effect?

5. (a) What kind of supporting evidence supplied by the society does Heinrich present in paragraph 4? How does it compare with the kind of evidence presented in paragraphs 5 and 6? Why might she choose to present that contained in paragraph 4 first?
   (b) How does Johnson, as cited in paragraph 7, try to convince people? How well does he succeed? Justify your answer.

(c) Examine the ideas Heinrich quotes from Johnson in paragraph 8. Why do these explanations fail to convince the reader?

(d) Review the "hoaxes" Johnson is cited as attacking in paragraph 10. How do his arguments against the hoaxes differ from his argument for his own ideas as presented in paragraph 8? Which arguments are more effective? Why?

(e) Select any two methods of presenting or arguing for his ideas that Johnson uses as cited in paragraphs 4 to 10. For each, suggest one or two ways in which he could have made his case more convincing, particularly for the type of person who is the intended reader of this article.

6. In paragraph 9, how does Johnson try to refute those who scoff at his ideas? How effective is he? Why?

7. In what ways does paragraph 11 act as a conclusion for this essay?

8. (a) Identify three techniques Heinrich uses in paragraph 8 to show that she does not agree with Johnson's ideas. What benefits does she achieve by using these techniques rather than simply stating that she herself does not support Johnson's beliefs?

(b) Again, in the opening sentences of paragraph 10, Heinrich clearly attacks Johnson. Yet she never uses the word "I." What advantages does she gain by using this indirect approach instead of making a statement such as "I think the society is ridiculous"?

# Warm-up

1. Write a short refutation of Johnson's argument that the U.S. National Aeronautics and Space Administration's space program is a hoax (paragraph 10). Before revising it, compare your first draft with those written by one or two others in the class, pointing out weaknesses in the arguments and making suggestions for improvements in the presentation.

    Working in groups of five or six, examine the refutations you have created. What types of evidence or methods of argumentation best refute Johnson's claim? Why?

# Thinking and Writing

a. People may ridicule the Flat Earth Society, but its members may have a point: we unquestioningly accept all kinds of scientific theories as fact, even when they seem to contradict what we see. When we talk about the sun "rising," our words reflect what we actually see: the sun appears on the horizon and rises higher in the sky. The sun, in other words, appears to go around the earth, just as the moon does. Yet we accept as true the scientific statement that the earth revolves around the sun (though the same scientists tell us the moon really does revolve around the earth).

On the other hand, we live in a society that prides itself on being skeptical. Most people think nothing of questioning religious truths that have been held for centuries. Even small children challenge their friends' claims with "prove it."

Write an essay in which you try to explain this apparent contradiction in our society. Why do we accept scientific theories as fact but question almost everything else?

**Audience:** someone who, like most of us, has never thought about this behaviour.

Submit all drafts of your essay to your instructor for evaluation.

b.  Whenever people hold beliefs that are different from those of the main-stream (whether they believe that the world is flat or that people should wear unusual clothes), others tend to laugh at them or reject them rather than try to understand their position or disprove it realistically.

Write an essay that explains why people generally react negatively to others who are "different." Provide arguments that will convince your reader that these reactions should be avoided.

**Audience:** an average person who, like most of us, could easily fall prey to the tendency to ridicule people who are "different."

Submit all drafts of your essay to your instructor for evaluation. Send a copy of your final draft to a local newspaper and ask if the editor is interested in publishing it.

# Teen Runaways: Should We Force Them Home?

## by Brian Weagant

Although the majority of runaways return voluntarily within two days, a small percentage find the harshness of street life an acceptable alternative to home or Children's Aid care. Some have run from abusive or dysfunctional families, others from institutions or foster homes where their needs were not being met. Still others find running the easiest way to resolve authority struggles with parents or child-welfare organizations. All of these children see running as the answer to their troubles. And until we recognize this fact, I see little hope of bringing them back home.

The press has made much of the risks facing runners, some of whom turn to panhandling, prostitution, and drug peddling in order to survive. According to conventional wisdom, these problems are exacerbated by toothless child-welfare legislation that hampers the police and the social services. But stricter and more intrusive laws are in my view both ill-conceived and unconstitutional.

Returning the teenager to the abusive family or inadequate institution or foster home fixes absolutely nothing. Moreover, legalizing the "arrest" of adolescents who are not at risk and then allowing them to be detained against their will may have the unfortunate effect of breeding more crafty runners, who are less likely to surface for help because of the response they expect from the authorities.

We make it legally and practically impossible for these adolescents to survive on their own, and then we hypocritically voice shock when they resort to crime or prostitution. If adults suddenly find themselves on the street without a penny, it does not take them long to find some welfare assistance, a meal, and a bed. Further, going for help does not result in being apprehended as "in need of protection" and sent to a group home with other adults in a similar situation. Teenage runners do not have the same options.

If we are truly committed to better lives for these young people, we must develop a legal procedure that allows them to emancipate themselves from parental or child-welfare care. Several jurisdictions in the United States have such legislation in place. Minors wishing to live apart from their parents or legal guardians can make an application to a court. If they show both a workable plan for living and a legal means of obtaining support or income, the court

1

2

3

4

5

can grant a declaration of emancipation allowing a youth to find employment and housing, enter into contracts, sue, obtain welfare, and get medical treatment without someone else's consent. Surely, a similar mechanism could give many young Canadian runners a safe and legal alternative to crime and prostitution.

6      Our legislators must face the constitutional implications of allowing competent adolescents to be effectively arrested simply because they have flown the nest. Such strong intervention should be reserved for the apprehension of alleged criminals or incompetents. By subjecting adolescents to this type of legal intervention, we would be denying them their constitutional right of autonomy not because of their lack of capacity or maturity but solely because of their numerical age. This is dangerous.

7      Arbitrary exclusions from the civil rights guaranteed by the Canadian Charter of Rights and Freedoms can only be justified if there is no other way to meet society's need. Yet there are plenty of other ways to protect teenage runners — and legally sanctioned emancipation is only a first step. We can develop social-service programming that offers runners a functional alternative to street life. We can provide shelters that are safe but noncoercive. Until we introduce these measures, we have no business considering a new law that makes running equivalent to a criminal offence, and we have no justification for curtailing the civil rights of runners.

8      The ability to make life decisions depends on the capacity to understand the alternatives. Accordingly, our common law recognizes no magic age at which one becomes competent to determine one's livelihood. Some argue that we can justify denying competent adolescents the right to make decisions about their own liberty because of their tendency to make bad or stupid choices. If this is the test for infringing basic civil rights, then most of us are in trouble.

# Style and Structure

1.     Write a one-paragraph description of the intended reader of this essay. Base your conclusions on specific evidence in the text.

2.  (a) Write a one-sentence summary of this essay's **thesis**.

    (b) Identify the sentence that contains the **thesis statement**. Examine this sentence carefully. How does it also serve as a statement of the essay's organization? How does such a statement of organization help the reader?

3.  (a) Given the intended reader, why might Weagant have chosen to open his essay with the contents of paragraph 1?

(b) What advantages does Weagant gain by presenting the other side's arguments in the first two sentences of paragraph 2?

(c) Identify two passages in paragraph 2 that contain words that will subtly influence readers to question the opponents' arguments. Briefly explain how each achieves its effect.

4. (a) Compare the use of **topic** and **concluding sentences** in paragraphs 3 and 4. Which paragraph is more effective in conveying its main point to the reader? Why?

   (b) Write a **topic sentence** and a **concluding sentence** for paragraph 3.

5. (a) How effective in influencing the reader's thinking is Weagant's strategy of placing the contents of paragraph 5 after paragraphs 3 and 4? Why?

   (b) What reasons might he have for choosing not to open the body of the essay with the contents of paragraph 5?

6. (a) What aspect of the topic does Weagant discuss in paragraphs 6 and 7?

   (b) What is the advantage of saving the contents of paragraph 7 for the end of this section *and* the end of the body?

7. (a) Some conclusions simply summarize the contents of the body. What does Weagant do in this **conclusion**?

   (b) Write a short **concluding paragraph** that does simply summarize the essay. Which approach is more effective, this new conclusion or Weagant's original? Why?

   (c) Explain the effect of using the word "us" in the essay's last sentence.

8. Select any paragraph in the body of this essay (except paragraph 3). Write a short summary of each sentence in the paragraph, then comment briefly on the logical development (**coherence**) of the paragraph.

9. Identify three passages in which Weagant's word choice influences the reader almost subconsciously to agree with his position (e.g., "we *hypocritically* voice shock. . . . " in paragraph 4). Explain how each works.

10. Brian Weagant is staff counsel for a children's legal-aid clinic. How does this position allow him to break the rule of never using the first person ("I") in an essay?

# Warm-up

Weagant points out that "all of these children see running as the answer to their troubles" (paragraph 1). Discuss with a group of three or four others in the class the alternatives that runaways might have explored as options to running. Write a paragraph that presents alternate solutions. **Audience:** a potential runner.

Test your first draft of the paragraph by asking two or three people from the class to review its ideas (and presentation of them) with you.

# Thinking and Writing

a.  In an essay written to counter Weagant's, Howard Crosby (Conservative member of Parliament for Halifax) wrote the following:

> All the activities of our legal system have a price and the change I advocate [a law enabling police to apprehend runaways] is no exception. Besides the financial cost of searching for runaways and returning them to parents, there would be more work for overloaded police officers and hassles for youths hanging out in parks and shopping malls. There would certainly be restrictions on young people's freedom. But that is a small price to pay for saving countless children from exploitation.
>
> Responsible Canadians should realize that children are not small adults. They do have rights, but those rights are not licences to destroy future opportunities. And like everyone else's rights, theirs ultimately depend on a strong family unit, which will always be the heart of Canadian society.

Obviously, Crosby and Weagant represent completely different views on the abilities and rights of adolescents.

Make two lists, one representing the view of adolescents conveyed in Crosby's comments and the other, the view presented in Weagant's essay. Write an essay in which you compare and contrast these two views of adolescents. Even though you may support one view more than the other, be objective in your presentation of both. As you write, do not refer to the individuals (Crosby and Weagant) but simply use their ideas as representative of two different perspectives that are common in our society.

**Audience:** someone who holds one or the other point of view on adolescents and has never considered another way of thinking about them.

Submit all drafts of your essay to your instructor for evaluation.

b.  Write an essay that explains (1) the view of adolescents that predominates in our society and (2) the ways adolescents are treated in the community (and particularly in schools) because of this view. If you believe the treatment adolescents receive could be improved, point out ways the basic view of them would have to change to achieve this improvement.

**Audience:** someone who might be in a position to influence the treatment adolescents receive.

Submit all drafts of your essay to your instructor.

Send a copy of your final draft to the public relations officer of an organization in your community that helps teenagers.

# Turning Down the Danger

## by Ellen Roseman

1    "Turn down the volume and turn down the danger." That's the theme of a campaign by the Canadian Hearing Society, warning that walkaround stereos can be harmful to your health. The nonprofit group, which has distributed thousands of fact-sheets to high-school students, hopes to make them aware that permanent hearing loss can result from prolonged exposure to any intense noise — whether pleasant or unpleasant. "A lot of people think sound has to be annoying to damage your hearing — something like a jackhammer in the street," says Tani Nixon, an audiologist and researcher with the Canadian Hearing Society. "That's not true. It just has to be loud."

2    The power of a sound wave is measured in units called decibels. Normal conversations are about 60 decibels. Very busy traffic has been clocked at 80 decibels. A garbage truck operates at 100 decibels, a power saw at 110 decibels. The sound level at rock concerts and discotheques can go as loud as 120 decibels.

3    Research from industry indicates that prolonged exposure to sound over 85 decibels can cause permanent hearing loss. As noise level increases, exposure time should decrease. The Ontario Ministry of Labour recommends that at 110 decibels, no more than 15 minutes of unprotected exposure be allowed.

4    The Canadian Hearing Society measured the sound level of portable cassette players, most of which have volume control settings from one (softest) to ten (loudest). At two, the output is 85 decibels. At five, it's 104 decibels. At ten, it's 120 decibels. (Tapes are recorded at different levels, of course, and the sound output depends on the tapes used. If the input is 20 decibels lower, the output will also be about 20 decibels lower.)

5    Based on its research, the Canadian Hearing Society warns that prolonged exposure to any levels above volume two can permanently impair hearing. And short-term exposure can also be dangerous — damage can occur if the portable cassette player is worn at volume six for only 30 minutes daily. This is the same as listening to volume two for 40 hours a week.

6    How do you know you have a noise-induced hearing loss? The first sign is that you can't hear high-pitched sounds, such as "th" and "sh." Since 60 percent of speech intelligibility comes from the high-pitched consonants, you'll find that speech is no longer clear. People with a noise-induced hearing loss often say, "I can hear you okay, but you're mumbling."

When I asked manufacturers to comment, Doug Willock of Sony of Canada    7
Ltd. said he didn't think it was fair to single out walkaround sound systems.
The stereo in your living room can deliver more power when hooked up
to headsets than a portable stereo.

This point may be true, but portable stereos tend to be used in much noisier    8
environments. If you're listening to your headset on the subway or in traffic,
you have to turn up the sound to hear your music. This loudness tends to
be greater than 85 decibels, the Canadian Hearing Society points out.

Music-induced hearing loss is starting to show up in young people. Dr.    9
A.S. MacPherson, Toronto's medical officer of health, said there has been
at least one case where an eighteen-year-old claims to have lost 95 percent
of his hearing through the use of a walkaround stereo.

A Queen's University study of 60 students in Kingston, Ontario, ranging    10
in age from 16 to 25, found a significant proportion with noise-induced hearing
loss — 35 percent in the left ear, 28 percent in the right ear, and 12 percent
in both ears. "You don't expect young people to have this kind of hearing
impairment when they're not exposed to occupational noise," points out Janet
Hatcher Roberts, the community health professor who did the study along
with Dr. Ronald Lees and audiologist Zofia Wald.

When interviews with the students showed they liked to hunt, play in    11
rock bands, listen to stereo music at high volumes, and go to noisy parties,
the researchers concluded that leisure-time noise exposure was definitely associated with the hearing loss.

# Style and Structure

1. (a) Identify the sentence(s) in the introduction (paragraph 1) that best cap-
       ture(s) the central **thesis** of the essay.
   (b) Assume that the intended reader of this essay is someone who uses
       a walkaround sound system or who is close to someone who does.
       What would be the likely impact of the first two sentences of paragraph
       1 on such a reader?
   (c) The author refers to the Canadian Hearing Society early in the first para-
       graph. What other authorities on hearing are cited in the essay? Given
       the intended reader, why does Roseman cite these authorities?
2.     What information does the author present in paragraph 2? Given the
       intended reader and topic under discussion, why does she present this
       information at the beginning of the body of the essay?

3. (a) Using one sentence for each, summarize the information contained in paragraphs 3, 4, and 5.

   (b) How does the order in which Roseman presents the steps of her argument in paragraphs 2 to 4 lead the reader logically to the conclusion presented in paragraph 5?

4. What aspect of the thesis does the author develop in paragraph 6? Why is this a logical aspect of the thesis to discuss at this point?

5. Comment on how, in paragraphs 7 and 8, Roseman anticipates a likely objection from those who favour portable sound systems, and how she counters it in advance.

6. How does the evidence on hearing loss presented in paragraphs 9 to 11 differ from that presented earlier in the essay? Why would the author save this evidence for the closing of her essay?

7. For various reasons, Roseman has concluded her essay with a statement on the relationship of "leisure-time noise exposure" in general to hearing loss. Write a conclusion that specifically draws the reader's attention back to the danger of hearing loss due to walkaround stereos. Compare the two conclusions. Which do you think is more effective? Why?

# Warm-up

1. Keep a journal of the types of noise and their levels that you encounter during the next 24 hours. Record all types, not just music. Based on the data you collect and the information provided by Roseman in her article, write a brief explanation of the danger you personally may be in.

   **Audience:** someone who can effect some change in your environment.

   Compare your report to those written by two or three others. Have they forgotten any that you included? Did they include some that you didn't even think of? Be sure to revise your work.

2. Who should be responsible for controlling the noise levels of radios, stereos, and so on? Should it be the government? What about the responsibility of the manufacturer who is producing a potentially dangerous product? Or should the responsibility be left to the individuals who use the products (it's their hearing, after all)?

   Decide which alternative you prefer. Then join up with the others in the class who think the same way. Working together, generate as many points as you can to support your stand.

Working individually, use this list of points to write a paragraph that explains your personal point of view. Select what you consider to be the best arguments from the list.

When you have finished the first draft, exchange papers with two or three others from the groups that proposed *different* solutions. Point out any weaknesses in their arguments and in their presentations, and have them do the same for yours.

Revise your paragraph into its final form, taking into account the others' comments.

# Thinking and Writing

a. One implication of this essay is a criticism of the way in which people listen to rock music. Write an essay in which you explain why rock fans like their music to be loud. (Consider the psychological reasons as well as such things as quality of sound reproduction.)
**Audience:** someone, such as a parent, who has read the article "Turning Down the Danger" and has difficulty understanding rock fans' listening habits.

b. Write an essay in which you explain why an educational campaign that distributes fact sheets and articles such as "Turning Down the Danger" either will or will not be successful in changing the listening habits of people exposed to high levels of "leisure-time noise" (like rock). If you do not think that such a campaign will be successful, suggest alternate approaches that might be taken.
**Audience:** the person in charge of the educational campaign of the Canadian Hearing Society.

Send a copy of your final draft to the nearest branch of the Canadian Hearing Society.

# Peace at Any Price on Vancouver's Georgia Viaduct

by Ted Byfield

1   What is called the Georgia Viaduct in Vancouver is in fact a roadway accessing the downtown area. It is well illuminated, has a sidewalk, and is travelled by several thousand automobiles most hours of the day. It was on this thoroughfare one early evening last month that a young woman was brutally assaulted by two men, escaping with her life when she was able to leap over the pedestrian rail into the path of the oncoming traffic and a motorist finally stopped and picked her up. The police estimate that several hundred cars passed her by as the attack took place. So did several pedestrians. The case has been widely deplored in the Vancouver media. What's wrong with people, they want to know. It's a good question. It should be asked, not just by police, but by those in a position to shape our culture: television producers, novelists, journalists, literature professors, and, above all, the people who plan the social studies curricula in the school system. Why is it, they should discover, that these people did not stop — "these people" being you and I?

2   The sociologists no doubt will have an explanation. They will say that in a small community, where everyone knows everyone else, and where antisocial behaviour brings on social ostracism — meaning that if you beat up people on the street, no one will speak to you — law enforcement is largely handled by the citizenry. (A friend recalls a case of rape in a small Saskatchewan town. The nearest police were miles away. "So the men," he said, "took that guy out behind the barn and fixed him." There were no more rapes in that town.) But as small communities become big cities, relationships become distant. You encounter many people you'll never see again. You don't need to worry about being "shunned." Community self-policing becomes impossible and we increasingly entrust it to uniformed officers. The crime you might see on the street, therefore, is somebody else's problem.

3   Except that it isn't. The brute fact is that the police cannot function if all of us, as it were, "drive past." They depend upon a high degree of public co-operation. When they don't get it, crime starts to pay, then becomes rampant, and eventually renders large urban areas ungovernable. Already certain sections of most western Canadian cities are unsafe after dark, particularly for women. In other words, this phenomenon of ungovernability is already upon us.

Moreover, even as an explanation for our insensibility, this sociological account ignores a telling fact. Big impersonal cities existed and survived long before anything that resembled the modern police force had come about. Eighteenth-century London, for instance, was hardly a social paradise. Life was squalid, brutal, and dangerous, and the frequent hangings at Tyburn provided popular entertainment. You could buy good seats to see them. Policing was left almost entirely to the citizenry, and an assault or theft in the public market would set the whole crowd chasing the miscreant. Hence, I suppose, the phrase, "Stop thief!" If the poor wretch survived the beating and booting that followed, he lived only long enough to appear on the program at Tyburn. We today would dismiss such barbarity as all part of a brutish and uncivilized past. Yet in two ways those crude people demonstrated themselves more civilized than we are. That is, they understood two things that we do not seem to understand. 4

First, they knew that an attack on Joe Smith's fishmongering stand was an attack on the whole market, indeed on the whole city. If the assailant beats and robs Joe today, he will do it to one of the rest of us tomorrow. Stopping him and punishing him, therefore, is everybody's business. Joe isn't the only injured party. When a crime is committed, we are all injured. People knew that in London's Billingsgate market in the eighteenth century. They did not know it on Vancouver's Georgia Viaduct in the twentieth. This does not evidence social progress, but social decline. 5

Second, and more important, they knew that preserving the security of the city meant the distinct risk of violence and injury. The market thief was probably armed with a cudgel or a knife and, since his life was now in imminent danger, he would doubtless try to use it. Stopping him was therefore dangerous. But was that not always the way? To preserve peace you must be prepared to use violence. The eighteenth century knew this and taught it. The twentieth in theory knows it, but teaches something else. 6

Violence, we assure our children, is always wrong. We must cherish peace: we must eschew violence. Such is the message of our schools, and Remembrance Day exercises descend into an orgiastic deploring of the "waste and insanity of war." The fact is ignored that once the criminal is at large, whether on the international scene or on the Georgia Viaduct, then violence alone can stop him. We are not taught this, and therefore when we come face to face with the fact of it — as several hundred of us did last month on the Georgia Viaduct — we do not know what to do. Coming to the aid of that woman meant, purely and simply, involving ourselves in the immediate possibility of injury, even of death. So we drove on. We avoided violence, 7 as our teachers had so fervently urged us. By doing so, we have lost one thing for a certainty. That is the Georgia Viaduct. It is no longer safe for the citizen to walk there, and heaven help him if his car should break down on it, for he then stands the chance of joining company with that young woman. Thus, block by block and neighbourhood by neighbourhood, we cede our cities to the enemy. The eighteenth century didn't do this. We do. So has our sense of civic responsibility advanced from the eighteenth century? The answer isn't quite as self-evident as it once seemed.

8    Again, are we not ill-served in this matter by the luminaries of our media, the editorial writers, the columnists, the talk-show hosts, all those founts of civic wisdom who have been so busy deploring the timidity and apathy that left that young woman to her fate? Surely, if they are really going to confront this issue, instead of merely dabbling with it, then they must ask themselves whether the doctrines we espouse in the school system are correct. Curiously, those who most loudly deplore the viaduct incident are one and the same with those who endorse the "peace" program in the schools. They first urge pacifism upon us, and then deplore us when we behave pacifically. You get the impression they really haven't thought it through. Well it's time they did. The cure will not be quick, and the disease is far advanced.

# Style and Structure

1. (a) The writer refers to "you and I" and "we" frequently throughout his essay. Suggest who "you and I" might include — that is, who his intended audience might be. Give reasons for your response.
   (b) What is the effect of using "you and I"? What other possibilities might the writer have chosen? Are these possibilities as effective for his purpose?
2.    By the end of paragraph 1, do you have a clear idea of what this essay is about? Can you point to any one sentence that acts as a **thesis statement**? Explain.
3. (a) The **topic sentence** of paragraph 2 tells us, "The sociologists no doubt will have an explanation." What effect would have been lost if Byfield had used the word "reason" instead?
   (b) Point to other statements following the one above that indicate that Byfield intentionally used the word "explanation" rather than "reason."
4.    In the middle of paragraph 2, the writer includes a portion in parentheses. Give two reasons why you believe he has chosen to

use parentheses. Presented this way, what effect does this portion have upon the reader? Why?

5. In a well-developed paragraph, explain what the purpose of a **topic sentence** is and give examples from Ted Byfield's essay. Do you believe that the **topic sentences** in this essay do their job? Explain.

6. In paragraphs 6 and 7 of this essay, the writer addresses the question of fighting violence with violence. He makes the point that "once the criminal is at large, whether on the international scene or on the Georgia Viaduct, then violence alone can stop him." Was violence used to stop the crime committed on the Georgia Viaduct? What conclusions can you draw about (a) the suitability of the example of the incident cited and (b) the internal cohesiveness of the essay?

7. Is the writer of this essay offering any solutions to the problem of urban crime? How do you know?

8. Identify the question asked in paragraph 8. What might you say about the tone of this question? How does this question set the tone of the entire paragraph?

9. Are there any words in this essay that you did not immediately understand? What might these words tell you about the intended audience? Make a list of difficult words and, using a dictionary or thesaurus, suggest alternatives that the writer might have chosen.

10. Does the title of this essay accurately reflect the main ideas of the essay? Can you suggest alternative titles?

# Warm-up

Invite a representative of your local police force to speak about crime prevention to your class. Prepare in advance a list of questions that will help you understand the situation in your own community, as well as help you prepare for an essay on the subject. Be sure that the invited speaker knows your intended questions so that he or she may prepare. Explain also that the class will be taking notes during the presentation.

After the presentation, have a class member review for the speaker one set of notes taken to make sure they accurately reflect the speaker's ideas and to give an opportunity for clarification. Another class member should prepare a short speech to thank the presenter.

After the speaker leaves, hold a class discussion about what you have learned.

# Thinking and Writing

a.  Byfield makes the point that "the police cannot function if all of us, as it were, 'drive past'" (paragraph 3). But is that, in effect, what people generally do? Many citizens have established such programs as Neighbourhood Watch, Crime Stoppers, and Block Parents. In fact, the city of Vancouver itself instituted Crime Stoppers and reported that the number of solved cases doubled within a year, thanks to citizens' tips.* How is it that such programs are reporting overwhelming success at the same time that the media are reporting unprecedented violence and apathy in our cities?

   In a well-developed essay, discuss the effectiveness of neighbourhood programs for peace and protection. Examine a program that exists in your area, taking into account such factors as communication, co-operation, shared responsibility among neighbours, and their relationship with local police forces.

   Variation: If no such programs exist in your area, write an essay in which you argue why one should be set up.

   **Audience:** concerned citizens who live in your community.

   Send a copy of your final draft to the local police department for comment.

b.  Two essays in this book deal with social attitudes to violence: "Deliberate Strangers" (p. 124) and "Peace at Any Price on the Georgia Viaduct." However, the two writers differ in many ways in what they see as contributing factors and possible solutions to the problem.

   In a compare/contrast essay, examine these two essays. (For the compare/contrast organizational approach, see p. 302.) Look at both the similarities and the differences in the writers' attitudes to violence. Be sure to include a clearly recognizable **thesis statement** in your introduction, showing your reader not just that you are comparing these two essays but why you are doing so.

   **Audience:** your classmates, who have also read the two essays.

*Tim Gallagher, "Has Vancouver No Good Samaritans?" *Alberta Report*, December 12, 1988.

# Lighting Up and Looking Cool

## by Velvet Shelvock

I was eleven years old when it all started. My girlfriend and I were on our way to the store to buy some junk food when we got talking about smoking. She said, "I've been smoking since I was ten," lying through her teeth and trying to impress me. I couldn't let that go without a substantial comeback. "Well, I've been smoking since I was nine." I was also lying, to make her stand up and take notice that this was one cool chick she was talking to. She thought about my reply for a moment and then said, "Let's go buy some." The words still ring in my ears today.

First, my teeth started changing colour to a dull shade of yellow. So I thought, "I'll just cover my mouth when I smile." Then, bad breath intruded on my life, so I became an avid gum chewer, eventually making all my fillings fall out. Then, as if that weren't enough, a tiny cough took hold and never went away. Now it isn't so tiny anymore. That coughing has other undue effects that I won't bother to disgust you with. Finally, bronchial asthma has set in.

I can't comprehend why anyone smokes, when the habit causes such terrible things, including cancer. You can spot a smoker a mile away, panting up stairs, coughing as soon as the crisp cool air gets into his lungs. And, even though I smoke, I can always tell when someone's just had a cigarette — he has the unhealthy smell of a dirty ashtray.

Smoking also restricts behaviour. I won't go to the show, because I can't smoke there. Some people don't allow smoking in their homes, a practice that I fully agree with. But I won't visit them. I admire people who don't smoke. Why should they have to breathe in second-hand smoke? But, hypocritically, I get ticked off if someone asks me to put out one of my cigarettes.

It seems like only yesterday that I started smoking, but I'm sure that my lungs would tell a different story. I'm 27 now and for at least ten years I have wanted to quit smoking, but it seems to be a hopeless situation. I wish I could go back in time and say to my friend, "I don't smoke and I don't want to."

Smoking doesn't impress anyone these days.

# Style and Structure

1. (a) What **organizational approach** does the writer choose to begin her essay? Discuss the benefits of such an approach. (For **organizational approach**, see pp. 301–302.)

   (b) What other **organizational approaches** might she have investigated as possible openers? Choose one of your suggestions and write an alternative introductory paragraph for "Lighting Up and Looking Cool."

2. (a) In paragraph 2, the writer changes to a different **organizational approach**. Identify this approach.

   (b) What **transitions** does the writer use to link ideas in paragraph 2? Discuss how effective these transitions are and your reasons for thinking so.

3. (a) In paragraph 3, the writer uses two indefinite pronouns, "anyone" and "someone." Review the section on **inclusive language** (pp. 328–330), and rewrite the paragraph, making it more inclusive.

   (b) Compare classmates' rewritten paragraphs. How many different ways of rewriting can you find?

   (c) Discuss the original paragraph and the rewritten alternatives. What can you say about the effort required to write for inclusivity? Does inclusivity make a difference in the effect of the paragraph? Explain your opinions.

4. (a) In paragraph 4, Shelvock uses the expression "ticked off." This expression would normally be considered slang. How acceptable and effective is it here?

   (b) Make a list of alternative words and expressions that the writer might have chosen. Compare each of your suggestions with the expression chosen and evaluate in terms of effectiveness and appropriateness.

5. The last paragraph consists of Shelvock's reflection, "Smoking doesn't impress anyone these days." How does this sentence tie in with the **introduction**? How would you describe the tone of this **conclusion**?

# Warm-up

To generate ideas, writers often brainstorm on paper. For this essay, Shelvock would have considered smoking itself, then all of the effects that smoking has had.

Try a form of brainstorming by putting a key word such as "smoking" in the centre of a large blank page. Jot down ideas in whatever order they come to you so that they surround your central image. When you are finished, go back and read your "mind-map," drawing circles around ideas and linking one to the next where logical connections can be made. Make sure that all ideas relate to your central image.

With the whole class or in small groups, compare mind-maps and discuss the usefulness of this technique.

# Thinking and Writing

a.  With the possible exception of those in psychotherapy, we seldom take the time to examine how and why we have developed habits in the way that this writer has done. There are all kinds of questions we might ask ourselves about our own behaviour: How did I learn to drive a standard car, and why do I prefer standard to automatic transmissions? Why do I like work generally, but hate housework? Why do I go jogging to keep my body healthy, then pig out on soft drinks that I know are loaded with additives?

In a well-developed cause-and-effect essay, describe one such habit that you have developed. (Or, if your own habits are too embarrassing or too difficult to bring to light, look at someone else's!) Be sure to give a good deal of thought to the process of habit formation; do not assume that there is always a simple, straightforward answer.
**Audience:** write this essay just for yourself.

Have a friend look over your essay and suggest corrections and possible insights.

b.  When asked if she would like her essay published, Velvet Shelvock (a college student) was amazed. She protested that she still has trouble with grammar and has to refer constantly to a dictionary to keep herself on track. But, on reflection, she concluded, "I guess I couldn't survive if I didn't write, though."

During her essay-writing career at college, Velvet has found that writing is no longer just a tool for getting marks, but a way of pondering and expressing her ideas. Writing has become less of a chore and more of a personal need. "But there's still the *spelling*," she adds.

Write an essay in which you discuss the process of writing an essay and the changes that occur in you as a result of having to sort out your thoughts and get them down on paper. Examine both the positive and negative aspects of essay writing.

**Audience:** people like Velvet Shelvock, who enjoy writing but understand its hassles, too.

After proofreading, send your final draft to students who are just beginning a writing course at your school. Ask them to return the favour.

# In the Beginning: God and Science

## by Lance Morrow

Sometime after the Enlightenment, science and religion came to a gentleman's agreement. Science was for the real world: machines, manufactured things, medicines, guns, moon rockets. Religion was for everything else, the immeasurable: morals, sacraments, poetry, insanity, death, and some residual forms of politics and statesmanship. Religion became immaterial, in both senses of the word. Science and religion were apples and oranges. So the pact said: render unto apples the things that are Caesar's, and unto oranges the things that are God's. Just as the Maya kept two calendars, one profane and one priestly, so Western science and religion fell into two different conceptions of the universe, two different vocabularies. 1

This hostile distinction between religion and science has softened in the last third of the twentieth century. Both religion and science have become self-consciously aware of their excesses, even of their capacity for evil. Now they find themselves jostled into a strange metaphysical intimacy. Perhaps the most extraordinary sign of that intimacy is what appears to be an agreement between religion and science about certain facts concerning the creation of the universe. It is the equivalent of the Montagues and Capulets collaborating on a baby shower. 2

According to the Book of Genesis, the universe began in a single, flashing act of creation; the divine intellect willed all into being, *ex nihilo*. It is not surprising that scientists have generally stayed clear of the question of ultimate authorship, of the final "uncaused cause." In years past, in fact, they held to the Aristotelian idea of a universe that was "ungenerated and indestructible," with an infinite past and an infinite future. This was known as the Steady State theory. 3

That absolute expanse might be difficult, even unbearable, to contemplate, like an infinite snow field of time, but the conception at least carried with it the serenity of the eternal. In recent decades, however, the Steady State model of the universe has yielded in the scientific mind to an even more difficult idea, full of cosmic violence. Most astronomers now accept the theory that the universe had an instant of creation, that it came to be in a vast fireball explosion fifteen or twenty billion years ago. The shrapnel created by that explosion is still flying outward from the focus of the blast. One 4 of the fragments is the galaxy we call the Milky Way — one of whose hundreds of billions of stars is the earth's sun, with its tiny orbiting grains of planets. The so-called Big Bang theory makes some astronomers acutely uncomfortable, even while it ignites in many religious minds a small thrill of confirmation. Reason: the Big Bang theory sounds very much like the story that the Old Testment has been telling all along.

5      Science arrived at the Big Bang theory through its admirably painstaking and ideologically disinterested process of hypothesis and verification — and, sometimes, happy accident. In 1913, astronomer Vesto Melvin Slipher of the Lowell Observatory in Flagstaff, Arizona, discovered galaxies that were receding from the earth at extraordinarily high speeds, up to three million kilometres per hour. In 1929, the American astronomer Edwin Hubble developed Slipher's findings to formulate his law of an expanding universe, which presupposes a single primordial explosion. Meantime, Albert Einstein, without benefit of observation, concocted his general theory of relativity, which overthrew Newton and contained in its apparatus the idea of the expanding universe. The Steady State idea still held many astronomers, however, until 1965, when two scientists at Bell Telephone Laboratories, Arno Penzias and Robert Wilson, using sophisticated electronic equipment, picked up the noise made by background radiation coming from all parts of the sky. What they were hearing, as it turned out, were the reverberations left over from the first explosion, the hissing echoes of creation. In the past dozen years, most astronomers have come around to operating on the assumption that there was indeed a big bang.

6      The Big Bang theory has subversive possibilities. At any rate, in a century of Einstein's relativity, of Heisenberg's uncertainty principle (the very act of observing nature disturbs and alters it), of the enigmatic black holes ("Of the God who was painted as a glittering eye, there is nothing now left but a black socket," wrote the German Romantic Jean Paul), science is not the cool Palladian temple of rationality that it was in the Enlightenment. It begins to seem more like Prospero's island as experienced by Caliban. Some astronomers even talk of leftover starlight from a future universe, its time flowing in the opposite direction from ours. A silicon-chip agnosticism can be shaken by many puzzles besides the creation. Almost as mysterious are the circumstances that led, billions of years ago, to the creation of the first molecule that could reproduce itself. That step made possible the development of all the forms of life that spread over the earth. Why did it occur just then?

7      A religious enthusiasm for the apparent convergence of science and theology

in the Big Bang cosmology is understandable. Since the Enlightenment, the scriptural versions of creation or of other "events," like the fall of man or the miracles of Jesus Christ, have suffered the condescension of science; they were regarded as mere myth, superstition. Now the faithful are tempted to believe that science has performed a laborious validation of at least one biblical "myth": that of creation.

But has any such confirmation occurred? Robert Jastrow, director of NASA's   8
Goddard Institute for Space Studies, has published a small and curious book called *God and the Astronomers*, in which he suggests that the Bible was right after all, and that people of his own kind, scientists and agnostics, by his description, now find themselves confounded. Jastrow blows phantom kisses like neutrinos across the chasm between science and religion, seeming almost wistful to make a connection. Biblical fundamentalists may be happier with Jastrow's book than are his fellow scientists. He writes operatically: "For the scientist who has lived by his faith in the power of reason, the story ends like a bad dream. He has scaled the mountains of ignorance; he is about to conquer the highest peak; as he pulls himself over the final rock, he is greeted by a band of theologians who have been sitting there for centuries."

Isaac Asimov, the prodigious popularizer of science, reacts hotly to the   9
Jastrow book. "Science and religion proceed by different methods," he says. "Science works by persuasive reason. Outside of science, the method is intuitional, which is not very persuasive. In science, it is possible to say we were wrong, based on data." Science is provisional; it progresses from one hypothesis to another, always testing, rejecting the ideas that do not work, that are contradicted by new evidence. "Faith," said St. Augustine, "is to believe, on the word of God, what we do not see." Faith defies proof; science demands it. If new information should require modification of the Big Bang theory, that modification could be accomplished without the entire temple of knowledge collapsing. Observes Harvard University historian-astronomer Owen Gingerich: "Genesis is not a book of science. It is accidental if some things agree in detail. I believe the heavens declare the glory of God only to people who've made a religious commitment."

A number of theologians concur that the apparent convergence of religious   10
and scientific versions of the creation is a coincidence from which no profound meaning can be extracted. "If the last evidence for God occurred twenty billion years ago," asks Methodist W. Paul Jones of Missouri's St. Paul School of Theology, "do we not at best have the palest of deisms?" Jesuit philosopher Bernard Lonergan goes further: "Science has nothing to say about creation,

because that's going outside the empirical. The whole idea of empirical science is that you have data. Theologians have no data on God." There comes a point, somewhere short of God, at which all computers have no data either. With the Big Bang theory, says Jastrow, "science has proved that the world came into being as a result of forces that seem forever beyond the power of scientific description. This bothers science because it clashes with scientific religion — the religion of cause and effect, the belief that every effect has a cause. Now we find that the biggest effect of all, the birth of the universe, violates this article of faith."

11    Some scientists matter-of-factly dismiss the problem of creation. Says Harvey Tananbaum, an X-ray astronomer at the Harvard-Smithsonian Astrophysical Laboratory: "That first instant of creation is not relevant as long as we do not have the laws to begin to understand it. It is a question for philosophers and religionists, not for scientists." Adds Geoffrey Burbidge, director of Kitt Peak National Observatory: "Principles and concepts cannot be measured. A question like 'Who imposed the order?' is metaphysical." Still, virtually everyone — both scientists and laypeople — is taken by the sheer unthinkable opacity of the creation and what preceded it. Says Jastrow: "The question of what came before the Big Bang is the most interesting question of all."

12    One immense problem is that the primordial fireball destroyed all the evidence; the temperature of the universe in the first seconds of its existence was many trillion degrees. The blast obliterated all that went before. The universe was shrouded in a dense fog of radiation, which only cleared after one million years, leaving the transparent spangled space we see in the night sky now. The first million years are as concealed from us as God's face. There are many forms of knowing: science, experience, intuition, faith. Science proceeds on the theory that there is method in all mysteries, and that it is discoverable. It obeys, reasonably, what is called the "first law of wingwalking": "Never leave hold of what you've got until you've got hold of something else." Faith, by definition, is a leap. It must await its verification in another world.

13    If it has done nothing else, however, the new coincidence of scientific and theological versions of creation seems to have opened up a conversation that has been neglected for centuries. Roman Catholic theologian Hans Küng detects the beginning of a new period, which he calls "pro-existence," of mutual assistance between theologians and natural scientists. People capable of genetic engineering and nuclear fission obviously require all the spiritual and ethical guidance they can get. As for theologians, the interchange between physics

and metaphysics will inevitably enlarge their ideas and give them a more complex grounding in the physically observed universe. The theory of the Big Bang is surely not the last idea of creation that will be conceived; it does suggest that there remain immense territories of mystery that both the theologian and the scientist should approach with becoming awe.

# Style and Structure

1. What device does the writer use in paragraph 1 to create controversy? How is the overall organization of the essay reflected in the first paragraph?
2. Isolate the sentences in paragraph 2 that most effectively state the **thesis** of the essay.
3. The writer combines two expressions in the following quotation: "Render unto apples the things that are Caesar's, and unto oranges the things that are God's" (paragraph 1). How does this marriage of sayings relate to the **thesis**?
4. Examine the body of the essay (paragraphs 3 to 12) and plot out its development paragraph by paragraph. How does the order in which the writer presents his main points impart a logical development to his **thesis**?
5. How does Morrow emphasize that most scientists and theologians feel that the premise stated at the conclusion of paragraph 7 is superficial.
6. How does Morrow use his **conclusion** to propose a real as opposed to a superficial reconciliation between science and religion? In what ways is this type of **conclusion** more satisfactory than a simple recapitulation of the **thesis**?

# Warm-up

1. Each of the following terms appears in the essay "In the Beginning":

| | |
|---|---|
| the Enlightenment | the Maya |
| metaphysical | the Montagues and Capulets |
| *ex nihilo* | Aristotelian |
| hypothesis | primordial |
| Einstein's Theory of Relativity | enigmatic |
| black holes | Palladian |

Prospero's island          Caliban
agnosticism                condescension
neutrinos                  biblical fundamentalists
deisms                     empirical
opacity

Choose one and write a formal explanation of its meaning and its significance in its context in the essay. (Make certain that each of the terms is chosen by at least one person in the class.) Make an overhead of your explanation to show the class so they can make notes. (Encourage them to ask questions about any points they do not understand.) Once all of the presentations have been made, you should have a complete glossary of these terms.

Make any revisions necessary to your explanation before submitting it to your instructor.

2.   Write a one-paragraph abstract (direct summary) of "In the Beginning."
     **Audience**: your classmates.

Distribute copies of your abstract to two or three classmates so they can check the accuracy of their reading of the essay.

# Thinking and Writing

a.   In his article, Morrow states the following opinions:

> Science was for the real world: machines, manufactured things, medicines, guns, moon rockets. Religion was for everything else, the immeasurable: morals, sacraments, poetry, insanity, death, and some residual forms of politics and statesmanship. (paragraph 1)

> Science and religion proceed by different methods. . . . Science works by persuasive reason. Outside of science, the method is intuitional, which is not very persuasive. In science, it is possible to say we were wrong, based on data. (paragraph 9)

> People capable of genetic engineering and nuclear fission obviously require all the spiritual and ethical guidance they can get. (paragraph 13)

Write an essay in which you either support or refute *one* of the quotations.

**Audience:** a layperson who is not directly involved with the sciences.

b. Write an essay on your personal view of what the ideal relationship between science and religion should be in the future.

**Audience:** someone who has strong religious convictions and is involved in trying to help others come to grips with religious doubts caused by their perception of science.

Send a copy of your paper to a member of the clergy that you know.

# Fashionable Ideas

## by Barry Estabrook

1    An Inuit hunter insisted I write this column. I never learned his name, and little distinguished him from the other young men: he was in his early twenties, was sprouting a thin, black moustache, and wore a cap advertising a snow-mobile company. But knowing his name, given the circumstances, didn't seem important.

2    A feast had just started in the village of Pangnirtung, tucked halfway up the eastern coast of Baffin Island. The excuse for the gathering was, officially, the opening of the Angmarlik Centre, a building that was to house a multiplicity of functions that, in the Inuit world view, belonged under the same roof: outfitters' office, community centre, drop-in centre, teen hangout, museum, library, art gallery, tourist information booth, and senior citizens club. To mark the occasion, five ringed seals had been killed, and a woman had just removed their meat from a cauldron bubbling over a bonfire when the Inuk accosted me.

3    "Never had seal before?" he asked, seeing my uncertain look as I gazed at the fatty, steaming gobs. "Here." With two fingers, he scooped up a piece that revealed too much of its original anatomical function for sensibilities shaped by buying cellophane-packaged meat at the local Loblaws.

4    I didn't want to lose face. So I swallowed quickly and was assaulted by a taste that combined the tang of mutton and the pungency of fish that has sat too long in the refrigerator.

5    "You a journalist?" the hunter went on, emboldened by my little act of complicity.

6    "Yes."

7    "Then tell your readers Inuit need to hunt seal."

8    Looking through Fred Bruemmer and Brian Davies' book *Seasons of the Seal*, I was reminded of my conversation with the young hunter. As an editor of a magazine that, in its pages, has tramped the length and breadth of Canada's Arctic, I admit with some embarrassment that last summer's government-sponsored junket was my first visit to that captivating land. But even under those less than favourable circumstances, the Arctic worked the magic so many visitors describe. The landscape, with surging rivers, tide-swept fiords and soaring snowcapped mountains, produced waves of awe I felt in my gut. It made me as proud to be Canadian as anything I have encountered.

It also gave me respect for the people who for the past 1000 years have made a living there. With respect came genuine liking. It's enough that a culture can survive in frozen desert, but Inuit do so with humour and generosity.

I am reminded of the two nine-year-olds who, in the twilight of 11:45 P.M., followed me down to the rock-strewn edge of the tidal flats. They had a few laughs trying to trap me in a game of twenty questions, then, tagging along as I made my way back to the town, insisted that they give me a lesson on how to hand-capture the little minnows trapped in puddles.

And there was the last piece of luggage checked onto our outbound commercial flight. Without my knowledge, the Inuk who had taken me fishing had frozen the single char I had managed to catch, mummified it in green garbage bags wrapped with duct tape, and then rushed it out onto the tarmac minutes before the flight attendant closed the airplane door.

Against a dozen such memories, the young hunter's request stands out as the one time an Inuk was brusque with me. But with the brusqueness came a clear note of desperation. His demand, simple as it was, echoed the burden of a century of mistreatment at the hands of Europeans. From about the time the Normans crossed the English Channel until the mid-1800s, the young Inuk's ancestors had survived by hunting in the waters of Cumberland Sound. That changed in 1857, when British whaler William Penny established a permanent station at Kekerten, near present-day Pangnirtung. Lured by an annual salary of one gun, one harmonica, and a steady supply of tobacco, many Inuit dropped their traditional way of life and moved to the settlement. For 50 years, things went well, even as the whale populations were hunted to the brink of extinction. Fashion — European fashion — demanded that women slim their waists with whalebone corsets. The desire to look right pushed the price of whalebone to $5.25 per pound ($11.50/kg) in the 1890s. By 1912, the fad had passed. Whalebone fetched a meagre eight cents per pound (17¢/kg). The Europeans went home, leaving behind decimated whale and seal populations, disease, lots of mixed-blood children, and a population no longer able to survive by hunting.

The next seven decades are the story of a long struggle back for the people of Pangnirtung. But by the early 1980s, the town was being described as a "model" Arctic community. Its economy was anchored on government jobs, printmaking, commercial fishing, and the beginnings of a tourist industry. A referendum banned booze from town, so Pangnirtung faced fewer of those problems than many Arctic communities. Most Inuit still went onto the land to provide food for their families, keeping the social fabric together. And the sale of sealskin enabled the people to fund hunting trips — no small consideration in a land where hamburger is $8 per pound ($17.75/kg) and a wilted cabbage is worth $6.

14      In 1983, leaders of the European Economic Community banned the import of pelts from harp seal pups. No matter that the hunters of Pangnirtung shot mature seals, the market for all sealskin collapsed. A hunter could get $40 for a good pelt in 1982. Today, he would be lucky to get $5, if he could find a buyer. The Pangnirtung Hudson's Bay Company outlet used to be one of the biggest sealskin dealers in the Arctic, employing one full-time fur grader and sending out planeloads of pelts. Today, the company is not buying. The grader is gone. The fur room is used to store excess stock. People can no longer afford to go out on the land, and the pelts of seals shot for food are thrown away, allowed to rot on the beach.

15      Northerners are convinced those are but the first ramifications of a campaign that will eventually destroy their way of life. Recent studies of native Greenlanders support this view. Examining suicide and accidental-death statistics that exceed those of virtually all the world's cultures, Greenland experts concluded that a genocide was under way, the inevitable result of a more powerful culture imposing its values on a weaker one. Canadian sociologists say the studies apply equally to our Arctic.

16      Conflicting cultural values are, of course, at the crux of the native-rights-versus-animal-rights debate. There is certainly no ecological explanation for why someone living in Liverpool or Lyons should object to a Pangnirtung hunter shooting a seal. At last count, more than five million ringed seals swam in the waters of the Canadian Arctic, making them the area's most abundant marine mammal. Some resource experts are even beginning to worry whether increasing seal populations will begin to cut into another important source of Inuit livelihood — char populations.

17      I recently put the question directly to a French friend of mine. Why does the average European support the seal ban? She shrugged and replied: "Fashion." It was an ironic use of the word. For it seems that once again, fashion is the villain, this time in the guise of fashionable ideas, but ideas no more applicable to life in the high Arctic than were whalebone corsets.

18      On the last full day of my visit to Pangnirtung, I was part of what has to be one of the strangest flotillas the eastern Arctic has seen. Two hundred people climbed into twenty-odd boats, ranging from open freighter canoes to Cape Islanders to heavy scallop draggers. We set sail in a blinding July snowstorm. The dozen Inuit aboard my boat included a two-year-old boy, who slept the entire voyage up under the foredeck on a pile of life jackets,

and a 103-year-old woman, who joined us midvoyage, passed hand over hand from a bobbing adjacent boat so that she could talk with a friend. Our destination, some three hours away over the ice-studded waters of Cumberland Sound, was the ruins of Kekerten, Penny's whaling station. Our purpose was to consecrate them as a historic site.

It seemed like an odd thing to me: consecrating the site that in many **19** ways marked the beginning of the end of a way of life for Pangnirtung Inuit. But Inuit take some pride in their accomplishments as whalers. The elders remember Kekerten as their birthplace.

As I looked about, I realized I was ashamed. Aside from some ruins and **20** rusting machinery, the main historic artifacts at Kekerten are bones, the bones of the great whales and, strewn across the barren hillsides, the bones of Inuit employees of the whalers, shoved into broken barrels and rifle crates. (The remains of the white men rest in a nearby cemetery.) The symbolism was not lost. One of the world's great creatures, and one of its most resilient cultures, both nearly driven to oblivion because of a whim of Victorian European fashion.

On the way back from Kekerten, a pair of ringed seals made the mistake **21** of sticking their heads above the water near one of the boats. They were killed with two shots from a .222. I won't pretend there was anything romantic about the killings or what followed. The boat immediately pulled up to the edge of an ice floe to allow its passengers to disembark. In an instant, the seals were split up the bellies and Inuit began to eat, offal and all, sans benefit of the boiling pot. Ten minutes later, the snack was finished. The people continued home, leaving two bloodstains on the white ice and two discarded sealskins.

The skins are what stuck in my mind. It seemed like such a senseless **22** waste.

# Style and Structure

1. (a) "An Inuit hunter insisted I write this column." What effect does this opener have on you, the reader?
   (b) Make a list of ten words that the writer might have chosen instead of the verb "insisted." Why do you suppose he chose as he did? What impact does the word "insisted" have that those on your list do not?
2. (a) In paragraph 3, the writer describes seal meat as it is offered to him by the Inuit hunter: "he scooped up a piece that revealed too

much of its original anatomical function for sensibilities shaped by buying cellophane-packaged meat at the local Loblaws." What does the writer mean?

(b) How would you describe the tone here? What does this tone reflect about the writer himself? Why do you think he chose such a tone?

3. (a) Estabrook gives his **thesis statement** in paragraph 7: "Then tell your readers Inuit need to hunt seal." What are the effects of having someone other than the writer give the **thesis**? Mention at least three effects. (Hint: Consider the answer you have given in 2(b).)

(b) Do you believe that the delayed **thesis statement** in this case is a successful strategy? Why?

4. In paragraphs 8 to 11, the writer speaks of the beauty of Canada's Arctic and the kindness of the people who live there. What relationship do these paragraphs have to the **thesis**? Why do you think the writer includes them?

5. In paragraph 12, Estabrook begins to trace the history of Inuit fortunes. Why do you suppose he chose not to begin his essay with this piece of historical background?

6. Count the number of words in each sentence in paragraph 14. What would you say about the writer's ability to vary sentence lengths? Looking over the paragraph once more, would you say that he has also used a variety of structures?

7. (a) Paragraph 17 is pivotal in this essay. Read it once again, and describe your immediate reactions to the French friend referred to there.

(b) Compare your reaction to this woman with your reaction to the Inuit hunter introduced earlier in the essay. With whom do you more readily sympathize? How do you think the writer has prompted your reactions?

8. This essay uses a number of **organizational approaches** in order to achieve its particular effect. Identify areas that are primarily

   (i) description;
   (ii) comparison;
   (iii) cause and effect;
   (iv) narrative.

   Which **organizational approach** do you believe best typifies the entire essay? Give reasons for your answer.

9. (a) The last part of the essay, paragraphs 18 to 22, tells of the writer's last day in Pangnirtung. Summarize what points the writer is trying to make in this section.

(b) As a **conclusion**, this is a fairly lengthy one. Taking into account the points you made in (a), do you believe that the strategy is effective?

# Warm-up

This essay makes excellent (although brief) use of direct quotations to bring home to the reader central ideas. Experiment with the use of direct quotations by imagining an old-timer who could report the information given in paragraph 13, the last seven decades of Pangnirtung's development. Rewrite the information, putting it into the words of the imagined character instead of the narrator.

Read your composition to the class or members of a study group. Compare the effect of reported conversation with that of the narration used in this essay.

# Thinking and Writing

a. In paragraph 16 of his essay, Estabrook writes, "There is certainly no ecological explanation for why someone living in Liverpool or Lyons should object to a Pangnirtung hunter shooting a seal." And yet the Europeans do object, and the effects of their objections have drastically altered the way of life in Canada's Arctic.

It is said that we live in a global village, that with communications networks and modern technology, no part of the world is remote from any other part. What happens in Alice Springs, Australia, may have an effect on Montrealers, for instance. We are, in short, "in this together."

Take one issue of ecological importance, such as the burning of rain forests in South America, the hunting of elephants in Africa, the water shortage in the southern United States. Why should the issue you have chosen have any significance to the average Canadian citizen? For your essay, follow Estabrook's model, showing a concerned participant speaking out.

In order to research your topic, you might wish to consult with a magazine that has an ecological or conservation-minded approach, such as the one from which this essay was taken (*Equinox*).

b.      Make a list of the useful facts found in this essay. Once your list is completed, go back and rank the facts in order of least to greatest importance. From your list, develop the outline for an essay in which you argue for more understanding of the Inuit's hunting of seals and the effective promotion of the sealskin trade. Take as your **thesis statement** the words of the Inuit hunter who addressed Estabrook: "[The] Inuit need to hunt seal."

     After your first draft, check your paragraphs to see that you have provided colourful examples and variety in sentence length and structure. Be sure to use proper documentation, giving credit to the author of this essay.

**Audience:** someone who is in a position to influence policy in native affairs.

     Send a copy of your essay to the Department of Native Affairs and ask for comment.

# Where's the Bargain?

## by Susan Hirshorn

Most of us, at one time or another, have felt deceived by a misleading ad or sales pitch. The untrue merchandise description, the salesperson's misleading assurance, the fine print that disclaims an offer too good to be true — all are ways unscrupulous or negligent retailers dupe unwary consumers. Some of the scams eventually prompt complaints to Consumer and Corporate Affairs Canada's Marketing Practices Branch (MPB), the body that enforces federal legislation on deceptive marketing practices.  1

The MPB gets its authority to take action on complaints from the federal Competition Act, which forbids business people from making misleading "representations" to the public. (Several provinces, notably Quebec, also have legislation that further covers the consumer against misleading sales pitches.) A representation is a radio or TV commercial, printed ad, sign, or any literature included with a product or service. It can, in theory, also be a verbal statement from a salesperson, but proving that such a representation was made can be a tall order.  2

The number of complaints received annually by the MPB has increased steadily over the past few years. Last year, consumers sent in more than 12 000 of them. Most were general complaints, but a significant number of consumers said that retailers made misrepresentations by using comparisons to an "ordinary" selling price. For example, a retailer might sell an appliance at a price that "was" $100, but "now" is only $50.  3

While truthful comparative advertising can give you useful information and help you make more intelligent buying decisions, the tactic is open to abuse. The many consumer complaints about price comparisons have prompted an increasing number of convictions of retailers in court. The conviction statistics demonstrate that there's a lot of confusion among consumers and retailers as to what true "regular" and "sale" prices are. In fact, "sales" are so common these days that it's hard for the consumer to tell when a bargain is really a bargain.  4

Buyers should be wary of some retailers' comparative price tricks. One of the more common ploys is for a store to persuasively compare its own prices with those charged by competitors. Phrases such as "rock-bottom prices" and "best deal in town" may sound good, but they're illegal under the Competition Act. Specific prices don't even have to be mentioned. Take, for example,  5 the case of Wacky Wheatley's TV and Stereo of Mount Pearl, Newfoundland. The retailer stated in a radio commercial that "if you don't buy from Wacky Wheatley's, you will pay too much." Wacky was fined in 1987 because investigation by the MPB revealed that competitors sold the same item for less.

6      Even if the retailer's price *is* (for the moment) the lowest in town, the advertisements may still be misleading customers. Let's say a supermarket ad states, "You'll save with us," and accurately compares its prices with those of local competitors. If some of those competitors have a policy of immediately lowering prices as soon as better ones are advertised elsewhere, the ad could be misleading. Rather than take an advertiser's word on "lowest" prices, shop around, quote that low price to other dealers, and find your own bargains.

7      To avoid doing detailed, up-to-the-minute fact checking of competitors' prices, retailers often instead make comparisons with their own regular prices. In doing this, the store must not rely on ancient history. Advertisements should report recently established regular prices. Take, for example, a store that sold a camera for $700 in September and October, lowered the price to $500 in November, then raised it to $600 in December. If the retailer wants to offer the camera "on sale" for $500 again in January, he or she must not mislead customers into thinking the regular price is still $700. The store's true regular price would likely be $600. Some retailers believe that offering the item at the higher price for a period of, say, two months is sufficient to establish a regular selling price. However, the MPB has stated that a more accurate gauge is the actual quantity sold at that price. That leaves the definition of "regular prices" somewhat open to interpretation. To make things more clear, the House of Commons committee has proposed that the wording of the definition be reviewed.

8      Even when retailers make accurate comparisons with their own regular prices, you still may not be getting a bargain. If a store regularly sells a brand of cookware for twice its competitors' usual price and then holds a "50-percent-off" sale, you obviously won't be saving a cent. Had you shopped around before this apparent sale, you could have bought the cookware at the lower price from one of the store's competitors.

9      As well, sales offering comparisons with manufacturers' suggested retail prices may violate sections of the act. That's because most goods are never sold at those prices, which are intended only as a guideline for retailers. But if a merchant can prove that the goods are normally sold at the suggested retail price by other dealers in the area, the comparison is acceptable. Competitors' prices did not faze Vancouver's Stereo People of Canada Ltd. They offered stereos at "incredible" savings off suggested list prices, until the

MPB pointed out that those list prices were higher than the ordinary selling price in the area.

"At cost" prices are equally difficult to pin down; be skeptical when they're mentioned in advertisements. Consider Eastern Sports Limited of Saint John, New Brunswick. The retailer advertised the entire stock of bicycles on sale "at cost price." An MPB investigation found that the firm's cost for the bicycles was below the sale price. 10

Comparison shopping can be difficult with normal goods, but when the retailer is offering seconds at reduced prices, you may have trouble deciding if the item is worth its price. Seconds are imperfect merchandise with minimal flaws that don't affect the article's basic durability, "wearability," or appearance. To help consumers know the quality of the items they buy, all seconds advertising should indicate the nature and extent of the imperfections (such as minor defects or variations in colour). Of course, it's always possible for goods to get rough treatment in transit or on the shelves. Thus, the term "seconds" doesn't include goods soiled or damaged by wholesalers or retailers. However, if the retailer knowingly accepts flawed items from a supplier, they should always be identified as seconds, regardless of the price at which they are offered. 11

The price of a second is usually not a true reduction, because the quality is not as good as that of the regular item. Therefore, retailers shouldn't include the words "save" or "savings" in seconds advertisements. They may, however, compare the second and regular prices, as long as the regular price is identified as being for first-quality merchandise. (As with other comparatives, the first-quality regular price must have been established beforehand.) Here's an example of a typical seconds advertisement: "Seconds Boys' Jeans. If first-quality, price would be $12.98. XYZ Store price, each $10.38." 12

No matter how good a product is — or how low its price — it isn't a bargain unless you can find it. There's nothing more frustrating than rushing across town for an advertised special, only to learn that the store is out of stock. The MPB regards the "nonavailability of advertised bargains" to be an offence. Failing to stock enough items to cover the demand created by an advertised special can be a variation of the old "bait-and-switch" scam. In the classic version, the merchant lures customers into the store with a nonexistent advertised special. Once the buyers are in, he or she tries to switch them to a more expensive item. 13

Even if the merchant doesn't actively try to sell a costlier item, failure to stock enough of the sale item may be a violation in itself. The list of the accused is not limited to small-town retailers. In May 1987, the MPB won 14 a conviction against Air Canada for failing to supply a reasonable quantity of advertised bargain seats for flights to Florida. The company was fined $15 000 (and is appealing the conviction). Some Toronto-area Chrysler dealers got an even worse scorching. After failing to provide an adequate supply of K-cars to support sale advertising, the 21 dealers were fined a total of $132 000. (This is a relatively large total fine. Most fines are much smaller.)

15    The critical term here is "reasonable quantity." Exactly how much is reasonable in the eyes of the courts depends on the size and category of the retailer and the type of merchandise in question.

16    Limited quantity is a risk consumers face with the "limited-time offer." Retailers often advertise such an offer to encourage you to snap up a product quickly. This tactic may be used with seasonal items (snow throwers, for example) as an "opener" to create momentum for a marketing campaign. As well, the limited-time offer is often applied to items the retailer has not previously sold — an introductory deal. A typical advertisement might run as follows: "XYZ Brand Snow Thrower, $699.00. After November 10, our XYZ Store regular price will be $750.00." An alternative wording — less risky because it's less specific — is, "For three weeks only. XYZ Store price: $699.00."

17    In order to avoid misleading consumers, the XYZ retailer has to be careful that the price and time predictions implied in the advertisement are accurate. That is, it all hinges on how long the product is available at the sale price. The XYZ Company must do three things. First, as mentioned above, it should ensure that it has enough snow throwers to supply consumer demand until November 10. (The dealer may choose at a later date to hold the sale over "due to popular demand," but should again ensure availability of the product.) Second, to be true to its time prediction, XYZ company should raise the price of the item to the regular price ($750) as soon as the sale is finished. Third, it should maintain that higher price to allow it to become established as a regular price.

18    Despite the retailer's good intentions, there may be legitimate reasons for not supplying the goods. Bad weather or strikes may have delayed delivery. Advertising foul-ups may have occurred. The best way for retailers to avoid prosecution is to prove that they offered to compensate customers for their inconvenience. One acceptable form of compensation (according to the legislation) is substituting a product of equal or better value for the advertised special. Another is the offer of a "rain check": a written promise to provide the advertised special at a later date. (Since seconds are "off-batches," and may be limited in quantity, getting a rain check if supplies run out can be

a problem. In that case, the retailer should be willing to provide you with comparable first-quality goods.)

However, the rain check has become so common that we wonder whether some retailers are deliberately using it as a legal way to practise bait and switch. Klaus Decker, director of MPB, suspects that some retailers may indeed be abusing the rain-check defence. "But," he adds, "it's difficult to prove in a court of law that the retailer's actions were deliberate." Deceptive tactics are even more difficult to prove if the store owner has stated in advertisements that quantities are limited. Your best defence against such abuses is to avoid buying from stores that always seem to have more rain checks on hand than advertised specials. If these merchants lose enough business, they may feel compelled to clean up their acts. 19

Whether it's a deceptive price comparison or a scarce special that lurks behind the advertisement you read, the lesson is the same. Be skeptical of bargains and come-ons that seem too good to be true. And if you catch local merchants at pricing trickery, report it to your nearest Marketing Practices Branch field office. They're listed in the blue pages of your telephone book under Consumer and Corporate Affairs Canada. 20

# Style and Structure

1. (a) Beginning with paragraph 5 and ending with paragraph 19, identify the **topic sentence** in each paragraph. (Be particularly careful in your examination of paragraph 5.)
   (b) Based on your analysis of these **topic sentences,** what two main points does Hirshorn want to convey to her reader?
   (c) Identify a sentence in the **conclusion** (paragraph 20) that presents an accurate summary of the main points of this essay.
   (d) Do any of the paragraphs or sentences in the introduction (paragraphs 1 to 4) qualify as an appropriate **thesis statement** for this essay? Give a reason for each rejection.
   (e) What is the effect on the reader of not presenting a **thesis statement** until the **conclusion**? Does it benefit or harm the reader's understanding of the **thesis**?
   (f) As it stands, what purpose does the introduction have?
2. Which organizational format does this essay employ? Cause and effect? Argument? Classification? Process analysis? Compare/contrast? Support

your answer with evidence from the essay. ("Organizational Approaches," pp. 301–302, will help you in answering this question.)

3.   When using this format, writers must do three things to help the reader:
   (i) clearly distinguish all the categories to be considered;
   (ii) arrange the categories in a logical order that avoids confusion;
   (iii) use **transitions** to act as guides.

   (a) Review the **topic sentences** you identified in 1(a). Name the seven categories of "deceptive price comparison[s] or . . . scarce special[s]" that Hirshorn presents. How clearly has she distinguished each for the reader?

   (b) Review the order in which the seven categories are presented. Does this order of presentation help the reader understand and solve the complexities of making intelligent buying decisions? Give specific evidence to justify your answer.

   (c) Examine any three **topic sentences** in the body of the essay. How does each establish the relationship of its ideas to those in the paragraph preceding it? What effect does the use of these **transitions** have upon the reader?

4.   **Conclusions** can serve a number of purposes. What two things does Hirshorn do in this **conclusion**? Is it an effective **conclusion**, given her intended reader and her overall purpose in the essay? Justify your answer.

# Warm-up

1.   Working with a group of three or four classmates, select one of the types of misleading ads described in the essay (e.g., comparative price tricks). Have each person in the group look through a different newspaper to find one or two good examples of an ad that might be using this type of trick. As a group, select from the ads you have gathered the one that seems the most suspect.

   Write a one-paragraph explanation of how this ad might be misleading the public.

   **Audience:** someone who has not read the original essay and may not be aware of the trick.

   Use materials from the group's paragraphs to prepare an oral presentation on this ad. (Use an overhead to display the ad itself.) After finishing the presentation, rewrite your own paragraph into a final draft.

2.   Hirshorn writes that "truthful comparative advertising can give you useful information" (paragraph 4). Select any two ads from a national magazine that present a similar product (e.g., two different cars). Write a one-

paragraph explanation of the usefulness of the text in the two ads in helping the reader make a decision.

**Audience:** someone who might be emotionally swayed by the ads.

Before revising your paragraph into its final form, show some of your classmates the ads, along with your paragraph, and discuss your conclusions with them.

# Thinking and Writing

a. The writer opens her essay by saying, "Most of us, at one time or another, have felt deceived by a misleading ad or sales pitch."

Write an essay in which you warn unsuspecting buyers about a case that happened to you or someone you know. Use the third person (rather than "I") and try to be as objective as you can.

**Audience:** someone who might fall prey to the same deception.

Send a copy of your final draft to the Canadian Association of Consumers.

b. Review the television commercials you have seen in the past few weeks. Jot down a point or two about each one that stands out in your mind. Try to identify any aspects of each that might mislead a consumer. Does the ad present cold, objective facts about the product, or does it promise a life filled with fun, friends, adventure, excitement, or passion, if only you buy the product? How does it try to attract you to its product?

When you have finished your review, write a classification essay that explains the ways in which television ads may mislead people, even if they say nothing about price.

**Audience:** someone responsible for television advertising.

Send a copy of your final draft to the public relations department of the company that produces an ad you find particularly offensive. You can find its address in one of the trade indexes in the reference section of your library.

# Policewomen on Patrol

## by Cynthia Brouse

1   On a Saturday night in October 1985, two constables in a patrol car cruised through the quiet Montreal suburb of Dorval, on the lookout for a man who had been seen loitering in backyards. Suddenly the patrol car's driver saw a man rise up out of a clump of shrubbery and aim a rifle at them. Before the officers could take cover, a bullet shattered the rear window of the car, and the constable in the driver's seat died instantly, shot in the neck.

2   She was Jacinthe Fyfe, 25, and the first Canadian policewoman to die in the line of duty. Her death is dramatic evidence of women's new share in the fight against crime.

3   Traditionally, policewomen have worked behind the scenes, rarely being assigned to situations that might involve them in violence. Now, women are valuable additions to *all* phases of law enforcement, and especially to what many officials call "the hub of police activities" — patrol duty.

4   Until the early 1970s, only a few Canadian policewomen were entrusted with patrol duties. Today, all 2200 perform the same work as their male counterparts: they routinely patrol beats, operate in vice squads, handle undercover work, and serve in traffic control. In 1986, Const. Rose Budimir of the Downsview detachment of the Ontario Provincial Police became its first female motorcycle officer. Constable Cheryl Schneider pilots a Twin Otter airplane to cover her beat among the remote Indian reserves of the Hudson Bay and James Bay coasts. Constable Kathy McLaren patrols Vancouver's Stanley Park on horseback. In British Columbia, 377 out of 5780 police are women, the highest percentage in the nation.

5   True, the shift in policewomen's status has not come without controversy. Many male officers have stubbornly resisted the assignment of women to "field" duties on the grounds that they are "emotional" and physically unfit for the rigours of patrol. But the resistance is steadily ebbing in the face of day-to-day evidence.

6   Constables Kimberley Greenwood and Theresa Rynn, for instance, were staked out at a bank that had been robbed twice by a man wearing a ski mask. Greenwood, posing as a teller, and Rynn, who waited outside in an unmarked car, kept in constant radio contact. When Greenwood saw the robber enter the bank and vault over the tellers' counter, she alerted her partner.

Rynn rushed into the bank with her gun drawn to find that Greenwood had already grabbed the robber. In seconds the two women had him handcuffed and were soon hauling him outside to a waiting police cruiser.

When Geramy Field was with the Vancouver Police Department's canine    7
unit, she followed her dog across a busy intersection in pursuit of a six-foot-five-inch, 210-pound (195-cm, 95-kg) car thief. Turning into an alley, she saw the suspect kicking the dog. Detective Field grabbed the man's arms, pinned him against a wall and handcuffed him.

Policewomen were working in Canada as early as 1911, when Edmonton    8
became the first city in the country to hire "lady officers." Vancouver, Toronto, and Winnipeg followed soon after; however, in these cities women were, for the most part, limited to answering phones, searching, escorting, and guarding female prisoners, and once in a while posing as prostitutes in undercover operations. Policewomen in Canada were not routinely given firearms until the early 1970s. In 1974, the first troop of women began training at the RCMP "Depot" Division in Regina.

Until about ten years ago, many female candidates for police forces were    9
eliminated by minimum-size requirements. Female recruits in Ottawa, for example, had to be five feet ten inches (178 cm) tall. In 1977, the RCMP adopted an evaluation system for recruits that placed less emphasis on stature and more emphasis on education, experience, age, and physical fitness. Now most police forces use similar systems, and many, such as Ottawa, Saskatoon, and St. John's, Newfoundland, have abolished height restrictions altogether, requiring instead that candidates meet height-to-weight ratios.

Little by little, male resistance toward female officers is moderating. The    10
men in the force realize that in many cases, particularly those involving young children, getting information from victims of sexual attacks, and defusing family free-for-alls, policewomen can be a definite asset. "Policewomen often have a greater ability to deal with areas of extreme sensitivity," says Phil Crosby-Jones, director of the British Columbia Police Academy.

Officers in the field point to women's preference for verbal mediation over    11
physical aggression. Norman Wickdahl, president of the Winnipeg Police Association, says, "The women I've worked with were able to talk their way around situations that may have resulted in an altercation if my partner had been a man."

Female officers command as much respect from the public as their male    12
colleagues, but some experts feel citizens stay calmer with women. Deputy Chief Keith Cole of the Dartmouth, Nova Scotia, police department explains:

"Most men will not hit a woman. In something like a barroom brawl, a woman may be able to get things under control more quickly than a male officer can. Sometimes a male officer walks in like he's the macho guy. But if a woman officer walks in, the party seems to cool down."

13    Everywhere, law-enforcement officials are closely scrutinizing traditional "tough" attitudes to policing. They are finding that skill in personal relations may be just as important as physical strength in equipping an officer to cope with potentially dangerous situations. Inspector Walt Bennett of the Royal Newfoundland Constabulary — the only force in North America whose police officers don't carry guns — points out that all good officers, male and female, use force only as a last resort. "Police officers need good communication skills — they have to rely on their wits."

14    Most professional law officers applaud the work of policewomen. A study by University of Manitoba criminologist Rick Linden showed that female police officers did their jobs as well as male officers — and that their supervisors rated them highly. Says Keith Cole, "They perform excellently. We're no longer hiring policemen and policewomen — but police officers."

# Style and Structure

1. (a) What is the relationship of the first two paragraphs to the central **thesis** of this essay?
   (b) What is the effect of concealing the driver's identity until the second paragraph?
   (c) For what type of reader would this opening be effective? Why?
   (d) Identify this essay's **thesis statement**. Does it summarize all of the points made by the **topic sentences** of the body's individual paragraphs?
2. (a) Identify the two paragraphs in this essay that do not have a **concluding sentence**.
   (b) Write an appropriate **concluding sentence** for each.
   (c) How would the sentences you have written help the reader?
3.    Brouse makes extensive use of examples in the body of this essay.
   (a) Identify three different points that she supports by use of examples.
   (b) For each point identified, explain how she prepares the reader to understand the significance of the examples used to support it.
   (c) Comment on the appropriateness of the examples offered in each case. How does each help the reader to understand the point Brouse is trying to convey?

4.  In the last half of the body of her essay, the writer depends heavily on the testimony of experts.
    (a) Identify three paragraphs in which such quotations are used.
    (b) Identify the **topic sentence** in each of these paragraphs.
    (c) Comment on the way each quotation contributes to the point being made in its paragraph. Is each appropriate?
    (d) Was it a good idea for Brouse to include the credentials of each person quoted? What effect does this strategy achieve?
5.  (a) How do the statements made in the final paragraph help the reader grasp the significance of the points made in the body? Do they form an effective **conclusion** for the essay? Why?
    (b) How do the statements made here compare to the **thesis statement** in the introduction?
6.  Identify three **topic sentences** in which Brouse uses words or phrases to make **transitions** from the ideas of the preceding paragraph. In each case, explain how the **transition** helps the reader.
7.  Identify two places in the essay where Brouse uses dashes to set off groups of words. Explain the effect of each. If this is an effective technique, why would she not use even more dashes?

# Warm-up

1.  Write a list of the assets that officials say policewomen bring to the job (paragraphs 10 to 13). Make another list of the characteristics attributed to policemen in the same paragraphs. Compare these lists to those written by two or three others in the class: try to account for any differences in your respective lists.

    Write a three- or four-paragraph essay in which you explain whether these characteristics are typical of the behaviours taught to all men and women in our culture.

    **Audience:** someone who has never thought very seriously about these differences in behaviour.
2.  Discuss with several of your classmates the positive behaviours and attitudes that each sex could learn from the other in our culture. Write a short essay on the topic.

    **Audience:** an adult who has been exposed to our culture's typical sex-role training.

# Thinking and Writing

a. Identify another occupation that has traditionally been associated with one sex (e.g., nurse, electronics technician, day-care worker, construction worker). Write an essay that explains

  (i) the reasons one sex has dominated this occupation;

  (ii) the benefits the other sex could bring to it;

  (iii) suggestions for the process by which the other sex could be encouraged to enter this occupation.

  **Audience:** someone who knows of the occupation but may never have questioned its being dominated by one sex.

b. Make two lists of jobs, one under the heading "Predominantly Male" and the other under the heading "Predominantly Female." Examine each list to identify patterns or types of occupations that attract primarily one sex.

  Write an essay that explains why the various types of occupations have traditionally been associated with one sex and not the other. Be sure to discuss the role of stereotyping, cultural training, and biological differences, in addition to any other factors you can identify.

  **Audience:** someone who has never considered this situation.

  Send a copy of your final draft to either your school newspaper (if there is one) or a newspaper in your community. Ask the editor whether the paper would be interested in publishing it.

# If You Toss In a Dollar, He'll Do Tricks

*The Globe and Mail*

Miami's Metrozoo has scored a remarkable coup by securing for exhibit a specimen of the world's most dangerous creature. Look at the menace in those beady eyes, the destructive potential of the opposing thumb; shudder at the unappetizing sight of hairless skin and the clumsy — albeit infrequent — attempts at locomotion on two limbs. (Stand back from the cage, sonny; annoy this one and he'll bite your head off.)   1

In the remarkable rush to the *Homo sapiens* exhibit, the lion has been spurned, left to prowl his lonely cage and ponder bitterly the ironies that can so quickly depose him as king of the beasts. Tigers, gorillas, bears, and elephants have also been left far behind in the popularity listings as the crowds hurry along to the Urban Man enclosure to gawk from a safe distance at the most treacherous of beasts.   2

The exhibit drew a crowd of 10 309 over a single weekend, and visitors are reported to have waited for hours for an opportunity to see man in his natural habitat, reading the newspaper, eating, drinking, sleeping, watching television, and using a telephone.   3

We can only guess how his keepers feel about having to clean out his cage — though any parent who has picked his way gingerly over the floor of a teenager's bedroom will have some idea. For the moment there is only one specimen in captivity, but zoo officials are probably looking around for a suitable mate. Trouble is, they're like pandas — very fastidious sometimes, especially when being watched by large crowds. Still, throw them a couple of bamboo shoots and a bottle of bubbly and hope for the best.   4

There have been protests, of course, about the cruelty of keeping any creature in a confined area where it must watch television and answer the phone. It's a jungle in there. No wonder they go wild and develop a taste for fermented fruit juice. Since this particular specimen pulled in $10 000 for a weekend stint at Metrozoo, he has not exactly been gnawing the bars and howling for freedom.   5

It may strike us as odd that members of a single species should line up for a look at one of their own kind, but we must suppose this is one of the very few situations in which a good, hard stare will not be resented.   6

Although *Homo sapiens* is far from well understood, he does have a surprisingly elaborate social structure in which, among other taboos, eyes are averted in subway cars. The fully authorized ogle accounts for the great success of the Miami exhibit.

7    As a zoological experiment, however, it would have been far more interesting to set things up so that the regular zoo animals could stroll, or slither, past the Urban Man cage and enjoy the simple diversion of inspecting a real *Homo sapiens* — perhaps throwing him peanuts and cigarette butts, laughing at his antics, and feeling thankful that he was safely under lock and key.

## Style and Structure

1. (a) What would be the likely reaction of the average reader to the first sentence of paragraph 1? Why is this an effective way to open an article in a popular newspaper? Would the same type of opening be suitable for a formal essay?

   (b) At what point did you first realize that the zoo exhibit is a man? What effect upon the reader does the author wish to achieve by withholding this information?

2. Identify the sentence in paragraph 2 that best states the **thesis** of the essay.

3. Why does the author choose to present the information contained in paragraph 3 before making the other points contained in the body of the essay?

4. One type of humour involves describing something in language one would normally use to describe something quite different (i.e., describing a small canoe in language normally reserved for an ocean liner). Identify passages in paragraphs 4 and 5 that use this technique.

5. Irony is a humorous device that involves saying one thing and meaning the opposite. Identify passages in paragraph 5 that use irony to make a point.

6. What effect does the writer wish to achieve in paragraph 6 by referring to himself and his readers in the first person ("us", "we") and to *Homo sapiens* in the third person ("he")? Why would he want to create this effect?

7. (a) What serious point about human nature does the author make in paragraph 7 even though he uses a humorous approach?

(b) What devices does the author use to get the reader to accept this unpleasant comment about the human species?

(c) Does paragraph 7 form an effective **conclusion** for this essay?

# Warm-up

1. In a group with three to five of your classmates, develop a short (five-
   minute) skit that portrays two parent animals taking their children to
   see the *Homo sapiens* display at the zoo. Perform the skit for the rest
   of the class.

2. Keep a point-form journal of all the activities you and your family perform
   at home in any two-hour period. Then write a report on the activities
   as if you were an anthropologist or biologist observing a different species.
   Draw conclusions about the significance of the behaviour you observe.

   **Audience:** a group of professional biologists wanting to learn about a
   new species.

   Working with four or five classmates, select one or two of your reports
   for presentation to the rest of the class.

# Thinking and Writing

a. By using humour, the writer of this essay was able to get many readers
   to accept, or at least think about, a number of concepts about *Homo
   sapiens* that they might have rejected immediately in a serious essay.

   Choose a controversial topic and write a humorous essay that would
   have a similar effect upon your readers.

   **Audience:** the same "average" reader as the one for whom the author
   of "If You Toss In a Dollar, He'll Do Tricks" wrote.

b. Write an essay in which you argue either for or against the proposition
   contained in the last paragraph of the article, that the other animals in
   the world would be better off if *Homo sapiens* were "safely under lock
   and key."

   **Audience:** someone who would disagree with your stand on the topic.

   If you are in favour of the proposition, send a copy of your essay
   to a group that is damaging animal populations; if you are against it,
   send a copy of your essay to an environmentalists' group.

# The Kiddie-Vote Campaign

## by Stephen Lequire and Mathew Ingram

1    Ian Hunter discovered "oppression" seven years ago. He was then the twenty-year-old editor of the Douglas College student newspaper in Burnaby, British Columbia. Following what he calls a "personality clash" with a female campus newspaper colleague, Mr. Hunter became the target of a Canadian University Press Commission inquiry into alleged oppression of his co-worker. "It was eventually resolved that Ian Hunter was a sexist tyrant," he confesses. "When you're slammed by a feminist collective and branded a woman-hater, you develop a better understanding of the issue of oppression." Having confronted his own sexism, he says, he developed a keen awareness of other forms of discrimination. Now a freelance journalist, he has of late focussed on another kind of social oppression — ageism.

2    Children, says Mr. Hunter, 27, are the most disadvantaged members of our society. They have the lowest income and the fewest rights. The root of their problems, he observes, is that they play no active role in the political process. In short, they cannot vote. For the last year or so, Mr. Hunter has championed the cause of voting rights for children. So far, his efforts appear to have done little to advance an idea many adults consider ridiculous.

3    But he has succeeded in attaining a measure of notoriety he hopes will enable him to be taken seriously. For starters, the crusader managed to parlay a discussion with a CBC producer on a Toronto subway into a freelance radio documentary that aired on the network's *Ideas* program. Then, *Globe and Mail* columnist June Callwood brought him to further national attention with a profile of him and a story about his campaign.

4    Mr. Hunter, who produces a weekly program on children's issues for Vancouver co-op radio station CFRO, contends that because Section 3 of the Canadian Charter of Rights and Freedoms guarantees the vote to all Canadian citizens, all youngsters ought to be included. He argues that as the bulk of Canada's population becomes older, children will become an increasingly oppressed minority. Beyond political clout, the franchise would afford children an opportunity to learn about democracy in a way that is just not possible in what he calls the "fascist totalitarian system called school."

5    Vancouver lawyer David Cruickshank, who co-authored *Admittance Restricted*, a 1975 Canadian Council on Children and Youth report on society's treatment of the young, says he and his colleagues opted not to push for

a youth vote in their recommendations only because they feared being branded a "loony group." Mr. Cruickshank thinks Mr. Hunter's proposal is rather extreme, but he suspects a charter challenge could obtain voting rights for children as young as thirteen. Christopher Harris, a Vancouver lawyer and Simon Fraser University political science instructor, thinks a case could be made for extending the vote to employed, tax-paying sixteen-year-olds, for example. However, he notes the preamble to the charter imposes "reasonable limits" on the guarantee of specific rights, and he speculates the courts would see age restrictions as a reasonable limit on voting rights.

Edmonton South MP James Edwards notes there was a controversy recently    6
when the federal Conservative party lowered the age for voting delegates at candidate-selection meetings to fourteen. "We had some problems with that, but it went through and I do know of at least one riding where fourteen-year-olds were bussed in to take part in the selection process." (That has also happened in several Liberal ridings, he hastens to add.) "This raises the question of whether the children should be prevented from selecting a candidate in a national vote when they have done so already at a nomination meeting," he says. "I suppose the theory is, it's a good way of initiating younger people to the political process, but I certainly don't think they should be able to vote federally at fourteen."

Vancouver lawyer Harris speculates that, without age restrictions, Canada    7
might have to look at using some sort of competency test for voters. And according to Todd Ducharme, executive director of the Centre for Constitutional Studies at the University of Alberta, the concept of a voter-competency test is fraught with legal, political, and ethical hazards. "Who would decide what determines competency?" wonders Mr. Ducharme. "The end result would be that some segments of the population would be disenfranchised — most likely the poor, those with lower education levels, the marginalized, and so on." He thinks it would be too much like the literacy requirements and poll taxes used in the old South of the United States, which effectively disenfranchised blacks. "Even if there was only a competency test for kids, it would no doubt favour middle- and upper-class kids, [because] they have access to a [better] education system, the social benefits, and so on."

Although virtually all Canadian citizens over eighteen have the right to    8
vote in federal, provincial, and municipal elections today, enfranchisement in Canada does not have a particularly democratic history. Throughout the 1800s, the vote was restricted to male property owners. Women were not granted the federal vote until 1918, and not all females were able to vote provincially until 1940. Many immigrants faced voting restrictions until the last of these

barriers came down in 1948, when Japanese Canadians were federally enfranchised. The Inuit and status Indians were barred from voting federally until 1950 and 1960 respectively, while nonstatus Indians slowly gained voting rights in all provinces, ending with Quebec in 1969. A year later, Ottawa reduced the voting age for all Canadians from 21 to 18.

9    Despite Mr. Hunter's efforts, it does not seem likely the voting age will drop much further. Even youthful political activists are at best lukewarm to the idea. Laurel Lawson, vice-president of B.C.'s Young New Democrats, says, "[Mr. Hunter] presented the idea to us, but it wasn't really given serious consideration. We have more immediate problems, such as youth unemployment, to deal with."

10   The reaction of most Canadians to the child-vote crusade was perhaps best summed up by a "letter-to-the-editor" writer who had the following tongue-in-cheek observation to make after reading the Callwood column in the *Globe*: "We cannot claim to live in a truly humane democracy until the day the vote is extended to the following disenfranchised minorities: the unborn, the recently deceased, small furry pets, and dolphins."

## Style and Structure

The authors of this essay faced a problem: they wanted to explain in a fairly serious way "an idea many adults consider ridiculous." They had to do two things: avoid arousing the reader's preconceived ideas and provide enough evidence to convince the reader of the idea's serious implications.

1. (a) What advantages, if any, do the authors gain by opening the essay with the story of Hunter's earlier experience with another form of "oppression"?

   (b) How does the order in which they present their points in the opening paragraph help them?

   (c) What is the central **thesis** of this essay:

     (i) Mr. Hunter's story?

     (ii) the definition of "kiddie vote"?

     (iii) the progress toward giving children the right to vote?

     (iv) the implications of giving children the right to vote?

   Justify your answer with evidence from the body of the essay.

Identify, if you can, the sentence that states this **thesis**. If you cannot, write a sentence that provides an appropriate **thesis statement**. Does including such a sentence help or hinder the reader's understanding of the ideas presented in the body? Why?

(d) How does the order of the sentences in paragraph 2 prepare the reader to consider the **thesis** seriously?

2.   Paragraph 3 gives no direct information about the arguments for or against children's voting rights. Why might the authors have decided to include it at this point in the essay?

3. (a) Examine the authors' presentation of Hunter's arguments in paragraph 4. Does the order in which they are presented help or detract from the reader's acceptance of these arguments? Why?

   (b) What reasons might the authors have for placing these arguments in the middle of the essay?

4. (a) How many authorities do the authors cite in this essay? How does this number affect the reader's attitude to the topic?

   (b) How often do the authors name the professions of the people they cite? Why might they choose to refer to them by profession rather than by some other characteristic, such as the number of children they have dealt with in their jobs?

   (c) Suppose the authors had not sought out the opinions of these experts and had simply presented the points in terms of "we think. . . . " What differences would there have been in the reader's acceptance of the ideas presented? Do your conclusions support or contradict the advice often given that a writer should never use "I" or "we" in a formal essay or business report?

   (d) Sometimes, inexperienced writers introduce every quotation with "says" (e.g., Smith says, " . . . ." Jones, on the other hand, says, " . . . ."). List the different words that the authors of this essay use to introduce quotations. How does this variation in word choice help the reader?

5.   Paragraph 8 makes no mention at all of giving children the right to vote. How does it relate to the central **thesis** of the essay? What purpose does it serve?

6. (a) Do the last two paragraphs of the essay provide an adequate and appropriate **conclusion**? Support your answer with specific references to the body of the essay.

   Write a different **conclusion** for this essay, drawing conclusions from the opinions of the experts cited as well as from the public's reaction to the idea of giving children the vote.

Which **conclusion**, yours or the original, creates in the reader a reaction that is more in keeping with the body of the essay? Why do you think so?

# Warm-up

1. Working with a group of three or four classmates, identify a number of political issues that would be of interest to people between the ages of fourteen and eighteen. On your own, write the text for a short campaign brochure aimed at this age group. (Use a fictitious political party and candidate.)

   Exchange your brochure with the others in your original group. Discuss the ways in which their appeals to readers differ from yours.

2. Make two lists, one about the dangers of irresponsible behaviour by the driver of a car and one about the dangers of irresponsible behaviour by a voter (or group of voters). Based on your lists, write a four- or five-paragraph compare/contrast essay in which you draw conclusions about the ages at which people should be given these responsibilities.
   **Audience:** someone in the age group of fourteen to eighteen.

   Read several essays written by classmates. How does the way each of them organized his or her essay compare with your own method? Discuss ways your respective papers could be improved.

# Thinking and Writing

a. Write an essay in which you outline your stance on giving children the vote. Support your stand by describing what our country would be like if all children were given the right to vote. (If you prefer, write a humorous essay on the topic.)
   **Audience:** someone whose opinion on the topic would be strongly opposed to yours.

b. Most of the arguments that could be used against giving children the right to vote have been used at some time or other against giving it to the people mentioned in paragraph 8 of the essay. It was once argued, for example, that women should not be allowed to vote because they would make emotional decisions rather than thinking through the issues; moreover, it was argued, they were not aware of the issues, as, of course, all men were.

Write an essay in which you argue for or against lowering the voting age to fourteen. If you oppose the idea, try to think of ways of presenting your arguments so they could not give rise to the criticism "But they said the same thing about . . . ." If you support the idea, try to meet and counter your critics' comments in advance.

**Audience:** someone between the ages of fourteen and sixteen.

Give a copy of your final draft to someone in this age group and discuss your arguments with that person.

# Earth's Biggest Blast

## by Walter Sullivan

1    A Czechoslovakian scientist has come up with a new explanation for what was by far the largest — and most mysterious — explosion ever recorded on earth.

2    The blast, high in the air over the remote region of Podkamennaya in Siberia on June 30, 1908, blew down trees for 40 to 50 kilometres in all directions. Horses 650 kilometres away were blown off their feet, and residents of a trading station 65 kilometres away were knocked unconscious and suffered flash burns.

3    The explosion was equivalent to a ten- to fifteen-megaton nuclear device and devastated an area of about four thousand square kilometres.

4    Investigation of the event was hampered because its location was so remote that no scientist reached the area until nineteen years later, although probably no phenomenon in history has evoked so much scientific speculation, ranging from suggestions of spontaneous nuclear explosions to theories of alien space ships crashing to earth, and falling comet heads.

5    The comet-head theory has now received support through a little-noticed proposal from L. Kresak of the Slovak Academy of Sciences in Bratislava, Czechoslovakia. He suggests that the blast occurred when a huge "boulder" shed by Comet Encke exploded in the atmosphere. Mr. Kresak noticed that the June 30 explosion coincided with the peak of an annual meteor shower. Such showers of "shooting stars" occur when the earth passes through debris left by a comet that has been partially torn apart during repeated close passes by the sun.

6    The shower that peaks on June 30 each year originates in the constellation Taurus and is attributed to debris from Encke, a comet that orbits the sun every 3.3 years.

7    Mr. Kresak believes that the components of comet fragments that make comets and their tails glow are gradually boiled away by solar heat, leaving only "cometary boulders." These, he reported in the Bulletin of the Astronomical Institute of Czechoslovakia, probably constitute "an overwhelming majority" of interplanetary objects one to a hundred metres in diameter.

8    According to his hypothesis, such an object would become so hot during its plunge through the atmosphere that it would explode in a catastrophic

manner. When large meteorites hit the earth, they generate explosions sufficient to gouge out craters, but no crater was formed by the Siberian blast, possibly because the "boulder" was not large enough to do so.

Scientists have noted many features of the 1908 blast that resemble those    9
of a powerful nuclear explosion. According to an account in the British journal *Nature*, a small amount of excess radioactivity has been found in the area.

Furthermore, the trees at ground zero — the point directly below the    10
explosion — were not blown down but were stripped of bark and branches like telephone poles, an effect also seen at Hiroshima after the atomic bomb.

In 1967, the prestigious scientific journal *Soviet Physics — Doklady* pub-    11
lished an analysis by Alexei V. Zolotov of the Ioffe Physio-Technical Institute of the Soviet Academy of Sciences, who had accompanied an expedition to the site. He concluded that the effects were those of a thermonuclear explosion, such as that of a hydrogen bomb. The nuclear-explosion idea was again argued in 1975 by Prof. Ari Ben-Menahem of the Weizmann Institute in Israel. He analyzed records of shock waves recorded around the world both in the atmosphere and within the earth — the entire planet trembled from the blast — and concluded that the explosion was probably "an extra-terrestrial nuclear missile" of ten to fifteen megatons.

The theory that the blast was the explosion of a nuclear-powered space    12
ship was revived in reports widely circulated by Tass, the Soviet press agency. Despite all these arguments, most scientists have found the nuclear-explosion idea far-fetched and prefer such explanations as the fall of a comet head.

But, in 1965, the Nobel laureate Willard Libby and two colleagues questioned    13
the comet theory because no comet had been seen approaching the earth. They suggested, instead, the fall of an "antirock" — a meteorite formed of antimatter.

Each atomic particle has a twin that is identical but opposite in such char-    14
acteristics as electrical charge. This is the particle of antimatter, and when such a particle meets one of matter, they annihilate each other in a violent burst of gamma rays.

This reaction would account for the explosion and also create a large amount    15
of radioactive carbon, which should later have become incorporated into the trees in the blast area. Dr. Libby and his colleagues found a small excess of the carbon in rings formed in two trees during 1909, but they concluded that it was not sufficient to support the antimatter idea.

In 1973, two scientists at the Center for Relativity Theory of the University    16
of Texas proposed that the event was caused by a tiny black hole, a hypothetical

object compressed to such density that its gravity would not permit the escape of light. Such an object, they reasoned, would go through the earth.

17    Their much-publicized proposal helped bring the concept of black holes wide public attention, but did not gain any scientific adherents.

18    The most widely accepted view of comet heads is the "dirty snowball" hypothesis of Fred L. Whipple at the Smithsonian Astrophysical Observatory in Cambridge, Massachussetts. He sees them as a mixture of dust and frozen gases but adds that, although he is not convinced of Mr. Kresak's boulder theory, he "has an open mind."

19    While the comet-fragment proposal is the front-runner at the moment, the mystery may never be settled to the satisfaction of everyone. At least not, as Professor Ben-Menahem has pointed out, until there is a recurrence. In that case, though the mystery may be cleared up, the other consequences may be disastrous, especially if the explosion occurs over an inhabited area and is mistaken for a nuclear attack.

# Style and Structure

1.    Here is another possible opening statement for this essay:

> A Czechoslovakian scientist has introduced a new theory about the 1908 explosion in Podkamennaya, Siberia.

From the point of view of the reader, would this introduction be as effective as the one in the essay? Give reasons for your answer.

2.    What purposes do paragraphs 2 and 3 serve in the introduction? How does Sullivan's choice of words and illustrations heighten the dramatic effect?

3.    List in order the different explanations for the explosion presented in the essay.
   (a) Can you detect a logical reason why the writer has presented the theories in the order he has?
   (b) Underline the first sentence in each explanation. How does this sentence function in relation to the rest of the explanation?
   (c) Where does the sentence appear in the section dealing with antimatter?

4.    How does paragraph 18 help to unify the essay?

5.    In the first sentence of the concluding paragraph, the writer summarizes the essay. For what purposes does he use the remainder of his **conclusion**?

# Warm-up

Working with a group of three or four classmates, use the reference section of your library to identify another mysterious unexplained event. (Make certain that you do not choose one that another group has already selected.) You may have to ask the librarian for assistance.

Have each person in the group write a short account of this mysterious event. The group can then use these accounts to put together a short oral presentation to the rest of the class. Challenge the class to come up with a good explanation for the event.

Revise your account into a final draft.

# Thinking and Writing

a.  Write an essay in which you either support or refute the proposition that the Podkamennaya blast was the result of extra-terrestrial visitation. Although you may never have heard of this explosion before, there is quite a large amount of material written on it. The newspapers, magazines, and books in your library should provide extensive information. (Be sure to use such aids as *The Reader's Guide to Periodical Literature*, *The Canadian Index*, or the index to a major newspaper to save yourself time and effort.)
    **Audience**: an average "nonscientific" reader who is aware only of the sensationalized aspects of the blast and yet would oppose your position on the proposition.

b.  Write an essay in which you argue either for or against the theory that the earth has been visited by extra-terrestrial beings. You will find such books as *Chariots of the Gods* and *Crash Go the Chariots of the Gods* useful when researching the topic, but be careful to document your sources of information.
    **Audience**: the "average" reader of a science magazine who could be expected to have some knowledge about the topic, would prize logical thinking, and would oppose your position on the theory.

    Send a copy of your essay to the editor of a science magazine.

# A Cry for the Beloved Country

## by Alan Paton

*No one has fought apartheid as long or as ardently as the South African novelist Alan Paton, whose* Cry, the Beloved Country *took the world by storm when he wrote it 40 years ago. When some of his colleagues quit the fight, or migrated to fight apartheid from abroad, Paton stayed and fought at home. His passport was confiscated for eleven years. He never bowed, never wavered.*

*With* Cry, the Beloved Country, *Paton became a symbol — courted, admired, idolized as one with the courage to fight an oppressive policy. His opinion was sought by those with conscience, his words reached every corner of the world. But when violence, ideology, and lust for sanctions overtook the antiapartheid campaign and seemed to dominate conventional wisdom abroad, Alan Paton began to be treated as a virtual nonperson — ignored and rejected by the very people who were once so admiring.*

*This fall from grace came primarily because Paton opposed violence, was not an ideologue, and rejected sanctions as the best way to help blacks achieve equality and dignity in South Africa. His wisdom was no longer welcome in some circles. Yet it is even more relevant today than it was in the past.*

*Here, in an article written shortly before his death in 1988 at his home near Durban, Alan Paton appealed again to those who really want to enhance freedom in his nation to support constructive change.*

1    I live in a very strange and beautiful and, in many ways, a very sad country. Its future is unpredictable. The great plan of Apartheid or Separate Development, or whatever you call it, so eloquently stated by our prime minister from 1958 to 1966, Hendrik Verwoerd, is falling to pieces about our ears. Although — in my opinion — Verwoerd did more harm to South Africa and to Afrikanerdom than any other person in our history, we cannot put the blame for all our troubles on him and his National Party. For, in reality, the National Party came to power on April 6, 1652, the day that Jan van Riebeeck and his three ships from Holland landed in Table Bay.

2    Our written history since that date is a history of conquest. The first conquests were easy, but the white settlers, called the trek-boers (or trek-farmers), encountered a much tougher enemy as they moved away from the shelter of Cape Town and Table Mountain. This enemy was the Xhosa people, who

resisted their northward movement. Their struggle lasted for 100 years; both of them were cattle owners and both wanted land. These were the years of the interminable Frontier Wars, and they left a mark on the minds and souls of both black and white.

Let me give an example of that mark on the Afrikaner mind. When I was appointed principal of Diepkloof Reformatory for black boys in 1935, many of my white staff were young Afrikaners who lived in the single quarters. It gave me a weekly shock to go into one of their bedrooms and see a wall with a large painting that depicted an almost naked black warrior in the act of jumping through a window of a trekker's house and impaling a white infant on the point of his assegai. The young Afrikaner who occupied the room slept under this picture almost every night of his life. He had never experienced such an event, which had occurred about 150 years earlier on the frontier. The young man nursed a feeling for black people that was a compound of fear and hatred, and this painting dominated not only his room but his thoughts. It is not a feeling cherished by all Afrikaners, and no doubt the hatred has much abated, but the fear is still there, and if we do not understand that, we do not understand the politics of South Africa today, and in particular the politics of the National Party.

In 1910, eight years after the end of the Boer War, the last conflict between the Afrikaners and the expanding British Empire, the British granted a new constitution to the Union of South Africa — formed by the coming together of the Transvaal, the Orange Free State, Cape Colony, and Natal. This was a generous act, but it was deeply flawed because the British government agreed to a colour bar in the constitution. And this British generosity did not mollify the diehard Afrikaners who were later to congregate in the National Party.

In 1948 came the greatest conquest of all, the coming to power of the National Party government on May 26. The greatest consequence of this was the Grand Plan of racial separation in every possible sphere, whereby the conqueror decided the future forever and forever of the conquered; the Grand Plan that is now falling to pieces about our ears.

And where do we stand now? We are going into a world where conquest has to be undone. Why does it have to be undone?

The first reason is that, after 300 years, the black people of South Africa, largely through their children, have said to the whites, "You can't do this to us anymore." And this is true; they are not going to behave like conquered people anymore. When did they say this? Well, if you must fix a date, it is June 16, 1976, the day Hector Petersen, aged thirteen, was shot dead by police in Soweto during a demonstration by school children against instruction in certain subjects in Afrikaans. The compulsory use of Afrikaans merely triggered the rebellion; the deep-seated cause was the decision by black children that they would not be treated as the conquered anymore.

8    A second reason why conquest has to be undone is that the outside world demands it more and more forcibly. I do not believe that the outside world always acts with wisdom. I do not believe that you can persuade our government to behave better by threatening it with punitive measures. These self-righteous people abroad think they can fix a date by which South Africa must do away with apartheid completely. Americans forget that they themselves only did away with segregation when the Supreme Court ordered them to do so in 1954, in the historic case of *Brown v. The Board of Education*, Topeka, Kansas.

9    A final reason why the age of conquest is coming to its end is that more and more white South Africans realize that their privileged position has to be given up, and that the alternative is to go back to the times of the Frontier Wars.

10   I believe the future holds three possibilities. The first is armed revolution, which the prophets of doom say is coming. I don't think it is. Those who may want to wage revolution have neither the money nor the arms. They would be fighting the most powerful army in Africa. A revolution could succeed only if there were armed intervention from abroad, and I think this is unlikely.

11   The second possibility is the continuance of the unrest and hatred that have disfigured our national life, the declaration of states of emergency, and an endemic ungovernability. It is true that when people are trying to burn down your house, you have to oppose them with violence. But your real problem is to do something that will make them not burn down your house.

12   The third possibility — and the one I think is most likely — is that we have entered an evolutionary period that will be difficult, and often painful. That is the poet Christina Rossetti's road that winds uphill all the way. It is in fact the period of the undoing of conquest. Our state president, P.W. Botha, has said that there are three urgent needs, and, in order of urgency, they are the preservation of order, the development of our resources, and political and constitutional reform. What non-Nationalists fear is that the government will not get beyond the preservation of order. Our present state of emergency is well over 500 days old.

13   We South Africans must be prepared for the uphill road, and our friends in other countries must remember that it *is* an uphill road, and must not expect us to reach the summit on any specific date. When things are bad, we can remember these words of William the Silent: "It is not necessary

to hope in order to undertake, and it is not necessary to succeed in order to persevere." Stoical advice indeed.

Disinvestment and sanctions are the weapons that many people in the outside world think will bring an end to apartheid. Some of these people are very powerful, such as the members of the U.S. Congress and the Commonwealth prime ministers. They are mistaken. 14

I have lived for 40 years under a National Party government. For thirteen years of my life, as principal of Diepkloof Reformatory, I spoke more Afrikaans than English. I was once a sympathizer with Afrikaner nationalism, and attended the centenary of the Great Trek on December 16, 1938; but I was forever alienated by the exclusivity and the racial fervour of that celebration. I can claim to know the Afrikaner fairly well, and I believe that my own archbishop, the Most Reverend Desmond Tutu, is quite wrong when he claims that sanctions will determine the political future; he is arguing, not from reason, but from passion, just as Verwoerd did before him. 15

There is another powerful reason against sanctions. In my years as principal at Diepkloof, I learned that you cannot save a boy from a criminal career by punishing him. Do the sanctioners not realize that you cannot effect a moral revolution by economic means? If they succeed in destroying our economy, that will not bring utopia. Our railways will stop running; our cities will decay; worst of all, our agriculture will be destroyed and we will become one of the begging nations of Africa. 16

I have one last and compelling reason for opposing sanctions. I will not put a man out of a job for any principle, however noble. It may be possible to be happy in London and Washington when people are starving in South Africa, but it would not be possible to be happy if you lived, as I do, on the edge of the Valley of a Thousand Hills, whose people depend for their living on the industries of Pinetown and Durban. 17

I hope our critics will come to realize that disinvestment and sanctions will not bring about the liberation of the oppressed, but will only add to their sufferings. I hope they will realize that the greatest help they can give to this country is to give understanding and encouragement to those many South Africans who are trying to make this a more just society. 18

I shall close by giving one example of such an endeavour. For eight months of 1986, a group of representative citizens of Natal — Zulus, Afrikaners, English-speakers, Indians, and Coloured people — met in the Durban city-council chamber to plan a joint legislative body for the province. This project is called the *KwaZulu-Natal Indaba*, the word "Indaba" being the Zulu name for a solemn and serious discussion. 19

20      It proposed a constitution for the joint assembly, composed of two houses. The lower house was to have 100 members elected by universal suffrage, and therefore it would have been overwhelmingly Zulu in composition. The upper house was to have 50 members: ten Zulus, ten Afrikaners, ten English-speakers, ten Indians, and ten others. The constitution therefore recognized two so-far incompatible ideals, namely a universal suffrage and a guarantee of the preservation of racial identity. The constitution further embodied a bill of rights.

21      That such a solution could be reached in orderly fashion can be regarded only as a miracle in these days of civil unrest. It is endeavours of this kind that need the encouragement of the outside world. It is grotesque to think that they can be helped by sanctions. I write this article in the hope the outside world will realize that it cannot punish South Africa into utopia.

## Style and Structure

1.  Who is the intended reader of this essay? How do you know?
2.  Inexperienced writers sometimes make the mistake of repeating their introductory **thesis statements** word for word in their conclusions.
    (a) Write down the sentence in Paton's introduction that acts as his **thesis statement**.
    (b) How does the **conclusion** in paragraphs 19 to 21 relate to this **thesis**?
    (c) Why is this approach an effective way of convincing the reader to accept the essay's argument?
3.  Well-constructed paragraphs in expository writing have **topic** and **concluding sentences**.
    (a) Identify the **topic sentence** in each paragraph of the body of this essay. Write a one- or two-word summary for each. Make special note of any idea in the paragraph that does *not* relate to the **topic sentence**.
    (b) Identify the **concluding sentence** in each paragraph. Write a point-form comment on how each relates to the ideas presented in the body of its paragraph (e.g., summarizes, comments on, draws conclusions from).
4.  (a) Review, in order, the summaries you made in 3(a) of the ideas contained in the **topic sentences**.
        Place the number 1 beside the summary representing the first **topic sentence** in the essay. Place 1's beside all other summaries that deal with a similar aspect of the main topic.

Place the number 2 beside the summary representing the first **topic sentence** that deals with a *different* aspect of the essay's main topic. Place 2's beside all the other summaries that deal with this new aspect.

Continue this process through the body of the essay (using 3, 4, and so on) until you have accounted for all of the summaries.

(b) For each of the numbers used in your answer to (a), write one word that summarizes the aspect of the topic dealt with by the **topic sentences** listed under it.

(c) In a sentence or two, explain the progression of ideas (1, 2, 3, etc.) that Paton has used as the basic structure for his essay.

(d) Why is this structure an effective strategy for presenting the essay's argument to the intended reader?

5.  Place an asterisk beside the summary of any **topic sentences** that do not fit into the **thesis** announced in the introduction of the essay. What does the number of asterisks tell you about the essay?

6.  **Transitions** are important devices in a piece of expository writing. They lead the reader carefully through the development of the ideas. A **transition** may be a single word (e.g., thus or therefore) or a sentence or short paragraph.

(a) Identify the word(s) in each **topic sentence** that help(s) the reader make the **transition** from the ideas of the paragraph preceding it. Make a list of these **transitions**. Select three or four that you think do their job well and explain how each helps the reader.

(b) Identify one paragraph in the body that acts as a **transition** between sections of the essay. How does it help the reader?

# Warm-up

1.  Work on one of the following topics with two or three others from the class, making certain that each topic has been chosen by at least one group:

| | | |
|---|---|---|
| Afrikaner | Afrikaans | apartheid |
| divestment | economic sanctions | universal suffrage |
| Desmond Tutu | Nelson Mandela | Steven Biko |

Using encyclopedias, magazines, and other reference materials in the library, discover the significance of your topic to the problems of South

Africa. On your own, write a paragraph that explains the topic and its significance to someone who has never heard of it.

Use this paragraph and those written by the others who worked in your group as the basis for a short oral presentation to the rest of the class. (Be prepared to answer questions at the end of your presentation.)

2. Using newspapers, magazines, and other reference materials from the library, collect at least three different articles on the recent problems in South Africa. Write a brief summary of the article that you believe deals with the most important issue. Distribute copies of your summary to your classmates.

# Thinking and Writing

a. According to Paton, the racial problem in South Africa is based to a great extent on hatred and fear among the white population. Yet he does not suggest ways in which these two elements can be overcome. Write an essay in which you outline practical approaches to overcoming this hatred and fear that could be put in place in South Africa.
**Audience:** someone who is aware of the problems in South Africa, but does not see any solution.

Send a copy of your final draft to the South African Consulate nearest to you. Ask for a response.

b. One person who read this essay responded by saying, "It's hypocritical for Canadians to get as excited as we do about the racial problems in South Africa. All we have to do is look at the way we have treated and still treat our native Indians if we want something to get excited about. We're too bloody smug and self-satisfied to see the racial problems in our own backyard! But we're more than ready to condemn the same behaviour in others."

Write an essay in which you argue the validity of this statement. (You may want to read over the essay "An Alternative to Incarceration," p. 45, for some interesting ideas related to this topic.)
**Audience:** a Canadian who may not be aware of the plight of Canadian native people.

# What TV Does to Kids

*Newsweek*

His first polysyllabic utterance was "Bradybunch." He learned to spell Sugar    1
Smacks before he could spell his own name. Recently, he tried to karate-
chop his younger sister after she broke his Six Million Dollar Man bionic
transport station (she retaliated by bashing him with her Cher doll). His nursery-
school teacher reports that he is passive, noncreative, and has almost no attention span; in short, he is very much like his classmates. This fall, he will
officially reach the age of reason and begin his formal education. His parents
are beginning to discuss their apprehensions — when they are not too busy
watching television.

It is only in recent years — with the first TV generation already grown    2
up — that social scientists, psychologists, pediatricians, and educators have
begun serious study of the impact of television on the young. According to
television survey-taker A.C. Nielsen, children under five watch an average
of 23.5 hours of TV a week. Today's typical high-school graduate has logged
at least 15 000 hours before the small screen — more time than he has
spent on any other activity except sleep. At present levels of advertising and
mayhem, he will have been exposed to 350 000 commercials and vicariously
participated in 18 000 killings. The conclusion is inescapable: After parents,
television has become perhaps the most potent influence on the beliefs, values,
and behaviour of the young.

Unquestionably, the plug-in picture window has transmitted some benefits.    3
In general, the children of TV enjoy a more sophisticated knowledge of a
far larger world. They are likely to possess richer vocabularies, albeit with
only a superficial comprehension of what the words mean. Research on the
impact of *Sesame Street* has established measurable gains in the cognitive
skills of many preschoolers.

Nonetheless, the overwhelming body of evidence — drawn from more    4
than 2300 studies and reports — is decidedly negative. Michael Rothenberg,
a child psychiatrist at the University of Washington, has reviewed the 50 most
comprehensive studies involving 10 000 children from every possible background. Most showed that viewing violence tends to produce aggressive behaviour among the young. "The time is long past due for a major, organized
cry of protest from the medical profession," concludes Rothenberg.

5    An unexpected salvo was sounded last winter when the normally cautious American Medical Association asked ten major corporations to review their policies about sponsoring excessively gory shows. "TV violence is both a mental-health problem and an environmental issue," explained Dr. Richard E. Palmer, president of the AMA. In defence, broadcasting officials maintain that the jury is still out on whether video violence is guilty of producing aggressive behaviour. And network schedulers say they are actively reducing the violence dosage.

6    But televised mayhem is only part of TV's impact. TV has at the very least pre-empted the traditional development of childhood itself. The time kids spend sitting catatonic before the set has been exacted from such salutary pursuits as reading, outdoor play, even simple, contemplative solitude. Few parents can cope with its tyrannical allure. Recently, Dr. Benjamin Spock took his stepdaughter and granddaughter to New York to see a concert and a Broadway show. But the man who has the prescription for everything from diaper rash to bedwetting had no easy solution for dislodging the kids from their hotel room. "Of all the attractions in New York," recalls Spock, "they seemed to find the TV set the most fascinating."

7    Small wonder that television has been called "the flickering blue parent." The after-school and early-evening hours used to be a time for "what-did-you-do-today" dialogue. Now, the electronic box does most of the talking. Dr. David Pearl of the U.S. National Institute of Mental Health suspects that the tube "has displaced many of the normal interactional processes between parents and children which are essential for maximum development."

8    Even more worrisome is what television has done to, rather than denied, the tube-weaned population. A series of studies has shown that addiction to TV stifles creative imagination. For example, a University of Southern California research team exposed 250 elementary students to three weeks of intensive viewing. Tests found a marked drop in all forms of creative abilities except verbal skill. Some teachers are encountering children who cannot understand a simple story without visual illustrations. Nursery-school teachers who have observed the pre-TV generation contend that juvenile play is far less imaginative and spontaneous than it was in the past. "You don't see kids making their own toys out of crummy things like we used to," says University of Virginia psychology professor Stephen Worchel. "You don't see them playing hopscotch, or making up their own games. Everything is suggested to them by television."

9    Too much TV too early may also instil an attitude of spectatorship, a withdrawal from direct involvement in real-life experiences. "What television basically teaches children is passivity," says Stanford University researcher Paul

Kaufman. "It creates the illusion of having been somewhere and done something and seen something, when in fact they've been sitting at home."

Conditioned to see all problems resolved in 30 or 60 minutes, the offspring   10
of TV exhibit a low tolerance for the frustration of learning. Grade-schoolers are quickly turned off by any activity that promises less than instant gratification. "You introduce a new skill, and right away, if it looks hard, they dissolve into tears," laments one first-grade teacher. "They want everything to be easy — like watching the tube."

The debate over the link between TV violence and aggressive behaviour   11
in society has had a longer run than *Gunsmoke*. Today, however, even zealous network apologists concede that some children, under certain conditions, will imitate antisocial acts seen on the tube. Indeed, a study of 100 juvenile offenders commissioned by ABC found that no fewer than 22 confessed to having copied criminal techniques from TV. Behavioural sleuths are also uncovering evidence that the tide of TV carnage increases children's tolerance of violent behaviour in others, because they have been conditioned to think of violence as an everyday thing.

And now a word about the sponsors. The hottest battle in this area involves   12
the impact of child-directed commercials on their audience's eating habits. Many of the ads on Saturday and Sunday morning "kidvid" peddle sugar-coated cereals, candy, and chewing gum, hooking children on poor eating habits long before they develop the mental defences to resist. "This is the most massive educational program to eat junk food in history," charges Sid Wolinsky, an attorney for a San Francisco public-interest group. According to a study by Columbia University psychology professor Thomas Bever, misleading TV ads may also be "permanently distorting children's views of morality, society, and business." From in-depth interviews with 48 youngsters between the ages of five and twelve, Bever concluded that by the time they reach twelve, many find it easier to decide that all commercials lie than to try to determine which are telling the truth.

A few daring parents have counterattacked by simply pulling the plug. For   13
example, Charles Frye, a San Francisco nursery-school teacher and the father of five boys, decided he would not replace his set after it conked out. Frye's brood rebelled at first, but today fourteen-year-old Mark fills his afternoon hours with tapdancing lessons, scout meetings, and work in a gas station. Kirk, his thirteen-year-old brother, plays a lot of basketball and football and recently finished *Watership Down* and all four of the Tolkein hobbit books.

Short of such a draconian measure, some parents are exercising a greater   14
degree of home rule. Two years ago, the administrators of New York's Horace

Mann nursery school became distressed over an upsurge of violence in their students' play. Deciding that television was to blame, they dispatched a letter to all parents urging them to curb their children's viewing. "After we sent the letter, we could see a change," recalls principal Eleanor Brussel. "The kids showed better concentration, better comprehension, an ability to think things through."

15    Clearly, there is no single antidote. For the children of today, and their progeny to come, TV watching will continue to be their most shared — and shaping — experience. Virtually all the experts agree, however, on one palliative. Instead of using TV as an electronic babysitter, parents must try to involve themselves directly in their youngsters' viewing. By watching along with the kids at least occasionally, they can help them evaluate what they see — pointing out the inflated claims of a commercial, perhaps, or criticizing a gratuitously violent scene. "Parents don't have to regard TV as a person who can't be interrupted," says behavioural scientist Charles Corder-Bolz. "If they view one show a night with their kids, and make just one or two comments about it, they can have more impact than the whole program."

16    Reduced to the essentials, the question for parents no longer is: "Do you know where your children are tonight?" The question has become: "What are they watching — and with whom?"

## Style and Structure

1.   In the first paragraph, what device does the writer use to emphasize the power of TV?
2.   (a) Reverse the order of the first two paragraphs. How would this affect the impact of the **introduction** on the reader?
     (b) Why does the author in his version place the **thesis statement** at the end of his introduction?
3.   Why does the author include the ironic comment in the last sentence of paragraph 1?
4.   Why does the writer employ statistical evidence in paragraph 2?
5.   Examine the section of the essay from paragraph 4 to paragraph 12. What persuasive technique does the writer use? Is this an effective technique to employ given the topic and the intended reader?
6.   Select two sections in which the writer employs direct quotation; rewrite them changing the direct quotation into an indirect quotation. Which has the greater impact on the reader?

7. If the writer is convinced of the harm that TV does, why does he include paragraph 3?
8. How does the subject of the last four paragraphs differ from the previous nine? Why is this an effective way to conclude this topic?

# Warm-Up

1. Reread paragraph 7, in which TV is described as "the flickering blue parent." Form a group of four or six classmates, and have half generate arguments supporting, and the other half arguments opposing, the ideas presented in paragraph 7.

   Write a paragraph based on the best arguments produced by your half of the group. In pairs, one "for" and one "against" the ideas in paragraph 7, present your paragraphs to the rest of the group. Stop after each pair has finished their presentation and try to point out flaws in the arguments presented by your opponent's paragraph.

   After everyone has finished presenting, revise your paragraph into a final draft, taking into consideration any objections raised by your opponents.
2. Repeat the exercise outlined in exercise 1, this time concentrating on the ideas presented in paragraph 8.

# Thinking and Writing

a. As you may have noticed, the author of this article is concerned with the effect of television on *you*, i.e., on the generation that has grown up with television as part of its everyday reality.

   Write an essay in which you examine the charges made in this article about the influence of television by relating them to your development and to the type of person that you have become. Be careful to avoid the all-too-common reaction of saying, "There's nothing wrong with me," and then rationalizing that researchers are making mountains out of mole hills. Be as honest and careful as you can, especially when you find yourself disagreeing with the charges. We are not saying, of course, that you cannot disagree with the article, but simply warning you against falling into an obvious pitfall. Try to use reason rather than emotion to make your points.

**Audience:** "average" readers who have built up prejudices because of the sensationalized reports they have encountered in the media. Thus your readers have come to hold opinions completely opposite to yours, but have never thought the problem out in terms of a real individual's development.

b.    "If even half of the contentions of this article are true, then some controls should be placed upon what may be broadcast; or, the people creating, sponsoring, and broadcasting should be made legally responsible for the results of their actions," was the comment of one person who read this article. Write an essay in which you either support or refute this comment. If you support it, include in your essay concrete suggestions for legislation and/or controls. If you are going to refute the comment, include concrete evidence to support your argument. You might, for example, find supporting evidence in a television trade magazine.

**Audience:** someone who is familiar with the television industry and is in a position to influence the type of programming being broadcast.

Send a copy of your essay both to the company that sponsors a program that you find particularly obnoxious *and* to the CRTC.

# Respect: At the Heart of Successful Marriage

**by Annie Gottlieb**

Respect is not mentioned in the marriage vows. No illustrated books show 1
how to achieve it. Yet it is central to a lasting, satisfying marriage.

Yes, respect. It seems a quaint, almost formal word today. But it's one 2
that couples who are successfully married mention with impressive consistency.
For her book *Married People: Staying Together in the Age of Divorce*, author
Francine Klagsbrun interviewed 87 couples who had been married fifteen years
or more. She hoped to identify the factors that had enabled these marriages
to survive and thrive in a time when some 40 percent end in divorce. Respect
turned out to be a key element. "The vast majority of people I interviewed
said, 'I respect him' or 'I respect her,'" says Klagsbrun.

What is this thing called respect? It's not the same as admiration. Says 3
Dr. Alexandra Symonds, associate clinical professor of psychiatry at the New
York University School of Medicine, "When you fall in love, you *admire* the
other. You look *up* to someone, much the way a child idealizes a parent."
Such romantic admiration thrives and even depends on the illusion that the
other is "perfect for you." That's why it doesn't last. "You come to see that
the person you married *isn't* exactly what you expected," says Francine Klagsbrun. "There are differences of personality, of approaches to life; different
ways of doing things." It's now that real respect has a chance to develop.

You can try to change your mate back into your fantasy. But for the marriage 4
to last, you must agree to disagree, learning to let the other be. For respect
is between peers. It is for something really there, tested and proven.

The put-down is the chief symptom — and weapon — of lack of respect, 5
or contempt. "Contempt is the worst kind of emotion," says Dr. Symonds.
"You feel the other person has no worth. I have one patient whose husband
loves sports. She would prefer to go to the theatre or to stay home and
read. She could simply say, 'We have different tastes.' Instead she says, 'How
can he waste his time and money that way?' She puts him down."

We've all seen marriages in which one or both partners attack the other 6
quite savagely in the guise of "It's for your own good." Any "good" is undone
by the hostile tone of what claims to be constructive criticism. A wife nags
her husband to be more ambitious and makes him feel like a failure because

he prefers craftsmanship or community projects to the competitive business world. Or a husband accuses his wife of wasting time whenever she gets together with a friend: "Why isn't she doing something productive?" In good marriages, partners nurture each other's self-esteem. They never make the other person feel like an idiot.

7    Respect, then, is appreciation of the *separateness* of the other person, of the ways in which he or she is unique. These things take time to discover, accept, and finally appreciate. That's why respect is a quality of maturity in a marriage, not of the first heat of romance. But this doesn't mean that married couples who respect each other are simply saying, "You go your way, and I'll go mine." On the contrary, says Francine Klagsbrun. "Respect often helps you to learn from each other, because you've taken on some of each other's ways of thinking."

8    My husband and I are from different worlds and generations. He's a European, eighteen years my senior. Sometimes we clash. But we've learned to respect each other even for some of the differences that once annoyed us most. As a result, we've grown more alike. I've absorbed some of his authority and definite standards; he's absorbed some of my tolerance. I've gained a genuine appreciation for jazz, he for rock'n'roll. That's the paradox of a good marriage. Only by respecting each other as you are do you open the door to change.

9    The root meaning of the word *respect* is "to look at." Respect is a clear yet loving eye. It sees not only what is really there, but also what is *potentially* there, and helps bring the latter to fruition. Respect is the art of love by which married couples honour what is unique and best in each other.

## Style and Structure

1.  (a) Identify the sentence in the first paragraph that acts as this essay's **thesis statement**. Give reasons to support your choice.
    (b) Examine the other sentences in paragraph 1 and the first two sentences of paragraph 2. What point are they trying to convey to the reader? What do they reveal about the writer's attempt to deal with the attitudes her intended readers may have toward her **thesis** before they read her essay?

2.  Given her intended reader, why might Gottlieb have chosen to begin the body of her essay by referring to Klagsbrun's book?

3. (a) In this essay, the writer defines respect in several ways. What method does she use in paragraphs 3 to 6?

(b) Considering her intended reader, what reasons might she have for beginning this definition by talking of love and admiration?

(c) What reasons would she have for following up this definition with the contents of paragraphs 4, 5, and 6?

4. (a) In what ways does the definition of respect offered in paragraph 7 differ from those offered in earlier paragraphs?

(b) What method of definition does Gottlieb use in paragraph 8? Why is it effective?

(c) What benefits does Gottlieb gain by saving the definitions presented in paragraphs 7 and 8 for so late in the essay?

5. In what ways does paragraph 9 act as an effective **conclusion** for the essay? Why would the writer begin her **conclusion** with a definition derived from a dictionary?

6. Count the number of words in each of the sentences in the first two paragraphs. How does this variation in sentence length help drive home to the reader the points being made?

7. The tone of an essay may be friendly or angry, formal or informal. The tone chosen can subtly affect the reader's acceptance of the ideas being presented.

(a) Identify three passages in which Gottlieb uses contractions. What tone do these contractions help establish? Is it an effective way of dealing with her intended reader?

(b) Given this tone, in what kinds of writing would it *not* be appropriate to use contractions?

# Warm-up

1. Working with a group of four or five others in your class, choose a word that represents a concept important in our society (e.g., "friendship," "hatred," "equality," "democracy").

(a) Write a paragraph that defines the word by describing what it does *not* mean (as Gottlieb does in her essay).

**Audience:** someone who may not have thought very seriously about the implications of the word.

(b) Write a paragraph that defines the word by describing what it does mean.
**Audience:** same as above.

(c) Write a paragraph that defines the word by using an example.
**Audience:** same as above.

(d) Compare your paragraphs to the ones written by the other members of your group.

# Thinking and Writing

a. As Gottlieb points out, most people enter marriage without knowing the most important ingredient for success. Most of us who fall in love never realize *its* most important elements either. Write an essay in which you define "Romantic Love." Use a number of different methods of definition. (Suggestion: you might want to write a humorous essay.)
**Audience:** a typical Canadian who is amazed at the array of emotions involved in loving.

b. Gottlieb draws a clear distinction between romantic admiration and a successful married relationship. Yet in our society most people marry because they are in love (i.e., share romantic admiration). Write an essay in which you briefly define romantic love and explain the role it plays in a successful marriage.
**Audience:** someone who is in love and plans to be married.

Send a copy of your final draft to someone who deals with people having difficulties in their marriages, such as a priest, minister, or marriage counsellor. Ask for comments on your ideas.

# Second Opinion

## by Ivor Shapiro

In a conference room on the top floor of an Ontario hospital, a group of staff members are discussing starvation. Their undernourished patient is not an Ethiopian refugee but a 77-year-old woman who has spent more than a year in hospital and now lies dying in a nearby ward. There is an intravenous tube in her arm, but it provides no nutrients, only dextrose and water. An ethicist quietly takes notes as nurses and therapists recount the case history. A month ago, after meeting with Mrs. X's family in the wake of her unexpected recovery from the complications of a stroke, the attending physician instructed staff to stop feeding her. Then, the day before yesterday, again with the family's consent, a new order appeared on her medical chart: when the last available intravenous site deteriorates in a few days' time, the water supply will end with it. No attempt will be made to lead a life-giving tube into her stomach.

Mrs. X herself has taken no part in the series of decisions that guarantee her imminent death. She suffers from dementia and floats in and out of mental clarity. Dementia does not kill, but Mrs. X's chronic frailty seems to amount to an agonizingly prolonged death. After the latest crisis passed, her family confessed to feeling worn out by deathbed scenes, and her son told the doctor that his mother would want to make an end of it. It is 31 days since the physician agreed that there was no point in continuing to feed her, and now, with the decision to stop providing water, the doctor may as well write out a postdated death certificate. Her nurses and therapists, distressed by that stark reality, decided to ask for a second opinion — not on a matter of medicine, but on the ethics of beckoning death.

Abbyann Lynch was at another hospital, leading the first of a series of staff discussions on "bioethics case studies," when the manager of Mrs. X's nursing team phoned the Westminster Institute for Ethics and Human Values, where she works. When the message reached Lynch, she rearranged her schedule and set up a meeting. This is not the first time Lynch has dropped everything to lead a discussion about whether or not a patient should be "allowed" to die. Over the past decade, it has become accepted practice for physicians to disconnect life-support systems in advance of patients' inevitable deaths — accepted, but never routine.

The legal and customary conditions for terminating treatment can be quite vague, so in these and other cases, an ethicist will often be called in to help doctors (or, as in the case of Mrs. X, the lower ranks in the health hierarchy) cut a moral Gordian knot.

5    Over the past decade or so, clinical ethics has become one of North America's growth industries. Most ethicists say the main stimulus for the increase in their business is an abundance of new technologies that present ever-widening choices — and dilemmas — to physicians and patients. But Benjamin Freedman, ethicist at Montreal's Jewish General Hospital, says the issues he and his colleagues most often tackle were around long before the advent of high-tech medicine. There is nothing new about patients' rights: receiving full information about risky medical procedures, having the power to refuse any or all treatment, and being guaranteed confidentiality by medical professionals. What is new is that patients and their families have become increasingly more aware, and therefore more demanding, of their rights.

6    From the doctor's point of view, there is no harm in taking out an extra piece of malpractice insurance by getting an ethical opinion on a tricky judgment call. For whatever reasons, the nation's hospitals are following the U.S. example of establishing ethics committees, and a dozen or so, mainly in central Canada's biggest cities, have hired professional ethicists to teach and counsel. An important part of the ethicist's job is to sort out the conflicting feelings and needs of patients, their relatives and friends, and the doctors and nurses. George Webster, ethicist at three Catholic hospitals in Toronto, says of the family's role in deciding about ending the treatment of an unconscious patient: "We do not routinely ask what they want, but rather ask them to reconstruct what the patient would want done." And who is family? A dying AIDS patient's estranged wife, his hostile parents, or his current lover?

7    Freedman says the proliferation of applied-ethics positions is reducing "a glut of philosophers." The new career options have been welcomed by a generation of philosophy Ph.D.s like himself, who, uninspired by the idea of a life spent probing ageless metaphysical questions, were looking for new markets for their wares. The jobs have also been a godsend for theologians who find earthly debates more attractive than spiritual exercises in a secular society. At the same time, says Abbyann Lynch, medical schools have been churning out a new kind of graduate class: more women, more members of minorities, older students with a background in the social sciences. Today's medical graduates, she says, are more willing than many of their forebears to think about the meaning of their vocation and to seek help in dealing with the agonizing questions about life and death with which their jobs confront them.

8    Some of these questions can be seen in the seven faces that watch Lynch

with a touch of disappointment as she tells the troubled nursing team that her role is not to provide clear-cut answers but to ask more questions and try to help them clarify issues. She is not here, she says, to make judgments.

Not all consulting ethicists would agree with so limiting a definition of their profession. It's a matter, perhaps, of personal style. Lynch has the manner of a teacher of philosophy, which is exactly what she has been since 1954. Her present assignments include sitting on hospital ethics committees, teaching groups of doctors and nurses, and conducting "ethics grand rounds," a monthly meeting at which hospital clinicians discuss complex cases — "The Case of the Extremely Low-Birth-Weight Infant" or "AIDS: Ethical Dilemmas." But with her gentle questions and tentative, self-effacing suggestions, she still plays convincingly the role of tame philosopher, criticizing logic and probing diagnostic assessments in the light of policies and laws. 9

By contrast, David Roy hunches over his pipe and delivers unambiguous epigrams with a punchy fluency oddly reminiscent of Joe Clark during Question Period. Roy runs the Centre for Bioethics at Montreal's Clinical Research Institute and provides consultancy services upon physicians' requests. His basic task, he says, is to build accurate descriptions of patients and their conditions. Is a particular brain-damaged child capable of experiencing happiness (and should she therefore be given the chance offered by an emergency operation), or is she a virtual vegetable who should be allowed a merciful death? Discovering the answer to such questions is not a job for a detached philosopher, he says, but a case for an "espionage agent." 10

The investigation requires detailed discussions with everyone involved: a shy nurse may hold the crucial piece of information about the patient. And then "a point comes in consultation when I put my opinion down on the patient's chart just like anybody else," Roy says. "To put it crudely, I've got to put my ass on the line." 11

When invited to put her opinions on charts, Lynch always refuses. "I'm not a clinician," she says. "I help people sort out and order their thinking and give them possible avenues to discuss." Similarly, because she is not a psychologist or social worker, she refuses to get involved in meetings with families. 12

But Roy says he would never consider doing a consultation without talking to the patient's family. He says ethicists cannot do their jobs properly without some of the skills of clinician, philosopher, and psychologist. The profession requires, he says, a broad humanities training "with a strong dose of, and interest in, science." 13

14   Lynch presses on with her questions to the nursing team about Mrs. X. What are the patient's chances now? Could she survive if feeding were to be resumed? Was she dying a month ago, before her food was withdrawn? Was she in pain?

15   She reads from a draft policy statement still under consideration by the hospital's ethics committee. Treatment must not be withdrawn, it says, unless the patient's death is imminent. She reads quickly through the rest of the document, pausing before the last sentence, which says: the purpose of withdrawing treatment must not be to hasten death but to prevent needless suffering.

16   A competent patient has a legal right to refuse treatment, Lynch reminds her listeners, and if the patient is not competent, the family may be consulted about what to do. But unless the patient is dying anyway, and the decision will affect only the timing and the circumstances of her death, the family's wishes should not necessarily be the "first priority."

17   In the case of Mrs. X, Lynch suggests to the hospital group (in the first indication of her opinion in nearly an hour of discussion) that the family's wishes may have dominated the decision. Over a month ago, before her feeding was stopped, Mrs. X was not about to die, was not even in any great pain. She was recovering from a respiratory infection, and while her dementia affected the quality of her life, her illness was not a terminal one analogous to cancer or AIDS, where, in the final stages, all a medical team can do is provide comfort and perhaps adjust the timing of an imminent death.

18   "This patient may be dying," Lynch says quietly, undramatically, "but she may be dying because she is not being fed." The starkness of that statement is greeted by a slightly dazed silence. No one disagrees. Lynch seems to have put into words a possibility no one at the table was eager to face: that a patient has been condemned to die for no good reason other than relieving her family of their burden of responsibility. But now it has been said, and within five minutes there is consensus about the next step: Lynch should raise the matter with the hospital authorities. Later, having visited Mrs. X, the hospital administrator will ask the ethics committee to consider the case.

19   The array of ethical paraphernalia available to hospitals — committees, consultants, guidelines, teachers, patient-advocates — may not always be an advance over old-fashioned agonizing on the part of patients and their families and doctors. Whatever else they do, the new procedures can have the effect of shifting decision making further away from vulnerable people in beds and closer to the people who have power over them. And the process offers doctors a chance to shuck off a burden of guilt.

Michael Yeo, a researcher on Lynch's staff, says people have a disturbing    20
tendency to relinquish moral authority to other people: priests and rabbis
in the past, now ethics committees and ethicists. He thinks there is something
"potentially dishonest or cowardly" about doctors deferring to a committee
on a matter of morality. "I shudder when I see someone quoted as 'an expert
in medical ethics,'" Yeo says. "I'm inclined to say the guy's just a schmuck
like anyone else."

For good or ill, the age of the ethical consultant has dawned. The specialty    21
is still so young that its practitioners' tasks, methods, and qualifications are
far from standardized, but ethicists are likely to contribute ever more frequently
to medical decisions — at best influencing them, at worst simply lending
them moral weight. Since the ethicists can only function effectively with the
goodwill of physicians, they potentially have a conflict of interest when their
consciences call them to stand up for patients. While today's consultants seem
to possess a compensating bias toward recognizing patients' interests, the un-
enviable tightrope they must walk could make them reluctant to recognize
abuses that are not glaringly apparent.

The ethics committee's ruling on the case of Mrs. X may help resolve some    22
future dilemmas. A shadowy area of policy has been illuminated, and if a
revised draft statement is passed, the hospital will clearly forbid the arbitrary
withdrawal of treatment from a patient who is neither about to die nor already
rendered vegetative by an irreversible illness. But things have moved somewhat
more quickly in the starving body of Mrs. X than in the hospital's body politic.
Within 48 hours of the emergency ethics consultation, she has had "a cerebral
accident," lost consciousness, and died. No one is suing the doctor or the
hospital. No one is pressing for a public inquiry.

And no one enjoys dwelling on the question of what would have happened    23
if the ethicist had been called in earlier. No one enjoys thinking about whether
being without food for the last month of her life may have helped to kill
Mrs. X.

# Style and Structure

1. What type of person does Shapiro expect his typical reader to be (e.g,
   medical professional, legal expert, philosophy major, etc.)? How can you
   tell?

2. (a) Identify the main topic of this essay:
   (i) the story of Mrs. X;
   (ii) the customary conditions for terminating treatment;
   (iii) the increase in the number of ethicists;
   (iv) the role of an ethicist.
   Write down the sentence in which Shapiro announces his **thesis.**
   (b) How does the presentation of Mrs. X's case in paragraphs 1 to 3 relate to this **thesis?**
   (c) Reread the **thesis statement** as if it were the opening sentence in the essay. Then reread paragraphs 1 to 3 as if they followed this **thesis statement.** Given the intended reader, which opening, Shapiro's or this new variation, is more effective? Why?
3. (a) What information does Shapiro include in paragraphs 5 to 7? How does knowing these facts near the beginning of the essay benefit readers as they continue through the later sections?
   (b) Paragraphs 9 to 13 use a compare/contrast format. What advantages does Shapiro achieve by presenting these contrasting opinions at this point?
   (c) Paragraph 8 takes the reader momentarily back to the case of Mrs. X. Why do you think Shapiro might choose to do so?
4. In what ways do the events presented in paragraphs 14 to 18 relate to the paragraphs preceding and following them? How important are these events to the reader's understanding of Shapiro's **thesis?**
5. (a) In what ways do the final three paragraphs of the essay act as a **conclusion?**
   (b) Shapiro returns to Mrs. X's case in the last two paragraphs. How effective is this technique in helping to convey his message to his reader?
   (c) How many times does Shapiro use the word "no one" in the last four sentences of the essay? What effect does this repetition have on the reader? How does the length of these sentences reinforce this effect?
6. Half of this essay is devoted to the case of Mrs. X. Reread the sections that do *not* deal with her specific situation (paragraphs 5 to 7, 9 to 13, 19 to 21). In what ways did including Mrs. X's case help the reader come to grips with this essay's **thesis?**

# Warm-up

1. Make a point-form summary of an ethicist's work. Then write a one-paragraph job description for an ethicist aimed at someone who has never heard of the profession.

When you have finished, look at two or three of the job descriptions written by others in the class. Compare them to yours for completeness and accuracy. Suggest details that might be added or changed in the others and make any changes to your own paragraph that would improve it.

2. Should an ethicist work in the way that Freedman does (see paragraph 11) or as Lynch does (see paragraph 12)? Write a paragraph that explains your preference and the reasons behind it.

**Audience:** a classmate who prefers the other way.

Find someone in the class who disagrees with your preference. Read each other's paragraphs and then try to convince the other person that your choice is preferable. When you have finished, make any revisions to your paragraph that might make it more convincing.

3. Working with the class as a whole, create a list of the types of cases in which an ethicist might play a role. Then write a short report on the class's findings.

**Audience:** someone who has never heard of an ethicist.

# Thinking and Writing

a. Shapiro's essay raises serious questions about decision making in the field of health care, particularly when those decisions involve such life-and-death choices as the ones in his example. Who should decide whether or not to remove life-support systems — the doctor, relatives, nurses, a team of people? Should such decisions be made at all? Should they be reviewed both before and after being put into practice? By whom? How often? At what stages should family members, doctors, nurses, ethicists, and ethical committees be a part of the decision-making process? What role should each play? Who should have the final say?

Write an essay in which you outline the process you would like followed if you or a member of your family were the patient in such a situation.

**Audience:** a medical professional.

Send a copy of your final draft to your family doctor and ask for a response.

b. The case of Mrs. X brings us face to face with the dilemma of euthanasia, or causing death to end suffering. Some people see euthanasia as an act of mercy. They believe a quick, painless death is preferable to facing extended periods of suffering from a terminal illness or from mental incompetence. However, another large segment of our society considers any act that speeds the process of dying to be a form of murder.

The dilemma becomes even more complicated in such cases as that of Mrs. X, where patients cannot tell others what they would like done, and those who are left to make the decisions may have opposing ideas on what course to follow.

Underlying this dilemma, of course, are the fundamental questions: "Who has the right to take life? Should euthanasia be practised at all?"

Write an essay in which you argue either for or against the practice of euthanasia. (Do not try to present the arguments for both sides.) As part of your planning process, try to identify the objections that would be raised by someone who holds a view opposed to yours, and deal with them in your essay.

**Audience:** someone who has not given much thought to euthanasia.

# When P.E.I. Joins the Mainland

## by Sue Calhoun

It was the summer of 1977, and a friend and I were racing madly in my    1
Volkswagen beetle to make the Cape Tormentine–Borden ferry to Prince Edward Island for a weekend camping trip. Of course, as we should have guessed,
so were hundreds of others. Stuck in the ferry-terminal parking lot, we waited
and waited while a hot summer afternoon faded to a chilly Maritime evening.
We boarded finally late that night. Still ahead of us was a long drive in the
dark to find a campsite.

Although the ferry service between New Brunswick and Prince Edward    2
Island has improved in the past decade, delays and stoppages are not un-
common. There are few passengers who don't have a story to tell about taking
the ferry across Northumberland Strait to this island of 126 000 residents.
Whether it was a long wait in the hot sun at the peak of the tourist season,
or being stranded for hours in winter in heavy ice in the strait, such tales
are almost the stuff of folklore in the Atlantic region. Lives on Prince Edward
Island are significantly influenced by the arrival and departure of ferries.

So when someone suggests abandoning the ferry and building a bridge,    3
or a fixed link, as it is called, it is almost instinctive for many to nod yes.
It would certainly make life easier. But, as is so often the case, things are
never quite as simple as they appear, a fact many people have discovered
during lively and emotional debate on the issue in the past few years.

The promise that the federal government would establish a passenger and    4
mail service to the mainland was one of the conditions under which Prince
Edward Island reluctantly joined the Dominion of Canada in 1873. Since then,
the idea of building a fixed crossing has come up regularly.

Senator George Howlan was one of the first to promote the idea — in    5
1885. In those days, winter transportation was by iceboats, which were al-
ternately rowed through open water and hauled over the ice by rugged crew
members, assisted at times by passengers. That winter, three iceboats with
fifteen passengers and seven crew members were caught in a blinding snowstorm and forced to camp overnight on the ice. No lives were lost, although
one individual became delirious and several lost limbs because of frostbite.
The incident served to remind Islanders that the winter service was treacherous
at best.

6      Senator Howlan said it was a disaster waiting to happen and asked the federal government to build a rail tunnel under the seabed of the strait. "We should never be imprisoned in the future as we have been in the past," he said. "Not only would the old industries be stimulated and put on a level with the other provinces, but quite a large number of new industries would be inaugurated."

7      In 1957, the Diefenbaker government tried to promote the idea of building a rock-fill causeway across the strait, leaving only a 300-metre bridged gap for shipping. Shipping companies complained it would be too dangerous. Eight years later, the Pearson government announced plans for a $148 million combined causeway and bridge. Construction actually began on both sides of the strait. Land was cleared, and approach roads and two overpasses were completed. (The roads have since been neglected, but the overpasses are in use today.) The project was cancelled by the Trudeau government in 1969, mainly because tenders for building the causeway were much higher than expected.

8      Now the idea is again being promoted. In 1985, inspired by Prime Minister Brian Mulroney's challenge to the private sector to come up with new ideas, two Nova Scotia businessmen submitted a proposal to build a combined bridge-causeway-tunnel across Northumberland Strait. Such a project, they said, could create a lot of jobs. Two other unsolicited proposals followed a year later — one for a bridge, the other for a tunnel.

9      In 1986, the government instructed Public Works Canada to assess the feasibility of the suggestions and to update engineering studies. Since then, more proposals have been received and numerous evaluations have been completed. In October 1988, the government announced that three finalists had been chosen — all recommended building a concrete bridge. The tunnel option was quickly discarded because the government was not satisfied that the only developer who suggested it could build the tunnel on time and within budget; discussions did not go so far as to consider the possible technical problems of building a tunnel under the seabed. A causeway is not being considered because it is generally agreed that the environmental risks would be too great. In the meantime, the fixed-link project has been postponed while an independent panel of experts reviews the effects the bridge would have on the environment and hears from the public.

10      A fixed crossing appeals to the federal government for two reasons: it would provide Islanders with better access to the mainland, and, equally important, it would eliminate the subsidies now paid for the ferry service. Marine Atlantic,

a Crown corporation that runs the ferries, receives $35 million in capital and operating subsidies every year.

The bridge is to be built over five years and initially funded by a private   11
company at an estimated cost of $1 billion. The company will then receive an annual subsidy from the federal government comparable to what is now being paid for the ferry service. This will be paid for 35 years, after which time the bridge will belong to the government. Tolls on the bridge will be equivalent to current ferry charges, roughly ten dollars one way for a car, its driver, and one passenger. (About one-third of Marine Atlantic's operating costs are covered by tolls.)

All along, the federal government has promised it would not proceed without   12
the blessing of Islanders, so in January 1988 a plebiscite was held. In the lively campaign leading up to the vote, the pro-link group, "Islanders for a Better Tomorrow," asserted that a bridge would mean convenience and cheaper transportation costs. The anti-link "Friends of the Island" were concerned about the environmental risks and the loss of the Island way of life. In the end, Islanders voted 60 percent to 40 in favour of a fixed crossing.

The issue has not been clear-cut for either side. It is not simply a question   13
of whether or not to build a bridge. The proposed fixed link has forced Islanders to think about their future. It has made them reflect on the question of progress, and what progress means as Canada moves into the 21st century. "Even if it doesn't go ahead, the fixed link has obliged us to think about what we want to be as a province," says Jim Larkin, a spokesman for the tourism industry.

Northumberland Strait is about 300 kilometres long and between 13 and 55   14
kilometres wide. It is covered with ice from January to April, although the sturdily built ferries usually manage to get through. Marine Atlantic, with four vessels, makes some 12 000 crossings a year. In 1986, it carried 1.6 million passengers in 550 000 cars and 175 000 commercial vehicles. (There is also a privately owned and government-subsidized ferry service that operates between Wood Islands, Prince Edward Island, and Caribou, Nova Scotia. It is expected to continue even if the fixed link is built.)

The proposed fixed link would span the strait at its narrowest point, between   15
Borden, Prince Edward Island, and Jourimain Island, New Brunswick, making it in winter the longest bridge over ice-covered waters in the world. Jourimain Island is three kilometres north of the ferry terminal at Cape Tormentine.

The water is relatively shallow there, about 30 metres. Although specific details of the three proposals are confidential, the bridge is expected to be a two-lane high-level structure over the entire crossing with piers about 200 metres apart. There would be a wider opening in the middle for large ships to pass underneath.

16   The bridge would use the approach roads on both sides of the strait that were built in the 1960s. Jourimain Island is linked to the mainland by one of these roads, which is well nigh impassable at present. Designated a national wildlife area, the island is home to many species of birds, and concern has been expressed about the effects a major flow of traffic would have on them. The Cape Tormentine terminal would continue to serve as a harbour for fishing vessels and may be adapted for other, yet undetermined, uses.

17   Northumberland Strait is one of the richest lobster-fishing areas in Atlantic Canada. Of the $70-million worth of fish and shellfish landed in the area in 1986, 73 percent was lobster — a quarter of Canada's annual lobster catch. Scallops, herring, mackerel, clams, mussels, and oysters are also taken in significant quantities. The area is fished by approximately 5500 inshore fishermen from the three Maritime provinces.

18   How a bridge would affect the fishery, both during construction and in the future, is clearly a major concern. During construction, there would be disruption of the ocean floor caused by dredging for the installation of concrete piers. Once the piers are in place, the main question then would be their effect on the ice. Many believe piers would increase ice jamming and delay break-up in the spring. That could lead to a change in water temperature and currents and postpone the start of the fishing season.

19   Fishermen are worried because life cycles of most marine species are influenced by temperature and currents. Newly hatched lobster larvae, for example, float to the surface where they spend from three to six weeks feeding on microscopic animal and plant life. Their dispersal depends on wind-driven surface currents.

20   Once the lobster larvae descend to the bottom, their growth is sensitive to water temperature. Lobsters require at least 9°C to begin moulting, the process by which a lobster sheds its shell in order to grow. Northumberland Strait, with its relatively warm waters, is a favourable environment for lobsters; a large proportion moult twice a year, meaning they grow twice as fast as those that moult once a year in other locations.

21   These issues have been the subject of many studies. Most have concluded that, once built, a bridge would have little lasting effect on the fishery. The most recent study done by ice specialists in Ottawa, for instance, says the

effects of the proposed bridge on ice jamming and temperature are likely to be minimal. Some reports suggest, however, that the construction phase could harm some species. Important scallop beds near the bridge alignment, as well as herring spawning beds at Cape Tormentine, risk being smothered during dredging operations. This would mean that neither species would reproduce during the years when dredging takes place. Most studies conclude that the greatest threat to the fishery would be an accident, such as an oil tanker hitting a pier and spilling its cargo into the strait.

Although generally positive, the studies are sometimes contradictory. And this has made a lot of fishermen on both sides of the strait very nervous.    22

Ansel Ferguson takes another sip of coffee as he settles into a comfortable    23
chair in his home in Hampton on the south shore of Prince Edward Island. An inshore fisherman, Ferguson was born a kilometre or so up the road, and spent eight years in the Royal Canadian Air Force and working in the Arctic on the DEW Line before coming home in 1961 to go fishing. Since then, he's fished everything — scallops, mackerel, herring — although in the past few years, because he's "getting older," he fishes only crab in the spring and lobster in the fall. Like many Maritime fishermen, Ferguson has an innate distrust of government officials and studies. He does not like the idea of a fixed link to the mainland. "Over the years, we've seen too many things happen," he says. "Numerous small projects, like bridges or causeways, that have ended up affecting the environment. Oyster beds have been destroyed, currents changed, siltation builds up. The government always comes back and says there was no evidence that that would have been detrimental. Well, I have no evidence that the fixed link will be detrimental either. But no one has ever built a bridge across Northumberland Strait before. All you can do is make an educated guess about the effects."

The Canso Causeway, built in the early 1950s to link Cape Breton Island    24
to the mainland of Nova Scotia, is often cited by fishermen as an example of what can happen. Over the years, scientists have had differing opinions about how the causeway has affected the fishery. "Some biologists say the Canso Causeway has not had any detrimental effects," Ferguson says. "Well, when I was young, we fished herring here (in Northumberland Strait) very early in the spring. It's only been the last few years that the herring have come back, but now they come in from the west, they circle around the island. So they have changed their patterns because of the causeway."

Ferguson is a member of the Prince Edward Island Fishermen's Association,    25
which initially did not oppose a fixed link outright, but wanted a tunnel because

it would be less disruptive to the marine environment. Since the tunnel option was discarded, the association has been campaigning to stop the project. It does not believe it is possible to predict the effect a bridge would have on the fishery.

26   Until recently, studies have suggested that the piers, placed 270 metres apart, would dam up nine percent of the strait. The fishermen's association argues that this would result in more frequent and longer ice jams. But now the federal government says the piers would be about 200 metres apart. If that is so, the fishermen say, the problem would be worse. Furthermore, once the ferry is taken out of service, its contribution to breaking up the ice will be eliminated.

27   On the other side of the Island, Henry Compton stomps the snow from his boots, then slips them off as he enters the large kitchen of his home near Bangor. Compton, 54, is a potato farmer, one of the largest producers on the Island. He and his two brothers farm 560 hectares, employ 25 people during the peak period, and produce a million five-kilogram bags of potatoes a year, 60 percent of which goes to Ontario and Quebec.

28   For Compton, getting his potatoes off the Island faster, and on a more regular and reliable basis, is reason enough for a fixed link. "It's terribly hard for our truckers to keep to a schedule when there are so many variables getting on and off the island. Schedules can be thrown off by the volume of the traffic and the lineups. And then there's the ice. For us, it's not so much the cost but the inconvenience, the problem of delivering a product on time. When we make a commitment to deliver, the customer wants it that day, not the next day or two days later. If you can't meet your deadline, you lose your customer," he says. Business people like Compton have been the major supporters of the project.

29   Government employment, agriculture, fishing and related food processing, and tourism are the major economic activities on Prince Edward Island. The proposed fixed link would affect them all.

30   The Atlantic Provinces Transportation Commission, for example, estimates the link would save the trucking industry from $5 million to $6 million a year — mainly in time saved. And a recent study predicts that 125 000 more tourists would visit the Island each year (over and above the 716 000 who visited in 1988). Those extra visitors would spend between $5 million and $10 million annually. Not surprisingly, the 750 members of the Tourism Industry Association of Prince Edward Island are in favour of the link.

31   Moreover, there would be an immediate boom during the construction

phase: an estimated 2000 jobs for five years, contracts for suppliers of construction materials, not to mention the multitude of consultants who have already been employed and would continue to find work on the project. When finished, the bridge is expected to employ 75 people for collecting tolls, clearing snow in winter, and providing emergency services.

However, the ferry service — and its 600 jobs — would disappear. These **32** jobs are full time and well paid by P.E.I. standards, and about 90 percent of them are filled by Islanders (the remainder of the workers are from New Brunswick). These wages contribute $15 million a year to the Island's economy, and the loss of these jobs would be a serious blow. Borden, where half of the labour force works for Marine Atlantic, could become a ghost town.

Some people suggest that the province's resources could not handle an extra **33** 125 000 tourists a year, most of whom would come in July and August. The pressure that increased traffic might put on beaches, sand dunes, and parklands concerns Diane Griffin of the Island Nature Trust, a group dedicated to the preservation of natural areas. Griffin is also worried that outsiders wanting to build cottages will drive up prices, making it harder for her group to buy up wild land. Concern about land speculation as a result of a fixed link was one reason why the provincial government recently announced a royal commission on land ownership and use.

Others fear that rather than helping business, the crossing could make Island **34** businesses more vulnerable to competition from outsiders, or, worse, that there would be no reason for some to stay on the Island; Cavendish Farms, an Irving-owned company that produces frozen french fries in Charlottetown, is an example. "The electricity bills alone are enough to drive businesses to Moncton," says Gerard Sexton, the union representative for Marine Atlantic workers.

As much as Northumberland Strait has been a physical barrier, it has also **35** been a psychological buffer for the people of Prince Edward Island. The isolation, especially in winter, has given them a character all their own. Some say it has allowed Islanders more independence and more control over their own affairs than otherwise would have been the case. People often talk about the "Island way of life," although it is a concept difficult to define. "A little more friendliness, a little more community closeness, a little less crime," says fisherman Ansel Ferguson. Throughout the debate, many Islanders have felt themselves on the verge of making a decision that will ultimately change the course of their history, and with it the nature of their way of life.

On the one hand, business people believe that the link will "stimulate **36** and inaugurate" new opportunities, as Senator Howlan suggested a century ago, and that the effects will be positive for the Island identity. "Cape Bretoners haven't lost their identity because of the causeway," says Jim Larkin of the Tourism Industry Association of Prince Edward Island. "If anything, they're even more individualistic today than they were before. I think the link may help us to focus our identity." Farmer Henry Compton believes that without the link the Island economy risks stagnation. "If we don't look after our economy, the Island could become a welfare state," he says.

37    On the other side are people like David Weale, a history professor at the University of Prince Edward Island. Weale ran as an independent candidate against the environment minister, Thomas McMillan, in the last federal election. Both were defeated by Liberal George Proud, who supports the fixed-link project. Weale conducted a one-issue campaign, because he felt that the federal government was trying to rush the fixed-link project without enough debate. "The identity of this province is profoundly tied up with its insularity. As one of my friends said, it would be like selling a bit of our soul to support a fixed link, especially when there seems to be so little evidence that it is really beneficial." While Weale concedes that some sectors, like the trucking industry, could benefit, he believes that a bridge would be the worst thing for tourism. "Our whole tourism industry here is based on image, on a certain ethos," he says. "If you greatly increase road traffic and cottage development on Prince Edward Island, what does that do to your tourism in the long run? How long is it before that intangible quality of being a clean, pastoral place is eroded?"

38    Perhaps, in the end, that is what the fixed-link debate is all about — progress, and how to define it. For Weale, it is a crucial question, given the increasing universal concern about the environment. "All over the world, technological development has placed an enormous strain on the environment. We all know that, and we're going to see it more and more each year. Now we have a major technological project planned for Prince Edward Island with environmental implications. It seems to me that you only proceed with these kinds of things if there are compelling reasons to do so. That ought to be part of our consciousness in the latter part of the twentieth century."

39    Construction of the fixed link had been planned to start in 1989. The schedule was delayed because of the federal election and the defeat of two key individuals, former public works minister Stewart McInnes and former environment minister McMillan. It has also been thrown off by the overwhelming concern of many Islanders for the environment. If the recently formed panel

of experts can deal with these apprehensions, construction could begin in 1990, unless, of course, the panel decides the project should not proceed at all, or if the price is too high.

For Islanders, this is an intense emotional issue, comparable perhaps to the free-trade debate. Now, as the independent panel prepares to hold public hearings, the intensity of Island opinion is not expected to wane. The issue is just too fundamental to the future of Canada's smallest province.    40

# Style and Structure

1.  Write a one-paragraph description of the intended reader of this essay. Use such evidence as the type of information included, the general approach to the topic, and the choice of words to justify your points.
2.  (a) Summarize, in one sentence, the main **thesis** of this essay.
    (b) Identify the passage in the introduction that presents this **thesis** to the reader. What techniques does Calhoun use to make the **thesis statement** itself more interesting?
    (c) In addition to stating her **thesis**, what else does Calhoun do in her introduction?
    (d) Write a one- or two-word summary of each point in the **introduction** that the writer uses to lead the reader from her opening story to the final sentence of paragraph 3. How well does the progression of ideas achieve **coherence** (logical development)? Justify your answer.
3.  (a) This essay's body has been structured into five major sections. Identify the aspect of the topic that is discussed in each.
    (b) Identify the paragraphs that serve as the **introductions** and **conclusions** for the first two sections of the body of the essay (paragraphs 4 to 22). In what ways do these paragraphs help the reader?
4.  (a) In the third section of the body (paragraphs 23 to 28), Calhoun uses someone from each side of the debate, a fisherman and a farmer, to present the reader with arguments for and against a fixed link. What advantages does she gain by doing so?
    (b) How does she convince the reader of the credibility of each representative? Why would she bother to do so?
    (c) Why might Calhoun have decided to follow Ansel Ferguson's observations with a description of the concerns of the Prince Edward Island Fishermen's Association?
    (d) Write a short **introduction** and **conclusion** for this section of the essay. How does their presence affect the section's impact on the reader?

5. (a) How does the final section of the body (paragraphs 35 to 38) relate to the sections that precede it? Given the intended reader and the number of subjects covered earlier in the essay, why is including this section an effective strategy?

   (b) What is the effect on the reader's thinking of presenting Weale's ideas at the very end of the body?

6. In what ways do the final paragraphs act as a **conclusion** for the essay? On a scale of one to ten, how would you rank this **conclusion's** effectiveness? Why?

# Warm-up

1. Some people argue that all major government decisions should be based on plebiscites such as that held in Prince Edward Island on the fixed link (see paragraph 12). Others say that once we have elected our representatives to office, we should stand back and let them do the job they have been elected to do.

   Hold a formal debate on this subject, with half the class developing arguments for the three debaters who will support plebiscites and the other half helping the three debaters who will argue for the other side.

2. Write a formal explanation of your own arguments for or against the frequent use of plebiscites.

   **Audience:** someone who would disagree with your stand.

   To try out the effectiveness of your first draft, have one or two people who disagree with your position read it over. Ask them to find weaknesses in your arguments and presentation. (Don't be satisfied with "It looks okay." Persist until you get some real help.) Use their reactions to help you revise.

# Thinking and Writing

a. As Calhoun points out, "Perhaps, in the end, that is what the fixed-link debate is all about — progress, and how to define it" (paragraph 38). Everywhere in Canada, the same kind of problem is being debated: should there be economic and technological development at almost any cost, or should we put our concern for the environment first?

Identify a project in your own community that is causing a similar discussion. It may be a new highway or the widening of an old one; it may be a new subdivision, factory, or mall, or the construction of a new communications system; or it may be pollution or other environmental damage caused by a long-established industry.

Write an essay in which you describe, as objectively as possible, both sides of the debate over this project.

**Audience:** someone new to the community who does not know the details of the problem.

b. Write an essay in which you suggest approaches that should be taken whenever there is a confrontation between technological or economic development and environmental concerns. Should one be given preference over the other? Is there some way to resolve the two sides? You may want to use specific examples to illustrate your points, but do not restrict yourself to trying to resolve one specific situation: deal with the problem in general.

**Audience:** someone who is involved in a very practical way with trying to resolve such problems.

Send a copy of your final draft to the public relations officer at the local office of Environment Canada or the Ministry of Natural Resources.

# Acid Rain: Scourge from the Skies

## by Robert Collins

1  Lumsden Lake, on the north shore of Ontario's Georgian Bay, twinkles like a sapphire in a setting of verdant forest and sparkling quartz. Blue, incredibly clear, and seemingly pure, just twenty years ago it abounded in fish.

2  But now this exquisite lake is dead, its fish wiped out, the other creatures and plants in its aquatic food chain dead or dying. Like hundreds of other lakes and rivers in North America, Lumsden has been ravaged by acid from the sky.

3  From the smokestacks of power plants, smelters, and factories across eastern Canada and the United States, and from vehicle exhausts in major cities, invisible clouds of sulphur dioxide and nitrogen oxide gases soar across provincial, state, and international boundaries. They settle, sometimes 1500 kilometres from their sources, as acid rain, acid snow, or dry particles that mingle with surface water to become acidic. The fallout erodes building surfaces and automobiles, may harm trees, crops, and soils, and could pose a threat a human health.

4  Already 140 Ontario lakes are dead or dying. An additional 48 000 are sensitive to acid rain because of the natural acidity of surrounding soil. In Nova Scotia, acid rain has killed all the salmon in seven rivers, threatening a $2-million-a-year salmon-fishing industry. In New York State's Adirondacks region, more than 150 lakes are fishless. Acid rain, concludes an intensive study by a committee of the Ontario legislature, is "a national emergency." Says John Fraser, former federal minister of the environment, "It is the most serious environmental problem now facing Canada."

5  Approximately one-third of the acid falling from North American skies is nitric, mostly from motor-vehicle combustion; about two-thirds is sulphur, produced mainly by coal-burning plants and nonferrous smelting. In Canada, the International Nickel (Inco) and Falconbridge smelters near Sudbury, and the Noranda Mines smelter at Noranda, Quebec, are notable offenders. Inco, the largest single source in North America, accounts for twenty percent of the sulphur dioxide emitted in Canada, and one percent of known sulphur-dioxide emissions in the world. In the United States, two-thirds of sulphuric acid rain comes from power-generating plants, particularly those burning high-sulphur coal. Each year the eastern United States belches forth 48 million metric tons of sulphur dioxide and nitrogen oxides; Canada emits seven million tons.

North Americans have been smelting ore and burning fossil fuels for gen-    6
erations. In the past, the gases went up ordinary chimneys or small smokestacks, to descend upon nearby areas and pollute them. In time, governments
and industries opted for taller smokestacks, and Inco's 350-metre one near
Sudbury, the tallest in North America, was one such vain attempt to disperse
pollution harmlessly into the atmosphere. Instead, these gases may ride the
winds for days — time enough for critical chemical reactions to take place.
Within three days aloft, for example, half of a sulphur dioxide ($SO_2$) emission
will oxidize into sulphate particles ($SO_4$). A rainstorm or snowfall, settling
through these particles, produces sulphuric acid ($H_2SO_4$), which falls to the
ground, usually far from the source.

Nitric oxides similarly turn into nitric acid, but the chemical reaction is    7
more complex and the pollutant more difficult to "track." Environment Canada's atmospheric environment service, feeding twice-daily weather reports
from a North American network into computers, can track an acid storm
fairly accurately back to its point of origin. We know that each year about
two million tons of sulphur come drifting across the border into Canada aboard
prevailing winds that in summer sweep north up through the United States
from the Gulf of Mexico, then curl in an easterly direction over Ontario,
Quebec, and the Maritimes. In the meantime, winds carry half a million tons
a year of Canada's pollution into the eastern United States.

The lethal fallout is measured on a "pH" scale (referring to the concentration    8
of hydrogen ions), wherein 0 is acid, 14 is alkaline, and 7 is neutral. But
because the pH scale is logarithmic, a pH of 5 is 10 times more acidic than
a pH of 6. The *mean* pH rainfall in Ontario's Muskoka-Haliburton lake country
ranges between 3.95 and 4.38, about 40 times more acidic than normal rainfall,
while storms in Pennsylvania have registered 2.8 — almost as acidic as vinegar.

Some lands and waters, according to their natural acidity, are particularly    9
susceptible. Lake Ontario is safe with a pH8 reading. Southern Ontario's farmland, much of the central United States, and Canada's prairies have well-buffered
soils. But environmentalists worry that vast Athabasca oil-sands developments
will acidify sensitive northern Albertan and Saskatchewan lakes. Most of the
Precambrian shield, including large portions of Quebec, are of a bedrock ge-
ology, low on alkalinity and easily harmed. Although damage reports from
Quebec are scarce, federal scientists fear that Quebec is *at least* as badly off
as Ontario.

New York State's beautiful Adirondack Mountains region, says park agency    10
commissioner Anne La Bastille, has become "an atmospheric cesspool." It receives large amounts of rain and snow, because it is the first easterly mountain

range to be hit by prevailing winds from the Midwest. As a result, half of the Adirondack lakes 600 metres or more above sea level are no longer able to support fish.

11    From studies of dying North American lakes and thousands of already-dead Scandinavian lakes, scientists know acid rain kills aquatic life by direct action on fish, by releasing toxic metals, and by depleting aquatic foods. In Canada, some species, such as lake trout, fail to reproduce below pH6. Scores of lakes on our continent fit into this killer category. Harold Harvey, University of Toronto zoologist and one of Canada's foremost experts on acid rain, can tick off the tragic life-and-death history of such lakes by name: "Tyson Lake was pH7.4 in 1955 and 4.9 by 1971, a horrendous change. . . . George Lake: 8 species left out of 13. . . . O.S.A. Lake: all fish extinct. . . . "

12    Below pH5.5, nearly all shrimplike organisms, essential diet for certain fish, disappear. Frogs and aquatic insects may be dying off, too. Part of the slaughter is caused by metal poisoning; aluminum, manganese, and possibly other metals are released by chemical action from lake beds or surrounding soils. Inevitably, the deadly chain reaction touches other wildlife: fish-eating ducks, loons, ospreys, otter, and mink.

13    Paradoxically, a trace of acid rain can actually improve the growth of certain plants in some soils, providing nitrate or sulphate nutrients. But rains of between pH4 and pH3 damage the foliage of almost all plants and reduce the yields of carrots, radishes, beets, and broccoli. Acid rain leaches calcium and potassium from plant tissues and erodes the waxy coating that protects their leaves from disease.

14    On the ground, acid rain leaches essential calcium, magnesium, potassium, and sodium from the soil. It also prevents the decay of vegetation, depriving the soil of valuable nutrients. It kills earthworms, encourages unwanted fungus, prevents some seeds from germinating, and releases toxic quantities of metal to be absorbed by roots.

15    More alarmingly, authorities fear acid rain in municipal water systems dissolves particles of copper or lead from pipes into drinking water. In one area of the Adirondacks, says park commissioner La Bastille, residents are advised to let their taps run five minutes every morning to flush out water that may have become toxic overnight.

16    What should be done? North America has been slow to recognize the problem and scientists across the continent deplore the lack of research funds. Scandinavia spends about 50 cents per capita on research, compared to ten cents in North America. "Acid rain is not a 'jazzy' problem," complains David

Schindler of the federal Freshwater Institute in Manitoba. "Unfortunately," says Minnesota Congressman James L. Oberstar, "it's easier to get $2 billion for a nuclear aircraft carrier than $6 million to protect the environment." Scores of studies *are* underway, but new technologies must be applied, existing laws and controls tightened, and a Canada–U.S. agreement reached.

If acid rain is not to get the upper hand, we will have to apply the best available technology, with all the political will we can muster. The U.S. Environmental Protection Agency (EPA) is experimenting with a burner assembly for pulverized-coal boilers that could reduce nitrogen-oxide emissions by 80 percent.    17

Technology for reasonable control of sulphur dioxide already exists, says EPA's David Hawkins. "All we have to do is apply it." Basically it consists of washing coal before combustion or cleaning emissions during combustion. Grinding coal and putting it through a liquid bath can remove as much as a third of the sulphur, says Lowell Smith of EPA. Yet about half of the high-sulphur coal presently used in the eastern states is not washed. Ontario Hydro, one of the largest coal users in Canada, buys washed coal but admits it would be improved by a further washing.    18

Of several techniques to remove pollution during industrial coal combustion, perhaps the most effective is "scrubbing," in which the gases are washed in a desulphurizing bath before going into the atmosphere. Scrubbers can remove at least 90 percent of sulphur dioxide. Yet only the *newest* coal-burning plants in the United States and *none* of the major Canadian utility plants are so equipped. To remove a further 12 million tons of $SO_2$ by fitting scrubbers to some eastern U.S. power plants would cost $3 to $4 billion a year, says Lowell Smith.    19

Many new processes are under study in both Canada and the United States. But will they be used any more than the existing pollution-removal devices? Industries tend to put off such expensive items until they are pushed by government. Governments, hectored by industrial lobbies or by regions whose economy depends on mining, tend to drag their feet until the public demands action.    20

"We must not give up on acid rain," says Tom Brydges, supervisor of limnology and toxicity with the Ontario Ministry of the Environment. "We must not be bamboozled by six-figure clean-up costs. If industries and utilities are pressed, they often find solutions that are better for the ecology and more efficient for them. We citizens must look these industries in the eye and say *'This won't do!'*"    21

22    An international agreement that serves as the framework for national, provincial, and state standards is essential. Canada and the United States are now inching toward it, but action is unlikely in the near future. The core of such an agreement would be *enforced* reduction of emissions in both countries.

23    "We must at least get an agreement for huge cutbacks in emissions, maybe by state or province," suggests Ontario's Brydges. But Ron Reid, staff environmentalist with the Federation of Ontario Naturalists (FON), is one of many who sees enormous difficulties in reaching international accord: "The United States seems to be going in the opposite direction, in its trend to coal usage and the demands in some parts of the country for *relaxed* emission standards. Yet the American *people* seem sympathetic whenever they hear about what's happening to Canadian lakes."

24    In both Canada and the United States, laws governing emissions are often ineffective and ambiguous. Whether a community in one country could sue a polluter in the other, for instance, is a question that causes jurists to shudder. In Canada, pollution-control laws are primarily a provincial matter. Thus, Canada's federal Clean Air Act is of very little direct benefit, says John Swaigen of the Canadian Environmental Law Association. The federal government can set emission standards where emissions would clearly endanger human health or violate an international agreement, but for acid rain there is yet no international agreement, nor is the threat to human health fully documented. Nevertheless, says Ray Robinson, assistant deputy minister at Environment Canada, this country could cope with acid rain without changes in the laws, given the co-operation of the provinces.

25    The U.S. federal Clean Air Act of 1970 and a subsequent amendment do lay a firm hand on all new coal-burning plants. Utilities will have to invest several billion dollars to remove 70 to 90 percent of the sulphur from coal. They will be required to reduce $SO_2$ emissions by 55 percent and nitrogen-oxide emissions by twenty percent over the current standard.

26    The trouble is, the new standards do not apply to existing plants. They are exempted on the premise that the stiff new regulations, requiring additional multimillion-dollar equipment, would impose a crushing financial burden on the companies and their customers. Yet by 1995, these older plants will still account for 73 percent of all $SO_2$ emissions from coal-fired utilities in the United States. Unless new rules are applied to existing plants, they will continue to pour acid rain on Canada and the eastern United States for the remainder of this century.

27    Canada wants the United States to amend its Clean Air Act. In the United

States, Robert Rauch, staff attorney with the nonprofit Environmental Defense Fund, wants EPA to get tougher by implementing a provision in the Clean Air Act that would prohibit interstate pollution and allow injured states to sue polluters, and by refusing to relax state limits. Lax application of the Ohio standard, he says, enables ten or twelve large coal-burning plants to legally emit five to ten times as much $SO_2$ as new plants would be permitted to do. "EPA may have to be given the flexibility to regulate particular coal-burning facilities," adds Gus Speth of the President's Council on Environmental Quality.

The annual cost of curbing emissions until the end of this century has been estimated at $350 million to $500 million in Canada and $5 billion to $7 billion in the United States. But the cost of not cleaning up is surely worse. "We're not talking about the damage to date," says Harold Harvey, "but about the potential loss if nothing is done now — and that is truly horrendous!" 28

Who can assess the value of a living lake, the splash of trout, the croak of frogs, or the cry of an osprey? These are lost forever already in some lakes. Yet, as Minnesota Congressman Oberstar says, "We have a rare opportunity to see a disaster coming." We have had a taste of it in the Adirondacks and we can learn from Sweden and Norway where, without any international controls, 15 000 lakes have been denuded by acid rain. There is time to stop it here, if enough citizens in *both* countries care enough to insist on quick decisive action. 29

Says Ontario's Tom Brydges: "It would be a crime to pass on to our grandchildren 50 000 lakes without fish, without loons, without fish-eating ducks. Dammitall, we're *not* going to let the environment go down the tube!" 30

# Style and Structure

1. (a) What image of Lumsden Lake does the writer present in paragraph 1? Which specific words and phrases create this image? How does this description fit the reader's expectations of a northern lake?
   (b) What image of Lumsden Lake does the writer present in paragraph 2? Which specific words and phrases create this image? How does this description fit the reader's expectations of a northern lake?
   (c) Why does the writer keep paragraphs 1 and 2 separate instead of combining them?

2.    The appeal to the reader in paragraphs 1 and 2 is mainly emotional. On what level does the writer appeal in paragraphs 3 and 4?

3.    Assuming that the **thesis statement** comes at the end of paragraph 4, what purpose do paragraphs 1 to 3 and the first half of paragraph 4 serve?

4.    What information is contained in paragraphs 5 to 8? Why does the writer choose to include this information at this point in the essay? What does this organizational strategy indicate about the intended reader of the article?

5.    What information is contained in paragraphs 9 to 15? How does the writer give the problem of acid rain impact for a reader who may not be very concerned about wildlife and the ecology?

6.    What information is contained in paragraphs 17 to 28? How does paragraph 16 help prepare the reader for this long section?

7.    In paragraphs 17 to 28, the writer presents three things that "should be done" about acid rain. Do you detect any parallels in the way in which he develops these sections? (Pay particular attention to **transitional** words such as "but" and "yet.")

8.    How do the final two paragraphs of the essay act as an appropriate **conclusion**? Why does the author use quotations?

# Warm-up

1.    Make notes on the kinds of damage caused by acid rain as they are reported in this essay. Then write a one-paragraph summary of the effects of acid rain.
      **Audience:** someone who doubts the effects of acid rain.
      Compare your summary to those written by two or three of your classmates. Try to help one another identify (1) any key points left out and (2) any passages in which the ideas are not expressed clearly. Revise your summary in the light of the suggestions made.

2.    Choose one of the following topics:
      (i) the extent of the damage caused by acid rain in Canada;
      (ii) measures already taken to control acid rain;
      (iii) the geographic regions of Canada affected by acid rain;
      (iv) the impact of acid rain on your own community.
      Collect at least three newspaper or magazine articles on the topic. Then write a brief summary (an abstract) of the most comprehensive and up-

to-date article you have found. (Make certain that at least two or three people in the class do each topic.)

Make enough copies of your summary for each person in the class, so that everyone has a resource booklet of up-to-date material on acid rain.

# Thinking and Writing

a.  Environmentalists frequently criticize industrialists for not doing enough to clean up pollution. Research the industrialists' point of view on acid rain, and write an essay in which you present their arguments sympathetically.

    **Audience:** an average citizen who has a minimal knowledge of the problem of acid rain.

b.  Write an essay in which you argue for or against new measures to control acid rain.

    **Audience:** a legislator or business executive in a position to do something about the problem.

    Send a copy of this essay to your representative in the provincial Parliament or to the president of your local or provincial hydro company.

# Integrated Sports: A Question of Fair Play

## by Fran Rider

1 Full integration for all ages and in all sports will mean drastically reduced opportunities for female athletes. With uncontrolled emigration of girls to boys' teams, girls' teams will fold, and many girls unwilling or unable to compete with boys will have no chance to play. This is equality?

2 Sports-minded girls already have enough trouble honing their abilities. Too often, boys' teams monopolize both practice time and funding dollars. But the way to correct such problems is to promote and develop a female sports system leading to Olympic competition and professional events. This effort is now well under way.

3 Time was when girls either played against boys or hung up their hockey skates. As recently as the mid-1970s, ten-year-old goalie Gail Cummings of Huntsville, Ontario, had no girls' team available to her and was rejected by a boys' team because of her sex. The OWHA helped Cummings take her cause to the Ontario Human Rights Commission. Although she lost, girls have since gained the right to play on boys' teams when no local girls' teams exist. They have also gained teams of their own that equal or even surpass the boys' in coaching and calibre of competition — and are much more sports-manlike to boot.

4 Take the teams open to Justine Blainey. The Toronto and surrounding area offers the world's best female hockey opportunities, ranging from provincial championship teams at the novice level (girls aged nine and up) through to the senior A Team Canada, which captured the McCallion World Cup last year.

5 Blainey has been touted in the press as an exceptional player simply because she qualified for a male team. Few noticed that the team was playing at the lowest competitive level in boys' hockey, and this kind of shortsightedness has coloured the entire debate about sports integration.

6 Many people now assume that the best female athletes should be moving up to male events. What an insult to world-class athletes like runner Angella Issajenko, skier Laurie Graham, and our Canadian Women's Field Hockey Team, who are every bit as skilled as their male counterparts! Should we dismiss these women as second-rate just because they can't outmuscle equally trained men?

No one disputes the notion more forcefully than female athletes. In most 7
sports, the vast majority of girls want to play in an all-female environment
where they can enrol at an early age and progress to the upper levels. They
want to match their competitors in size and strength as well as dedication
and mental acuity.

Integrated teams may meet girls' needs in a few sports, such as shooting, 8
where a more muscular opponent cannot dominate competition. But in many
others, integration would make females the losers. Each sport's promise for
integration is best evaluated by its own governing body, not by ill-informed
feminists.

Like it or not, male and female bodies do not perform identically. Medical 9
evidence indicates that the differences are negligible until puberty, when girls
gain a temporary edge in size and strength. But the situation reverses at
about age fourteen. And if teenage girls are to have the teams they deserve,
we must nurture and protect the entire female stream.

If we allow girls like Justine Blainey to play on inferior male teams, how 10
can we deny boys the chance to play on often-superior female teams? Last
season, the OWHA's male applicants included a fourteen-year-old boy who
felt that the girls' program offered better opportunities than the boys'. But
letting boys in creates a new problem: displacement of girls by more powerful
players.

Integration will lead to exploitation of female athletes. Girls will be lured 11
from top female teams by coaches of male teams who want sensationalized
media coverage and increased funding (often allocated on a per-capita basis).
These girls will be recruited at puberty to help bring the male team a championship, and will then be discarded when biology overtakes them.

Meanwhile, the loss of girls from the female system will leave their former 12
teammates with fewer opportunities. The defection of one or two players
has been known to kill a team, and those that survive such blows will then
face a shortage of money. Cost-slashing governments will likely decide to fund
only one team per sport. Universities, now fending off requests for increased
funding of women's teams, could well go the same route.

In Quebec, which has allowed integration since 1978, female sporting op- 13
portunities have not expanded. Only 35 girls' hockey teams exist, compared
with 286 in Ontario, and almost 300 girls play on boys' teams, compared
with 55 in Ontario.

If we really want more opportunities for female athletes, then let's start 14
giving girls more funding, facilities, media coverage, corporate sponsorships,
and elite opportunities. And let's stop demeaning female teams with cheap

talk about integration. We need not defeat men in head-to-head combat on the playing field to prove we're their equals.

# Style and Structure

1. (a) The writer has chosen to begin her essay with her **thesis statement:** "Full integration for all ages and in all sports will mean dramatically re- duced opportunities for female athletes." Do you believe this is an effective opener? Explain your answer.

   (b) Regardless of whether you like the opener or not, you can experiment with alternatives. Review the suggestions on introductory techniques (pp. 303–307) and choose two different approaches that might work in this instance. Write two new beginning paragraphs on this subject, proposing the same **thesis.**

   (c) Which of the three introductory paragraphs you now have do you prefer? Why?

2. (a) Count the number of sentences in each paragraph of this essay. What might you conclude about the variety of paragraph lengths?

   (b) Taking the information provided and using appropriate **transitions,** com- bine paragraphs 4 and 5. Do you feel that the longer paragraph formed this way is more satisfactory? Give reasons to support your decision.

   (c) Contrast the paragraph formed in (b) above with some of the writer's shorter paragraphs, such as paragraph 2. What tone do short paragraphs give to the essay?

   (d) Review one of your recent essays, looking for short paragraphs. Do you believe that you could now improve the tone by developing the para- graphs further? Choose one and rewrite for fuller development; then compare with your earlier attempt. Which do you prefer?

3. In paragraph 13, the writer presents statistics regarding women's sports in the provinces of Ontario and Quebec. What impression do these sta- tistics make upon the reader? Do they strengthen the writer's case? Why?

4. (a) Point out areas in this essay in which the writer uses different **organizational approaches** to help further her argument. (See pp. 301–302 if you need to review **organizational approaches.**)

   (b) Which approaches do you think are most helpful in proving the writer's case? Would you suggest others that might also be effective? If so, which?

5. (a) In her **concluding paragraph,** Rider introduces the pronoun "we." To whom does "we" refer?

(b) How does the use of the pronoun "we" change the tone of the essay? What impressions will the reader likely take away from the essay, in light of this change? Do you believe that the strategy is effective? Explain your answer.

# Warm-up

Investigate the difference between primary and secondary research techniques. Divide the class into two groups. The first group will conduct primary research by polling other students and staff outside the class about their attitudes toward government funding in the area of sports. This will involve meeting together first to compile a list of questions to ask participants. The second group will conduct secondary research by going to the library to find as much current information as possible on what Canadians believe their government should be doing about funding organized sports.

Bring the two groups together for a class discussion of findings and experiences. Investigate such questions as which technique produced more helpful information and which technique was more enjoyable. Try to draw some conclusions about the use and the effectiveness of each of these two techniques.

# Thinking and Writing

a. A poll among readers of the magazine in which this essay was published showed that 60 percent favoured integration of males and females in sports teams, 29 percent opposed, and 11 percent were undecided. Evidently, those favouring numbered more than twice those who opposed.

Write an essay in which you explain why you believe there is such a large proportion of people favouring integration. Give specific examples of social attitudes that you feel might have promoted the response given. You might also cite cases such as that involving Justine Blainey, mentioned in this essay, to support your opinion.

**Audience:** anyone interested in community team sports.

b. In her essay, Rider speaks of "cost-slashing governments" (paragraph 12), suggesting that they are looking for ways to reduce the amount of funding they give to sports.

Many people suggest that governments are frequently less than generous when dealing with the needs of sports. On the other hand, there are those who maintain that, particularly in times of economic slowdown, governments have far more important issues to address, and that sports should be the last of their considerations.

Write an essay in which you argue for or against increased government spending in the area of sports. You will probably find information to support your ideas if you look through the pages of the sports section of your local newspaper. Organize the research material you find, using a number of approaches.

**Audience:** a local member of parliament.

Choose two essays expressing opposing opinions and seek publication for them in the school newspaper.

# Crowd Control

## by John Colapinto

George "The Animal" Steele and Bam Bam Bigelow hit the spotlit ring, and     1
Marilyn is up out of her seat bellowing. "Tear his eyes out! Rip his ribs out
of his chest! Hey, ref! That wasn't fair! What're you, blind?"

A cashier at a restaurant, Marilyn usually attends wrestling matches with     2
a couple of friends. She's a small-boned woman in her forties with beige hair,
beige glasses, beige slacks, and a beige sweater. She's been a wrestlemaniac
since the age of fifteen, when she attended her first show. Except for karate
(she says her bedroom is wallpapered with Chuck Norris posters), Marilyn's
favourite sport in the whole world is wrestling.

It's a passion she shares with millions of others in 26 countries who have     3
caught wrestling fever. NBC-TV's monthly wrestling show is now a top-rated
program; *Piledriver* (an LP of wrestlers growling pop tunes) went platinum
in 1988; sales are brisk for Ricky "The Dragon" Steamboat baseball caps, King
Kong Bundy posters ("Suitable for Framing!"), and even the plastic Hulk Hogan
light-switch cover ("HULKASIZE YOUR ROOM!"). Wrestling may not be making the cover of *Sports Illustrated* and *Newsweek*, but the sport is more
popular than ever.

The question is, "Why?" Why does Marilyn spend her nonworking hours     4
combing The Sports Network for wrestling updates? Why drop fifteen dollars
on a ticket?

Seen live, without the flash and dazzle of TV editing and the distracting     5
commentary, wrestling seems an unusual sport indeed. A match between two
of wrestling's biggest stars, Greg "The Hammer" Valentine and Jake "The
Snake" Roberts, is little more than a listless, slow-motion tussle in which
lumbering, sun-lamped men with shaven chests and Spandex bottoms execute
somersaults with the assistance of their "opponent." Jake throws a "punch"
that misses by a yard, yet sends Valentine flying against the ropes. When
the now "enraged" Valentine retaliates, tossing his tormentor out of the ring
(onto the conveniently placed foam mat), the "victim" is seen to give a little
*hup* with his legs to help himself over the ropes. Frequently, it's possible
to see the supposed adversaries communicating with each other to agree on
the next move: a knee drop, a body slam, or that ever-popular but mystifying
moment when both wrestlers, in tandem, trot back and forth across the ring,

"bouncing" off the ropes, narrowly missing one another in the centre until they pretend to collide and one of them falls down.

6      Wrestling is often compared to the throwing of the Christians to the lions — a communal outlet of violent tendencies. But if it's blood-letting people want, they don't go to wrestling. There's always hockey or, better still, boxing, where the athletes are sometimes killed. Marilyn, for instance, grimaces at the mention of boxing. "Can't stand it," she says, mere minutes after hurling her invective at Jake and Valentine. "Too violent!"

7      It can't be the spectacle that draws the crowds. Occasionally a wrestler will perform an impressive acrobatic leap or fall, but such moments are rare. The wrestlers can't be blamed. They're simply too exhausted to do much except roll around a bit. Billy "Red" Lyons, now retired from the ring, recalls what it was like working the North American wrestling circuit in the 1950s, during the sport's earlier boom. Wrestlers fought five nights a week without benefits or health insurance, and they were paid only for their time in the ring. "It's a tough life," Lyons says. "In some ways it's even worse for the boys today, because they work all over the world. Jet lag. Monday they're in Toronto, Tuesday in Tokyo, Wednesday in Australia." If the travelling doesn't wear them down, injuries do. (Just because the fighting is faked doesn't mean they don't get hurt.) Wrestlers are often performing with torn ligaments, twisted joints, bruised muscles, sprains. Or worse. "I knew guys who'd broken a leg," Lyons says. "They'd get it put in a cast. Then, after a day, they'd cut the cast off, tape up the fracture, and go into the ring. You had to. You only get paid when you fight."

8      Signs of this frantic life are clearly visible in today's top stars. When the "titans" enter the ring, you can see the boredom, fatigue, and pain that makes the skin on their faces sag. They trudge into the spotlight, favouring swollen knees, limping on twisted ankles, growling like very tired and unconvincing bears.

9      And yet. . . . The audience is rapt. A half-hearted knee drop in a bout between two unknowns can raise a more ear-splitting shriek of joy from the crowd than an overtime goal by the home team in hockey. Ask Marilyn why she screams herself hoarse, and she shrugs and smiles. "That's just the way I am. I'm very excitable when it comes to this. You get caught up in it. I know it's fake," she adds cheerfully. "But that's okay. I still love it. I JUST *LOVE* IT!"

10     In 1952, the French philosopher Roland Barthes pondered wrestling and con-cluded that it is a "sum of spectacles, of which no single one is a function."

Possibly — but this isn't much help in explaining wrestling's appeal to fans like Marilyn. Anthropologist Jim Freedman, in his book *Drawing Heat*, offers a class explanation for the sport's popularity. Wrestling often presents a simple drama. A rule-abiding good guy is pitted against an unscrupulous bad guy who has supposedly rigged the contest by bribing the referee, using concealed weapons, or working in collusion with one or more colleagues outside the ring. The struggle is a metaphor for the real-life injustices and inequities suffered by simple, hard-working folk. Freedman says that wrestling's predominantly blue-collar fans "recognize [in the ring] an economy that's rigged against its basic [free-market] principles of opportunity for everyone, and rigged against them and their jobs in factories and small businesses." But Freedman doesn't explain why people angry about being duped by society will pay fifteen dollars for the privilege of being further duped by the powers that rig wrestling.

Philosophers, academics, and even fans can go only so far in solving the 11 riddle of wrestling. As with everything else about the sport, answers can be arrived at only through the promoters. At 53 years old, Jack Tunney is one of the most successful wrestling impresarios in the world. A bearlike man six feet three inches tall, Tunney likes to show people how far a kid from Toronto's tough east end can go on a high-school diploma. He wears a dark blue business suit with a gold World Wrestling Federation lapel pin, a chunky gold pinkie ring, and a gold bracelet. His salt-and-pepper hair is conservatively cut, except for the hint of Elvis in the curling wave that crests over his forehead.

Tunney has been in the wrestling game for more than 30 years, having 12 apprenticed with his uncle, Frank Tunney, the legendary promoter who, in the 1930s, was one of the first to recognize the vast potential for profitability in the sport. Together, Frank and Jack built a wrestling empire unparalleled in Canada. In the early 1980s, after his uncle's death, Tunney threw in his lot with the New York–based World Wrestling Federation, and in 1984 was elected its president. Tunney is as vague about his role as WWF president as he is about all aspects of his business. "Well, I'm kind of like the head of the Kiwanis Club," he says, "or the Lions Club . . . I chair meetings . . . and so forth . . . make decisions on the rules. . . . "

Tunney has been a major player in creating the worldwide wrestling boom 13 of this decade. It was the WWF that came up with the highly successful marriage of rock'n'roll and wrestling. (Cyndi Lauper was hired to act as "manager" to a woman wrestler, generating immense publicity.) The WWF has crammed cable-TV airwaves with wrestling extravaganzas. And the WWF has, for better or worse, made Hulk Hogan a household name.

14        At heart, Jack Tunney is a promoter, and when he's feeling particularly expansive (which, admittedly, isn't often), he can be slyly sardonic about the sharp young MBAs who have invaded wrestling's back rooms with their flow charts and demographics and marketing strategies. "Those are smart guys," Tunney says. "They come up with some real good ideas. But they don't know how to sell tickets."

15        Tunney does. He has spent 30 years filling arenas with hysterical fans. He's done it, he explains, by giving people exactly what they want. Tunney actually stands at the exit as the fans file out after a show. He eavesdrops on what they are saying to each other, trying to learn what moments they enjoyed, which wrestlers they liked. "The *fans* choose the favourites," Tunney says. "Give 'em what they want, and they keep coming back."

16        And what *do* they want? "Well," Tunney says, "put it this way. Hulk Hogan won all his matches for four years. Obviously, people weren't coming to see him lose."

17        It has been revealed by renegade wrestlers that promoters not only rig the outcome of each match, they can stage-manage every moment of the struggle. Tunney, of course, denies this, just as he denies any role in engineering the offstage dramas that run like a soap opera through the wrestling season. "Natural tensions develop between the wrestlers," Tunney explains, patiently. "What we do, as promoters, is *play* on those tensions. By hanging around in a dressing room, you can tell who doesn't like who." For instance, "Ravishing" Rick Rude and Jake "The Snake" Roberts have a running dispute over the overtures "Ravishing" repeatedly makes toward Jake's wife. "Ravishing" often approaches her at ringside in full view of the fans and wriggles his pelvis suggestively. Invariably, Jake, wielding his trademark eight-foot boa constrictor, hurtles himself from backstage and chases "Ravishing" around the ring. Though this scenario is repeated in city after city, Tunney insists it is perfectly spontaneous. "There's very bad blood between those two," he says. "Naturally the fans are looking forward to a big match between them. So, at the appropriate time, we'll schedule one. You give the people what they want."

18        Tunney prides himself on being a keen observer of human nature. "I really make a study," he says. "I can sit in an airport, watch the people, and really enjoy myself. You look at them, size them up, try to guess where they came from, where they're going, what they have at home, what they do." Tunney calls this his hobby ("like stamp collecting"), but it's the same skill he uses as a promoter — probing the buried desires, dreams, and frustrations of total

strangers. Not that Tunney and his promoter cronies are always successful in tapping those deep-seated feelings. Sometimes they guess wrong about the way the fans' sympathies will go. He gives the example of the Honky Tonk Man, an Elvis impersonator who was originally conceived as a "baby face" (promoter jargon for good guy). But audiences reacted differently. They turned on him, jeering, booing, and railing against what they took to be an overweening arrogance. "We made a mistake," as Tunney puts it. But he and his fellow WWF officials decided to play on the outrage of the crowd, converting Honky Tonk Man into an arch heel by pitting him against baby faces whom he threatens with his "killer guitar." In this modified incarnation, Honky Tonk Man has become one of the sport's top stars, the fighter a crowd loves to hate. "What you want," Tunney explains, "is some strong reaction — love *or* hate. Doesn't matter which. The worst thing is *no* reaction. They hate Honky Tonk Man," Tunney adds, permitting himself a rare chuckle. "So they *love* him."

Listening to Jack Tunney, you come to realize that wresting isn't about wrestling at all, or about class anger, or the struggle between good and evil, or even about fakery. It's about the dialogue between promoter and fan. Why don't audiences mind that the outcomes of matches are prearranged and the dramas fabricated? Because they want them to be. Everything is tailored to their own desires, shaped according to the fluctuation of their every mood, all in the interest of bringing them back for more. This accounts for why the crowd doesn't mind the awful tedium of a live show. They yell, scream, jump up and down — because wrestling is about being *heard*. 19

It's the last match of the night, a tag-team duel between the Killer Bees and the team of Bobby "The Weasel" Heenan and Ted "Million Dollar Man" Di-Biase. Marilyn is heaping special scorn on "The Weasel," an aptly nicknamed heel who continually interferes with the match from ringside. "Get outta there, &#!*!" Marilyn screams. Turning to her companion, she adds, "He calls us humanoids. But he should look at himself. He's the biggest humanoid of all." 20

To the uninitiated, Marilyn's harangue might seem futile. Busy pretending to fight, "The Weasel" is clearly paying no attention (even if he could hear her voice above the 14 000 others screaming at the same time). But this doesn't bother Marilyn, or shut her up. Like everyone else in the arena, she seems to have an implicit understanding that someone is listening to her, that she's making some kind of difference, that she's affecting events in some way. And, of course, within wrestling's specially constructed universe, she is. 21

# Style and Structure

1. Describe, in detail, the intended reader of this essay. Use specific evidence taken from the text to support your description.

2. (a) Marilyn probably said many things at this wrestling match. Why might the author have chosen the specific quotation he uses in paragraph 1? What is the effect of saying she was "bellowing" (as opposed to, say, "yelling" or "shouting")?

   (b) Colapinto presents a detailed description of Marilyn in paragraph 2. Why would he describe her as "small-boned" and repeat the word beige? What is the effect of ending the paragraph with the phrase "Marilyn's favourite sport in the whole world"? What general impression of her does this paragraph convey? Why would the author want to create this impression?

   (c) How does paragraph 3 relate to the paragraphs that precede it? How does Colapinto make the **transition**?

   (d) The author makes extensive use of parentheses in the first three paragraphs. What effect do you think he is trying to achieve by using them?

   (e) What purposes do the first three paragraphs of this essay serve? Are they effective, given their intended reader?

3. What is the function of paragraph 4? What are the benefits of using questions here?

4. Identify the **topic sentences** in paragraphs 5 to 11. How does their relationship to the **thesis statement** contribute to the **unity** and the impact of this essay?

5. What aspect of the thesis does Colapinto explore in paragraphs 11 to 17?

6. (a) In what ways does the opening sentence of paragraph 11 help the reader?

   (b) The author devotes two paragraphs to a detailed description of Jack Tunney (paragraphs 11 and 12). How does he avoid having this description distract the reader from his central **thesis**?

7. In spite of the announced **thesis**, more than half the paragraphs in the body of this essay refer to Jack Tunney (paragraphs 11 to 18).

   (a) How do these references add to or detract from the **unity** of the essay?

   (b) List the ways in which Colapinto uses references to Tunney to develop this part of his **thesis**. For each, explain the benefit he gains from using Tunney.

   (c) What methods does he employ to get readers, almost without their realizing it, to accept the fact that using Tunney in these ways is valid?

8. (a) As part of the **conclusion,** paragraph 19 fulfils several functions. What are they?
   (b) How does paragraph 19 complement the introduction's presentation of the **thesis?**
   (c) What is the effect on the reader of Colapinto's choosing to return to Marilyn in paragraphs 20 and 21? How does he capitalize on her behaviour?
9. Colapinto uses several interesting stylistic devices in his final paragraph to give impact to his ideas.
   (a) How does the variation in the length of the sentences help him convey his message to his readers?
   (b) What contribution is made by the repetition of "that she's . . . " in the second-to-last sentence?
   (c) Normally, it is not a good idea to begin a sentence with "and." Why would Colapinto have chosen to break this rule in his final sentence?

# Warm-up

1. Make a brief list of the things a professional wrestler must do (and put up with) according to Colapinto. Discuss with some of your classmates the kind of personality someone would have to have to become successful in this field.

   Write a short character sketch of what a person must be like to become a successful professional wrestler.

   **Audience:** someone who has not read Colapinto's article.

   Compare your character sketch to those written by the others. Can you see any ideas or techniques you could use as you revise your work?
2. Write a one-paragraph description of a person you know, which subtly makes a point about that person as Colapinto does about Marilyn in paragraph 2.

   Before you begin, jot down a number of your acquaintance's physical features. Then identify some character trait, interest, or behaviour that can be related to a number of these features.

   **Audience:** someone who has never met the person being described.

   Test the success of your first draft before revising it: give it to two or three people to read. Then ask them questions that will tell you how well they have understood your point.

# Thinking and Writing

a.  Choose a sport you enjoy watching and write an essay explaining its popularity (or lack of it). Try to outline the underlying reasons rather than falling back on such old excuses as "it's fun," or "it helps people relax." (If you are not a sports fan, choose a popular sport such as hockey, football, or baseball and explain why people would enjoy watching it.)
    **Audience:** someone who is not a fan of that sport.

b.  Sports viewing is so popular in North America that it has spawned multi-billion-dollar businesses. Write an essay in which you explain why so many people in our society watch professional sports.
    **Audience:** someone who is familiar with sports.

    Send a copy of the final draft of your essay to a sportswriter for one of your local newspapers.

# How to Write Fiction

## by W.P. Kinsella

The title, of course, is a lie, as fantastical as any of my fictional creations. I cannot teach anyone how to write fiction. No one can teach anyone how to write fiction. What I can do, in my capacity as a professional fiction writer, is to smooth the road for those people I find who show talent as storytellers, to show them a few tricks of the trade — how to market their material, how to deal with publishers, editors, agents, and the like. 1

I can never suggest what a would-be fiction writer should write about. If you don't have a few dozen ideas for stories floating around in your head, stories that have to be told, then stick to your other hobbies and forget fiction writing. But if you have your heart set on writing fiction, consider the following: fiction writing, I tell my students, consists of ability, imagination, passion, and stamina. Let's consider each individually. 2

By "ability" I mean the ability to write complete sentences in clear, straightforward, standard English. This will not pose a problem for most of the people in the Writers Union, but it is surprising how many university students are unable to write simple sentences. If you can't express yourself clearly, abandon hope unless you are prepared to take a remedial English course. I've been known to suggest to my university students that they get a Grade 5 grammar book and begin their study there. 3

"Imagination" involves the ability to create stories. Little children can create wonderful, uninhibited stories full of fanciful characters. But as the years pass, the regimens of school and community kill the storyteller that lives within each of us. To write fiction you have to dig deep and discover that storyteller. 4

Some writing instructors tell students to "write of what you know." I disagree with that. In 99 cases out of 100, writing about what you know will fill pages, but fill them with dull and uninteresting material. Let's face it, for nine out of ten of us our lives are so dull that no one would care in the least about them. The tenth person has a life so bizarre no one would believe it if it were written down. The secret of a fiction writer is to make the dull interesting by imagination and embellishment, and to tone down the bizarre until it is believable. 5

I belong to the nine. I live a very quiet life; I have a lovely wife who is a true helpmate and ultrasupportive of my career; we have a nice home on the ocean; we have the freedom to travel. In other words, we are very 6 happy. If I wrote about that I would soon be back selling life insurance, or something equally vile. People don't want to read about happy people. Conflict is an absolute must in every story or novel.

7    I think I clipped the following statement from an American Amateur Press Association publication a few years ago: "The master plot of all novels and stories is: 'An appealing character struggles against great odds to attain a worthwhile goal.'" "Struggles against great odds" are the key words. Something must be at stake, and the character must take some action. What will the conflict be? What action will the appealing character take? That is up to the author. Authors spend half their time writing, and the rest looking at their story and saying, What if? What if? What if? What if I take the story this way? What if I take it that way?

8    "Passion" is an almost nebulous ingredient. It is what an author does to make you love a character. It takes very hard work to analyze it. When you find a novel or story in which you absolutely loved a character, where you had a sweet tear in your eye at the end of the story, or where you found yourself laughing uncontrollably, read it again for pleasure. Then reread it ten more times for business; analyze every line to learn how that author made you laugh or cry. When you learn the secret, use it in your next story.

9    Never forget that fiction writers are entertainers. Fiction writing comes from the days when the cavemen were gathered around a campfire and Ugh stood up, pounded his chest and said, "Listen to me! I want to tell you a story!" If his story wasn't interesting and suspenseful, his companions soon wandered off to their caves.

10    Fiction writers are not philosophers, or essayists, or pushers of causes religious or otherwise. And above all they are not navel-gazers. All of these are types of nonfiction, and should never be confused with storytelling.

11    One important point to remember is called Valgardson's Law (after B.C. writer W.D. Valgardson): Stories or novels are not about events, but about the people that events happen to. The fact that the Titanic is sinking or a skyscraper toppling — or even that the world is ending — is not important unless you have created an appealing character who is going to suffer if the dreaded event happens. If you want to write fiction, cut out this paragraph and paste it on the wall in front of your typewriter. It will save you weeks, months, maybe even years of struggle.

12    The final ingredient is "stamina." Each of the others I have described is about 5 percent of the writing process. Stamina is the final 85 percent. Stamina is keeping your buns on the chair and writing even when you don't feel like it. I know it's a cliché, but though inspiration is nice, 98 percent

of writing is accomplished by perspiration. Stamina is doing as I have done — sitting down to write my 50th short story, the previous 49 having been unpublishable, knowing that number 50 will also be unpublishable, but that it will be 2 percent better than the previous 49. Stamina is getting up at 5 A.M., running water over your fingers, so they will make the typewriter keys work for an hour or two before you go off to your hateful job. I did that for twenty years while I beat my head against the walls of North American literature.

If your head is still full of stories and you are still determined to write **13** them down, lots of luck. You'll need that, too.

# Style and Structure

1. (a) Identify the paragraph(s) that make up the **introduction** of the essay and underline the sentence(s) that best state(s) the **thesis** of the essay.
   (b) How does Kinsella organize the information presented in paragraphs 1 and 2 to give emphasis to those aspects of fiction writing he feels can be taught?
   (c) In the **introduction,** how does he prepare the reader for the organization of the material presented in the body?

2. What aspect of the **thesis** does Kinsella deal with in paragraph 3? Why would he choose to deal with this aspect of the thesis first in an essay dealing with fiction writing?

3. (a) What aspect of the **thesis** does the writer develop in paragraphs 4 to 7?
   (b) What is the relationship between the information contained in paragraph 5 and that contained in paragraph 6? Given the intended reader, why is this an effective technique? How does the fact that Kinsella is a well-known fiction writer increase the effectiveness of this technique?
   (c) What is the relationship between the last sentence in paragraph 6 and the information contained in paragraph 7? Assuming that the most likely reader of this essay is a novice fiction writer, why would Kinsella include the information contained in paragraph 7?

4. (a) What technique does Kinsella use in paragraph 8 to define the term "passion" for the average reader?
   (b) What two techniques does the writer employ in paragraphs 9 and 10 to develop his definition of fiction writers? Given the intended reader, why would he choose to use both of these techniques?

    (c) What is the relationship between the first and second sentences of paragraph 11? How does sentence 2 help the average reader grasp the point being made in sentence 1?

5. (a) What aspect of the **thesis** does Kinsella discuss in paragraph 12?

    (b) Why does he choose to deal with this aspect of the writing process last in the body of the essay?

    (c) The average person would not associate "stamina" with fiction writing. What techniques does Kinsella use to help the reader understand the importance of stamina for a writer?

6. (a) Where else in the essay does the author refer to the reader's head being full of stories?

    (b) Why is this second reference a good technique to use in a **conclusion**?

# Warm-up

1. In paragraph 3, Kinsella places great importance on knowing the basics of grammar. Yet most people see learning grammar as a boring waste of time. Write a paragraph that argues for or against *one* of the following topics:

    (i) grammar should be taught only to those wanting to be professional writers;

    (ii) grammar is so worthwhile we should all put up with having to learn it;

    (iii) there are painless ways to learn grammar.

    **Audience:** your English instructor.

2. Compare paragraph 7 of Kinsella's essay with paragraphs 18 to 20 of "From Quill to Computer" (p. 26). Then write a short explanation of how the advice given in these essays compares with the writing practices of most of the people you know. Try to explain their motives for writing the way they do.

    **Audience:** your English instructor. (You can be honest! English teachers are all too aware of the writing practices people use.)

    Use your written work as the basis for a general class discussion of the way people revise their writing and their reasons for behaving that way.

    Be sure to revise your report before you hand it in!

# Thinking and Writing

a.    Write an essay in which you compare Kinsella's description of the components of fiction writing ("ability, imagination, passion, and stamina") with the popular image that some people have of "a writer."

      **Audience:** someone who has serious misconceptions about how a fiction writer creates.

b.    Kinsella's essay vividly describes the amount of effort and devotion required to be a successful fiction writer; it also describes the need for most beginning writers to spend more time at "hateful" jobs to support themselves than they spend writing. Write an essay in which you argue either for or against the proposition that young writers should be given grants so that they can devote themselves completely to the job of writing.

      **Audience:** someone in a position to create government grants to support artists.

      Send a copy of your finished essay to the federal minister of culture.

# Who's Going to Read This Anyway?

Many hours of research, writing, and rewriting are frequently wasted simply because the writer has forgotten one cardinal rule of good writing: *Research into your topic must be accompanied by research into your reader*. Put another way, with the possible exception of creative writing, we do not write to communicate with ourselves; we write to communicate with others. Consequently, any insight we can get into the strengths, weaknesses, and prejudices of our readers may well improve the effectiveness of our writing.

The very worst thing a writer can do is to follow the misleading advice that it is somehow dishonest to employ a certain style, vocabulary, and format that you know is preferred by an instructor, on the grounds that it does not reflect your normal style — whatever that is. Surely our conversations reflect our *attention to audience* every day. Imagine some of the problems that would arise if we employed the same vocabulary, jokes, and tone of familiarity that we use with our friends in our conversations with teachers and employers. By all means write what you think you should write, but do not forget that your readers' knowledge of the topic, their preference for certain styles, formats, and vocabulary, and, in some cases, their attitudes must be judged, and the style varied accordingly.

"But how," you may ask, "can I hope to research my reader?" Obviously in some cases you cannot, and in those situations you would be best to adopt the middle road (employ generally accepted styles, formats, and vocabulary). On the other hand, most of your writing, both in school and at work, will be going to the same few people, so you should have little trouble following these three guidelines.

### A. Pay careful attention to the instructions that precede the writing assignment.

No one in the business or academic world wants to read poor writing. In the workplace, supervisors generally have time to explain to new employees how they want reports, time sheets, and correspondence written. If you ask, some supervisors will provide you with examples of formats and styles peculiar to their company. They may even be willing to comment on the appropriate technical level of writing for various situations. Certainly instructors are willing to give students detailed information concerning format, documentation, style, and vocabulary requirements. Remember, if you are unclear on any of the above points — ask.

B. Seek the advice of more experienced employees or students.

If no one else is available to discuss your writing with you, you can always seek out a more experienced employee or student for advice. Most of us are genuinely flattered when someone approaches us for advice, and we are frequently more than willing to help.

C. Request an evaluation of your writing.

Evaluations need not be a threat; put them to work for you. In school, we get used to instructors evaluating our written work, but even here keen students can improve their chances for success. Ask the instructor to take ten minutes to go over your work in detail. Go prepared with a set of intelligent questions, not just complaints or pleas for a higher grade. Ask your instructor how the paper could be improved and if there are any elements missing. Supervisors in the workplace are not in the habit of evaluating your written work unless there is an obvious problem, such as poor spelling or incomprehensible sentences. In any case, it is a good idea for junior employees to request a few minutes of a supervisor's time to discuss their first few reports. Again, most people are pleasantly surprised to be asked for advice and will generally comply with any reasonable request.

If you are tempted to sit down and write before carefully considering your audience, please remember the Edsel. The Ford Motor Company spent millions to design, build, and market this luxury automobile, only to see it fail miserably in the marketplace. Eventually, it cost the company several hundred million dollars to learn that they had produced a well-engineered and -constructed automobile for which no appreciable market existed. You can avoid the same mistake for nothing.

# Planning Your Written Communication

Whenever you talk to people, you use all kinds of nonverbal devices to clear up for your listener any ambiguities that may arise from imprecise communication. You make gestures with your hands, face, and body, you alter the tone of your voice, you watch for puzzled looks, and so on. If you want proof of just how much we all depend upon such devices to help convey our verbal messages, watch people talking on the telephone: everyone using the phone will still gesture, smile, and use body language as if the person being spoken to were present in the room.

When you turn to written communication, on the other hand, you no longer have such nonverbal devices to rely on, so you can no longer get away with the spontaneous and vague language you use in verbal communication. You must be much more precise in the words you choose, and must therefore give careful consideration to how the material is going to be presented to your reader.

Many people make the mistake of just sitting down and beginning to write. Yet charging ahead in this way is actually the hardest way to write effectively. The writer has to keep too many things in mind at one time, thinking ahead to what will come next, thinking back to what has gone before, trying to find just the right wording for the idea that is being dealt with right now, and making certain that the relationship of all of these words is complete and clear to a reader. In short, the sit-down-and-write technique almost guarantees failure. Once you have tried another approach to the task of writing, you will understand why most people who say they can't write are actually saying they cannot communicate effectively using the sit-down-and-write technique. Unfortunately, since these people are not aware of any other technique for writing, they make the mistake of giving up all hope of ever writing well.

As a matter of fact, there are a few easy steps you can take before you begin to write that will greatly improve the effectiveness of your expository writing. At first they will take a little extra effort, but after you have used them a few times, they will actually speed up the process of writing for you. Think, for example, how often you have had to waste time going back over what you have written to add some point that you left out when you used the sit-down-and-write approach. How often have you later discovered that you wandered away from the main point into some alluring but relatively unimportant side issue? How often have you wasted time putting down far more information than the situation called for? How often have you found that you have ended up putting ideas down in a piecemeal way that actually confused your reader? Thus, although many people who have never used a preliminary planning stage think that it will waste too much time, the steps outlined below will in fact *save* a great deal of time, worry, and confusion, while going a long way toward guaranteeing that your reader will understand your point exactly as you intended it.

## Step 1: Decide on your subject and thesis.

In school, you are usually either assigned a specific **subject** or given a choice of predetermined subjects on which you are asked to write. This procedure corresponds far more closely to what will happen to you in the working world than you may think. Your employer may assign a report on a specific subject; a customer may present you with a specific problem to be solved; or your job itself may present a difficulty that can be overcome only by a written explanation to a superior. All these situations provide a subject on which you may write.

Whatever the source of your subject, the best way to proceed is first to define your **thesis** as precisely as possible. For example, jot down at the top of a piece of paper

> Subject:  office efficiency
> Thesis:  office efficiency and its positive relationship to em-
> ployee morale
>
> *or*
>
> Subject:  pollution
> Thesis:  cheaper, more efficient urban mass transit and how
> it will improve air quality in cities

Notice that the thesis reflects your angle, your interest in the broad topic at hand. Your thesis will form the basis of a **thesis statement** when you come to writing the essay (see p. 304).

Remember that at this stage of your planning you may not know all the implications of the problem or all the details of a process, so you may have to modify the thesis as your research proceeds. You may, for instance, define your thesis in the second example above still further by considering only Canadian cities or referring to only one specific type of urban transit. Still, you have a solid starting point.

Be careful not to choose a thesis that is too broad or too narrow for the situation or for the length of the report. Ask yourself: What thesis will reflect the needs of my reader? What thesis fits the context of the problem? If your employer asks for a report on how to improve office efficiency, a thesis such as "The History of Employment Practices and Their Effect Upon the Morale of the New Employee" will be far too general to suit the context — your employer wants a solution, not a history lesson.

In short: (i) determine the *appropriate* subject;
(ii) determine the *appropriate* thesis.

**Step 2: Explore the subject and the thesis.**

a. If you are not certain of all the details involved in the subject, do research. Read and make notes on what you read. But remember to write down titles, authors, publishing information, and page numbers for your sources. You will need them later to give credit to your sources and to give authority to your opinion. Also, be sure to write on one side of the page only, to avoid confusion later.

b. Think about your subject and your thesis. Consider how the information that your research has turned up relates to them. Are you going to have to modify your original statements? Are you going off on a tangent with your present line of research?

c. Discuss your subject, your thesis, and your research materials with someone else. In the process of defining the material for this person, you will gain clearer insight into it yourself.

d. Complete your research.

These steps may at first sound as if they are meant to be used only for a major project on a subject that you do not know well. However, they hold just as well for small projects or familiar subjects. Even when you know the subject thoroughly, you need to think over the process, the situation, or whatever it is you are going to explain. What details are really involved? Are there any underlying factors that may not at first be visible? Is your approach too one-sided?

Discuss your ideas with someone else. By talking them over with another person, you will get a clearer concept of what the ideas really entail and the process you need to use in order for someone else to understand them.

Jot down your ideas as they come to you, in point form and at random. Put down everything that has any relationship at all to your subject and thesis. Often such a brainstorming session will bring to light all kinds of interesting insights.

**Step 3: Select material from your collected data that is appropriate to your subject and thesis.**

When your research has been completed, whether it is a list of random thoughts or a pile of extensive notes taken from outside reading, review the material that you have collected.

For each item or point, ask yourself whether it really does relate to your subject and thesis. If it does not, throw it away or scratch it from your list. If it does, jot down beside it in a word or two exactly how it relates to, explains, or illustrates your subject and thesis.

What you are doing in going through this step is ensuring that your finished product has **unity**.

### Step 4: Group related points into clusters.

Go through the items that still remain in your collected research material and look for points that relate to the general subject and thesis in the same way. This should be a relatively simple process because you have already noted in a word or two how each point relates to the main idea.

If you are working from a revised list for a subject that you know well, you may find it easier when you first try this stage of planning to rewrite your list completely so that the clusters of related ideas are physically near each other.

With a little practice, you will soon find that simply writing the same number or letter beside related points will be adequate at this stage for such material.

If you are working with extensive research notes, now is the time to get out the scissors and cut out the various points that you have collected: you can then deal them into piles of related points in the same way that you would sort out the suits of a deck of cards. Remember, however, to note on each scrap of paper where the material came from, or you may find yourself doing a great deal of rereading so that you can give credit to your sources.

Whichever method you use for arranging your points into clusters, make certain that the points in any one grouping do not cover too wide a range of ideas. These clusters are going to form the basis for your paragraphs, and if a paragraph tries to cover too many points, the importance of each will be lost in the crowd. If you find that a cluster is becoming too broad in its range, divide it into two or three important subcategories.

Write a point form summary of the concept that binds each cluster of points together in their relationship to your subject and thesis.

### Step 5: Choose an organizational approach that gives your ideas their strongest impact.

At this stage you must decide upon the order in which you are going to present your clusters or paragraphs to your reader. Usually your subject and material will suggest the most logical **organizational approach**. A report concerned with declining office morale might well suggest the chronological or time-sequenced organization. On the other hand, an essay on air pollution and urban mass transit might require a cause-and-effect organization. In addition, an attempt to convince someone to follow your proposed plan of action might call for an organizational structure in which you present your second-weakest argument first, followed by your weakest, and conclude with your strongest point.

There are other approaches that you might take as well. Generally, essays are organized in one of the following methods:

process analysis — shows a sequence of steps or stages taken to produce a result

cause and effect — shows why and how a particular result has been achieved

compare/contrast — shows the similarities and/or differences of two or more ideas, objects, or processes

classification — identifies the categories contained within a topic and sorts data into these categories

argument — presents evidence to support a hypothesis and draws conclusions

example — illustrates a concept by giving one or more examples

narrative — illustrates a concept by telling a story

description — explains or illustrates by providing vivid details

definition — explains the unfamiliar by using a clear and detailed definition

Keep in mind, however, that while most essays follow one overall approach, good writers combine elements of other approaches to give their ideas maximum effectiveness. For example, a writer choosing to discuss the effect of urban mass transit on a city's air quality might well, in order to really set the scene for the reader, decide to begin with an extensive description of the city before mass transit was introduced. Depending on the projected readership's familiarity with the subject, the writer might also decide that a working definition of urban mass transit is necessary. Both of these approaches are worked into an essay that is primarily organized to investigate cause and effect. Invariably, your purpose in writing and your readership's needs will determine the best approach, or approaches, to use.

The important thing to remember at this point in planning your written work is that this is the stage that is going to "make or break" the impact of your final product. A well-organized work will impress your points upon readers. A work that lacks organization, logical development, and, hence, **coherence** will at best cause readers to question your competence to tell them anything worthwhile; at worst, they will simply stop reading (an unfortunate event in the case of an employer, who may stop reading your work *permanently*).

Step 6: Within each cluster, arrange the points into an order that gives them their greatest effect.

Taking each cluster separately, examine each point you have included. Make certain that they do indeed have a direct relationship to the other ideas within that cluster and, by extension, to the overall thesis of your essay.

In deciding how to arrange these points, always place your binding idea first. This will become your **topic sentence**, setting out the main idea of the paragraph (see p. 307). Next, ask yourself the same questions that you asked when deciding upon the arrangement of the clusters themselves within the overall organization. Each paragraph thus becomes a mini-essay, with a logical, coherent organization to give ideas their most effective presentation.

Step 7: Begin to write.

By going through these stages or "steps" of planning, you will have saved yourself a great deal of anxiety, turmoil, and wasted time. You will have ensured that you stay on the topic when you come to the writing stage and that you present your material in an orderly fashion. You will also have helped to ensure that the rest of your task is easier, because now all you have to worry about is the actual wording of the paper and the creation of an appropriate introductory and concluding paragraph.

# The Writing Stage

## I. The introductory paragraph

A good opening paragraph, or **introduction**, serves three purposes in getting your message across to your reader: it focusses the reader's attention on your subject; it provides the reader with an idea of the specific stand you wish to take (in other words, your thesis), and it impresses and interests the reader by showing the importance of your subject.

### A. Focussing the reader's attention

Many inexperienced writers make the mistake of beginning their written work simply by presenting the data they have gathered without first focussing their reader's attention on the general topic that this data is supposed to present or explore. The result is inevitably disastrous, for the writer has forgotten that although he may know the topic well enough to understand the significance of the data, the reader is probably coming to the topic for the first time. Attempting to read an essay that lacks a clearly defined **thesis statement** is like setting out on a journey without any idea of your destination: it is a frustrating experience that is more likely to arouse anger than provide knowledge.

If you have been following our steps of preliminary planning for your work, the construction of this thesis statement should be relatively easy, because all you really have to do is expand the idea that you jotted down as your thesis. (See Planning Your Written Communication, Step 1, p. 299.)

The placement of your thesis statement, however, is a matter of great concern. Consider the essay that aims to convince supervisors to buy a Merit X-2000 copier. The essay might be written in any one of the following circumstances:

(i) managers know nothing about the Merit X-2000;

(ii) managers have been briefed about the Merit X-2000 and are willing to hear arguments about its benefits;

(iii) managers are facing a tight budget and are openly hostile to the idea of a large purchase, unless it is absolutely crucial to the well-being of the firm.

Chances are very good that beginning the essay with the thesis statement "The Merit X-2000 copier would be the best purchase for our company" would not sit well with supervisors in situations (i) and (iii). The question "Who's going to read this, anyway?" is of great importance to the writer facing these situations.

Reader preparation is generally necessary before one introduces the thesis statement: the more likely the reader is to be resistant, the more preparation is necessary. For most situations, you will find it helpful to introduce your subject in the first paragraph, leading up to a thesis statement as the last sentence. The writer facing situation (i) would likely decide to prepare the reader with some information about the Merit X-2000 before setting out a thesis statement.

> On June 12, our printshop copier broke down for the fifth time in six months, causing a backlog of 200 unprocessed orders that sat until repairs could be made. In all, four days were lost before the orders could be sent out. Mike Mackinnon of the printshop suggests that the model presently in use is adequate for general use. It is not, however,

capable of meeting the demand from each of six departments on an ongoing basis. A small but efficient copier would do much to keep business at the front desk moving smoothly. <u>My study suggests that the Merit X-2000 would be the most cost-efficient machine for our needs.</u>

Notice that the writer situates the reader, showing what the problem is and why the purchase of a copier is necessary, before actually suggesting which copier to buy. The thesis statement focusses the reader's attention, without giving a nasty surprise.

## B. Providing the reader with a general idea of your approach

If an essay is like taking a journey and the thesis statement provides the reader with a map, the next few sentences of the introduction provide an idea of the roads to be taken. This information reveals the organizational approach, enabling the reader to grasp some idea of the scope of your essay before setting out in earnest. For example, the writer of the essay on the Merit X-2000 might continue into the second paragraph in the following manner:

> Compared to the other machines available to us, the Merit X-2000 will give the highest efficiency at the lowest initial, and operating, costs. The capacity of the machine is slightly larger than we need now, but with our proposed expansion next year we will quickly find additional need. Moreover, the service policy of the company would give us cheap and efficient maintenance.

In this way, the writer outlines the direction the rest of the essay will take. The reader will look for a compare/contrast of the Merit X-2000 with other machines on the basis of (a) costs, (b) capacity, and (c) maintenance.

As with the construction of your thesis statement, the construction of this section of your introduction should be relatively easy if you have been following our steps of preliminary planning: all that will be involved now will be the expansion of your organizational approach with the addition of the main points of your paper. Be sure, however, that the sentences that present your approach to your reader have a logical order, preferably an order that reflects in a general way the order in which you are going to present your data in the body of your essay.

## C. Capturing the reader's interest

Whenever you are writing in the working world, your subject is most likely to be one that is important to you for one reason or another. If you are going to impress the importance of your subject upon your reader, you are going to have to make certain that your introduction arouses interest. This may not seem an easy or appropriate task in vocational writing, but it can be done fairly easily by the careful wording of the paragraph. Nothing is more boring, for example, than an introduction that begins "The topic that I am going to write about in this paper is. . . ." Although such a sentence may present your idea to the reader, the dryness of the presentation does nothing to encourage the reader to become involved with your ideas on any more than a very superficial level. Simply by providing a more stimulating wording, you can change your reader's attitude from bored perusal to interested exploration of an idea. The earlier example of the copier, for instance, invites the reader to become involved because it speaks to the self-interest of a manager who wants life to be problem-free and profitable. The sense of discovery will capture this reader's interest.

There are of course even more dramatic techniques that you can use, but you must be careful that they are appropriate for the situation for which you are writing. There is nothing wrong, for example, with starting off your introductory paragraph with a provocative quotation, question, statement, or other dramatic device to stimulate your reader's interest. The effectiveness of this technique can be appreciated by an examination of the following opening sentences:

> This essay is going to deal with the topic of child beating.

> Would you turn your head the other way and try to ignore a neighbour who was beating his child into insensibility? Of course you wouldn't. Yet with the present attitude of our society toward child beating in the community, that is precisely what we are all doing.

The personal involvement called for by the presentation in the second example will arouse far more interest and, it is hoped, action than will that in the first.

On the other hand, you must always be very careful that your attempt to capture interest does not distort the message you want to convey. You must still make certain that the introduction says precisely what you mean. Too often, inexperienced writers fall into the trap of melodrama or exaggeration and render their topic ridiculous rather than important. An opening statement such as "The beauty and symmetry of the Merit X-2000 put it in the ranks of Taj Mahal" would make your report more appropriate for a comedian than for an employer searching for machinery.

# II. The body or development section

The **body** of your written communication is the section that carries the burden of your exploration of your topic. By organizing your material into a series of paragraphs that lead logically from your introduction to your conclusion, you are verifying and expanding on your observations in the introduction.

The writing of this section of your paper should be just as simple as the writing of your introduction was if you followed our preliminary planning process. You will have already collected the information that you want to convey and have arranged it in clusters that are going to form the basis of the paragraphs of this section. In fact, if you have followed Step 6 of our planning stage, you have even guaranteed that the writing of each paragraph is reduced to the problem of worrying about using just the right words to capture your exact meaning. Make certain that these words are grouped together in such a way as to make your readers hear your voice in their head, with all of the proper pauses and inflections; that is, make certain that you have used complete sentences and proper punctuation. See the two sections of this book that deal with these topics if you have any doubt at all about your abilities to do either.

# III. The parts of the body: the paragraph

Every paragraph in the body or development section of your paper forms a complete unit of ideas that develops, explains, illustrates, or contrasts with one aspect of the thesis that you are presenting. In order to be complete, each paragraph needs a **topic sentence** that focusses your reader's attention on the aspect of the topic to be dealt with in this paragraph; since you have already noted the binding idea of each cluster of points as you went through the planning process and since each of these clusters is going to form the basis of a paragraph in the body of your paper, you simply have to expand this binding idea into a complete sentence to create the topic sentence for each paragraph. In other words, the topic sentence presents a generalized outline of the material to be dealt with in the paragraph.

The sentences that follow the topic sentence develop the aspect of the topic and approach introduced by that sentence. You have already ensured that these sentences will have a unified and logically developed impact upon your reader because you have eliminated unrelated points and arranged the remaining ones in Step 6 of that process. All that remains to be done is the expansion and/or combination of these points into complete sentences. As you write, of course, you can double check to make certain that the arrangement of the points you have chosen earlier is in fact the most effective. Ask yourself, "Do the sentences in this paragraph present the reader with a clear, logical sequence so that the real importance of my ideas is felt and understood?"

You will find **transitions** useful in helping the reader follow the flow of your ideas. Transitions are words or phrases that show the reader the connection between ideas, as illustrated below:

| Relationship | Transition |
|---|---|
| result | therefore, thus, consequently |
| contrast | however, otherwise, on the other hand |
| example | for instance, for example, namely |
| addition | furthermore, moreover, besides |
| similarity | likewise, similarly |
| summary | in other words, in short |
| sequence | then, next, finally |

The last sentence of each paragraph rounds the paragraph off by refocussing the reader's attention on the main idea that the other sentences of the paragraph were explaining, illustrating, and so on. Without this **concluding sentence**, you will leave your readers hanging in mid-air. They will either have to try to draw their own conclusions or go on to the next paragraph without really thinking about the importance of the points you have made. In either case, by omitting a concluding sentence, you undermine the impact of your idea.

From these recommendations, it should be quite clear that a one-sentence paragraph rarely does the job. Your reader will expect you to develop your thoughts. The one-sentence paragraph can, however, be used to isolate one idea you want to emphasize. But you do not want to overuse a technique that draws attention. In short, use the single-sentence paragraph sparingly, if at all.

Examine the structure of the preceding paragraph if you want an illustration of a well-designed paragraph: the topic sentence introduces the subject, and the concluding sentence summarizes and drives home the point. The following paragraph, on the other hand, shows effective use of a one-sentence paragraph.

Only when all three components — the topic sentence, body, and concluding sentence — are present in your paragraph will your idea appear complete to your reader.

# IV. The concluding paragraph

Just as a paragraph will lose its impact upon the reader if you omit a concluding sentence, so too will the entire work lose much of its impact if you forget to end it with a **concluding paragraph.**

A concluding paragraph may do many things for your essay. For one thing, it may serve to refocus your reader's attention on the thesis by restating your original thesis statement in other words. A mere repetition of what you said in your introduction, however, is not going to do much to show off your ideas. The reader has been following your organized and expanded ideas throughout the essay and is now prepared for a somewhat fuller, more reflective look at the specific aspect of the subject you have chosen.

A conclusion can be used to perform many other duties as well. Many writers prefer to look toward the future, having satisfied themselves and their readers that all aspects of the thesis have been explored throughout the body of the essay. This technique is especially helpful because it shows readers something of the ongoing importance of the subject, while leaving them with something to think about after the essay is finished. As the reader continues the thinking process and remembers the essay, the writer's task is accomplished. No one, after all, wants to write forgettable essays!

The essay writer might use the conclusion to suggest ways of implementing the ideas raised in the essay, even to challenge readers to do so. Whatever the conclusion does, it provides a **clincher**, a sentence that (a) satisfies the reader that the essay is finished and (b) gives the reader something to remember. The conclusion does not, however, raise unrelated issues that will confuse the reader because they cannot be dealt with satisfactorily. A conclusion that leaves the reader on edge may work very well in a murder mystery, but it is highly unsatisfactory in expository prose.

With a little practice you will find that these procedures will become a natural part of your writing and actually speed up the process for you (to say nothing of simplifying the task by breaking it into smaller, more easily managed units). The steps become natural so easily because they really only reflect what your mind is trying to do with any idea when presenting it to a reader: they break the overall topic into its component parts, give these parts a logical order, and then put the parts back together again in a unified whole that is easily understood by your reader.

The first few times that you plan your writing according to our suggested planning stages, make certain you do not take on large topics. Narrower topics will be easier to manage at first and will give you the opportunity to go through the process more often.

Always remember that just going through the motions of planning will not accomplish anything: think the problems through as you go. Nor should you expect planning to remove all of your difficulties the first time that you use it, although it will remove many of the difficulties that you have experienced when using the sit-down-and-write technique. In any case, don't be discouraged: like any other art form, writing needs to be practised.

Finally, you will notice as you read through the essays in this book that the authors use a variety of approaches to constructing introductions, development paragraphs, and conclusions. These examples will no doubt give you a wealth of ideas to draw from, once you have mastered the foundations of expository writing provided in this section. Practise the basics according to the steps outlined above. Then, after you are more confident, explore some of the other formats — perhaps even invent a few of your own.

# Proofreading Your Composition

## I. Sentence errors

People usually define the sentence by saying that it expresses a complete thought. However, don't "Wow," "Beautiful, man," and "Dumb" express complete thoughts? In one way, of course, such expressions are complete in themselves; indeed, they are often used in creative writing, where their context gives them appropriate significance. Nonetheless, for more formal situations calling for the clear, precise, and complete explanation of an idea to a reader, such expressions are not normally adequate. In short, good expository writing calls for the use of complete sentences, because the structure of sentences demands a clear definition of the ideas being presented to the reader; the sentences require that something (a *subject*) be carefully defined as *being* or *doing* something. A complete sentence, that is, demands a subject and a predicate.

Thus, if you read "The growling dog" you find yourself waiting for more information: What about the growling dog? Did it bite the writer? Did it turn tail and run? The fragment lacks an action (i.e., a verb or predicate) that would give you a complete idea about the dog.

If, on the other hand, you read "The growling dog stood across the body of his fallen master," you have a complete idea of the situation; you have read a sentence.

Although in informal writing occasional sentence fragments are not unacceptable and can be used quite effectively, most people use complete sentences in formal writing. In fact, *talking* in formal situations, such as job interviews, demands complete sentences, so writing them in similar circumstances is usually quite natural. Occasionally, however, you will find that in the effort to put words down on paper, you use incomplete sentences or run several sentences together into one: you must carefully reread everything that you write to make certain that in your haste you have not actually obscured your meaning by presenting your reader with ideas that are incomplete or that have been run together with others.

## 1. The sentence fragment

> My experience in sales management has taught me a number of important skills over the years. Organizing my time for one thing.

Read the second so-called sentence of the above example again, without rereading the first sentence. Obviously this "sentence" does not really tell the reader anything by itself, for it depends on the first sentence for its meaning. Such partial sentences are called **sentence fragments**.

Sentence fragments are usually created in only three situations:

a. You have isolated words in apposition to the last words in the previous sentence:

> Several machines will fit our present needs. Compton's Model XT-20, the Rainville 300, or the compact Watson 210.

The writer of this fragment tried to stress the number of machines available, but instead created a sentence fragment. The writer should have used the dash, as its purpose is to give dramatic impact (see, pp. 336–337).

b. You have isolated a subordinate clause (used to expand upon the idea of the previous or following sentence):

> Our second production line will be out of service during July. Because of routine maintenance.

Such words as *when*, *if*, *since*, *as*, and *because* alter the meanings of the sections of a sentence that they introduce by making them subordinate, or secondary, in meaning to the main idea of a sentence:

> Our second production line will be out of service during July [main idea] because of routine maintenance [secondary or subordinate idea].

A subordinate idea always needs a main idea to expand upon: "Because of routine maintenance" means nothing by itself.

c. You have isolated verbal phrases containing a verb ending in "ing." Consider, for a moment, the following:

> having been there already
> being an example of professionalism
> doing what should have been done
> after having arrived in Hong Kong

Obviously none of these statements makes any sense: "ing" verbs depend upon other words for their meaning; used alone, as they are in these examples, they are meaningless. Yet how often in our rough drafts do we write such things as the following:

> We must never use verbs ending in "ing" as independent verbs. *The reason being that they depend on other words for their meaning.*

(If you didn't catch the problem with the second "sentence" the first time you read the example, reread it without looking at the first sentence.)

### How to recognize sentence fragments

As you have seen in examining the examples given above, you subconsciously know already how to recognize a sentence fragment when you view it in isolation from the sentence that precedes it: it leaves you wanting more information so that you can form a complete idea. The way to recognize sentence fragments in your own revised drafts, then, is to isolate them from the rest of the work.

One approach you can try is to put the work away for a day or two; rereading a paper some time after you originally wrote it makes you more objective (i.e., it tends to place you in the situation of a reader coming upon a work for the first time); you will more easily recognize fragments. Reread your work aloud, making certain that you say what you have actually written. (Keep in mind that all too often we "see" with our minds; that is, we know what we meant to write and this knowledge causes us to think that we read things like complete sentences when indeed we have written only sentence fragments.)

If you still encounter difficulty identifying sentence fragments, there is a second approach that will help you to catch them: read the entire work over, sentence by sentence, *backward*. Almost every sentence fragment depends upon the sentence that precedes it to give meaning to its incomplete idea: hence, when you read your work backward, you encounter the fragment *before* you have read the sentence containing the idea to which it refers. This approach can effectively isolate the fragments and make them far easier to identify.

## How to correct sentence fragments

Since the sentence fragment is not independent because it usually depends upon the sentence that precedes or follows it for its meaning, there are two methods for correcting fragments:

(i) Make the fragment independent by adding a subject or a verb; for example, change

> From that time on, he was a perfect citizen. *Doing what should have been done from the beginning.*

to

> From that time on, he was a perfect citizen. He did what should have been done from the beginning.

(ii) Incorporate the fragment into the preceding or following sentence; for example, change

> From that time on, he was a perfect citizen. *Doing what should have been done from the beginning.*

to

> From that time on, he was a perfect citizen, doing what should have been done from the beginning.

## 2. The comma splice

The **comma splice** is an error that occurs when a writer uses a comma to replace the period at the end of a sentence. In almost every instance in which such an error occurs, you will find that the comma has been used to replace a period between two sentences that are very closely related in their meanings (the second sentence may illustrate the point made in the first; add additional information about the point made in the first; or give the effect of a cause that was outlined in the first). Example:

> We aren't that intelligent, our ideas and opinions are seldom our own.

Writers of comma splices try to create a certain effect but unfortunately fall into a trap. They want to drive home a certain idea and subconsciously realize that a period will bring the reader to a full stop, destroying the dramatic impact of the second point. Therefore, they mistakenly resort to the comma. They should use the dash or semicolon instead (see A Short Guide to Punctuation, p. 330).

### How to recognize comma splices

The easiest way to spot comma splices is to listen to yourself carefully as you read your written work *aloud*. Make certain that you read exactly what is written on the page (the mind has a strange way of fooling the eye into thinking that it has seen something that it knows should be there but that, in fact, is not). Most people, when they try to explain something with precision to someone else, think in sentences; thus, you will find that when you encounter a comma splice and read it aloud as it is punctuated (i.e., giving only the short pause that is symbolized by the comma), the passage will not sound right; your mind will recognize the confusion that the use of the comma can create. You will see the point being made if you read the following "sentences" aloud:

> I knew that I had made a mistake when she slapped my face, it was all too obvious.
> Whenever I came to call, no one seemed to be at home, maybe they were giving me a hint.
> Many recent films have tried to imitate *Star Wars*, not one has succeeded.

In many cases the identification of comma splices is made much easier by the fact that they very often occur just before adverbial connectives:

> I had no warning about the test, *therefore*, I was not prepared.
>
> A person who owns a small piece of land can save money, *for instance*, one might grow vegetables.

Some other **adverbial connectives** are

| | | |
|---|---|---|
| hence | however | thus |
| consequently | henceforth | moreover |
| nevertheless | otherwise | furthermore |
| on the other hand | namely | therefore |
| that is | for example | for instance |

*N.B.:* Do not confuse adverbial connectives with **co-ordinate conjunctions** (*and*, *or*, *but*, *for*, *nor*, *so*, *yet*), which take commas.

> I was late for work; *however*, I wasn't put on report.
>
> I was late for work, *but* I was not put on report.

If you still have difficulty recognizing comma splices, you may have to use a special trick, which will take a little extra time, until you become better at finding them. As you proofread your revised draft, every time you encounter a comma reread the part of the sentence that comes before it to see if that part makes sense on its own. If it does, read the part of the sentence that comes after the comma to see if it makes sense on its own. If either part does not make sense on its own (i.e., is *not* a complete idea), the use of the comma is correct. If both parts do make sense on their own, look for the possibility of a comma splice. Examine the following examples:

> Stereo-system enthusiasts will enjoy this magazine, it features articles on getting the most from your system. (*comma splice*)
>
> Cutting corners in research is never advisable, but there are some short-cuts that will help you. (*correct*)

The second example shows two complete ideas joined with a comma and a co-ordinating conjunction. When no such conjunction joins complete ideas, as in the first example, a comma splice occurs.

### How to correct comma splices

You can correct the comma splice by using any one of the following methods:

(i) Subordinate one of the ideas to the other, that is, one of the sentences to the other, by introducing a subordinate conjunction. For example, change

> Environmentalists have become upset recently, there have been a number of serious oil spills. (*comma splice*)

to

> Environmentalists have become upset recently because there have been a number of serious oil spills.

(ii) Join the two sentences with a co-ordinating conjunction.

> Environmentalists have become upset recently, for there have been a number of serious oil spills.

(iii) Use a semicolon. It is designed to draw the reader's attention to the close connection of the ideas that precede and follow it, and thus gives impact to the second idea without creating a comma splice.

> Environmentalists have become upset recently; there have been a number of serious oil spills.

Or, you may choose to vary the emphasis as follows:

> There have been a number of serious oil spills lately; environmentalists have become upset.

(iv) A fourth possibility involves the use of the colon. In cases where your second idea amplifies or expands upon the first, you may choose this method of linking your ideas.

> Oil spills have become a menace to coastal life: both waterfowl and fish stocks have been threatened.

### 3. The run-on sentence

The run-on sentence occurs when a writer uses no punctuation at all at the end of a sentence:

> Environmentalists have become upset recently there have been a number of serious oil spills.

Actually, the run-on sentence is exactly the same error as the comma splice, except that here even the comma has been left out. The writer is trying to achieve the same effect as with the comma splice (i.e., to point out the connection between the ideas of two sentences by speeding the reader through to the second idea). If you find a run-on sentence in your own work, you should be able to use exactly the same methods outlined in the section on the comma splice to identify and correct it.

# II. Agreement

### 1. Agreement: Subject and verb

The subject and the verb of any sentence must always have the same number (i.e., singular or plural).

Most of the time, we have no difficulty with subject/verb agreement, because our use of the language has so accustomed us to using correct agreement that errors immediately strike us as not sounding right. Few of us would have difficulty recognizing the problem in such sentences as "He go to the store" or "They goes to the store."

Occasionally, in more complex sentences or in constructions that we do not use frequently, we become confused or forget just what word is the subject of the verb, or what the number of the subject really is. The following section outlines the most common instances in which writers make errors in subject/verb agreement and suggests how they can be corrected and avoided.

### Common problems of subject/verb agreement in number

| Situation | Example of Error | Correct Form |
| --- | --- | --- |
| (i) A group of words comes between the subject and the verb, one of which is a noun of a different number than the subject. | One of the eggs are rotten. | *One* of the eggs *is* rotten. |
| | Life with all its trials and tribulations are hard to bear. | *Life* with all its trials and tribulations *is* hard to bear. |

| | | |
|---|---|---|
| (ii) The word *there* begins a sentence. In such expressions as *there is, there are, there was,* and *there were,* the number of the verb (e.g., *is* or *are*) is determined by the number of the noun that *follows* the verb (the real subject). | There is many cases of unnecessary surgery.<br><br>There was times when I almost gave up. | There *are* many *cases* of unneccesssary surgery.<br><br>There *were times* when I almost gave up. |
| (iii) A collective noun is the subject of the sentence. (Collective nouns are nouns that represent groups of people or things: e.g., *group, herd, crowd, jury, audience, class.*) | The class are late for the examination. | The *class is* late for the examination. |
| If the group is acting as a unified whole, use a *singular* verb. | The jury agree on the verdict. | The *jury agrees* on the verdict. |
| If the members of the group represented by the collective noun are not acting as a unified whole, use a *plural* verb. | The crowd disagrees on what to do. | The *crowd disagree* on what to do. |
| You can avoid the entire problem of awkward-sounding plural verbs in these circumstances by rewording the subject of the sentence. | | |

*Remember:* (a) When the members of the group agree, use the singular verb.

| | | |
|---|---|---|
| (b) When the members of the group are not unified, *change the subject* to a plural noun that identifies the members of the group. | The herd are going off in all directions. | The *cows* are going off in all directions.<br><br>The *members* of the herd *are* going off in all directions. |
| (iv) When the usual order of the sentence is reversed so that the subject follows the verb, make certain that you have the same number for the subject and the verb. | In the doorway was standing two gigantic police officers. What was I to do? | In the doorway *were* standing two gigantic police officers. What was I to do? |
| (v) Indefinite pronouns such as the following are *always singular* and therefore always have *singular* verbs: *one, each, everybody, no one, nobody, none, someone, somebody, either, neither, anyone, everyone.* | | *Neither* of the men *is* able to do the job.<br><br>*Someone* representing the colleges *is* to blame.<br><br>*None* of the topics *is* interesting.<br><br>*Each has* its proper place.<br><br>*One* of the women who won the lottery *is* my aunt. |
| (vi) Two separate subjects of the same verb, joined by *and*, form a *plural* subject; they require a plural verb. | | *My brother and I are* going to travel this summer.<br><br>*Halifax and Quebec City have* citadels. |

An exception to the
rule in situation (vi)
occurs in the following
situations:

(a) If the subjects
joined by *and* refer
to the same person,
place, or thing, they
take a singular
verb.

*My old comrade and
close friend has*
insisted that I stay
with him and his
wife. (*Comrade* and
*friend* in this sentence
refer to the same
individual.)

(b) If the subjects
joined by *and* are
commonly considered to
be singular (e.g., rock
and roll, ham and eggs,
Browning and Bowles Ltd.),
they take a singular verb.

*Browning and Bowles is*
the most prestigious
insurance firm in
Saskatoon.

(c) Although subjects
joined by *and*
generally take plural
verbs, singular subjects
linked by such
expressions as
*in the company of*,
*assisted by*, or *as
well as* always take
singular verbs.

*My cousin*, assisted
by a friend, *has*
opened a used
book store. (The real
subject of this
sentence, *cousin*, is
singular and requires
the singular form of
the verb, *has*.)

---

(vii) Two subjects of
the same verb, when joined
by a *both . . . and*
construction, always
form a plural subject;
they require a plural
verb.

*Both* my father *and* I
*are* going.

(viii) Two subjects of the same verb, when joined by *either . . . or,* *neither . . . nor,* or *not only . . . but also,* may take either a singular or a plural verb: if the subject *closer* to the verb is singular, use a singular verb.

Neither mother nor *Aunt Helen* is able to go.

Neither the children nor *Aunt Helen is* able to go. (Note that even though *children* is plural, *Aunt Helen,* which is singular, is closer to the verb; therefore, the verb is singular.)

If the subject closer to the verb is plural, use a plural verb.

Either the instructor or the *answers* in the book *are* wrong. (Note that even though *the instructor* is singular, *answers,* which is a plural subject, is closer to the verb; therefore, the verb is plural.)

*Remember:* When in doubt, or when you get caught up in an awkward, confusing situation, take the easy way out: reword the sentence so that *either* comes before one subject *and* its verb, and *or* comes before the second subject and another verb.

Either *the textbooks are* wrong, or the *instructor is.*

| | |
|---|---|
| (ix) *Who, which, that* (relative pronouns). When these words introduce a subordinate clause *and* act as the subject of the verb in that clause (e.g., "the man who was coming to dinner"), they always refer to a specific word used earlier in the sentence (e.g., in our example, to "man") and take their number from that word. Thus, if the word referred to is singular, use a singular verb after *who, which,* or *that*; if the word referred to is plural, use a plural verb. | The *stories* that *are* told about him are all lies.<br><br>The *story* that *is* being told about him is a lie.<br><br>The *person* who *is* telling the story is a liar.<br><br>The *people* who *are* telling the story are liars.<br><br>One of the *men* who *were* imprisoned was my uncle. (In this case, *who* refers to *men,* not to *one;* therefore, the verb directly following *who* is plural. The verb for *one* comes later in the sentence and is singular: *was*) |

## 2. Agreement: Pronouns and antecedents

A pronoun always agrees in number (i.e., singular or plural) with the noun to which it refers.

The *men* said *they* were tired.

Most of the time, you will have no difficulty with pronoun/antecedent agreement, but there are four situations that might cause you confusion:

| Situation | Example of Error | Correct Form |
|---|---|---|
| (i) Collective nouns (*crowd, jury,* | After the jury deliberated for six | After the *jury* deliberated for six |

| | | |
|---|---|---|
| pack, *group*, etc.) are considered singular if all the members of the collection are acting as a unified whole. | weeks, they reached a verdict. | weeks, *it* reached a verdict. |
| (ii) Collective nouns are considered *plural* if the members of the collection are *not* acting as a unified whole. | The jury still disagreed on whether it should ask for advice. | The *jury* still disagreed on whether *they* should ask for advice. |
| (iii) Indefinite pronouns (*one, each, everyone, either, neither*, etc.) are *always* singular. | Everyone did as they were told. | *Everyone* did as *he* or *she* was told. (But see Inclusive language, p. 328.) |
| (iv) Make certain that you know to which word the pronoun refers. | Neither of the boys knew what they wanted to do. (The word to which the pronoun refers is not *boys* but *neither*.) | *Neither* of the boys knew what *he* wanted to do. |

## 3. Agreement: Possessive pronouns (my, your, his, her, its, our, their)

Just as a pronoun takes its number from the noun that it replaces, so too does the possessive pronoun.

Usually a writer has little difficulty in recognizing the appropriate number of the pronoun to use; we do it almost every time we speak:

Where is Hilda's hat? It's with *her* coat.
Here come the kids. Do they have *their* coats on?

A problem normally occurs only in the same four situations that we have encountered when discussing pronoun agreement:

| Situation | Example of Error | Correct Form |
|---|---|---|
| (i) Collective nouns (*crowd*, *group*, *jury*, etc.) are considered singular if all the members of the collection are acting in a unified way. | The flock was sleeping quietly in their fold as the wolf crept closer. | The *flock* was sleeping quietly in *its* fold as the wolf crept closer. |
| (ii) Collective nouns are considered *plural* when the members of the collection are *not* acting in a unified manner. | The flock ran off in all directions as the wolf attacked its fold. | The *flock* ran off in all directions as the wolf attacked *their* fold. |
| (iii) Indefinite pronouns (*one*, *someone*, *somebody*, *everybody*, *each*, *either*, etc.) are *always* singular. | Each of the men did their homework. | *Each* of the men did *his* homework. |
| (iv) Make certain that in a complex sentence you know exactly to which word the pronoun refers. | | Ms. Evans is one of those *instructors* who never forget *their* students' names. (Here, *who* refers to *instructors*, not to *Ms. Evans*.) |

# III. Pronoun reference

Pronouns are used to substitute for, or take the place of, nouns. Using them frees us from the boring and unwieldy repetition of nouns. Without pronouns, we would have to write the following, for example:

> Kathleen is a doctor. Kathleen lives in London, Ontario. Many patients feel that Kathleen is the best doctor that these patients have ever had.

Since we can use pronouns to substitute for specific nouns, however, we can avoid the rigidity and childishness that using them brings:

> Kathleen is a doctor *who* lives in London, Ontario. Many patients feel that *she* is the best doctor *they* have ever had.

When using pronouns, be careful to observe the following two rules:
(a) There must be a specific noun to which that pronoun refers.
(b) There must be only one noun to which the pronoun could possibly refer.

Look at the confusion that the lack of a specific noun to refer to causes in the following sentences:

> My uncle, an old college friend, and Dr. Peter Smith came for a visit yesterday. *He* is from Montreal.

This sentence causes confusion by not clearly defining which person the pronoun *he* refers to. In this case, the pronoun in the second sentence would have to be changed to a specific noun: e.g., "*Dr. Smith* is from Montreal."

> *They* don't know what they're doing in Ottawa.

To whom does the pronoun *they* refer: the cabinet? the civil service? members of Parliament? the Ottawa tourists? The sentence would have to be changed to replace the first *they* with a specific noun: e.g., "*Our members of Parliament* don't know what they're doing in Ottawa."

> Runaway inflation, increasing unemployment, and a mounting trade deficit are three major problems our country faces. *This* often causes people to turn to dictators.

The failure to have one specific noun to which the pronoun *this* refers causes the reader confusion. To convey a clear meaning, the second sentence would have to be changed — to read, for example, "*Such economic difficulties* often cause people to turn to dictators."

# IV. Modifiers

Modifiers (i.e., words or groups of words that describe other words) attach themselves to the appropriate word closest to them in a sentence. Thus, unless you are very careful in placing modifiers, they may describe the wrong word and cause your reader to misunderstand your meaning, become confused, or end up laughing at what you intended to be a serious point.

Note how the change in the positioning of the following modifiers changes the meaning of the sentences:

| | |
|---|---|
| He handed the book to the customer with the leather binding. [*This would be a rather strange-looking customer.*] | He handed the book with the leather binding to the customer. |
| She took a loaf of bread from the refrigerator that Aunt Bessie had made. [*Aunt Bessie, we must suppose, had a job in a factory that made refrigerators.*] | She took a loaf of bread that Aunt Bessie had made from the refrigerator. |
| I only asked for one ticket. [I didn't demand, plead, or do anything other than *ask.*] | I asked for only one ticket. |
| He lived in the house built by his great-grandfather for ten years. [*Great-grandfather either didn't want to take up permanent residence or was a very slow worker.*] | He lived for ten years in the house built by his great-grandfather. |
| Walking down the street, a courthouse came into view. [*An advance in bionics has apparently been made; courthouses are walking now.*] | Walking down the street, I saw a courthouse. |

Such problems arise from the fact that *we* know precisely what we mean when we write the sentence, but we forget that *others* will not know what we mean unless we put our modifiers in exactly the right place. We know that Aunt Bessie never worked in a factory, so it doesn't occur to us that someone else could think that she did. We're just trying to get down on the paper that Aunt Bessie makes her own bread; doesn't everybody know that she does? The answer, of course, is no — not unless *you tell them.*

Make your modifiers say what you mean by placing them with the word that you want them to modify.

If modifiers are a problem in your writing, the easiest way to spot misplaced modifiers is either (a) to read your own work aloud, preferably a day or so after you wrote it, or (b) to have someone else read it aloud for you while you read to yourself over his or her shoulder. By putting yourself in the role of a stranger coming to the work for the first time, you will recognize the confusion or the change of meaning that results from "misplaced" modifiers.

*Remember:* Always ask yourself as you write and reread your work, "What will my reader take this passage to mean?"

# V. Verb-tense consistency

Whenever you write, you must make certain that you always present the reader with one consistent point in time (that is, verb tense) from which to view your material. In the following example, the writer mistakenly presents two points of time (one present, one past):

> In *The Edible Woman*, Marion *intends* to marry Peter until she *discovers* he *is* trying to dominate her. When she *realized* what he *was* doing, she *refused* to marry him.

In the first sentence, the writer views the book as existing in the present tense, and thus presents the action taking place in the book as occurring right now. Confusion arises when the second sentence shifts to the past tense, perhaps because the writer read the book some time in the past or because the author wrote in the past tense. This writer should have determined in advance which point of time (verb tense) would be used throughout the essay.

Not all cases of changes in verb tense are as obvious as the example above.

> How many times have you had to hit the brakes because other drivers decide they want to gawk at a roadside emergency?

The immediacy of the situation has caused the writer to switch tenses. Nevertheless, the change strikes the reader as awkward and disturbing, and detracts from the importance of the argument. To take the reader through a complete and unified experience, the writer should correct the sentence to read as follows:

> How many times have you had to hit the brakes because other drivers have decided they want to gawk at a roadside emergency?

# VI. Inclusive language

What is inclusive language? Not surprisingly, inclusive language is the opposite of exclusive language, which is language that excludes women by emphasizing gender bias or stereotypes. Gender bias exists in our language for several reasons, but three are particularly obvious:

1. In the English language, there is no neutral pronoun for a nonspecified person or being. Therefore, "Everyone has driven *his* car to work this morning" is technically correct, even though "everyone" may include a number of women.

2. Traditional sayings have preserved many phrases that suggest gender bias. A writer may refer to a "gentleman's agreement," for instance, thus implying that only men make honourable contracts. Similarly, the reference to an "old wives' tale" may reflect an attitude that women have little else to occupy them than the spinning of incredible stories.

3. Some writers, wishing to show women in active roles in society, mistakenly give an undue emphasis to gender. Few women like to be referred to as "lady lawyers" or "janitresses"; most prefer simply "lawyers" or "caretakers."

Once again, the title of this book suggests the overriding concern of every writer: *Who's going to read this anyway?* Is your reader likely to take offence at your choice of words, thereby missing the meaning of your entire message?

Manuals, textbooks, and similar materials are being rewritten using inclusive language because of the changes in our social attitudes toward gender. The following techniques will provide you with a handy guide to making your writing inclusive.

## 1. Substitute articles for pronouns.

*Not*    Everyone is expected to bring *his* own materials.

*But*    Everyone is expected to bring *the* necessary materials.

## 2. Combine sentences to avoid pronouns.

*Not*    The technician is responsible for supervising the process. He will arrange weekly meetings to assign tasks.

*But*    The technician is responsible for supervising the process, and will arrange weekly meetings to assign tasks.

## 3. Repeat nouns.

*Not*    The manager will be required to make frequent out-of-town trips. He will also make a full report upon return.

*But*    The manager will be required to make frequent out-of-town trips. The manager will also make a full report upon return.

## 4. Use plurals.

*Not*    Every student will prepare his own summary.

*But*    Students will prepare their own (individual) summary.

## 5. Use the passive voice.

*Not*    The manual provides the reader with a suitable background, and the instructor will give him more detailed information.

*But*    The manual provides the reader with a suitable background. More detailed information will be given by the instructor.

## 6. Avoid traditional expressions that preserve gender bias.

*Not*    in layman's terms
*But*    in easily understood language

*Not*    a weak sister
*But*    the weakest element

*Not*    mankind
*But*    all people

## 7. Avoid gender identifiers in professional titles.

*Not*    clergymen
*But*    the clergy

*Not*    policeman, police woman
*But*    police officer

*Not*    chairman
*But*    chairperson, the chair

Finally, try to avoid "he/she" except in isolated instances. For one thing, the expression is difficult to read out loud. Also, and more importantly, one must maintain consistency in the use of the pronouns throughout a paragraph, and the repetition of this awkward combination adds little grace to one's writing style. For example, consider the following paragraph:

There is a great deal the average student can do to preserve good relations with instructors. For one thing, he/she can simply attend classes. Furthermore, he/she can prepare questions to ask about his/her favourite element in the course, understanding that a teacher is kindly disposed to someone who shares an interest in the subject. Finally, he/she can remember to show simple signs of civility — a friendly "good morning" or "hi!" can do wonders.

# A Short Guide to Punctuation

Many people are confused by punctuation because they mistakenly think they are dealing with some abstract, unknowable set of rules. In fact, nothing could be further from the truth.

Whenever you use punctuation in your written communication, all you are doing is trying to convey to your reader the structure of your meaning — which, when speaking, you supply by pauses, inflections, tone of voice, and so on. If you were talking to someone, the differences between the two following sentences would be immediately understood by your listener:

John [pause] is the cause of the problem here [rise in voice to indicate a question]

*and*

John is the cause of the problem here [no pauses, no change of tone]

When you are writing to someone, on the other hand, you use punctuation marks to make your meaning clear to your reader: if you intend the first meaning, you substitute a comma for the pause following "John" and a question mark for the rise in your voice at the end of the sentence; you do not use these punctuation marks if you intend the second meaning.

John, is the cause of the problem here?
John is the cause of the problem here.

Therefore, when you try to decide what punctuation to use in a passage, you are only thinking about how to represent on the page what you do all the time when you speak. For the most part, successful use of punctuation simply means conveying your meaning accurately by paying attention to how you would say the passage aloud, and translating that emphasis into a symbol.

In the following section, we summarize how each punctuation mark symbolizes a pause or an inflection. Refer to this guide if you encounter any situation in which you are in doubt about the correct punctuation symbol to use.

# I. The comma (,)

The comma represents the short pauses that are used in speech to give emphasis or to maintain the clarity of an idea within the sentence.

There are basically eight situations in which you would pause in such a way when speaking and, hence, for which you should use the comma when writing.

## 1. In lists

When you speak, you pause between the *words* (or *groups of words*) in a *list* (or *series*):

> I went out to buy *margarine* [pause] *tobacco* [pause] and *coffee*.
> What walks *on four legs in the morning* [pause] *on two legs at noon* [pause] and *on three legs in the evening?*
> I believe *that he worked hard* [pause] *that he played hard* [pause] and *that he lived a good life*.

When you write the same sentence, you insert commas to represent these pauses:

> I went out to buy *margarine, tobacco,* and *coffee.*
> What walks *on four legs in the morning, on two legs at noon,* and *on three legs in the evening?*
> I believe *that he worked hard, that he played hard,* and *that he lived a good life.*

RULE #1: Insert commas between the words (or groups of words) in a list (or series).

## 2. Between adjectives in a series

When you use only one adjective to modify a noun, you do not pause between them when you speak; therefore, you should not use a comma when you write:

> the faithful friend

However, when two (or more) adjectives in a series describe the same noun, you naturally pause between the adjectives:

the faithful [pause] kind friend

When you write, this pause must be represented by a comma:

the faithful, kind friend

In the above example, the adjectives in the series modify the same noun, "friend," independently. In other words, they do not depend on or change each other's meaning. Thus, you could reverse the order of the adjectives without destroying the meaning of the passage:

the kind, faithful friend

If you encounter a situation in which reversing the order of the modifiers destroys the meaning of the passage, do *not* use commas between the modifiers; for example,

the very faithful friend

cannot be reversed to the "faithful very friend." In this case, "very" is modifying "faithful, not "friend." Therefore, you should not insert a comma between "very" and "faithful."

**RULE #2: Insert commas between adjectives in a series when they (independently) modify the same noun.**

**3. Before the co-ordinating conjunctions** *and, but, for, or, nor, so,* or *yet*
Whenever you orally connect two main ideas by using *and, but, for, or, nor, so,* or *yet,* you pause before you say this connecting word to draw attention to the transition between the two ideas. You should normally insert a comma to symbolize this pause when you write:

The thin woman ate her dinner, *and* the fat man ate his heart out.
He ended his speech, *for* he found that his audience had left.
She needed an ace, *but* she drew a two.

Do *not* use a comma before any of these connecting words when the subject of the second main idea is omitted because it is the same as the subject of the first:

She needed an ace *but* drew a two.

**RULE #3: Insert a comma before the words *and, but, for, or, nor, so,* and *yet* when they join two main ideas that have separate subjects (i.e., when they act as co-ordinating conjunctions).**

## 4. To set off nonessential information in a sentence

If you add information to a sentence that is not essential for your listener to understand the main idea of the sentence, you invariably pause before and after that added information. Commas are inserted when such passages are written to symbolize these pauses.

## 4A. Apposition

If a word or expression is placed beside another to give more information about that other word or expression, and if both have the same grammatical construction (e.g., both are nouns), the added word or expression is said to be *in apposition* to the other. Since words or expressions used in apposition do not add information essential to the understanding of the sentence, they are set off with pauses in speech, and with commas in writing:

> *A post-secondary institution*, the college deals with mature students.
> The college, *a post-secondary institution*, deals with mature students.
> Joanne found herself going to college, *a post-secondary institution*.

**RULE #4A: Use commas to set off words or expressions used in apposition.**

## 4B. Nonessential phrases and clauses

*Clauses*

If you use clauses beginning with *who, whom, which,* or *that* (i.e., relative clauses) to add information that is descriptive but not essential to your audience's understanding of the main idea of a sentence, represent the oral pauses with commas that set off the clause:

> Arlene, who won the hundred-yard dash, is my best friend.

Although the information in the *who* clause adds an interesting detail, it is not essential to the main idea of the sentence "Arlene is my best friend." Note how you would normally pause before "who" and after "dash" if you were saying this sentence to someone.

Consider, on the other hand, the following sentence:

> The athlete who won the hundred-yard dash is my best friend.

The *who* clause has become essential to the basic meaning of the main idea, because the athlete is not named or given any other form of identification; without the information in the *who* clause, the audience has no way of knowing which specific athlete is referred to. Note that if you were saying this sentence aloud, you would not pause before "who" or after "dash."

*Phrases*
The same rule applies to verbal phrases. When the phrase contains nonessential information, commas are used to set it off from the rest of the sentence (as pauses would if you were speaking):

> John, wearing a silly grin, wiped the cream pie from his face.

If the information contained in the phrase is essential to the main idea of the sentence, commas are *not* used (just as you would not pause when speaking):

> The boy wearing the red cap is my cousin.

**RULE #4B: If a verbal phrase or a relative clause is vital to answering the question "which one or ones," then it is essential to the meaning of the sentence and does not require commas to set it off.**

**If a verbal phrase or a relative clause is not vital to answering the question "which one or ones," then it is nonessential and should be set off from the rest of the sentence by commas.**

### 5. Interrupters
If you interrupt the natural flow of a sentence by inserting a word, phrase, or clause, you pause when you are speaking to set off or give emphasis to the interruption. In writing, this pause is represented by a comma. The interrupter can occur almost anywhere in the sentence and can take many forms, including a personal name. Notice how the interrupter (in italics) is set off by commas from the rest of the sentence in the following examples:

> I decided, *therefore*, to go.
> Charles, *no matter how much he tried*, simply could not pass a driver's test.
> Both partners in a marriage, *not just the wife*, should be responsible for doing housework.
> *No*, I refuse to get involved with that kind of nonsense.
> *Martha*, I have loved you madly all of my life.

**RULE #5: Use commas to set off interrupters from the rest of the sentence.**

## 6. To avoid confusion

If you listen carefully when you speak to someone, you will find that you make brief pauses in your speech simply to prevent your listener from confusing your meaning. Note, for example, how the pause alters the meaning in the following sentences:

> Have it ready for April Nelson.
> Have it ready for April [pause] Nelson.

These pauses are represented by commas whenever they are necessary to avoid confusion for your reader.

> Call me Gary when you arrive.
> Call me, Gary, when you arrive.

**RULE #6: Use commas when necessary to avoid misunderstanding.**

## 7. To set off dates and places

You use commas to symbolize the pauses that you normally make between the elements of dates and places.

> On October 13, 1812, the Americans attacked Queenston Heights, Ontario.
> I moved to 197 Clarence St., Brantford, Ontario, on April 12, 1979.

**RULE #7: Use commas to set off dates and places.**

## 8. After long introductory phrases and subordinate clauses

In speaking, whenever you begin a sentence with a subordinate clause ("If . . . ," "When . . . ," "After . . . ," etc.), you pause at the end of that introductory element to allow your listeners to digest its meaning before you go on to the main idea of the sentence: for example,

> If you are going to be late [pause] please call to let us know.

When the introductory element is long, such a pause is particularly important because it prevents your listeners from becoming confused. It also allows them time to think about the meaning of the idea contained in the introductory element and to prepare to apply it to the idea coming next in the main clause of the sentence: for example,

When you find that you have a large number of assignments due at the same time and only a few days to do them all (pause) you must be highly organized in your approach.

When you are writing, you should use a comma after such introductory clauses or phrases to take the place of these oral pauses (as has been done in this explanation). When you do, you help your reader to understand the meaning of both parts of the sentence.

As soon as you arrive, call us to let us know that you are safe.
Because my car would not start, I missed my first class.
Since I did not have enough money to buy my textbooks, I fell far behind the rest of the class.
Until a few years ago, greenhouse gardening was considered a rich person's hobby.
In the absence of a better alternative, we decided to return home.

**RULE #8: Use a comma after an introductory element.**

Note: Everyday speech patterns occasionally suggest commas where none should be placed. The most noticeable example of this error occurs when the subject of a sentence is separated from its logical completion. For example, a comma should not appear in this sentence: *The student who spends six hours a night on homework or studying is probably not using time wisely.* In spite of the long subject (everything that precedes *is*), no comma should be placed before the verb. Subjects and verbs logically belong together. Except when an interrupter is added, they should not be separated.

# II. The dash (—)

Just as the comma is used to show a reader where we would pause in a sentence if we were speaking, so too is the dash. As long as you avoid excessive use of dashes, they can add variety to your punctuation.

You might at first think that such duplication is unnecessary, but the dash is used whenever we want to add a little extra dramatic effect to the pause:

I dashed forward to knock the gun from his hand — but I was too late.
History provides us with one overwhelming lesson — the silliness of the human race.

When you suddenly change the direction of the thought of a sentence, you might want to reflect the drama of that change by using a dash:

> My father was a man of infinite kindness — but he died the cruelest of deaths.

You might want to replace the commas with dashes in order to give extra emphasis to explanatory phrases, words in apposition, and so on:

> That young man — his own son — struck the old man.

You might also want to use the dash to give emphasis to the final words of a sentence when they sum up the preceding ideas:

> The backpack came complete with cooking equipment, sleeping bag, cook stove, and nylon tent — a complete outfit.

Most important, do not use commas to mark off an interrupter that forms a complete thought. Use a pair of dashes in such cases:

> Old Mark Hennessey — I'd almost forgotten him — turned up at the office yesterday.

# III. The semicolon (;)

When you have two complete sentences that are closely connected in meaning, you can stress this connection by using the semicolon to replace the period:

> The perfect spot was down by the river; I knew that from the time I was a child.
> He's not a bad dog; he's got a mean temper, though.

Whenever a semicolon is used in such situations, it is only reflecting the type of pauses that are made in oral communication; someone speaking tries to draw the listener's attention to the connection between the ideas of the sentences by pausing slightly longer than for a comma but not as long as for a period. As a matter of fact, it is the misinterpretation of this shortened pause between two sentences that causes people to write comma splices and run-on sentences.

One of the most common difficulties that inexperienced writers encounter is the omission of the semicolon before transitional words other than conjunctions. You should be careful to use the semicolon between two complete sentences (main clauses), when the second sentence begins with one of the following adverbial connectives:

| | | |
|---|---|---|
| indeed | consequently | then |
| instead | henceforth | likewise |
| thus | furthermore | for instance |
| hence | nevertheless | that is |
| however | otherwise | for example |
| moreover | therefore | |

Note that a comma is used to reflect the pause after such transitional words, except the very short ones ("then," "thus"):

> I was late; therefore, I had to do without breakfast.
> I know just how you feel; however, I still cannot agree.
> I did not have my car rust-proofed when I bought it; consequently, the car is now worthless.

Be careful *not* to use a semicolon in front of any of the adverbials listed above when they act as interrupters in the middle of a sentence (main clause):

> I know, however, just how you feel.

# IV. The colon (:)

Although the colon does not reflect a unique type of oral pause, it is not difficult to use because its purposes are so specialized.

### 1. To introduce a long list
If your list is relatively short and simple, try to incorporate it into your sentence and avoid the use of the colon:

> My greatest pleasures are a quiet lake, a snow-capped mountain, and the smell of pine trees.

If, on the other hand, your list is long and detailed, you should introduce it with a *complete sentence* and a colon:

> There are ten first-class dining rooms in Vancouver: . . . .
> My father would not allow me to have a motorcycle for the following reasons: . . . .

Avoid situations such as the following: losing your passport, having your pocket picked, or missing your train.

But note that there is no colon when you *end* the introduction with *such as*:

Avoid situations such as losing your passport, having your pocket picked, or missing your train.

## 2. To introduce a long quotation

If the quotation is relatively short, try to incorporate it into your sentence:

"From each according to his ability, to each according to his need" was the basic doctrine of Marx and his followers.

If, on the other hand, the quotation is longer than one sentence, you should introduce it with a complete sentence and a colon:

In her book *Roughing It in the Bush*, Susanna Moodie described in unrestrained prose her joy on first seeing Quebec City: "Canadians, rejoice in your beautiful city! Rejoice and be worthy of her — for few, very few, of the sons of men can point to such a spot as Quebec. . . . "

# V. The question mark (?)

The question mark is used to convey to your reader the inflection (the rise in your voice) that you can use orally when you ask a direct question:

Are you going to the pub?

Remember that a quotation that contains a direct question is read with the same inflection as was used by the speaker quoted. Thus, we use a question mark within the quotation marks:

Marlene asked, "Are you going to the pub?"

However, when a sentence contains an *indirect question*, you do *not* raise your voice and hence do *not* use the question mark.

Marlene asked if I was going to the pub.

# VI. The exclamation mark (!)

An exclamation mark is used only to point out to the reader the emphasis you would place on a statement that expresses surprise, shock, or some other sudden emotion. Be careful not to overuse it.

> Get out of the way!

# VII. Quotation marks (" ")

Quotation marks are another instance of punctuation marks that do not reflect a distinct pause or other change in your speech patterns. Once again, however, the very specialized function of quotation marks makes their correct use relatively easy.

### 1. Direct quotations

Use quotation marks to enclose the exact words that someone has spoken or written:

> The old-timer asked, "Who was that masked man?"
> "Who," the old-timer asked, "was that masked man?"

Do *not* use quotation marks around *indirect* quotations.

> The old-timer asked who the masked man was.

### 2. Extended quotations

If the passage that you are quoting is longer than *five* lines, you should use a completely different technique to show your reader that you are giving an exact quotation. For the entire passage quoted, indent approximately 15 cm from the left and right margins, single-space the entire passage, and *do not* use quotation marks.

> The following article, printed on July 1, 1867, illustrates the enthusiasm of the founders of our nation:
>
> > Upon the occasion of the birth of this great nation, stretching from sea to sea, from the temperate climes of the South to the frigid climes of the Arctic waste. . . .

3. The position of other punctuation when used with quotation marks

(i) Place periods and commas *inside* quotation marks:

"Come here," he shouted.
The reply came back, "Never."

(ii) Place colons and semicolons after the closing quotation mark.

The police officer shouted, "Hands up"; however, the burglar fled.

(iii) When you use question marks and exclamation points with quotation marks, observe the following rules:
(a) If the question or exclamation is found *only* within the quotation, the question or exclamation mark goes *inside* the quotation marks.

"Why are you so late?" John demanded.
Mary replied, "What's it to you?"

(b) If the question or exclamation takes in the entire sentence, the question or exclamation mark goes *outside* the quotation marks.

Did John say, "I am leaving for Saskatoon tomorrow"?

# VIII. Punctuation of titles

1. Whenever you refer to the titles of any of the following, use quotation marks around the title:
   (a) a chapter of a book (e.g., "The Advance of Democracy" in *A History of the Modern World*);
   (b) an article from a newspaper or magazine (e.g., "Motherhood Alone: A Choice and a Struggle" in *The Globe and Mail*);
   (c) an entry from an encyclopedia (e.g., "Shakespeare" in *Encyclopedia Britannica*);
   (d) a single episode from a TV series or a single song from a record album (e.g., "Arrival" from the TV series *The Prisoner*);
   (e) the title of a short story or a poem (e.g., "Daffodils" from *The Norton Anthology*).
2. Whenever you refer to the titles of longer works, such as books, plays, films, newspapers, magazines, and encyclopedias, *underline the title* to indicate that it would be italicized in print, as in the examples above.

# IX. The apostrophe (')

## 1. To denote possession

The concept of possession often presents difficulties for inexperienced writers, because the apostrophe itself is not heard when we speak. In fact, the failure to use the apostrophe for possession is perhaps the most common error in writing.

The concept of possession itself, however, is not difficult to learn, and, with a little practice in identifying specific examples of possession in your work, you should be able to avoid misusing or omitting the apostrophe.

"Possession" simply means that you are showing that one thing belongs to another (e.g., "John's hat" means "the hat belonging to John").

You should not have too much difficulty with the idea of possession when it applies to a person owning something (e.g., John's hat), but the problem becomes a little more difficult when you approach the idea that things and abstract ideas can "possess" characteristics or other things:

> The colour of (or belonging to) a rock is the *rock's colour*.
> The troubles of (or belonging to) life are *life's troubles*.

You may have to be careful not to go to the other extreme of placing an apostrophe after all words that end in *s*. If you are in doubt, apply the "belonging to" test:

> Reverse the order of the words (e.g., from "The country's borders" to "The borders — the country") and insert the words "belonging to" between them (e.g., "The borders belonging to the country").

If the meaning of the words remains the same, you know that you have a case of possession and should use the apostrophe.

The rules by which you determine the position of the apostrophe in the possessing word are the following:

(i) If the "possessing word" ends in any letter other than *s*, add *'s*:

> John*'s* hat
> the horse*'s* stall
> wome*n's* coats
> the ma*n's* shirts

(Note that both singular and plural words ending in a letter other than *s* take an added *'s*).

(ii) If the possessing word is plural and ends in *s*, add only the apostrophe:

> horses' stalls
> dogs' lives

(iii) If the possessing word ends in *s* or an *s*-sound, pronunciation is the key to forming the possessive:

> the class*'s* opinion
> Joyce*'s* new car
> Mr. Jone*s'* address
> Jesu*s'* followers

(iv) If two or more people (or things) possess the same thing, only the last noun is given the apostrophe:

> Fred and Joan's car [they jointly own the car]

If two or more people (or things) possess two of the same things, both receive apostrophes (and note that "car" becomes plural).

> Fred's and Joan's cars

## 2. In contractions

When one or more letters are left out of a word, the apostrophe replaces the omitted letter or letters.

> Don't [Do not] do that.
> Let's [Let us] go.
> I couldn't [could not] do that.
> I'll [I shall] go.

A word of warning is in order. Sometimes people confuse contracted words with possessive pronouns. *Remember:*

> You're [You are] doing well.
> *but*
> Your coat has been stolen.

> It's [It is] not too late.
> *but*
> Its fur was matted.

They're [They are] coming over later.
*but*
Their jobs were boring.

Who's [Who is] coming to dinner?
*but*
Whose lipstick is on your collar?

### 3. Plural forms of letters, figures, and signs

Styles of writing change over time. It was once fashionable to write plurals of letters or figures with an apostrophe.

Watch your P's and Q's.
All of the 6's and 12's go in this column.

However, the more modern style is to simplify writing by doing away with any punctuation that can be omitted without causing confusion. No confusion arises if the examples given are simplified.

Watch your Ps and Qs.
All of the 6s and 12s go in this column.

If there is any possibility of confusion, however, the apostrophe must be used.

SIN's are recorded next to the surnames.
I hadn't considered the expense of c.o.d.'s.

# Commonly Confused Words

There are a number of words that are often mistakenly interchanged or con-fused by people when they speak and write. Sometimes the mistake can bring a ridiculous meaning to the sentence that completely destroys the seriousness of the message that the writer intended the reader to receive.

"They found his body in the middle of the dessert" brings up an image in the reader's mind of a hulking detective found dead in a giant bowl of jello — a good scene from a Woody Allen movie, perhaps, but definitely not the tragic *desert* scene that the writer intended to depict.

The following section is intended to give you a quick reference to check the most commonly confused words whenever you have the slightest doubt about whether you have used the right word or not.

It is a good idea to read this entire section over a few times even if you have no doubts. All too often, people assume that they know the correct word or the correct form of a word when in fact they have been making an error for years.

## ACCEPT — EXCEPT

ACCEPT — means to receive something or to agree with something:

> I accepted the certificate from the Dean.
> I accept that concept.

EXCEPT — means "other than" or "but":

> Everyone except Joan had to rewrite the test.

## ACCESS — EXCESS

ACCESS — means "coming toward" or "a way to approach something," or "permission to approach something":

> I had access to the library.
> The only access to the mansion was through a guarded gate.

EXCESS — means "an extreme," "too much":

> His head felt like a race course for the Austrian cavalry because he had drunk to excess the night before.
> We have had an excess of rain during the last month.

## ALSO

"Also" is not confused with any other word, but it is commonly overused and abused. It is always best to try to find another word to replace "also."

## AFFECT — EFFECT

AFFECT — means to cause change or to influence something:

> Smoking affects your breathing.

EFFECT — as a *verb*, means to result in or to produce a result:

> The prime minister was unable to effect his legislation.

— as a *noun*, means the result of something:

> Troubled breathing is the effect of excessive smoking.

Note: "Effect" is most commonly used as a noun. Except in a few obsolete or technical cases, "affect" is *not* used as a noun.

## ALREADY — ALL READY

ALREADY — means "previously":

> "We were already there."

ALL READY — means that everyone or everything is prepared to do something:

> We were all ready to go.
> I was all ready to go.

## AMONG — BETWEEN

AMONG — means to be in the midst of more than two things, or to divide something for more than two people:

> The five of you will have to decide among yourselves.

BETWEEN — means to be located or to happen so as to separate two things; or to divide something for two people:

> I was caught between the devil and the deep blue sea.
> I divided the last of the wine between my girlfriend and her brother.

## AMOUNT — NUMBER

AMOUNT — means the quantity of something:

> The amount of snow that fell last night was incredible.

NUMBER — means a collection of persons or things:

> A number of people came to our house on Christmas Eve.

Note: Errors usually occur in the use of these words when a writer confuses a collection (i.e., a group of people or things) with a quantity, and puts down, for example, "The amount of people who favour abortion is changing."

> The correct wording recognizes that the people involved are individuals gathered into a collection, not a lump of undifferentiated flesh: "The number of people. . . ."

## ARE — OUR

ARE — is a form of the verb "to be":

> We are going to the store.

OUR — is the possessive form of the pronoun "we":

> Our house burned down.

The confusion of these two words results from the pronunciation of "our" in some Canadian dialects. If you are in any doubt about whether you have made the error when you reread your paper, see whether you can reword the phrase to read " . . . belonging to us"; if you can, use "our."

## A WHILE — A LOT

No one confuses these expressions, but they certainly are overused. Both are colloquial phrases and are not appropriate in many formal situations in expository writing. *Avoid* them if at all possible.

## CAN — MAY

CAN — means "to be able":

A cheetah can run at 130 km per hour.

MAY — means "to have permission":

May I go to the washroom? (The only time you should ask, "Can I go to the washroom?" is after being treated by a doctor for bowel problems.)

## CHOICE — CHOOSE — CHOSE

CHOICE — is a *noun* that means "selection," or "choosing," or "option":

What choice did I have?

CHOOSE — is a verb that means "to select." The "oo" is pronounced the same as the "oo" in "tool":

Choose the right tool for the job.

CHOSE — is a verb, the *past* tense of the verb to choose. The "o" in "chose" is pronounced the same way as the "o" in "elope":

They chose to elope.

## COARSE — COURSE

COARSE — means "rough":

This sweater is made of coarse wool.

COURSE — means a plan of action or direction:

No course will guarantee you a passing grade.
The golf course is a good place to meet people.

## DESERT — DESSERT

DESERT — as a *noun*, means "a place where there is little rainfall":

Cacti grow in the desert.

— as a *verb*, means "to abandon":

He deserted his family.

DESSERT — refers to those delicious, fattening goodies at the end of a meal:

No more dessert for me, thanks. I'm obese already.

## DEVICE — DEVISE

DEVICE — (the "-ice" is pronounced the same as the frozen substance, ice) as a *noun*, means "a tool, a scheme, an invention," etc:

That device will never fly, Orville.

DEVISE — (the "-ise" is pronounced the same as the "-ies" in "lies") means "to invent, to plot, to contrive":

You had better devise some good lies to account for the pies.

## EMIGRATE — IMMIGRATE

EMIGRATE — means "to leave" a country:

He emigrated from Canada to avoid paying his taxes.

IMMIGRATE — means "to come" to a country:

He immigrated to Canada to find a better life.

## EMINENT — IMMINENT — EMANATE

EMINENT — means "important, distinguished":

She is an eminent lawyer.

IMMINENT — means "about to happen":

From the darkness of the clouds we knew a storm was imminent.

EMANATE — means "to originate from, to come from a source":

Daylight emanates from the sun.

## FEWER — LESS

FEWER — is used to refer to a collection of things that can be counted:

Fewer people watch the late movie than watch *The National*.

Less — is used to refer to the amount of a material or thing:

Less time was lost when a stoplight replaced the stop sign.

*Remember:* Fewer people ski when there is less snow than usual.

# I — ME

I — is the subjective form of the first person pronoun:

When I forgot the punchline, I became the joke.

Me — is the objective form of the first person pronoun:

When he hit me with the pie, the joke was on me.

# ITS — IT'S

Its — is the possessive form of the pronoun *it*. Remember, *none* of the personal possessive pronouns (*my, your, his, her, our, their*) uses an apostrophe; therefore, *its* is no exception:

Its tail drooped between its legs.

It's — is the contracted form of "it is":

It's about time for supper, isn't it?

*Remember:* Only if you can substitute "it is" should you use an apostrophe.

# KNOW — NO

Know — means "to be aware of":

I know how to do trigonometry.

No — means "not in any way":

"No, no," she cried, "you must not give up."

# LATER — LATTER

Later — means "subsequently." The *a* in later is pronounced the same way as the *a* in "play:"

Stephanie can come out to play later.

Latter — means "the last-mentioned thing of two things mentioned." The *a* sound of latter is pronounced the same way as the *a* sound in "ladder."

John and Bert helped us elope. The latter brought the ladder.

## LAY — LIE

Lᴀʏ — in the *present* tense, means "to put something somewhere":

Lay the book on the table.

Lɪᴇ — means to assume a horizontal position, as opposed to placing something else in a horizontal position:

Lie down, please; it's time to go to sleep.

The problem: the past tense of the verb "to lie" is "lay":

John lay in bed thinking, "Shall I just lie here and hope that I laid the book on the table?"

*Remember:* You lie down each night.
You lay something down on a table.
You lay in bed last night.
You laid your coat down yesterday.
(There is no such word as "layed.")

## LESS — LEAST

Lᴇss — the comparative form of "little," it means "not so large," etc. "Less" is often used with adjectives and adverbs to create a "negative" comparative:

likely . . . less likely
beautiful . . . less beautiful
sure . . . less sure

Lᴇᴀsт — the superlative form of "little," it means "smallest in size, quantity," etc. "Least" is often used with adjectives and adverbs to create a kind of "negative superlative":

certain . . . least certain
costly . . . least costly

Do not make the mistake of thinking that adding an "-er" or "-est" suffix to the end of a word accompanied by "less" or "least" adds emphasis: it simply reduces your phrase to nonsense. *Never* write such things as "least likeliest" or "less fiercer."

## LETS — LET'S

Lᴇтs — means "allows":

She always lets him go early.

LET'S — is the contracted form of "let us":

Let's go to the show.

*Remember:* Only if you can substitute "let us" should you use the apostrophe.

# LIKE — AS — AS IF — AS THOUGH

LIKE — usually a preposition introducing a prepositional phrase, which *never* contains an independent verb; normally compares *things* or *people*:

I wish I were like him.
He was out like a light.

AS — usually a conjunction introducing a subordinate clause (containing a subject and a verb); normally compares *states* or *actions*:

I cook as my mother does.
*not*
I cook like my mother does.

Note: If you are unsure whether to use "like" or "as," look for a following verb. If there is one — or if one is *understood* — use "as."

In the following sentence, the final verb, *has*, is understood: *I'd be very happy to have the same salary as Joan.* Thus, *as* is correct. This would not be the case if no verb was understood, as seen in this sentence: *I'd be happy to have a salary like Joan's.*

You will often find that when your first impulse was to use "like" as a conjunction, the words you really wanted were "as if" or "as though."

He lay there as if he were dead.

# LOOSE — LOSE — LOSS

LOOSE — (the *s* is pronounced in the same way as the *s* in "moose") as an adjective, means "not tight," and as a verb, means "to untie":

Who let the moose loose?
Is the skin of a moose loose?

LOSE — (the *s* is pronounced in the same way as the *s* in "blues") means "to mislay":

I just can't lose the February blues.

LOSS — (rhymes with "toss") means "something lost":

The loss of the toss meant the end of the game.

The confusion between these words simply results from not knowing which spelling goes with which sounds: remember one and you have them all.

## MORE — MOST — -ER — -EST

MORE — is the comparative form of "much"; it means "greater in quantity or quality":

> I have had more to drink than I should.
> More haste makes more waste.

"More" is often used together with an adjective or adverb to create a "comparative" form for that word:

> likely . . . more likely
> certain . . . more certain

MOST — is the superlative form of much; it means "greatest in quantity or quality":

> I love you most of all.
> She had the most money of all of us.

"Most" is often used together with an adjective or an adverb to create a "superlative" form for that word:

> certain . . . most certain
> quickly . . . most quickly

ER — is a suffix added to the end of many adjectives and adverbs to create the comparative forms of those words:

> great . . . greater
> large . . . larger
> late . . . later

-EST — is a suffix added to the end of many adjectives and adverbs to create the superlative forms of those words:

> sure . . . surest
> full . . . fullest
> late . . . latest

People are often confused over which of these alternatives to use when they want to create comparatives and superlatives, but there is a relatively simple guideline to use that regularly works: *If the word that you want to make into a comparative or superlative form has* three or more *syllables, use* more *or* most:

> su-per-cil-i-ous . . . most supercilious
> ri-dic-u-lous . . . most ridiculous

(Any dictionary will give you the number of syllables in a word by breaking the word into its component syllables as we have done here.)

Never use both "-er" or "-est" and "more" or "most" with the same word: never write "most fiercest," "more faster," etc.

## PASSED — PAST

Passed — is the past tense of the verb "to pass"; it means "went by":

> We passed the bus.

Past — means that something happened earlier:

> That's all in the past, now.

## PERSECUTE — PROSECUTE

Persecute — means "to oppress, to harass, to cause someone trouble":

> Hitler persecuted the Jews.

Prosecute — means "to put on trial, to try to prove charges against someone in court":

> Trespassers will be prosecuted.
> Of course, you could always try to persecute trespassers, but you would probably be prosecuted for doing so.

## PERSONAL — PERSONNEL

Personal — means "private":

> These are my personal belongings.

Personnel — means "the staff that works for a firm, college," etc.:

> The personnel in the store are a pain.
> The personnel office is upstairs.

## PRACTISE — PRACTICE

Practise — is the *verb*, and means "to do, to do repeatedly in order to learn a skill," etc.:

> He must have practised in order to do that badly.

PRACTICE — is the *noun*, and means "a custom, a repetition of a skill in order to learn it well," etc.:

It is a good practice to check all buttons and zippers.
Make it a practice not to practise your drums after midnight.

## PRINCIPAL — PRINCIPLE

PRINCIPAL — as an *adjective*, means "the most important":

The principal cause of lung cancer is smoking.

— as a *noun*, means "the person in charge of a school":

The principal is your pal.

PRINCIPLE — is used only as a *noun*; it means "fundamental truth or rule of conduct":

This is the main principle behind our action: all people are created equal.

## STATIONARY — STATIONERY

STATIONARY — means "standing still":

The bus remained stationary.

STATIONERY — means "paper for writing":

Good stationery makes writing easier.

## THEIR — THERE — THEY'RE

THEIR — is the possessive form of "they":

They forgot their heir when they left their money to charity.

THERE — is an adverb, used in such constructions as "here and there," "over there," and "there are . . . "
THEY'RE — is the contracted form of "they are."

## TO — TOO — TWO

TO — is used as a preposition: "to the store," "to town," etc.
— is part of an infinitive: "to go," "to run," "to fall," etc.
TOO — is an adverb. It means (1) "likewise or also" and (2) "more than enough":

I, too, had had too much to drink.

Two — is a number:

I'll take two minutes.

## WERE — WE'RE — WHERE

WERE — is the plural form of the past tense of the verb "to be":

We were later than we thought.

WE'RE — is the contracted form of "we are":

We're in hot water now.

WHERE — is used to ask about the location of someone or something:

Where on earth are you dragging me now, Rover?

Make certain that you know where to use "were" and where to use "we're" (know which spelling goes with which sound).

## WEATHER — WHETHER

WEATHER — refers to the state of the atmosphere:

We have been having rainy weather lately.

WHETHER — is used in such constructions as "Whether you're ready or not, I'm going."

Note: the word *wether* does exist, but it means "a castrated ram."

## WHO — WHOM

WHO — is the subjective form of the pronoun:

Who is coming to the party?

WHOM — is the objective form of the pronoun:

Whom do you prefer?

## WHO'S — WHOSE

WHO'S — is the contracted form of "who is":

Who's going to Pub night?

WHOSE — is the possessive form of the pronoun "who":

Whose hat is this?

*Remember:* None of the possessive forms of pronouns uses an apostrophe: *my, your, his, her, its, our, their,* and *whose*.

## WORSE — WORST

WORSE — is used to compare two possibilities:

His condition is worse than it was yesterday.

WORST — is used to consider more than two options:

Of all those lazy bums, he is the worst.

## YOUR — YOU'RE

YOUR — is the possessive form of "you":

Here's your hat; what's your hurry?

YOU'RE — is the contracted form of "you are":

You're the cream in my coffee.

# Spelling

In the following chart, you will find the major rules for spelling. Most errors in spelling, however, occur in situations not covered by any rule: you may pronounce a word in such a way that when you go to spell it, you write down what you "hear" and make a spelling error (e.g., "prejudist" for "prejudiced"); you may even assume that you know the correct spelling for a word, only to discover later that you have been using the wrong spelling for years.

These points, together with the complexity of the rules themselves, should make you aware of one overwhelming fact: you should use a dictionary with great frequency. The authors of this book have often thought that they could easily win the prize for the world's worst spellers; yet very few things leave our desks with spelling mistakes in them. The way we do this is very simple: we *know* that we are terrible spellers; therefore, we set aside one final rereading of anything we are working on to do nothing but check for spelling with a dictionary open in front of us.

One word of warning about using the dictionary: make certain that you read the meaning of the word when you check for spelling. Many words sound similar and are near each other in the dictionary, but mean very different things. There is a world of difference between "cognative" and "cognitive," for example.

*Remember:* good spelling is the result of long practice.

### Some hints to help improve spelling

1. Correct misspelt words using a dictionary. Practise writing the word in several different sentences if you really want to drive the correct spelling home.
2. Check the pronunciation of words. Pronunciation is a good guide to English spelling more often than people think. *Note:* pronounce the word *carefully.*
3. Check the meaning of words. If you know what a word means, you will tend not to confuse the spelling.
4. Check the make-up of words. *Most* spelling errors stem from faulty word-building (e.g., addition of prefixes and suffixes).
5. Whenever possible, use memory devices. They may sound childish at times, but they work:

   "*i* before *e* except after *c*"
   "The principal is my pal."

   Make up your own memory devices.
6. Remember: *all* spelling rules have exceptions.
7. Never take a chance on spelling an unknown word correctly. *When in doubt, use a dictionary.*

The chart on the following pages outlines some spelling rules and their exceptions.

| 1. Rule | Examples | Exceptions |
|---|---|---|
| *i* before *e* except after *c*, when the "ie" or "ei" are pronounced "ee," as in "eerie." | achieve, chief, niece, belief, grief, siege, brief, fiend, yield, shield, etc.<br>After c:<br>ceiling, deceive, receive, conceive, perceive, etc.<br>**Note:** In all of these words, "ie" is pronounced as the "ee" in "eerie." | neither<br>either<br>sleight<br>foreign<br>sovereign<br>surfeit<br>counterfeit<br>forfeit<br>height |
| *e* before *i*, when "ei" is pronounced as in "eight" ("long" *a*). | neigh, neighbour, reign, sleigh, eight, etc. | sheik<br>weird<br>leisure<br>seize |

| 2. Plural Forms | Examples | | Exceptions | |
|---|---|---|---|---|
| For most nouns, add *s* to the singular to form the plural. | boy<br>hat<br>street<br>avenue | boys<br>hats<br>streets<br>avenues | man<br>woman<br>child<br>ox<br>sheep<br>fish | men<br>women<br>children<br>oxen<br>sheep<br>fish |
| For nouns ending in -*ch*, -*sh*, -*s*, -*x*, or -*z*, form the plural by adding -*es* to the singular. | rich<br>brush<br>gas<br>tax<br>waltz | riches<br>brushes<br>gases<br>taxes<br>waltzes | | |
| For nouns ending in a consonant followed by *o*, add -*es*. | echo<br>tomato<br>hero<br>tornado | echoes<br>tomatoes<br>heroes<br>tornadoes | Musical terms ending in a consonant +*o*:<br>piano<br>alto<br>**Note:** photo | pianos<br>altos<br>photos |
| For *most* nouns ending in -*f*, simply add -*s*. | hoof<br>grief<br>proof<br>belief<br>roof | hoofs<br>griefs<br>proofs<br>beliefs<br>roofs | calf<br>elf<br>half<br>knife<br>life<br>shelf<br>wife | calves<br>elves<br>halves<br>knives<br>lives<br>shelves<br>wives |

| Many words introduced into English from Latin and Greek have retained their original plural forms. | *Latin:* | | Some foreign words have acquired English plurals: |
|---|---|---|---|
| | datum | data | forum forums |
| | medium | media | maximum maximums |
| | bacterium | bacteria | geranium geraniums |
| | *Greek:* | | |
| | thesis | theses | |
| | crisis | crises | |
| | analysis | analyses | |
| | parenthesis | parentheses | |
| | criterion | criteria | |
| | phenomenon | phenomena | |

| 3. Prefixes | Examples | Exceptions |
|---|---|---|
| Prefixes are syllables added to the beginnings of words to change their meanings: *dis-*, *mis-*, etc. For a prefix ending with the same letter as the first letter of the word to which it is to be joined (e.g., "dis-" and "similar"), keep *both* consonants. | dissimilar misspell unnecessary unnerve overrun disservice dissatisfied | Some style books prefer to use a hyphen between two vowels when the first is part of a prefix: co-operate re-enter |

| 4. Final *e* | Examples | | Exceptions |
|---|---|---|---|
| A final silent *e* almost always makes the vowel (*a,e,i,o,u*) preceding it say its name — i.e., gives it a "long" sound. | mat | mate | Multisyllable words: composite estimate (the noun). |
| | man | mane | |
| | met | mete | |
| | sit | site | |
| | dot | dote | |
| | hop | hope | |
| | cut | cute | |
| | shut | shute | |

| 5. Suffixes | Examples | | Exceptions | |
|---|---|---|---|---|
| Suffixes are syllables added to the ends of words to change their meanings (e.g., from noun to adjective, verb to noun, present to past, etc.). | fire | firing | slice | sliceable |
| | live | livable | outrage | outrageous |
| | endure | endurance | marriage | marriageable |
| | hesitate | hesitation | | |
| | style | stylish | **Note:** In all of these words, the *e* is retained to keep the *c* and *g* "soft" before *a* or *o* (say the words aloud and compare the sounds to the "hard" *c* and *g* in "garbled" and "current"). | |
| A final silent *e* is *dropped* before a suffix beginning with a vowel: e.g., -able  -ed  -ing  -ion  -ish | | | | |
| A final silent *e* is usually *retained* before a suffix beginning with a consonant: e.g., -ful  -less  -ment  -ness | arrange | arrangement | nine | ninth |
| | love | lovely | true | truly |
| | state | statement | argue | argument |
| | bore | boredom | + all cases of *-ly*: | |
| | | | able | ably |
| | | | whole | wholly |
| A final silent *e* is retained in a few cases where dropping it would cause confusion. | singe | singeing | | |
| | dye | dyeing | | |
| For words of one syllable that contain a single vowel and end with a single consonant, *double* that consonant before a suffix beginning with a *vowel:* e.g., -able  -ed  -ing  -ion  -ish | *sit* | *sit*ting | **Note:** This rule does not apply to one-syllable words ending in two consonants (e.g., *start*) or to one-syllable words that contain two vowels and end with a single consonant (e.g., *sail*). | |
| | *hop* | *hop*ping | | |
| | *swim* | *swim*ming | | |
| | *swim* | *swim*mer | | |
| | | | start | starting |
| | | | sail | sailing |
| | | | mail | mailed |

| For words of more than one syllable (e.g., pre-fer) that end in a single vowel followed by a single consonant and that stress the *last* syllable, *double* the final consonant before a suffix beginning with a vowel (e.g., -able, -ed, -ing, -ish). | pre*fer* be*gin* per*mit* for*get* ful*fil* | pre*ferr*ed begi*nn*ing perm*itt*ed forge*tt*able fulfi*ll*ed | chagrin refer | chagrined reference |
| When the stress is placed on a syllable *other than* the last one, the final consonant is *not* doubled (e.g., for words such as "NAR-row" and "ex-HIB-it," where the most emphasis is placed on a syllable other than the last one). | transfer prosper | transference prospered | traveled jeweler **Note:** A few words have two different spellings; both are acceptable. | travelled jeweller |
| A final *y* after a *consonant* (e.g., -ty) changes to *i* before most suffixes. | beauty copy silly busy | beaut*i*ful cop*i*ed sill*i*ness bus*i*ness | dry sly **Note:** *y* is unchanged before *i*, as in beautifying, and in compound words, as in byway, citywide. | dryness slyly |
| A final *y* after a *vowel* (e.g., -oy) usually remains unchanged before suffixes. | boy employ play coy | boys employment playful coyness | day gay lay pay | da*i*ly ga*i*ly la*i*d pa*i*d |
| For a suffix beginning with the same letter as the last letter of the word to which it is to be joined (e.g., "ing" and "ski"), retain *both* letters. | sudden ski hopeful | sudde*nn*ess sk*ii*ng hopefu*ll*y | eighth | |

*-able / -ible*

| | | |
|---|---|---|
| If the word to which the suffix is to be added is complete in itself (e.g., "drink"), it is usually correct to add -able. | drink*a*ble<br>eat*a*ble<br>read*a*ble | inevit*a*ble<br>delect*a*ble<br>repress*i*ble |
| If that word is *not* complete in itself (e.g., "permiss-"), it is usually correct to use -ible. | poss*i*ble<br>permiss*i*ble<br>irrepress*i*ble | |

If you are still in doubt, the following guidelines may be helpful:

If a word ending in -ation can be made out of the root word, then -able is usually correct.

If a word ending in -ssion can be made out of the root word, then -ible is usually correct.

| | | |
|---|---|---|
| admire | admir*a*tion | admir*a*ble |
| consider | consider*a*tion | consider*a*ble |
| permit | permi*ssi*on | permi*ssi*ble |
| admit | admi*ssi*on | admi*ssi*ble |
| repress | repre*ssi*on | repre*ssi*ble |

**Note:**  perfect     perfection     perfectible

| *-ant* and *-ent* | Examples | Exceptions |
|---|---|---|
| The letters *t* and *v* are usually followed by -ant. | impor*t*ant<br>rele*v*ant<br>expec*t*ant<br>ser*v*ant<br>dis*t*ant | insis*t*ent<br>persis*t*ent<br>compe*t*ent |
| "Hard" *c* (as in cat) and "hard" *g* (as in good) take -ant. | signifi*c*ant<br>extrava*g*ant | |
| "Soft" *c* (as in nice) and "soft" *g* (as in rage), take -ent. | adole*sc*ent<br>intelli*g*ent | pa*g*eant |
| Often the name for a person requires -ant, and the word describing him requires -ent. | "A depend*a*nt is depend-ent on someone else." | superintend*e*nt |

| -sede, -ceed, -cede | Examples | Exceptions |
|---|---|---|
| *-sede*: "Supersede" is the *only* word in the English language to end in -sede.<br><br>*-ceed*: "proceed," "exceed," and "succeed" are the only words in the English language to end in -ceed. In *all other cases*, the word-ending pronounced like the word "seed" is spelled *-cede*. | cede<br>intercede<br>precede<br>concede<br>accede<br>secede | |

| -c and -ic | Examples | Exceptions |
|---|---|---|
| *-c*<br>Words ending in a hard *c* (e.g., pani*c*), add *k* before suffixes beginning with *e, i,* or *y* (the *k* keeps the *c* "hard"). | traffic<br>mimic<br>panic | trafficking<br>mimicked<br>panicked<br>panicky |
| *-ic*<br>Words ending in -ic (e.g., authentic), add *al* before the suffix -ly. | authentic<br>magic | authentically  public    publicly<br>magically |

**Rogues and Demons: those problem words that haunt us all**

*-ery* and *-ary*
Stationery is made of paper.
Stationary means to stand still.
A corpse belongs in a cemetery.

For words that are commonly misspelled because people confuse them with other words, see Commonly Confused Words, p. 344.

# Index

Agreement: 317–324
   of possessive pronouns 323–324
   of pronoun and antecedent 322–323
   of subject and verb 317–322
Apostrophe: 342–344
   in contractions 343–344
   in plurals of letters and numbers 344
   of possession 342–343
Body (of the essay) 307–309
Coherence 302
Colon 338–339
Comma: 331–336
   with adjectives in series 331–332
   with appositives 333
   for avoiding confusion 335
   before co-ordinating conjunctions 332–333
   with dates and place names 335
   with interrupters 334
   with introductory phrases 335–336
   in lists 331
   with nonessential phrases and clauses 333–334
Comma splice 314–316
Concluding paragraph 309
Concluding sentence 308
Conclusion (concluding paragraph) 309
Dash 336–337
Exclamation mark 340
Inclusive language 328–330
Introductory paragraph 303–307
Modifiers 325–327
Organizational approaches 301–302
Paragraphing 307–309
Planning 297–303

Pronoun reference 324–325
Punctuation 330–344
Question mark 339
Quotation marks 340
Run-on sentence 316–317
Semicolon 337–338
Sentence errors 310–317
Sentence fragment 310–313
Spelling 356–363
Thesis 299
Thesis statement 299, 304
Titles, punctuation of 341
Topic sentences 303, 307
Transitions 308
Unity 301
Verb-tense consistency 327
Words that present difficulty 344–356

## To the owner of this book:

We are interested in your reaction to *Who's Going to Read This Anyway?* Fourth Edition, by Donna Kerrigan, Ray Matthews, and Gary Webb.

1. What was your reason for using this book?
   ☐ high school course     ☐ continuing education course
   ☐ college course     ☐ personal interest
                                           ☐ other (specify)

2. In which school are you enrolled? _____

3. Approximately how much of the book did you use?
   ☐ ¼     ☐ ½     ☐ ¾     ☐ all

4. What is the best aspect of the book?

5. Have you any suggestions for improvement?

6. Is there anything that should be added?

**Fold here**

------------------------------------------------------------------------------------------------------------------------